ARMY FILM AND THE AVANT GARDE

ARMY FILM

and the

Avant Garde

CINEMA AND EXPERIMENT IN
THE CZECHOSLOVAK MILITARY

ALICE LOVEJOY

INDIANA UNIVERSITY PRESS

Bloomington & Indianapolis

This book is a publication of

Indiana University Press
Office of Scholarly Publishing
Herman B Wells Library 350
1320 East 10th Street
Bloomington, Indiana 47405 USA

iupress.indiana.edu

Telephone   800-842-6796
Fax   812-855-7931

♾ The paper used in this publication
meets the minimum requirements of the
American National Standard for Information
Sciences—Permanence of Paper for Printed
Library Materials, ANSI Z39.48–1992.

Manufactured in the United States of America

Library of Congress
Cataloging-in-Publication Data

Lovejoy, Alice.
   Army film and the avant garde : cinema
and experiment in the Czechoslovak
military / Alice Lovejoy.
      pages cm
   Based on the author's dissertation
(doctoral)—Yale University, 2009.
   Issued with a DVD featuring
13 short films produced by the
Czechoslovak Ministry of Defense.
   Includes bibliographical
references and index.
   ISBN 978-0-253-01488-7 (pb : alk. paper)
— ISBN 978-0-253-01483-2 (cl : alk. paper) —
ISBN 978-0-253-01493-1 (eb) 1. Experimental
films—Czechoslovakia—History—20th
century. 2. Československý armádní film.
3. Documentary films—Czechoslovakia—
History—20th century. I. Title.
   PN1993.5.C9L68 2014
   791.43'61109437—dc23

2014022233

1 2 3 4 5   20 19 18 17 16 15

In memory of my father, David Beaton Lovejoy.

CONTENTS

ACKNOWLEDGMENTS

THIS PROJECT has taken shape over more than a decade, across two continents. In the process, I have benefited from the support, generosity, and wisdom of numerous people.

It is in many ways marked by its beginnings in Yale University's Film Studies Program. I can think of no more dynamic and rigorous environment for the study of cinema and cultural history, at the heart of which were always films themselves. I am grateful to Dudley Andrew, Katerina Clark, John MacKay, and Charles Musser for their generous, imaginative intellectual guidance and for the models of scholarship that they continue to provide. I thank Marci Shore and Timothy Snyder for expertly shaping the project's foundations in East Central European history and Pericles Lewis for thoughtful feedback in its early stages. Over the course of this project, I was privileged to work with Peter Demetz, who generously offered his unparalleled perspective on the story it tells. I owe my deepest debt of gratitude to Katie Trumpener for her unwavering faith in the project, insightful readings and critiques, the towering example of her own work, and the wide-ranging conversations that are an ongoing source of inspiration.

The Film and Media Studies Program at Colgate University and the Department of Cultural Studies and Comparative Literature and Moving Image Studies program at the University of Minnesota provided supportive environments in which to revise the manuscript. In particular, I thank my Minnesota colleagues John Archer, Hisham Bizri, Cesare Casarino, Gary B. Cohen, Keya Ganguly, Eva Hudecová, Rembert Hüser, Richard Leppert, Jason McGrath, Verena Mund, Paula Rabinowitz, Matthias Rothe, and Christophe Wall-Romana for comments and advice from numerous disciplinary and linguistic perspectives, and the CSCL staff, especially Barbara Lehnhoff, Claire Anderson, and Kate Gallagher, for indispensable logistical expertise. John Mowitt deserves special thanks for steadily encouraging me to make this project's stakes ever clearer.

I could not have completed this book without my colleagues and friends in cinema and media studies and in East Central European culture and history, who have helped me understand its intersection with numerous other stories and disciplines. Rossen Djagalov, Krista Hegburg, Joshua Malitsky, Lisa Peschel, and Masha Salazkina have been invaluable readers and interlocutors. Bradley F. Abrams, Rachel Applebaum, Luca Caminati, Shawn Clybor, Sarah Cramsey, Kevin B. Johnson, James Krapfl, Jessie Labov, Jindřich Toman, Cristina Vatulescu, Daniel Vojtěch, Ondřej Vojtěchovský, Tara Zahra, and Kimberly Zarecor generously shared knowledge, references, and material. Stimulating conversations with Haidee Wasson helped me sharpen and refine the book's arguments. In Prague and Brno, some of the finest film and media historians I have met—Jindřiška Bláhová, Lucie Česálková, Ivan Klimeš, Pavel Skopal, and Petr Szczepanik—offered incisive feedback and discussed the finer points of postwar media history, while Vít Janeček and Pavel Jech made the Film Faculty of the Prague Academy of Performing Arts (FAMU) an institutional home-away-from-home. It is to Martin Švoma that I owe my knowledge of Army Film's existence. And in New Haven, Prague, Minneapolis, Montréal, Boston, and beyond, Laura Bohn, Susan Burch, Michael Cramer, Daniel Feldman, Elan Fessler, David Greenberg, Zdeněk and Hedvika Holých, Maryhope Howland, Noor Jehan Johnson, Casey Riley, Brangwen Stone, and Kimberly Strozewski, among others, provided good incentive to leave the archives and libraries.

In the project's later stages, it benefited greatly from the insight of scholars whose influence is legible throughout it: Nataša Ďurovičová, Tom Gunning, Anikó Imre, and Nancy M. Wingfield, all of whom read the manuscript in its entirety. My thanks in particular to Nataša for her expert translations and for seeing the story this book tells with crystal clarity.

A series of remarkable films was the impetus for this project, and I am grateful to Tom Gunning (University of Chicago), Andrea Slováková (the Jihlava International Documentary Film Festival), Dan Streible (the Orphan Film Symposium), and Yale University's 1968 conference for facilitating their presentation. The Czech Studies Workshop and conferences and talks organized by Muriel Blaive (Ludwig Boltzmann Institute for History and Public Spheres), Christiane Brenner (Collegium Carolinum), Nataša Ďurovičová (University of Iowa), and Irena Grudzińska Gross and Andrzej Tymowski (Princeton University) offered challenging and lively debate. Needless to say, any shortcomings in this book are my own responsibility.

This project would not exist without archives and libraries. I thank the superb staff at the Czech Republic's National Archive (Národní archiv), National Film Archive (Národní filmový archiv), National Library (Národní knihovna), Military History Institute (Vojenský historický ústav), and Ministry of Foreign Affairs Archive (Archiv Ministerstva Zahraničních věcí); the British Film Institute, Special Collections; the British Library; and the University of Minnesota Libraries for helping me locate material. The National Film Archive (NFA) and Military History Institute, where I conducted the majority of my research, deserve particular thanks. At the former, I am indebted to Michal Bregant, who first opened the doors to research on Army Film and has remained a stalwart ally. Vladimír Opěla wisely selected the first Army films I saw. Jarka Fikejzová and Eva Pavlíková uncovered essential resources, while Iwona Lyko provided invaluable assistance. Many of the images in this book are reproduced courtesy of the NFA. I am also grateful to the Military History Institute for providing me with access to films, which served as critical tools in my research and from which some of the images in this book were sourced. The Institute's archival staff, especially Alena Hrnčířová and Zuzana and Marcela Pivcová, provided a congenial space in which to work. At its film archive, David Černý and Milan Hrubý graciously endured my presence in their office for weeks at a time, locating and explaining countless films, while Václav Šmidrkal shared information and resources.

It would also not exist without the filmmakers who generously agreed to be interviewed: Rudolf Adler, Ivan Balaďa, Alois Fišárek, Ladislav Helge, Karel Hložek, Vojtěch Jasný, Jaromír Kallista, Rudolf Krejčík,

Jiří Krob, Jan Schmidt, Juraj Šajmovič, and Karel Vachek. In particular, I thank Antonín Liehm for an e-mail confirming that I was on the right track, Jaromír Kallista for the timely reminder that it is in imperfection that stories become more believable, and Karel Vachek, with whom it all began. It is with a sense of loss that I acknowledge the brilliant cinematographer Juraj Šajmovič, who did not live to see this book's completion.

I am grateful to the programs and institutions that generously supported my research: the Graduate School of Arts and Sciences and International Security Studies at Yale University; the Institute of International Education Fulbright Program; the Fulbright-Hays Program; the Fulbright Commission of the Czech Republic (especially Hana Ripková and Hana Rambousková); the American Council of Learned Societies; the McKnight Foundation; and the University of Minnesota's Center for Austrian Studies, College of Liberal Arts, Grant-in-Aid program, and Imagine Fund. The University of Minnesota Press and Oxford University Press kindly allowed me to reprint material that appears in chapters 4 and 5 of this book from "Surplus Material: Archives, History, and Innovation in Czechoslovak Army Films" (*The Moving Image* 2011: 2 [Fall 2011]: 1–20) and "A Military Avant-Garde: Experimentation in the Czechoslovak Army Film Studio, 1967–1969" (*Screen* 52:4 [Winter 2011]: 427–441), respectively.

At Indiana University Press, I thank my editor Raina Polivka for her enthusiasm and patience, and for helping me realize precisely the project I envisioned. Project manager Michelle Sybert expertly shepherded the book through its final stages.

My family provided the love, support, and excitement for intellectual challenge that fed this project. Igor Tchoukarine lived and breathed it with me and made its research and writing a source of great joy. It, in turn, owes more than I can express to his forbearance, encouragement, and historical acumen. This book is dedicated to the memory of my father, David Beaton Lovejoy, who died as I was completing it. A historian in his own right, his limitless curiosity about society and culture influenced all that is written here. He would, I know, have been the first to read it.

NOTE ON TRANSLATION

UNLESS OTHERWISE indicated, all translations in this book are the author's own.

ARMY FILM AND THE AVANT GARDE

Introduction

ON THE MORNING of January 25, 1969, a group of Czechoslovak Army directors and cinematographers set off, cameras in hand, for the center of Prague. There they joined over 500,000 others for the funeral procession of university student Jan Palach, who a week earlier had publicly immolated himself in protest of the results of the August 1968 Warsaw Pact invasion of Czechoslovakia and the occupation that followed it. Crowds ringed the city's streets, from Charles University's Carolinum, where Palach lay in state, through the Old Town, to the University's Philosophical Faculty, where he had studied. In luminous black and white, the filmmakers sketched a portrait of a city that is defined not by these landmarks, but by crowds alone, by stunned, somber faces and wringing hands. Soon afterward, director Ivan Balaďa wove the footage into *Forest* (*Les,* 1969), an elegiac city film and a portrait of a metropolis in mourning. *Forest,* however, is also an elegy of a different sort. The film represents one of the last in a series of nonfiction experiments made in the late 1960s by the Czechoslovak Army Film studio, films whose formal innovation, and social and political critique, rivaled those of the contemporaneous Czechoslovak New Wave. In the year and a half after *Forest* was made, this remarkable film culture would be dismantled, and the productions of the 1960s archived, largely forgotten, for over thirty years.

This book tells the story of the institution in which this "military avant garde" emerged. In the nearly five decades encompassed here, the military played a unique role within Czechoslovak cinema, helping shape its

1

institutional, conceptual, and even formal dimensions. In the 1930s, the Army's Film Group was a central force in the development of Czechoslovak documentary. In the early 1950s, what was then known as Army Film competed with Czechoslovakia's nationalized film industry for prestige, resources, and viewers, testing the limits of the socialist state's cultural policies in its earliest years. And in the 1960s, as works like *Forest* were taking shape, many of the filmmakers of the Czechoslovak New Wave carried out their military service in the studio. If Army Film thus permits a new reading of Czechoslovak cinema's history, films like Balaďa's tell a different story: that of an experimental film culture that not only emerged within a state institution but that took the form that it did because of its parent organization's culture and practices.

MILITARY FILM IN CZECHOSLOVAKIA

Czechoslovak military cinema existed before Czechoslovakia itself existed. During World War I, legionnaires in France, Italy, and Russia made the country's first military actualities, and in the newly formed Czechoslovak Republic, Army filmmaking remained, for a while, their province. It gained momentum and direction in 1929, when Jiří Jeníček was appointed chief of the Ministry of Defense's Film Group. Jeníček was both a career soldier and an active participant in Czechoslovakia's flourishing amateur cinematic and photographic cultures: He helped organize the 1936 International Exhibition of Photography in Prague and published extensively on film and photography. By the 1940s, his writings came to represent, in film critic Antonín Navrátil's words, the "first Czech excursion into the theory and aesthetics of documentary film."[1]

Jeníček read widely, and drawing, among others, on Central European and Soviet writings on film and photography, on the *Kulturfilm,* and on the institutional achievements of British documentary, his essays articulated a distinctive theory of military cinema, one that linked film's modern, optical nature with the tasks of propaganda and that saw the Army as a prime pedagogical space for both filmmakers and film language. At the same time, he fostered relationships with members of Czechoslovakia's cultural avant garde, who contributed to the Film Group's three major productions of the 1930s: the 1937 *Our Army* (*Naše armáda*), and the 1938 *Soldiers in the Mountains* (*Vojáci v horách*) and *In a New Life* (*V nový život*). These short films portrayed Czechoslovakia as modern, multinational, and prepared to defend itself from German aggression; financed, moreover, by the Ministries of Foreign Affairs and Defense, they helped to pioneer a role for the Czechoslovak state in film production and to crystallize the country's documentary tradition.

With German occupation in 1939, the Czechoslovak Army was dissolved, the Film Group with it. When it was reconstituted after World War II, Jeníček's legacy would persist alongside postwar transformations to the institution and to Czechoslovak cinema culture, both of which charted the development of military film in the following decades. Nineteen forty-five found the Army's Film Division (temporarily still headed by Jeníček) in a unique situation, exempted by president Edvard Beneš's 1945 nationalization decree from government control of film production, distribution, and exhibition. This at first constrained the Division (which in 1951 was renamed Czechoslovak Army Film [Československý armádní film]), and for the first five years after the war, beset by political infighting and lacking organization, it produced few films. Nationalization, however, also allowed military cinema considerable autonomy, as it was not subject to direct oversight from the Ministries of Information or Culture, as the country's primary film producer, Czechoslovak State Film, was.

Army Film's fortunes changed with Alexej Čepička's 1950 appointment as minister of defense. The notoriously megalomaniacal Čepička (son-in-law of Czechoslovakia's first Communist president, Klement Gottwald) saw military film not only as a means of training a more effective army or propagating Czechoslovakia abroad, but also as a source of institutional and personal prestige.[2] From 1950 until 1956, the Ministry devoted extensive financial and material resources to Army Film, as it did to a wide range of military cultural institutions, requisitioning space and equipment and instituting a program under which filmmakers—including recent graduates of FAMU, Czechoslovakia's newly founded national film academy— served their required years of military service in the studio. Many of these filmmakers would later become key figures in the New Wave: Among the well-known directors to serve in Army Film in the 1950s and 1960s were Zbyněk Brynych, Ladislav Helge, Vojtěch Jasný, Pavel Juráček, Karel

Kachyňa, Jiří Menzel, Jan Němec, and František Vláčil. For some, service
in the Army substituted for formal education in film. Vláčil is the best
known of these. As he notes in an interview, "I was never an assistant director to anyone, nor did I go to film school, and thus Army Film, for me,
was a 'journeyman's' school."[3]

As its technical, financial, and professional resources improved, the
studio's productions increased in number. At the same time, according to
Čepička's vision for the studio, Army films themselves "grew" and were
often cut to feature length. Among these were the 1953 feature documentary *People of One Heart* (*Lidé jednoho srdce*, dir. Vojtěch Jasný and Karel
Kachyňa), which chronicled a visit by the Czechoslovak Army's song-
and-dance troupe to China, and the socialist-realist epic *The Tank Brigade*
(*Tanková brigáda*, dir. Ivo Toman, 1955), which interpreted the end of
World War II in Czechoslovakia as the result of Soviet military strength.
In keeping with Čepička's interest in prestige, these—like the studio's
more common short films—were intended to be screened beyond the
military's extensive internal exhibition network, in prominent "civilian"
locations and new, grandly conceived events such as the Army's own film
festival.

Čepička was dismissed from office in 1956, the sole political casualty of
the Khrushchev Thaw in Czechoslovakia.[4] In the 1960s, under a minister
of defense (Bohumír Lomský) less concerned with cinema, and as the reform movement that would become the Prague Spring took shape, Army
Film's leaders worked to construct a new identity for the studio, one that
that acknowledged public mistrust of the military and allied itself with
the reforms. This identity was crafted in press screenings and conferences,
and in the domestic and international film festivals to which Army films
increasingly circulated. Drawing on Czechoslovak military cinema's interwar and postwar histories, it pictured Army Film as a training ground
for the country's young cinematic talent, an innovator in nonfiction film
form, and an institution that, by virtue of its very structure and military
nature, encouraged experimentation. The result was a series of inventive films, many of them explicitly antimilitary. Karel Vachek's segment
in *Army Newsreel 3/1965* (*Armádní filmový měsíčník 3/1965*), for instance,
ostensibly celebrates the twentieth anniversary of the Soviet liberation
of Czechoslovakia but in fact, using the director's trademark Brechtian

strategies, emphasizes the traumatic, and often absurd, nature of war. And the sole fiction feature that Army Film produced in this period, Jan Schmidt's 1966 *The End of August at the Hotel Ozone* (*Konec srpna v hotelu Ozon*), envisions the apocalyptic aftermath of a third, nuclear, world war, in which a band of women roam the ruined earth.

By the late 1960s, then, due to the confluence of institutional forces put in place at three distinct historical moments—the interwar years, the height of the Stalinist period, and the Thaw of the early- to mid-1960s— Army Film offered a uniquely rich context for film production in Czechoslovakia. It had also become a microcosm of sorts of Czechoslovakia's burgeoning film culture, with recent graduates of FAMU temporarily gathered in the studio's intimate space (for Army Film was comparatively small) during their years of military service. Many of the filmmakers who served in Army Film in the 1960s recall having a considerable degree of latitude—to choose topics and styles, and from strict censorship—during these years, as films like *Forest* attest. And thus the talents and infrastructure that Čepička had hoped would make Army Film an esteemed producer of feature-length films that followed "the Soviet model" ultimately enabled the studio to return to its roots in short nonfiction and experimental film. The institution, in turn, sketched a continuum from the interwar avant garde and the Griersonian documentary to socialist realism and the cinéma vérité and modernist documentary of the late 1960s.

ARMY FILM IN SCHOLARSHIP AND POPULAR MEMORY

In 1962, the Karlovy Vary Short Film Festival's jury praised Army Film as a "'young workshop' for Czechoslovak film."[5] Thirty years later, in his chronicle of Czechoslovak documentary, Navrátil dubbed the studio an "incubator of talents."[6] Nevertheless, Army Film is largely absent from histories of Czechoslovak cinema. The postwar studio is addressed in Václav Šmidrkal's 2009 *The Army and the Silver Screen,* published by the Czech Army, while the interwar period is the subject of proceedings from a 1992 conference, *The Image of the Military in Interwar Czechoslovak Cinema.*[7] References to Army Film can occasionally be found in the major histories of the Czechoslovak New Wave—Peter Hames's *The Czechoslo-*

vak New Wave, works by Antonín and Mira Liehm, and Josef Škvorecký's *All The Bright Young Men and Women*—typically, however, as footnotes to the feature film careers of New Wave filmmakers.[8] And from time to time, the studio is evoked in unexpected places: for instance, in Czech-born German author Maxim Biller's short story "When the Tomcat Comes" ("Wenn der Kater kommt"), which seems to meld Vláčil's military film career with the civilian career of Czech director Alfred Radok in the story of the titular "father" (*Vater–Kater*), whose last name is Radek.[9]

The lack of sustained attention to the studio, particularly in its postwar incarnation, has both practical and political roots. Army Film's institutional existence was, first, separate from that of Czechoslovakia's nationalized film industry, and it remains so in its archival afterlife. The majority of the studio's extant internal documents are archived not with other government files relating to cinema (in the Czech Republic's National Archive or National Film Archive), but in the Administrative Archive of the Czech Army in the city of Olomouc and in the Czech Central Military Archive's Ministry of Defense collection. Army films themselves are archived in two locations—in the Army Film Archive (a division of the Military History Institute in Prague), and the Czech National Film Archive. Archivists have not yet been able to reconstruct the studio's complete production history.[10]

Beyond these archival distinctions, at the time they were made, the studio's films were largely unknown to the general public. Most were made for internal use—some deemed "secret" or "top-secret"—while films released to civilian audiences (many of them newsreels or short nonfiction films) typically appeared as accompaniments to feature films, in festivals, in dedicated short-film cinemas, or on television. Army productions nevertheless had a vibrant life within the military, whose film distribution organs dispersed them to barracks classrooms, film clubs, mobile cinemas, specialized film festivals, and workshops, as well as to the official settings for which they were commissioned.

If the studio's neglect is thus that of nonfiction, short, and "useful" film worldwide, it also speaks to Army Film's institutional context.[11] The postwar Czechoslovak Army is typically remembered in opposition to the general public, as a conservative—and particularly in the 1950s, repressive—state-within-a-state.[12] In a 1966 interview with Army Film employees, film critic Antonín Novák stated as much, asking the filmmakers if the studio wasn't "one of the last remnants of a period when it seemed that the Army wanted to create its own republic, one with its own culture."[13] Under Čepička's leadership, indeed, the Czechoslovak Army was infamous for its financial excesses, internal purges, role in the country's show trials, and political and human rights abuses. It embodied, in short, the darkest and most tragic aspects of Czechoslovak Stalinism. However, the conception of the army as, effectively, a foreign body overlooks both this institution's wide social reach—nearly all of the country's male youth served in it—and the fact that in the mid- to late 1960s, its Main Political Administration, under whose aegis Army Film fell, was deeply involved in the reform movement.[14] Army Film's absence from the history of Czechoslovak film and media thus also reflects a more general mistrust of "sponsored" film—which, as Jan-Christopher Horak points out, highlights the ideological assumptions that often underpin assessments of film history and aesthetics.[15] In the Czech case, this is coupled with a deep-rooted antimilitarism embodied perfectly by the literary figure of the Good Soldier Švejk, a leitmotif in Army Film's productions and culture.

If one looks closely at the Army's productions, however, it is clear that they tell a more complex story than the paradigm of military versus society allows us to imagine. Here, Švejk, with his attendant paradoxes and contradictions, is doubly relevant: Even when they are not striking examples of cinematic experiments occurring in what might seem to be an unlikely location, the films are a testament to military cinema's close intertwining with "civilian" cinema in Czechoslovakia—whose history, I argue, this institution allows us to read anew. These two stories are the focus of this book, and I frame them through a dual lens: first, the studio itself, and, second, the relationship between its productions' form and their social, political, and discursive context.

Chapter 1 focuses on the tense years prior to World War II, charting how, at the intersection of Jiří Jeníček's organizational efforts, Ministry of Foreign Affairs funding, and shifts in Czechoslovak and world cinema culture of the 1930s, the Army's Film Group developed the institutional and aesthetic identity that would define Czechoslovak military cinema for most of the following four decades. The Group, in these years, was conceived akin to industrial film institutions—as a "workshop" for nonfiction film form and a space for young filmmakers to hone their skills—while its films were seen as a means through which to assert Czechoslovakia's military strength and political viability. This identity was marked equally by Jeníček's theories of film, photography, and visual propaganda and by his conscious modeling of the Film Group after the British Empire Marketing Board and General Post Office film units.

Chapter 2 follows this institution through the tumultuous years 1945–1955, chronicling how two developments—the 1945 nationalization of Czechoslovak cinema and Čepička's appointment as minister of defense—established the conditions for Army Film's postwar growth. Simultaneously, it traces the evolution of Czechoslovak cinema culture through the studio, focusing, in particular, on nonfiction film. Like much of Czechoslovak cinema at this moment, the Army's short nonfiction films served as pedagogy for a changing world. This entailed depicting the processes of postwar reconstruction and "building socialism," modeling a relationship between Czechoslovakia's military and civilian spheres, and picturing its shifting geopolitical alliances. Although such films have often been interpreted as an index of Soviet cultural influence, I call this into question, arguing that an institutional perspective allows us to read the films of the 1950s within a continuum that begins in the interwar period and makes visible the links between the pedagogical and practical projects of Czechoslovak and international—not only Soviet—documentary.

Chapter 3 investigates Stalinist-era cinema further, through Army instructional films of the early 1950s and their engagement with the formal and political concepts of the "example," "model," and "Soviet model." Describing a rhetoric of exemplarity in such films—which functioned as "models" for soldiers' actions, while themselves following strict formal "models"—I trace how, in the mid-1950s, certain instructional films (many made by future members of the New Wave) began to challenge the notion of the "model." These films presented behavior that deviated from military norms while also diverging from instructional filmmaking's strictly defined generic codes. The chapter, in sum, locates some of the New Wave's roots in instructional filmmaking, which, it argues, represented a dual form of pedagogy: for the soldier (who learned behavior) and the filmmaker (who learned to make films).

Chapter 4 turns to the late 1950s through 1967, when—with Čepička out of office, and as the Czechoslovak 1960s began—the military faced a crisis of legitimacy. In these years, Army Film's interwar identity as a "workshop" became a strategic tool for transforming discourse about its work and its films and crafting the image of an institution sensitive to the concerns of a largely antimilitary Czechoslovak youth, a hotbed of formal experimentation and radical new ideas about society. As part of this shift, Army filmmakers were encouraged to adopt a wide thematic and stylistic range in their films, while the studio developed exhibition strategies that focused on "civilian" film festivals at home and abroad, as well as on television. The chapter thus sheds further light on the history and politics of the "Czechoslovak film miracle" of the 1960s, underlining its deep and systematic links to governmental and industrial media practices and the ways in which its tradition of social and political critique, at times, reflected institutional demands.

The book's final chapter discusses Army Film at the height of the Prague Spring, before the studio's normalization in the wake of the August 1968 Warsaw Pact invasion. Moving beyond the strategic critique of earlier in the decade, Army Film, from late 1967 to 1970, engaged directly and intimately with the country's political and social reforms. In these years, indeed, a distinct mode of experimental nonfiction film emerged in the studio, one that drew on institutional, economic, and political factors within the studio and the Czechoslovak state, as well as on the broader cultural dynamics of the "exceptional" year of 1968. These films, the chapter argues, were among the most radical in postwar Czechoslovak cinema, a fact that—like Army Film's own history—asks us to think anew about the context and genesis of experimental and "oppositional" cinema and its relationship to the state.

INSTITUTIONS, CONTINUITY, AND THE COLD WAR

As these synopses make clear, I approach Army Film's history through the lens of the studio as a space of production: its emergence and development, its internal practices and discourse, its context. This institution's evolution over nearly fifty years, in turn, affords a new perspective on the history of postwar East European cinema, whose outlines are typically circumscribed by the arc of the Cold War and read in dialogue with its watershed moments: 1945 (World War II's end, the Yalta conference, and the nationalization of film industries), 1948 (the Communist Party's rise to power, and soon after, socialist realism's adoption as a standard "method"), 1956 (the "secret speech"; crises in Hungary and Poland), 1962 (Czechoslovak destalinization; the beginning of what András Bálint Kovács defines as "established modernism," both in Western and Eastern Europe), 1968 (the Prague Spring), 1989 (a return to "Europe" and to the market).[16]

This narrative has begun to shift as scholars have examined new aspects of the region's postwar media cultures; among them popular genre production, television, and the structure of film and media industries themselves.[17] Institutions like Army Film are a critical part of this reassessment, for their productions in fact represented the majority of media made in the region. Such institutions' production practices are equally important, for these oblige one to look beyond key dates and events and at the everyday concepts of budgets, materials, employees, and institutional wrangling-for-position in a system that exceeded the familiar binaries of—in Anikó Imre's words—"good and bad, liberation and oppression, authoritarianism and democracy, truth and lies."[18] Army Film, finally, asks us to modify this narrative by demonstrating how moments in the chronology of East European cinema and media history that are traditionally seen as caesurae in fact represent points of continuity. Most importantly among these, it makes clear that cinema of the Stalinist period—on which there is comparatively little criticism and scholarship—was an integral part of Czechoslovak media history, closely linked to the modernist film cultures that preceded and followed it.[19]

In this sense, drawing insights from recent work in film and media history and in the cultural and social history of Eastern Europe, this book addresses the question that almost all writings on the Czechoslovak New Wave have attempted to answer: to borrow Josef Škvorecký's tongue-in-cheek language, how the "miracle" of Czechoslovak film emerged, in the 1960s, from what the rest of the world saw as "some Eastern European country . . . eo ipso technically undeveloped and culturally impoverished."[20] The three classic English-language studies of the New Wave offer varying responses to this question. Škvorecký argues that the New Wave was "a synthesis, evolved from a dialectic situation formed by four factors of the post-war development": the nationalization of the film industry, the establishment of FAMU, the institutionalization of socialist realism in the 1950s, and audiences' subsequent lack of interest in domestic productions.[21] He argues, in short, that the New Wave was the product of the nationalized film industry, with both its pitfalls (government centralization, socialist realism) and its advantages (FAMU filmmakers were able to see, and learn from, international art cinema, and filmmakers had more resources).

In his *Closely Watched Films,* Antonín Liehm, like Škvorecký, writes of nationalization as a double-edged sword, on the one hand offering filmmakers possibilities unimaginable under the previous market-based production system, and on the other giving the government the ability to control film production absolutely. Liehm likens the relationship between the state and film production in postwar Eastern Europe to that of a valve or a leash: "Every relaxation of state control enabled film to utilize the advantages presented by nationalization. Every tightening of the state's grasp made nationalized cinematography into a prison with bars so dense that art could not slip through."[22] While it allows for multiple—both positive and negative—interpretations of the state's relationship to film, Liehm's metaphor still envisions the state in unitary terms and not as an institutional actor with multiple dimensions, a characteristic that this book argues is important. Peter Hames, too, in *The Czechoslovak New Wave,* interprets the New Wave's emergence as a product of both nationalization and the 1960s—"one aspect of a wider phenomenon of the growth of ideas in economics, politics, literature and the arts that made up the Czechoslovak Reform Movement."[23] He, like Škvorecký, reads the movement's films as a reaction to socialist realism: "The break with the normative traditions of Socialist Realism," he writes, "was an essential first phase in providing the opportunity to create freely and in accordance with an inner need."[24]

Although these studies remain the authoritative texts on the New Wave, Army Film's history suggests revisions to their arguments. First, as I discuss in chapters 2 and 3, the form of military films demonstrates that the innovative aesthetics and narratives that defined Czechoslovak cinema of the 1960s, in and beyond the Army, represented, in some measure, an evolution, not a break, from socialist realism and that Czechoslovak cinematic socialist realism itself did not solely reflect the "Soviet model" but rather built on a range of domestic and international practices and discourses. Second, the studio's history is evidence of the critical role that state institutions played in the development of the "Czechoslovak film miracle," even at politically repressive moments, thus underscoring the ways in which, as Haidee Wasson asserts, "politically radical, aesthetically conservative, and unrelentingly governmental forces have long shaped film culture."[25] This, finally, challenges the auteurist model that often defines literature on East European cinema, highlighting the multiple contexts, institutional, political, and material, in which its directors worked. In this sense, I take as a methodological guide Tom Gunning's reflection on the author: "The idea of an author can be valuable insofar as it opens texts to historical forces, and pernicious insofar as its insulates films in an ahistorical cult of personality."[26] Army Film's history, moreover, frames the issue of auteurism in productive ways, demonstrating how auteurs can be useful to institutions—and institutions useful to auteurs—as well as how institutions themselves can be "auteurist."

NONFICTION FILM AND THE STATE

If longue-durée institutional history thus makes clear the limitations of a common reading of postwar East European cinema—in which filmmakers struggle within monolithic media industries, isolated both from the industries and cultures that preceded them and from the rest of the world—the studio's development also nuances our understanding of documentary film history.[27] For fundamentally, Army Film's history is that of a government institution of nonfiction film.[28] As was the case elsewhere in the 1920s and 1930s, what critics came to understand as "documentary," in Army Film, developed as Bill Nichols describes in his seminal article "Documentary Film and the Modernist Avant-Garde," at the intersection of the avant garde and the state, "when cinema came into the direct service of various, already active efforts to build national identity."[29] In the 1950s, the studio's films continued in this path, echoing the form and rhetoric associated with documentary's international "institutionalized" format, which was, in Zoë Druick's words, "short, national, and didactic."[30] In the early 1960s, armed with new technologies, military filmmakers adopted the observational approaches of cinéma vérité and cinema direct. And at the decade's end, the same filmmakers reacted to this format, borrowing from the legacy of the interwar avant garde.[31]

This story's familiarity is significant. For outside of a scattering of works—among them Mikhail Romm's compilation films, Dušan Maka-veyev's fiction-nonfiction hybrids, and the Polish "Black Series" (*Czarna seria*) films—little postwar East European or Soviet nonfiction film has made its way into the canon of world documentary. The result has often been the reliance on Cold War frameworks to explain these films, which are interpreted in the familiar terms of "collaborator" or "dissident": as either supporting or resisting the Party and the state. This book aims not only to bring unknown aspects of postwar East European nonfiction film to light, but also, by highlighting the common roots and similarities between nonfiction film East and West, liberal and socialist, to frustrate these dichotomies and point toward an international history of postwar documentary.

There are nonetheless differences between Army Film's history and the history that Nichols discusses. While Nichols reads the British Documentary Movement's use of "innovative techniques" as a means of "urg[ing] preferred solutions to social problems," experimentation with film language was itself an institutional goal for Czechoslovak military cinema.[32] And where Nichols links the formal developments of the late 1960s to the "dissolution" of the state's "fixed, central place" in documentary, in Army Film, the state remained their site and center. These differences speak to what film critic Jaroslav Boček, in 1964, termed Army Film's "industrial" character: its mandate to continually improve the way it fulfilled its institutional charge.[33] As such, they also highlight documentary's deep intertwining with "useful" cinema.[34] For throughout the period this book examines, Army Film categorized its productions as, variably, "documentary," "newsreel," "instructional," "popular-scientific," "reportage," "promotional" films, and beyond. These works served purposes ranging from pedagogy to propaganda, entertainment to advertisement, internal communication to historical record keeping. "Purpose" itself, furthermore, reveals a media history that exceeds the Cold War's conceptual and physical geographies, as these films had a markedly cosmopolitan existence, frequently traveling to international film festivals (tourist film festivals, agricultural film festivals, etc.) defined less by bloc politics than by the more practical question of a film's function or subject: what it taught, depicted, or did.

Distinctions between Army Film and other state documentary institutions are also clear domestically, for the postwar nationalized film industry had a nonfiction film studio, Krátký (Short) Film, which produced a similar range of genres to Army Film on a wider array of topics. In Jiří Havelka's extensive catalogues of Czechoslovak cinema, Army Film's productions are listed under the heading "Films Made outside of Czechoslovak State Film," and as the comparatively short list of films in this column demonstrates, the military studio was small.[35] Yet it is in part because of its very smallness that Army Film is an apt case study through which to reassess the state's relationship to cinema, a relationship that has often been regarded with, to borrow Ben Kafka's phrasing, ambivalence: on the one hand, enthusiasm for public support as an alternative to the commercial film industry; on the other, a vision of the state as a force that suppresses radical aesthetics and politics—and in the case of instructional and propaganda films, often compels and coerces.[36]

Army Film allows us to investigate this relationship in structural terms. As a branch of the military, the studio was at the core of the state (the entity, in Max Weber's definition, that maintains a monopoly on the legitimate use of physical force).[37] However, while institutions like Krátký Film operated within the nationalized film industry, even before Army Film's omission from the postwar nationalization decree, the Ministry of Defense maintained an independent budget for film production, distribution, and exhibition, recognizing the military's distinct uses for the medium. This, coupled with its internal censorship processes, permitted the military film studio to pursue an idiosyncratic course, one that did not necessarily correspond to broader cultural policies.

With this, Army Film makes clear that the Czechoslovak state's relationship to cinema was not unitary but varied according to its institutions' priorities, policies, and practices. These, moreover, were often at odds, as even after nationalization ostensibly did away with the "bourgeois" interwar years' competition, Czechoslovak government film institutions vied with one another for the symbolic capital of prestige. If this competition, as chapters 2 and 4 demonstrate, helped shape Army Film's institutional identity and productions, the studio's internal documents and films reveal other ways in which the state's relationship to cinema was productive—in the memoranda that became channels for reflection on film as a medium and cinema as a cultural phenomenon; and in the institutional discourse that mirrored the critical aesthetics and politics in Army Film's late-1960s productions.

These documents are at the core both of this book's understanding of the state and of its methodology. As anthropologist Matthew Hull writes in his 2012 survey of literature on bureaucratic documents, such "material" objects "are not simply instruments of bureaucratic organizations, but rather are constitutive of bureaucratic rules, ideologies, knowledge, practices, subjectivities, objects, outcomes, and even the organizations themselves." This, in turn, makes the state "not simply . . . a bureaucracy of regulation, but also '. . . a spectral presence materialized in documents.'"[38] And it is, I argue, precisely through objects such as Army Film's productions, schedules, and budgets that we can ask what the state was for this cinematic institution. In keeping with these objects' materiality, the response to this question will be consistent neither with that of other institutions nor across temporal, geographic, or cultural contexts.[39]

VANGUARD

The state nevertheless has multiple facets in this book, which is also concerned with the space of the state—its geopolitical dimensions. This is in part due to its subject: As chapter 1 discusses, Czechoslovakia was a creation of World War I, a multinational space whose outlines were both politically vital and constantly challenged.[40] But the book's spatial preoccupations also reflect its subject, the Army, an institution charged both with preventing incursions into state territory and with making maps, whether charts of land or battlefields or propaganda that announces a country's existence and strength. As Paul Virilio and Friedrich Kittler have argued, film and other visual media have long been central to this process of military "mapmaking," serving as tools that sharpen perception and, as Kittler writes, "determine our situation."[41] In order to see clearly, these tools and the techniques for their use must constantly be improved, thus placing the military at the vanguard not only of media technology but also of media aesthetics.

This book does not focus on Czechoslovak military cinema's engagement with active conflicts, its management of, in Virilio's words, "tactical and strategic representations of warfare for the soldier, the tank or aircraft pilot, and above all the senior officer who engages combat forces."[42] Nevertheless, in the period it examines, the studio was consistently characterized as a laboratory for film form and language—in Thomas Elsaesser's words, emphasizing its links to industrial film, "research and development."[43] Indeed, in the 1920s, Army filmmaking was briefly housed in the Czechoslovak Ministry of Defense's Investigative and Experimental Division. And in his writings on visual propaganda, Jeníček anticipated Virilio and Kittler's arguments, positing the army as an institution whose innovation in the modern media of photography and film had "one entirely simple program: to awaken and strengthen stateness and the state."[44]

Although it emerged in the context of interwar sponsored and industrial film, this characterization persisted after World War II. Boček's 1964 description of the studio as "industrial," for instance, hinged on the fact that its experiments were rooted in its "purposeful" charge, which limited the subjects on which it made films but left open possibilities for the way that it treated these subjects.[45] This terminology thus allows us to reframe Virilio's and Kittler's arguments to account for what scholars have demonstrated in other geographic contexts: the military's role not only as film and media's technical or aesthetic vanguard but also as a pioneer in cinema's applications and institutions.[46] Indeed, for Army Film's Polish counterpart, the military film studio Czołówka (vanguard; as Dorota Ostrowska points out, an early pioneer of Polish cinema's production-group model), this understanding was embodied in its very name.[47]

It was thus that Jeníček, too—who preferred the term "experimental" to describe the Film Group's work, reserving the adjective "avant-garde" for pure formal experimentation—understood military cinema's function. Yet for him, this was not incompatible with the tradition of aesthetic innovation that developed in the Group as a result of both its "industrial" nature and its legacy of collaboration with the cultural avant garde. Nor, after his ouster in 1948, would it be incompatible with the dominant under-standing of the term "avant-garde" in postwar Czechoslovakia, where—as the interwar avant garde increasingly became the target of criticism—it indicated the progressive, revolutionary nature of a state in which social-ism was being "built," a process in which Army Film saw itself as a central participant.[48] As such, the aesthetics and politics of films like *Forest* must also be read as a product of Army Film's institutional mandate to picture Czechoslovakia's borders and position in the world, a process that, by the end of the decade, required piercing the evident surface of post-invasion reality, revealing its inherent strangeness. And thus if the studio's history challenges common genealogies of East European cinema, it also under-scores Michael Zryd's argument about the centrality of institutions to avant-garde filmmaking.[49] Indeed, not only did the Czechoslovak Army provide the material basis—salaries, film stock and equipment, distribu-tion, time—for the "military avant garde" to thrive; it also helped deter-mine its form.

This institution and its films are both the primary subject and the most complex aspect of this book. For although Army Film's history calls into question the epistemological framework of the Cold War, many of its pro-ductions used this framework as their guide. In the 1950s, films about border guards saw Czechoslovakia's western frontier as the dividing line between two "worlds," while in the early 1960s, compilation documenta-ries framed Sudeten Germans as a fifth column that threatened Czecho-slovakia and the socialist sphere. And throughout the studio's postwar history, yearly newsreels catalogued the "battle technology of the capi-talist armies" while others warned viewers about "ideological diversion" arriving from the West via magazines and movies. Yet the fact that, in their provenance, such films were entwined with radically different forms and modes of filmmaking testifies to the multifaceted nature of really exist-ing media in "really existing socialism," a fact to which Army Film itself also speaks.

1

A Deep and Fruitful Tradition:
Jiří Jeníček, the Film Group, and
Cinema Culture of the 1930s

"ON THE GOALS AND RESPONSIBILITIES of Military Film," a 1937 article by Czechoslovak Army filmmaker Jiří Jeníček, does not open—as one might imagine from its staid title—with the history of battles or proclamations about duty to country and flag. Instead, it begins with a quote from Béla Balázs's 1924 *Visible Man*: "Film is *the popular art* of our century."[1] This quote serves as pretext for Jeníček's contention: that militaries throughout the world have long been a central source for new understandings and uses of cinema. "A good eight years before Balázs," he writes,

> during the last part of the World War, soldiers recognized the advantages that film can bring to their work, sensing that it had all the characteristics of a popular communication medium. They did not, of course, place film as high on the hierarchical ladder as Balázs, but they recognized its exceptional importance for defense at a time when it was still considered a peripheral . . . entertainment; when a man of average education blushed if pressed to acknowledge that he spent his evenings at the biograph.[2]

This "recognition" was not, he notes, "sheer chance." Instead, it was the "result of a deep and fruitful tradition to which the names of numerous soldiers speak: for instance, the French Army officer Nicéphore Niépce, one of the inventors of photography; or general Uchatius [Franz von Uchatius], the inventor of the projection stroboscope . . . , who contributed very honorably to the history not only of military photography and cinema, but also of photography and cinema more generally." This history of innovation in visual technology, in Jeníček's estimation, is linked to military innovations in cinema's applications, of which he highlights three: propaganda, education, and technical.

If Jeníček's characterization of the military as cinema's advance guard prefigured by a half-century Paul Virilio and Friedrich Kittler's media theories, it also described Czechoslovak military cinema at this moment. In the 1930s, the Army's Film Group (Filmová skupina), with Jeníček at its helm, was a vanguard for Czechoslovak film: a space in which new social, political, formal, and institutional understandings of cinema were discussed, tested, and put into practice. As such, Jeníček's invocation of contemporary film criticism was doubly fitting, for this process was integrally connected to "civilian" film culture. The Group, indeed, brought together several of the interwar Czechoslovak figures most deeply and practically engaged in articulating a conception of cinema that extended beyond its popular associations with commerce or entertainment. Some of these figures were members of the country's cultural avant garde: musician, critic, and dramatist E. F. Burian; filmmaker Jiří Lehovec. Others, like diplomat Jindřich Elbl, were government officials. By the time Jeníček published his essay, the Film Group was on the cusp of being recognized both for these conceptual contributions and for, as film critic Antonín Navrátil would observe years later, its role as an "incubator of talent": an institution that allowed young filmmakers to hone their skills through practice.[3] This identity—which recognized Czechoslovak military cinema as a site of experimentation and education—would define Army filmmaking in the country for decades to come.

PROPAGANDA AND MYTH

"There are," Jeníček observes in his essay, "as many opinions and viewpoints on the function of military film as there are armies"—and in Czechoslovakia, military film's central "function" was "historical propaganda." This corresponded to long-standing cultural practices in Czechoslovakia, to whose very existence—as historian Andrea Orzoff has detailed—propaganda was critical. Long before 1919, when the new, democratic state was established by the Treaty of Saint-Germain, Orzoff writes, the country's founders "decided that international and domestic propaganda would have to be intense complementary efforts for the postwar Czechoslovak state. The world, particularly the Great Powers, had to be taught about this new parliamentary democracy at Europe's heart."[4]

These founders—chief among them philosopher Tomáš Garrigue Masaryk and sociologist Edvard Beneš (Czechoslovakia's first and second presidents, respectively)—led the process in which the First Czechoslovak Republic was carved from the former Hapsburg Monarchy, which, for centuries, had spanned much of Eastern and Central Europe. The republic was correspondingly diverse. At its west were the Czech lands (Bohemia, Moravia, and Silesia), which together had possessed two thirds of Hapsburg industry.[5] At the north, the mining region of Silesia bordered and shared population with Poland, while to its east were the largely agrarian and Catholic Slovak lands, historically part of Hungary. To Slovakia's east lay poor, religious, and rural Subcarpathian Ruthenia, formerly a Hungarian territory and today part of Ukraine.

The new state's heterogeneity was at once an advantage—with its mixture of developed industry, rich agricultural territory, and (in the Czech lands) literate, educated population—and a liability. While in the 1921 and 1930 censuses, roughly 65 percent of the state's population was identified as "Czechoslovak" (a term that itself comprised distinct populations and identities), a fifth of Slovakia's interwar population was ethnically Magyar (Hungarian), and a full third of Bohemia's interwar population German. Jews, Poles, and Ruthenians also made up a considerable part of Czechoslovak society.[6] Despite the practical fluidity between many of these identities, their populations were the subject of claims by Czechoslovakia's neighbors—primarily Hungary and, after the National Socialist (Nazi) Party came to power, Germany.[7] Moreover, the republic's official "national" culture proved in practice to be primarily Czech, leaving little room for the expression of other identities.[8]

Thus, while World War I propaganda had sought to justify Czechoslovakia's creation, propaganda remained a critical governmental tool after the war, when it helped present a coherent state identity to publics at home and abroad. This identity centered on a Czech national narrative, or "myth," dating to the nineteenth-century "National Awakening," when artists and intellectuals canonized a series of "national" personalities, works, and events—the fourteenth-century monk Dalimil's chronicle of the Czech people, religious reformer Jan Hus, and folk tales and proverbs.[9] Among the myth's central themes were the Czech language's function as a bearer of national identity; the characterization of Germans as, in historian Jiří Rak's words, an "ancestral enemy"; and most important, a vision of the country as exceptional among its neighbors for its deep-seated democratic values.[10]

As Orzoff describes, this "myth" was disseminated through a range of media (print, radio, the graphic arts, lectures) whose production and circulation the Czechoslovak Ministry of Foreign Affairs coordinated, but that was typically produced in collaboration with private institutions: Masaryk and Beneš, she writes, believed that "propaganda and cultural diplomacy were more effective when the state's hand was hidden."[11] Until the early 1930s, however, the Czechoslovak government limited its involvement with cinema. Pavel Zeman attributes this to the political elite's mistrust of new media and to its anxieties about foreign perceptions of the state's identity as a democracy (especially as cinema was nationalized in the Soviet Union, Italy, and Germany).[12] Governmental engagement in Czechoslovak cinema during the 1920s was thus largely limited to economic concerns (the Ministry of Industry, Trade, and Business managed film import and export and helped "cultivate" the domestic film industry) and censorship (managed by the Ministry of Interior), mirroring cinema's status in other interwar liberal democracies.[13]

The Ministry of Defense, however, was an exception to this rule and, throughout the interwar period, maintained its own production facilities and budget in order to support the military's unique needs for film and to ensure military secrecy.[14] Czechoslovak military cinema, in fact, effectively predated the First Republic itself, as the Czechoslovak Legions, volunteer forces that fought in World War I alongside the French, Italian, and Russian armies, had been heavily involved in filmmaking throughout the war.[15] Here, they performed a function similar to that of Czechoslovakia's World War I propaganda in other media, giving discursive shape to a state that did not yet exist.

For the first few years after the war, military filmmaking remained the province of former legionnaires, among them Karel Fiala, who led the Army's Photographic and Cinematic Division in Slovakia (where fighting against Béla Kun's Hungarian Red Army had just ended), making actuality films and assisting with Czechoslovakia's paternalistic "assimilation" of Slovaks.[16] In 1921, the film and photographic group was incorporated into the Ministry of Defense's Investigative and Experimental Division (Výzkumný a zkušební ústav), where it added films on military technical, industrial, and other subjects to its long-standing patriotic repertoire. An October 27, 1923, review in the daily *Národní listy* (*National Papers*), for instance, describes a screening of military films that day (timed, as many such screenings were, to coincide with Czechoslovakia's independence day, October 28) that included footage from the Army's training maneuvers of that year, showing the "life of a soldier, his training and military preparation" and various military athletic competitions.[17]

When, in 1925, the group was transferred once again—this time, to the General Staff's Training Division (Oddělení branné výchovy) and its Military Technical Institute (Vojenský technický ústav)—its production expanded to encompass, among others, nature and promotional films.[18] In 1930, it began producing a newsreel, *Military Bulletin* (*Vojenský zpravodaj*). And late in the 1920s, the Ministry of Defense produced three fiction features, all directed by Vladimír Studecký: the 1927 melodrama *Slavia L-Brox* (*A Pilot's Romance*) (*Slavia L-Brox* [*Románek letcův*]), the 1929 spy film *Mountain Calling SOS* (*Horské volání S.O.S.*), and the 1928 *For the Czechoslovak State* (*Za československý stát*), which, with its Legionnaire topic and title, returned the Group to its earliest intentions and institutional roots.[19]

In 1929, Jeníček—a career soldier since 1916—was transferred to Prague and to what was then known as the Film Group. Under his leadership, Czechoslovak military cinema further developed its newsreel, instructional, and propaganda production, modes that were central to Jeníček's understanding of military cinema.[20] Jeníček's instructional films ranged in form and approach, from expository to reportage to popular-scientific. Some focused on behavior and morale, employing fiction as a mode of instruction, among them the 1934 *Morning in the Barracks* (*Ráno v kasárnách*), a series of slapstick vignettes demonstrating proper conduct on military bases. (The intertitle "Rule: the alarm clock signals to the men to wake up and get ready for the day's work" is followed by a scene in which soldiers douse their oversleeping comrade with a bucket of water.)

Although, like their precursors, instructional films often had patriotic undertones (a night guard in *Morning in the Barracks*' first vignette contentedly reads Božena Němcová's *The Grandmother* [*Babička*], a literary classic of the Czech National Awakening), elements of the Czechoslovak "myth" were most prominent in the Film Group's propaganda. The 1935 *Our Soldiers* (*Naši vojáci*), for instance, opens with the title

> Remember the words of Karel Havlíček Borovský: "The soldier's vocation is beautiful and honorable when he puts his life at stake for his countrymen, when he endures discomfort for our many-hued homeland, when he guards the borders of the land, so that it may peacefully work." This is the spirit of the Czechoslovak soldier's work![21]

The film that follows sketches the "life cyle" of a Czechoslovak soldier through a compilation of scenes from military actualities and instructional films (youth at a scout camp, conscription, daily life on the military base, the work of different units), ending triumphantly, with a military parade.

DEPRESSION, SOUND, AND NATION

The Film Group's development in the 1930s was the result not only of Jeníček's leadership but also of political and cultural shifts that created synergy between the Czechoslovak state's economic interest in cinema and the national interests of its propaganda in other media. Two events of the late 1920s and early 1930s precipitated these changes: the Great Depression and the advent of film sound. The latter, in multinational Czechoslovakia, was an immediate lightning rod for nationalist rhetoric—as Nancy M. Wingfield has chronicled, the September 1930 screening of German-language sound films in Prague set off four nights of riots by Czech fascists.[22] In this context, as Czechoslovakia began to feel the Depression's effects, concern grew about the economic and ideological ramifications of foreign (primarily American and German) film's predominance in the Czechoslovak market.

In April 1932, the Ministry of Industry, Trade, and Business responded to this concern by implementing a "contingent" system, designed to retain money from foreign film exhibition and thereby bolster the domestic film industry.[23] As Petr Szczepanik has detailed, like similar systems that had been established elsewhere in Europe since the 1920s, Czechoslovakia's contingent stipulated that in order to import a specified number of films, a foreign company was required produce one film in Czechoslovakia or to purchase a "contingent voucher."[24] Yet Czechoslovakia's system was immediately less successful than its counterparts. Upon its implementation, the MPPDA (Motion Picture Producers and Distributors of America)—which, Szczepanik writes, deemed Czechoslovakia too small to merit "such strict measures"—began a boycott of the Czechoslovak market that lasted for over two years.[25] Making matters worse, the absence of American films from the market forced Czechoslovak cinema owners to rent German films—many of them either openly supportive of the Nazi Party or interpreted as such—in order to stay in business.[26]

With this, film import and export became pressing matters of national security and cultural identity. Indeed, it was not only economics (the fate of the domestic film industry) or the prospect of war (signaled by Nazi propaganda) that worried Czechoslovaks but also domestic politics. At the heart of these stood the country's northern and western, largely German-speaking, borderlands. Home to a substantial proportion of Czechoslovakia's industry, the region was hit particularly hard by the Depression, and in 1933, its economic concerns were channeled into politics by Konrad Henlein's newly founded Sudeten German Homeland Front. The latter, which transformed itself into a political party (the Sudeten German Party [Sudetendeutsche Partei or SdP]) in 1935, in Eagle Glassheim's words, blamed the region's economic problems on "perceived Czech discrimination, as well as Jews and global capitalism."[27] The SdP's appeals to solidarity with the Nazi Party and articulation of a distinct German national identity threatened the Czechoslovak government's carefully managed multinationalism.[28] And thus, as journalists and film professionals watched increasing numbers of films from Germany appearing on Czechoslovak screens, they began to call urgently for a two-pronged remedy: for Czechoslovakia to appease the American studios, and for the country to begin producing its own cultural propaganda films as a counterweight to the German films.[29]

One such call came at the end of October 1933, in a letter sent by František Papoušek—a prominent Prague lawyer and co-owner of the Fenix cinema—to Jindřich Elbl, the Ministry of Foreign Affairs' young Film Officer. Papoušek's letter described the situation that Czechoslovak cinema owners faced—"If we do not have American films," he explained, "we must rent and play German films"—framing it in terms of nationality, defense, and the intertwined issues of sound and language. Papoušek argued that film has greater "cultural importance and effect on the wider public" than media such as radio and literature, and used the Third Reich as an illustration, contending that "one simply has to look at Germany, and at how film, there, has become one of the primary means for psychological mobilization." "We, too," he wrote,

> are currently in a state of psychological mobilization. . . . At the very least, we should not help the enemy mobilize. For it is clear that every film that arrives from Germany, even if its subject is innocent, has an effect in Czechoslovakia in terms of language; in that it is in the German language with its German soul.

"Every cinema visitor who pays for a ticket," he concluded, "is . . . financing German film propaganda," a problem for which the "only defense for now is simple: not to work *pour le roi de Prusse* by needlessly removing its sole competitor."[30]

Papoušek's letter was decisive. Upon receiving it, Elbl recalled years later, he understood that concerted efforts needed to be made to use film for the purpose to which the Ministry of Foreign Affairs had long put other media: to, in his words, "propagate Czechoslovakia abroad."[31] Over the following six years, he and his allies in the public and private sector did just this, leading efforts to produce Czechoslovak cultural propaganda films, to expand governmental involvement in cinema, and to end the American boycott, with the goal of fostering an understanding of film as what he would later term a "product of national culture."[32] In November 1934, they convinced the Ministry of Industry, Trade, and Business to replace the contingent system with a "registration system," under which foreign distributors paid what was effectively an import tax on films shown in Czechoslovakia. This placated the MPPDA, which ended its boycott in January 1935.[33] The "registration funds," in turn, were distributed to domestic productions by the Film Advisory Board (Filmový poradní sbor), a government initiative also launched in November 1934, whose jurisdiction gradually extended to film production, distribution, and exhibition.[34]

In keeping with its origin as a response to the contingent system, which was primarily concerned with fiction features, this longer format was initially the Film Advisory Board's focus. The Board's purview expanded to short and nonfiction films on June 26, 1936, when the Commission Directing the Production and Distribution of Cultural-Propaganda Short Films (Komise pro řízení výroby a distribuce kulturně-propagačních dodatkových filmů) was founded, composed of representatives from various ministries and usually chaired by Elbl himself.[35] Intended to both financially support and articulate a common dramaturgical line for such films, the commission approved film treatments and distributed money from the registration fund to short film projects.[36]

CULTURAL PROPAGANDA

The Film Advisory Board and the Commission for Cultural Propaganda Films were indications of a broader transformation occurring in Czechoslovak cinema, as governmental and nongovernmental figures alike began to advocate for a film culture that was, in various ways, functional—political, pedagogical, and cultural—and not merely commercial.[37] As the Ministry of Foreign Affairs' extensive propaganda production in other media makes clear, such functional perspectives on culture had a long history in Czechoslovakia, to whose very founding they had been fundamental.[38] They were nevertheless also closely in step with interwar developments in international cinema culture, as, in Haidee Wasson's words, a range of institutions, movements, and individuals worked to "make films educational, useful, or even participatory."[39]

Nationalism and geopolitics were, as this chapter discusses above, critical driving forces behind such developments in Czechoslovakia, where a vital dimension of cinema's "function" was its ability to give shape to national and state identity.[40] Similarly, the Ministry of Foreign Affairs' initial mistrust of cinema was founded on a perceived equation between nationalized cinema and lack of democracy. The Czechoslovak press took up these issues as institutions like the Commission for Cultural Propaganda Films began their work, discussing the role that mass media, and particularly film, could play in—and for—democracies. Articles on the topic appeared from various ends of the political spectrum. In June 18, 1937, Bohumil Stašek of the Catholic Czechoslovak People's Party called, in *Filmový kurýr* (*Film Courier*), for Czechoslovakia, "as a democratic state," to take a greater interest in cinema and to centralize state film production (nevertheless leaving the Ministry of Defense's film operations autonomous). Inverting the Czechoslovak government's rhetoric about nationalized film industries, Stašek asked, "When dictatorships are using film for propaganda, why shouldn't a democratic state like Czechoslovakia use film to advocate for democratic principles, which are harmless?"[41] A week later, in the same journal, Elbl himself published an open letter to Czechoslovak film professionals, exhorting his colleagues to, in the words of the article's title, "Play Domestic Short Films." He, too, couched his argument in familiar terms, drawing on language's centrality to the national "myth." "Just as we would be at a disadvantage if we didn't have newspapers written in Czech and Slovak, or radio in our native language," he wrote, "we were and are at a disadvantage without Czechoslovak cultural-propaganda films at a moment when our cinema screens are flooded with similar films by foreign countries."[42]

The Czechoslovak Army, which had long used cinema as a mode of domestic and international propaganda, concurred with these proposals, and in the May 1938 issue of the Ministry of Defense's journal *Branná politika* (*Defense Politics*), Oldřich Kuba proposed that a "central organ" be formed to orchestrate Czechoslovak responses to German propaganda.[43] Like Stašek, Kuba called upon the state to produce "democratic propaganda," which he defined, after analyzing Soviet and Nazi propaganda in detail, as a form of propaganda that "convinces rationally . . . without noise and the apparatus of theatrical propaganda" and that is, "above all, factual."[44]

Jeníček, too, contributed to the debate, writing a passionate defense of film and photography as state propaganda in *Branná politika*'s February 1939 issue.[45] This was, however, not the first time he had written about the topic. In the fall of 1932, when the American boycott's effects were just beginning to be felt, Jeníček had laid the foundations of what would become a well-developed theory of visual propaganda in his essay "Photography and Film in the Service of Political Propaganda," published in the daily

Národní politika (*National Politics*). Seemingly in anticipation of govern-mental concerns, the essay praised film and photographic propaganda as "discreet, hidden, well-disguised," as useful tools for provoking "sympathy and interest" in a state and "creating understanding of its political inter-ests" both abroad and at home.

The examples Jeníček offered were strategically negative: The Central European states that lost territory in World War I, he wrote, had turned to film and photographic propaganda in an attempt to win back this land. Hungary had done so via international photographic salons and exhibi-tions. "In recent European photographic salons," he observed,

> there has been a mass collection of Hungarian amateur photographs, by more than sixty photographers.... The effect? Papers all over the world have ... emphasized their distinctiveness and value ... also, without fail, reminiscing about Hungary's harsh political fate. And the goal is achieved!

Here, Jeníček interpreted visual propaganda in existential terms, with the sheer number—not subject or form—of Hungarian photographs standing in for and corroborating the scale of the former Greater Hun-gary. Germany's achievements in propaganda, conversely, lay in its short cultural films (*Kulturfilme*). As an example Jeníček gave the 1930 five-part film *Das deutsche Land an der Saar* (*The German Land on the Saar*, about the Saarland, a German territory that the Versailles treaty established as a French and British protectorate, and whose later state identity was decided by a plebiscite in 1935). "There are two years to go before the vote," wrote Jeníček, and to help Germany win, "this new German 'cul-tural' film adopts the motto 'The Saarland must be rescued by Germany.' From this springs the film's concept, which communicates powerful and ancient Germanness; for instance, the region's Teutonic history, and its thousands-year old commonality with the German empire."[46]

By describing German and Hungarian propaganda as underhanded attempts to regain lost territory (parts of which were situated in Czecho-slovakia), Jeníček thus made an indirect case for the fragility of Czecho-slovakia's own borders and, by extension, for the country to produce "de-fensive" propaganda. Within Czechoslovak debates about propaganda, moreover, his approach to the subject was distinctive, framing propaganda not (as Kuba or Stašek did) as rhetorical "argument" but, rather, as a means of visually evoking the space of the state. While this concern with territory was apt for a soldier, it also subtly reformulated contemporary Czechoslovak discourse about national "language"—which Jeníček understood primarily as visual or media language. His critical writing on photography and film would continue to develop this idea.

OUR ARMY

Given his passionate support of visual propaganda and the Czechoslovak Army's long history of film production, it is little surprise that Elbl turned to Jeníček in his effort to develop Czechoslovak cultural-propaganda filmmaking, contacting the Army's General Staff in February 1937 with a proposal. Czechoslovakia's allies, he wrote, had been asking the Ministry of Foreign Affairs for "short, appropriate and high-quality films about the Army" that would emphasize its "modern technical equipment in such a way as to facilitate the film's propaganda effect but also be mindful of intelligence concerns." The Ministry of Foreign Affairs had already tried, numerous times, to produce such a film through private production companies and the Film Advisory Board, but owing to restrictions on civilians filming in military zones, the project had not come to fruition. He thus requested that such a film be made by Jeníček, who, he noted, "is known in cinematic circles as very professional, and whose work would be a guarantee of flawless photography and an understanding of film's propaganda effect." Elbl assured the military that the "Ministry of Foreign Affairs, whose representative on the Film Advisory Board is the chairman of the Commission for the Production of Short Cultural-Propaganda films [that is, Elbl himself], will furnish the means for the film's production through the commission."[47]

On March 17, Jeníček sent a treatment and screenplay for the film (originally titled *Czechoslovakia Is Prepared!* [*Československo je připraveno!*]) to the General Staff, which had agreed to produce the film for the Ministry of Foreign Affairs on the condition that it be sent to that year's World Exhibition in Paris.[48] The screenplay begins with the image of "fast-moving

clouds" (to be shot, according to Jeníček, "either in positive or in negative"), with the superimposed titles "Czechoslovakia / is a country / of
warm-hearted / honest / hard-working / peace-loving / people. It is a
country / of freedom and democracy!" The final title dissolves into a shot
of Prague Castle, and from there to a series of scenes depicting life in the
Czechoslovak Republic: Prague in panorama, shots of the modern, bus-
tling capitol, the countryside (Říp Mountain, the picturesque landscape
of northwest Bohemia, peasants at work), factories in industrial centers,
farmers gathering wheat in the fields, and workers leaving factories in the
evening. These scenes, Jeníček notes, are intended to "show the dynamism
of Czechoslovak life" and should be shot and edited to "a stirring tempo."

With the next set of titles—"The Czechoslovak people want / Peace /
Peace / Peace!"—the film shifts to an allegorical register. It is a beautiful
summer day. Children play in the countryside; cars "fly" down the high-
ways, and trains down railway tracks. A boy and a girl lie in a meadow,
watching the sky. A close-up on their eyes dissolves to storm clouds gathering above. Lightning flashes, and smoke rolls in from the distance. A third
set of titles appears, initiating the film's third section: "Czechoslovakia/
knows that peace is threatened / but it is not afraid / of anyone! / It has / a
wonderful / courageous / well / equipped / Army!" A series of shots then
presents the Czechoslovak Army in all its technological advancement: the
infantry, the artillery, cars and tanks, and finally "planes sweeping pow-
erfully overhead." "When the planes have disappeared," Jeníček writes,
"the image dissolves to one of a quiet countryside." The quiet, however,
is just the calm before the film's final storm. Soon after, scouts appear on
the horizon, and the Army engages the enemy with planes, explosions,
anti-aircraft guns, "a mass of attacking tanks," machine guns, anti-tank
cannons. At the end of the scene, the battle won, the final set of titles appears: "Czechoslovakia / is strong / is not afraid / is prepared / and above
all / loves / peace!"[49]

In its finished version, the film—ultimately titled *Our Army* (*Naše
armáda*)—only partially resembled its screenplay. Much of its imagery
had changed (the film opens, for instance, not over clouds, but over the
abstract image of a river—presumably the Vltava, which winds through
Prague—edited backward into the film), its allegorical scene was omitted,

and its battle scene was more extensive than Jeníček's screenplay suggested.[50] The intertitles for the Czechoslovak version were also designed differently than Jeníček had proposed. In place of interchangeable titles (with distinct versions, as he intended, in Czech, German, French, Russian, English, Serbian, Romanian, etc.), bilingual (Czech/German) titles appear, in an apparent appeal to the idea of Czechoslovakia as a state in whose defense each national community had an equal stake.

Our Army premiered on Czechoslovak independence day, October 28, 1937, and was distributed in cinemas alongside Otakar Vávra's fiction feature *A Philosophical History* (*Filosofská historie,* itself a patriotic work, adapting National Awakening author Alois Jirásek's novel of the same name).[51] It was a swift success: A Ministry of Defense report from early 1939 calculated that, in the first nine months of the film's release, it made a profit of 33,901 Czechoslovak crowns; the report also noted that, according to the director of MGM (which, along with United Artists, distributed it internationally), the film's "publicity value" was approximately one million dollars.[52] Although it was primarily intended to be shown domestically and to "friendly" countries abroad, *Our Army* was also unexpectedly useful in Germany, where it made censors so nervous that they would allow only Czechoslovak citizens to watch it at an event commemorating the Twenty-Eighth of October.[53] (Later, the Germans requested a copy for themselves, which, after some hesitation, the Czechoslovaks provided, reasoning that "the film can accomplish its propaganda goals in Germany as well—show what kind of an enemy Germans are facing—and fight against the German taste for war, in favor of peace.")[54]

In this sense, *Our Army* was a decisive victory for both the Ministry of Foreign Affairs and the Film Group. With its simple assertion of Czechoslovakia's existence and depiction of the military technology that assured its borders, Jeníček was able to put his conceptions of visual propaganda into practice. Meanwhile, it permitted the Ministry of Foreign Affairs to continue producing propaganda in its customary indirect fashion, with the added benefit of naturally arousing enemy interest in the film. The film, moreover, proved an effective conduit for the "Czechoslovak myth," simultaneously evoking national symbols such as Prague Castle and Říp (the mountain from whose vantage point, the legend holds, Father Czech first saw the lands that would become Bohemia) and the state's postwar modernity.

STATE MODERNISM

Such a vision of modernity—encompassing, at once, Czechoslovakia's advanced military technology; the updated infrastructure of a state with smooth, paved roads, fast cars and faster trains; and traditional "national" culture—is at the core of *Our Army*. In his screenplay, for instance, Jeníček specifies that the boy and girl in the film's allegorical section, who represent the Czechoslovak state threatened by its bellicose neighbors, should be wearing traditional dress (*kroj*). Yet he calls for their costumes to avoid "folklore" or "banality." They should be "stylized," he writes, "somewhat like the dancers' clothing in the first act of the new production of *The Bartered Bride*."[55]

This interpretation of modernity—in which national tradition itself was, in the context of the new state, "modern"—was indicative, at once, of the historical moment, geopolitical context, and Jeníček's own military, theoretical, and artistic concerns. Born in 1895, Jeníček had had a unique professional life, one that spanned his primary employment as a soldier and his parallel career in photography and film. As a soldier, he had fought at various fronts in World War I and its aftermath: in Italy from June 1917 to June 1918 and in South Bohemia and Slovakia until June 1919, when, in the battle against Béla Kun's Hungarian Soviet Republic, he was wounded. When the fighting ended, he was stationed in Slovakia, where he remained until his 1929 transfer to Prague.[56]

Even before his transfer, Jeníček had been active in Czechoslovakia's community of amateur photographers, which counted among its members many of the country's central figures in film and photography and overlapped with its cultural avant garde.[57] This community's institutions and events—journals, lectures, exhibitions—were crucial channels through which ideas and trends in photography and film circulated to Czechoslovakia from abroad, and vice versa. Although Czechoslovak photographers followed Soviet, Western European, and North American photography closely, the most salient of these exchanges were regional, involving the "new photography" that emerged in Central Europe (Austria, Germany, Hungary, Poland) in the 1920s and 1930s.[58]

Jeníček published photographs in amateur journals (his first appeared in *Rozhledy fotografa-amatéra* [*The Amateur Photographer's View*] in 1926) and served on the editorial board of *Fotografický obzor* (*Photographic Horizons*). He was also active in clubs, joining the Czech Amateur Photographers' Club (Český klub fotografů-amatérů) when he moved to Prague. A year later, he displayed a collection of ten photographs in the club's 1930 exhibition.[59] However, he was best known as a critic of photography (and later film), a reputation born from the numerous reviews and articles he published, from the early 1930s onward, in an impressively wide variety of publications (from specialized photography and military journals, to the weekly photo magazine *Pestrý týden* [*Colorful Week*], to the independently owned newspaper *Lidové noviny* [*People's News*], to the Agrarian Party's *Venkov* [*Countryside*]). The scope of topics about which Jeníček wrote was similarly broad, ranging from technical advice about lenses and tripods for the amateur photographer to treatises on propaganda, the social photography movement, military cinema, and realism.

Matthew S. Witkovsky characterizes Jeníček as a "modernist proselytizer," and indeed, firm convictions about modern photography drove the photographer-soldier's writings.[60] Like other critics affiliated with the "new photography," Jeníček's theory of photography was fundamentally a critique of pictorialism, the studio-centered and process-heavy style that had dominated Central European amateur photography since the turn of the twentieth century. Instead of employing "so-called plastic processes (bromoil; bromoil, gum, or oil printing)"—hallmarks of pictorialism— Jeníček wrote in the 1929 article "On the New Photography" that modern photography should "update itself," adopting techniques that relied on the camera's mechanical, optical nature and trading pictorialism's classical or romantic motifs for subjects drawn from contemporary life.[61] As he asked in *Photographic Horizons* in 1932,

> Why . . . do we only photograph beautiful old Prague, while modern Prague, living Prague, the Prague of today, does not exist for photographs? Grandmothers at the market, little boats on the Vltava, Prague passages, yes; but cars in motion, parking lots, electricians, workers, factories, the suburbs of Prague—those are foreign subjects to us.[62]

This "updated photography" (*aktuální fotografie*) must, finally, become "intellectual," which Jeníček described as "adapting photographic work to rational thinking," recognizing that photography is "a dispassionate imagistic critique of life."[63]

Though its terminology ("updated" and "intellectual" photography) was novel, Jeníček's writing on modern photography was broadly inspired by contemporary film and photographic theory and most closely resembled László Moholy-Nagy's "new vision" in its assertion that photography's fast, light-sensitive emulsions and mechanical nature suited the medium inherently to documenting modernity.[64] ("Nothing is more foreign to photography," Jeníček wrote in 1932, "than being out of time, not being current.")[65] In this, it also echoed the Constructivist interest in photography and film's technical and material dimensions, as well as the idea of *photogénie*—the likening, by Louis Delluc and Jean Epstein among others, of the camera to a revelatory apparatus that unveils parts of the world invisible to the human eye—concepts that were already familiar to Czechoslovakia's photography and film community, having been discussed by critics such as Karel Teige, Vítězslav Nezval, and Jiří Voskovec.[66]

The uniqueness of Jeníček's theories rested rather in the equation between vision and geopolitics that he outlined in his 1932 essay on propaganda. Indeed, for Jeníček, capturing modern life through the optics of photography and film not only was a matter of documentation but also entailed the more abstract concept of seeing the state and the "nation." "Updating the photograph," he wrote in *Národní politika* in 1934, "assumes that photography expresses a living interest in the time, in the state, in national society; that it is an echo of Czechoslovak life, of Czechoslovak society."[67] Revisiting this concept in 1947, he pointed to Soviet photography and film as interwar influences, recalling that their attraction lay in the way they "understood reality not only creatively and socially, but also in terms of the state [*státně*]."[68]

Soviet film, photography, and criticism, which were staples in Czechoslovak film and photographic culture by the late 1920s, were unquestionable influences on Jeníček's interwar thinking: He expounds, for instance, on Vsevolod Pudovkin's theories of acting in his 1937 article on military instructional film, "Soldiers Act in Film."[69] Yet the date of his 1947 text is significant, for this marked two years since the Soviet Union had been declared the "model" for the postwar Czechoslovak Army and since Jeníček, still precariously at the head of the military film studio, had come under increasing political pressure.[70] Given this, Jeníček's understanding of the ways in which the modern media of photography and film make the "state" or "nation" visible are better interpreted within the cultural and political context of interwar East Central Europe, in whose art, S. A. Mansbach writes, the "fusion of folkloric and modernist elements" represented a local response to an experience of modernity rooted in postimperial nation- and statehood.[71]

The applied arts, according to Mansbach, were a particular site for such "fusion," and given contemporary discourse about film as a medium with "functional" dimensions, it is unsurprising that we find similar tendencies in films such as *Our Army*.[72] In this sense, Béla Balázs—to whose *Visible Man* Jeníček referred in "On the Goals and Duties of Military Film"—is an illustrative analogue to Jeníček, for the notion of film's relationship to "national" culture was equally important to the Hungarian critic. As Balázs writes, "Just as folk songs and folk tales, [sic] have now attracted the attention of folklore studies and cultural history . . . so it will be impossible in future [sic] to write a cultural history or a national psychology without devoting a large chapter to film."[73]

Erica Carter traces Balázs's "alternative utopia of a Hungarian renaissance rooted in vernacular popular-cultural forms" to his relationship to composers Zoltán Kodály and Béla Bartók, whose compositions referred to "the musical traditions of the rural peasantry" in order "to develop a distinctively modernist and pentatonic compositional style."[74] These compositions, in which "tradition" determined the shape of "modernist" style, echo the "updated" folk costume that Jeníček proposes for *Our Army*, just as Balázs's idea of a "new Hungarian folk vernacular" does.[75] They also mirror the structure of the Czechoslovak "myth" itself, in which the modernity of the post–World War I state represented the culmination of a much longer "national" trajectory. Both Balázs and Jeníček, finally, took this intertwining of political modernity, aesthetic modernism, and "national" tradition to its logical end. Not only did they make and write about films; they also had political careers: Balázs served briefly in Béla Kun's government, where he worked under György Lukács.[76] Jeníček, for his part, recalled proudly in 1947 that while working for the Film Group, "I was serving the Army, the nation, the state! My photographs had become political expressions!"[77]

THE SHORT FILM, SPONSORSHIP, AND EXPERIMENTATION

Jeníček's theories of photography were echoed in his writings on film, which culminated in two books: *The Short Film* (*Krátký film*, 1940) and *The Alphabet of the Short Film* (*Abeceda krátkého filmu*, 1944), with the former book dubbed, by the critic Navrátil, the "first Czech excursion into the theory and aesthetics of documentary film."[78] The "short film" (*krátký film*), as Jeníček described it, derived from the *Kulturfilm* (whose Czech translation, *kulturní film*, was often used interchangeably with *krátký film*), a German exhibition category encompassing a wide range of productions—all of them broadly "cultural," educational, or noncommercial—that were screened before feature films.[79] William Uricchio underscores the term's breadth, noting that "terms such as Unterrichtsfilm, Lehrfilm, Industriefilm, Forschungsfilm, Populärwissenschaftlicher Film, Dokumentarfilm, and even Werbefilm and Propagandafilm, all make historical claim to inclusion within the overarching Kulturfilm."[80] In his writings on the format, Jeníček, too, discussed the "short film's" multiple purposes: "information, propaganda, science, folklore, culture, education, natural history, etc." A more decisive factor in categorization than a film's subject or purpose was its length (between 300 and 500 meters was ideal) and its use of "*film speech* [*mluva*], which is the means by which a short film's content is interpreted for the audience."[81]

In these texts, Jeníček's convictions about film and photography's documentary nature, his distaste for pictorialism's themes and processes, and his wide reading in contemporary criticism remain evident. The short film, he wrote in 1934, "must always be truthful and natural." It should not be filmed on a set, and—once again reflecting his interest in Pudovkin's theories of acting—it should feature "characters from the people" instead of actors. Such strategies would have geopolitical effects, resulting in a

"popular, national expression" of "Czechoslovak" identity that would, owing to film language's intrinsically optical nature, be comprehensible to
"all languages of the world."[82] Naturally, then, the short film would be
well suited to cultural or political propaganda. Jeníček emphasizes this in
his 1939 *Branná politika* essay, where, echoing his 1932 essay on the subject, he writes that film and photographic propaganda's "functionality"
(*služebnost*), its power to convince, lies in its use of "a clear language: film's
own language, photography's own language." When used properly, he
concludes, these languages "have one entirely simple program: to awaken
and strengthen stateness [*státnost*] and the state."[83]

The *Branná politika* essay also captures a second fundament of Jeníček's
theory of the short film, which understands the format in an institutional
light. In the essay, Jeníček argues that Czechoslovak film and photographic
propaganda's comparative weakness is due to the fact that it has "lacked
... leadership, a system, organization, which is the only thing ... that can
allow a perfect and valuable work of film or photography to emerge, and
with it, reliably effective propaganda."[84] Such institutions of propaganda,
he maintains, should not only organize film and photographic work but
also teach its techniques, thereby promoting experimentation in film language. Similarly, in *The Short Film,* Jeníček adds to the then-common calls
for a Czechoslovak film academy, holding that such an institution would
be doubly advantageous, ensuring the regular production of high-quality
short films, and educating young filmmakers.[85] The film academy's contributions to film language, too, would have geopolitical implications. For
"if short film consciously attempts to experiment," Jeníček writes, "it will
lead the little boat that is film to that island of cinematic fairy-tales: to a
truly national cinema."[86]

The term "experiment," a cornerstone of Jeníček's taxonomy of the
short film, had a distinct meaning, one that did not correspond to the pure
formal play he reserved for "avant-garde" film (e.g., the work of German director Oskar Fischinger): *The Short Film* states vehemently that the "short
film is, no matter what, not an avant-garde film!"[87] Jeníček nevertheless
at times used the term "avant-garde" to describe his own work: the Film
Group's 1938 film *Soldiers in the Mountains* was, in his telling, "*avant-garde
and aggressive.*"[88] Perhaps better translated as "vanguard," the latter usage
signals what he intended "experiment" to encompass: an institutional

process of trial and error in the pursuit of new understandings of and uses for cinema, the perfection of "film language," and, most important, the development of a "national" cinema. As he observed in *The Short Film,* "If the short film is to develop and grow, it must adopt a different word than 'avant-garde' to signify its quests for new islands [the 'island of cinematic fairy tales']. . . . This word is—*experiment!*"[89]

Jeníček's report on a September 1934 Paris screening of three British General Post Office (GPO) films contextualizes and clarifies these ideas. Organized by the author Maurice Rostand, Club cinématographique 32, and the French Communist Party weekly *Regards,* the screening was advertised as an evening of "avant-garde" films.[90] Jeníček was skeptical. Basil Wright's 1933 *Windmill in Barbados*—in which he saw similarities to Czechoslovak director Karol Plicka's pioneering ethnographic film *Zem spieva* (*The Land Sings,* 1933)—he described as a "beautiful documentary, ethnographic [*národopisný*] film, very well done, nothing more, nothing less. In no way avant-garde." Of Evelyn Spice's 1934 *Weather Forecast,* he wrote: "I must say that I have never before seen such an excellent, comprehensive—and yet still compelling—reportage film. Great applause reinforced the fact that young Spice's film was a success.—Avant-garde?" "The word avant-garde," he concluded, "was not used at all in the conversation [following the film], except by the master of ceremonies and in the printed invitations." Jeníček rather saw the evening's films and their institutional background—which, in his words, "allowed new young directors to thrive"—as prime exemplars of the "experimental" short film. He praised their producer in particular, asking, "Will we find another John Grierson in Czechoslovakia?"[91]

The preference for an active, applied definition of the term "avant garde" evident in Jeníček's descriptions of his work must be distinguished from the interwar Czechoslovak avant garde's own calls for an engaged film and photographic culture. These came largely from the socialist Left Front (Levá fronta), an association founded in 1929 upon the dissolution of the avant-garde group Devětsil, and whose political program was more explicitly revolutionary than its predecessor's. The Left Front's Film-Photo Group (Film-foto skupina, founded in 1933, and often simply called "fifo") was devoted to the promotion and practice of "social photography," a movement allied with "worker photography" movements elsewhere in interwar Central Europe; in its name and goals, the organization also resembled the Workers Film and Photo League, founded in 1930 in the United States.[92] Where Jeníček's writings described photography and film as modern, optical engagements with reality, reality was not, for social photography, inherent in the photographic image. Rather, it had to be pointed out, often dialectically, through captions, editorializing, and montage, echoing Walter Benjamin's words in his 1934 essay "The Author as Producer": "What we must demand from the photographer is the ability to put . . . a caption beneath his picture as will rescue it from the ravages of modishness and confer upon it a revolutionary use value."[93] As a graphic example of this, Witkovsky offers the cover of the catalogue for the 1933 Prague exhibition of social photography:

> Three photographs rise here in layers from a photographer's camera, like fragments of an expanding visual consciousness: a soft-focus landscape, a photogram, and uppermost an allegorical depiction of poverty. Pictorialism yielded to modernism, which must in turn yield to socialism.[94]

Petr Szczepanik and Jaroslav Anděl argue that this disagreement between approaches to film and photography hinged on the concept that drove so many developments in Czechoslovak cinema of the 1930s: the two media's "function." Fi-fo, Szczepanik and Anděl write, called for "social functionality" in cinema; Benjamin's "revolutionary use value." Critic Lubomír Linhart, for instance, wrote in 1931 of the necessity "to *organizationally* utilize the 'popularity of the most widespread mass art' and to give this art proper direction, in order to realize—as much as it is possible in a capitalist state—Lenin's slogan: 'Of all the arts, the cinema is the most important for us.'"[95] Conversely, for Jeníček and other branches of Czechoslovakia's film and photographic community (e.g., the Film Advisory Board, the Commission for Cultural Propaganda Films, and other "sponsored" film institutions), film was "functional" in other ways: as an aid to education and industry, national culture, and—in the case of the military—defense, training, and communications. These divergent understandings of "function," in turn, correspond to the two forms of interwar modernism that Thomas Elsaesser identifies—one industrial, "of advertising and design," and one "avant-garde high art, of revolt and

revolution"—allying the Film Group closely with the industrial film institutions that it resembled.[96]

As the Paris screening demonstrates, filmmaking's institutional and
financial dimensions—in particular, the question of sponsorship—were a
flashpoint for tensions between these understandings of function. Among
the screening's guests was Alberto Cavalcanti, director of the third film
screened, *Pett and Pott*. Though well liked, Cavalcanti's film was accused
by some in the audience as merely "selling the telephone." Called to respond to these accusations, Jeníček reports,

> Cavalcanti was, all of a sudden, nowhere to be found. He was finally lo-
> cated in the hallway . . . [and] was asked directly to name the company that
> sponsored this film. Still skulking in the hallway, Cavalcanti proclaimed
> that he had nothing to say about the film; that it spoke for itself. Finally,
> for the general entertainment of the club, an envoy was sent to the hallway
> to fetch the director of *Pett and Pott*. The latter, however, protested that his
> lawyer was not present, and thus he couldn't discuss it.[97]

Cavalcanti's reaction to these accusations reflects his own fraught relationship with the French avant garde, whose "aesthetic pretensions," in
his words, caused him to leave the country for England and the GPO. Yet
it also highlights the fact that conflicting conceptions of film's "function"
were not always incompatible in institutional terms. For Cavalcanti evidently saw little conflict between his political convictions and his sponsorship by "this singular organization," in which, he wrote, "we work in
conditions that recall the best communist practices" and whose turn to
"practical subjects" he viewed as cinema coming to "play its true role in
modern life."[98] The Film Group, too, speaks to this fact, for fi-fo member
Jiří Lehovec was a key collaborator on its late-1930s productions.

Despite his admiration for Grierson, however, it was not only the British film units that shaped Jeníček's conception of institutional experimentation and the short film. It was also a domestic context that included organizations such as the Baťa Company's film studio—founded in the city
of Zlín in 1936 and in which filmmakers like Alexander Hackenschmied,
Elmar Klos, and Otakar Vávra made innovative instructional, advertising,
and documentary films[99]—and writings by figures such as Jan Kučera, editor-in-chief of the newsreel *Aktualita*. In his 1928 essay "Advertising and

Cinematic Art," Kučera calls for advertising and newsreels to be "training" for "cinematic art." "Advertising," he writes,

> is and will always be an entirely technical and commercial system. Its power lies in the pureness of its supremely functional form. . . . Art, however, will take a different path. Once it is tamed by the craftsmanship of advertising films, the visual world will be put to use in another place where it will have a different value. . . . All contemporary arts eschew dilettantism, and the more modern film art becomes, the more it requires skilled craftsmanship.[100]

Kučera, here, makes an argument similar to Jeníček's own contention in *The Short Film* that the format would "prepare the path for feature-length Czech film."[101] His use of the term "craftsmanship," moreover, suggests another way to conceive of institutions such as the Baťa studio and the Film Group: as akin to Germany's Bauhaus in their use of commissions as the basis for, in Jeníček's words, "experimentation." This comparison is historically apt, for there were close connections between the Bauhaus and the Czechoslovak avant garde (Karel Teige, for instance, was invited to the Bauhaus faculty in Dessau, while as we have seen, Moholy-Nagy's writing was a touchstone for Czechoslovak photographers).[102] It is also structurally appropriate, for the Czechoslovak film institutions were equally understood in pedagogical terms. Like the Bauhaus, in short, they operated according to a "workshop" (*dílna*) model, a term that would persist in Czechoslovak military cinema's self-conception for long decades.

IN PRACTICE

In the five years after the GPO screenings, Jeníček consciously borrowed from these models in shaping the Film Group's work. The Group's military location, however, continued to influence its practices in ways that set it apart from its industrial or semi-private counterparts. Its staff, first, was formed in a way unique to the military: Each year, Jeníček sought out soldiers with filmmaking experience to work in the Group, and recruits typically served only during their required military service.[103] In the mid- to late 1930s, the Group was home to Jiří Lehovec, Vladimír

Novotný, and Jan Čuřík—all of whom would continue to well-regarded careers in "civilian" cinema—while its external collaborators included figures such as Burian, who composed the soundtrack for *Our Army.* This structure seems to have been generally agreeable to all parties: By having skilled filmmakers assigned to the Group, Jeníček was guaranteed a level of quality and professionalism, while for these film professionals, service in the Film Group may have been preferable to service in a regular military division.

Nevertheless, the compulsory nature of service in the Film Group at times caused conflicts, a fact to which Jiří Lehovec's experience attests. It was presumably Jeníček who secured Lehovec's position in the Group when he entered the Army in 1935—the two men had worked in the same photographic and critical circles for years. Lehovec's three years in the Film Group were crucial to his career: According to Navrátil in his 1984 biography, they helped him transform from a journalist and photographer into a filmmaker and allowed him a "fantastic perspective on professional film work," to "see how documentary film is made." They also "deepened his meticulousness and sense for responsibility, systematicity ... elements [that] became an integral part of Lehovec's creative character."[104] This kind of training was precisely what Jeníček, the self-styled "Czechoslovak Grierson," intended the Film Group to offer. Day-to-day work in the Group, however, was a different matter, owing to Jeníček's uncompromising opinions about how military films should be made, which relied on the same theoretical convictions that underpinned his writings on film and photography.

Jeníček's understanding of film as a fundamentally optical medium proved the most difficult standard. For while his ardent emphasis on visuality resulted in impressive films, it also placed extraordinary demands on cameramen—as became clear during the production of *Soldiers in the Mountains.* Like *Our Army,* this film was made in collaboration with Elbl's Commission for Cultural Propaganda Films, which agreed to fund the approximately 50,000 crowns that the film would cost.[105] In the screenplay, Jeníček described *Soldiers in the Mountains* using language that echoed his critical writings, stating that the film will have "its topicality. It will be free of *historicism* of any sort, and its guiding conception will be the principle: *One for all—all for one—all for the greatness of Czechoslovakia.*"[106] The film's "topicality" (a term for which Jeníček used the same word, *aktuál-nost,* that he used elsewhere to mean "updatedness") had to do with the growing domestic and international doubts, as the SdP grew in strength, about Czechoslovakia's viability as a multinational state. Jeníček's casting proposal also responded to these doubts: The film's actors, he wrote, will be "Czechoslovak soldiers—Czechs, Slovaks, Germans, and Hungarians."

Jeníček transposes the film's "principle" to a wintry mountain setting and to the allegorical tale of a border-guard company. The work of these soldiers is dangerous, for although they are accomplished skiers, the mountains present hazards. A soldier is buried in an avalanche, and in a daring, torchlit nighttime maneuver, his comrades rescue him. This slight story and the company of soldiers function as metonymy for the principle "one for all, all for one, all for the greatness of Czechoslovakia": Just as the soldiers work together for the greater good of their unit, so the country's nationalities must work together for the good of the state. This idea's metaphorical significance becomes clear in the film's final sequence, in which women wearing folk dress march in formation next to the soldiers. The title "all for Czechoslovakia" appears (see figure 1.1), and, finally—as military planes fly overhead and the national anthem plays—"all for a better future."

While, in a narrative sense, *Soldiers in the Mountains* speaks rather plainly to contemporary politics, formally, it is a showcase of Jeníček's talent as a photographer and a practical application of his theories of film—in particular his understanding of the terms "experimental" and "avant garde." "Despite all of its pragmatism and realism," he writes in the screenplay, "the film is conceived as fully *avant-garde* and *aggressive.* My idea for it is to use new possibilities in the filmic montage of sound and image, as well as of the image itself, and in general a new film style and expression."[107] Accordingly, the screenplay calls for recitatives in Czech and German by its soldier-actors that would reflect the film's multinational ideals (intertitles could be used for other languages, he notes in the treatment, although it would not be complicated to create a variety of sound versions).[108] Ultimately, however, the film included only a musical soundtrack by composer Jiří Srnka.[109]

In a visual sense, *Soldiers in the Mountains*—which was shot in Smrekovice u Ružomberoku, Slovakia, from February to March 1938 and employed

FIGURE 1.1

"All for Czechoslovakia" (*Soldiers in the Mountains*). Film still courtesy
of Národní filmový archiv/National Film Archive, Prague.

nearly eighty soldiers as actors (Jeníček had requested many more: "300
skiers, 50 good skiers, and 30 exceptional skiers")[110]—revolves around
its wintry setting and the graphic, chiaroscuro effect produced by the
play of shadows on snow. In the film's opening sequence, shot in brilliant
sunlight, the soldiers ski in formation down a hill, leaving sinuous tracks
in the fresh snow. Its nighttime rescue scenes depict them climbing the
mountain on skis, lit by sidelights, and descending in formation, carrying torches. Jeníček planned these shots meticulously, inserting diagrams
into the screenplay that indicated camera position, lighting, and blocking.
His meticulousness is also reflected in his shooting diary, in which he
recorded the precise times and conditions of filming, the meters of film
shot, and the grueling nature of work on a production for which natural
light, unsullied by a single cloud, was of utmost importance: "February

FIGURE 1.2

Soldiers in the Mountains. Film still courtesy of Národní
filmový archiv/National Film Archive, Prague.

27: Shot from 6:30 to 16:00 nonstop without a break for lunch. Continued
until 18:00. 300m shot."[111] This fastidiousness (a combination of Jeníček's
career-soldier's and photographer's personalities) evidently took its toll on
Lehovec: As Navrátil writes, "Jeníček, in good will, insisted on the *complete realism* of a situation, yet at the same time, as a soldier, overlooked
the comfort and physical hardships of his cameramen." Lehovec left the
unit in spring 1938, shortly after shooting finished, to work for the short
film division at the commercial AB Company.[112]

Soldiers in the Mountains' photography proved its main critical attraction. In a press release that equated the brave feats of military filmmakers with those of soldiers, the film was "sold" as a virtuoso work of
cinematography:

> All of its scenes were shot in nature—*that is, they were not staged or shot in
> studios*—and under the most unfavorable meteorological conditions, in

which our military filmmakers waited eagerly for days when the sun was shining. . . . Just imagine that the night scenes were shot using only two reflectors, and *even then, only laterally, thus without overhead lighting.*

The press release also pronounced *Soldiers in the Mountains* a major advance in the form of the short film:

> Jeníček's film . . . shows that the short film can be made according to the same filmic laws that govern the feature film. . . . We can truly say that both Jeníček and Srnka have . . . created a film filled with the purest Czechness, and have also shown the path that [Czechoslovak] film should take.[113]

The film was thus, in the eyes of this writer (who, although the press release is uncredited, we may assume was also the director), the practical culmination of Jeníček's theories of photography and film. It was shot off set, with non-actor soldiers; it was made through an "experimental" process, according to the "laws" of film language. It proved that the short film was a mode of production whose claim to the status of "art" was equal to that of the fiction feature. And the result of this hard-won cinematic vision was a product that was essentially *national* in character.[114]

Soldiers in the Mountains was even more popular than its predecessor. After bids by numerous companies, AB (whose studios and personnel had produced the film's sound) was chosen to distribute the film in Czechoslovakia, where it met with great acclaim: "When you see this film," one critic raved, "your heart will be aflutter."[115] International versions, meanwhile, circulated. Just as *Our Army* had played at the 1937 World Exhibition in Paris, *Soldiers in the Mountains* was among the films chosen to represent Czechoslovakia at the 1939 World's Fair.[116]

IN A NEW LIFE

Czechoslovak cinema was on edge during the spring and summer of 1938, after *Soldiers in the Mountains* had been shot but before its release. The registration fee for foreign short films that the Commission for Cultural Propaganda Films had implemented in 1937 (the funds from which went to the production of domestic short films) had staunched the influx of Nazi propaganda films.[117] Newsreels, however, emerged as a new battle-ground: In June 1938, the Ministry of Industry, Trade, and Business reported that clips from Czechoslovak newsreels were being cut, negatively, into German newsreels.[118] Earlier that month, the operator of a cinema in the Moravian village of Pohořelice reported, with great distress, discovering a segment commemorating Hitler's birthday in a UFA (Universum Film-Aktien Gesellschaft) Prague newsreel, just at the time that President Beneš's birthday was to be celebrated.[119]

These events mirrored politics at large: During the summer of 1938, tensions over Czechoslovakia's border regions escalated, culminating in the Munich Agreement of September 29, 1938, when France and Britain appeased Hitler by allowing him to annex the Sudetenland to the Reich. In October, with German occupation imminent, Beneš went into exile, and under the leadership of a new president, Emil Hácha, the state became known as Czecho-Slovakia. Finally, on March 15, 1939, Germany invaded, creating a clericofascist puppet state in Slovakia and, of the Czech lands, the Protectorate of Bohemia and Moravia.

During Czecho-Slovakia's brief existence, the Film Group continued to work, making the last propaganda film that Jeníček directed for the interwar military, *In a New Life* (*V nový život*). The film, which premiered on December 20, 1938, documented a military project of the previous spring and summer, in which troops moved a Slovak mountain village to make room for a military training camp.[120] The village is rural and poor—wheat is ground and hay is baled by hand; the residents are pious. It is, the film's voice-over remarks, "as if time stood still." Time, indeed, is the film's organizing logic, beginning with the cycles of seasons, life, and religion that structure experience in the village—a village unaware of the Czechoslovak state. However, when the state's vanguard—soldiers—arrive and move the villagers to a freshly constructed development, this all changes. Their modern houses now sit in orderly rows, their agricultural equipment is up-to-date and efficient, and their children attend school, where they learn to read and write. The cyclical time of tradition and religion has been replaced by the linear time of modernity, with the aid of the Army and the Czechoslovak state. As the film's final scene of the villagers dancing in *kroj* emphasizes, however, modernity is not incompatible with national and traditional life; rather, it supports and enriches it.

FIGURE 1.3

Before the Army's arrival (*In a New Life*). Film still courtesy of
Národní filmový archiv/National Film Archive, Prague.

With this, *In a New Life* reaches the same conclusion that *Our Army* and
Soldiers in the Mountains did, envisioning Czechoslovak state modernity
as an enhancement of traditional national (in this case, Slovak) culture—
here with the same paternalist overtones visible in early Czechoslovak
military actualities. It was nevertheless produced within a different political context. By the time *In a New Life* was in postproduction, in the fall
of 1938, the republic had been effectively dismantled, and Czechoslovaks
were awaiting German invasion. Jeníček thus turns away from his earlier
films' now fruitless focus on defense—which depicted the Army's ability
to protect the "outside" of the state; its borders—and toward the "inside"
of the state, in which (perhaps in a gesture to a postwar future) the Army
is an agent of progress and modernization.

FIGURE 1.4

After the Army's arrival (*In a New Life*). Film still courtesy of
Národní filmový archiv/National Film Archive, Prague.

In a New Life is also formally and rhetorically distinct from its predecessors. The film abandons the graphic framings (e.g., extreme high- or
low-angle shots) and transitions (360-degree or diagonal wipes) that had
defined *Our Army* and *Soldiers in the Mountains* in favor of temporal and
spatial orientation and continuity. This continuity is central to its argument, which is rooted not—as in the Film Group's previous work—in
staged, often abstract sequences, but within an historical event.[121]

According to Navrátil, Lehovec's departure from the Film Group
caused this shift—it is the avant garde's formal influence, he suggests,
that we see in the films on which Lehovec and Jeníček collaborated.[122]
However, the shift may also be read in light of the broader transformations
in interwar film culture that this chapter has chronicled, as the concept of

a "functional" cinema crystallized, in part, in what Grierson and others called the "documentary": a term that refers not only to the fact that *In a New Life* depicts an historical event but also to its role as, in Jonathan Kahana's words, "cinematic social pedagogy addressed by an individual or corporate author to the citizen of the modern industrial nation-state."[123] This understanding of documentary was also reflected in the film's reception, with a reviewer in *Filmový kurýr* observing that *In a New Life* was a "documentary film and a truthful film. It does not paint anything, it does not embellish anything. Its sole purpose is to show how the military, even in indirect ways, improves the social standards of the population."[124]

In a New Life was not the only such film to be made in Czechoslovakia at this moment—a year earlier, filmmaker Jiří Weiss had completed his *Song of a Sad Land* (*Píseň o smutné zemi*, 1937), which also depicts the Czechoslovak state's role in modernizing, transforming, and "improving" the republic, in this case Subcarpathian Ruthenia. Like Jeníček's film, Weiss's constructs its argument around infrastructure: the new dam that helps the Ruthenian timber industry develop, thereby both physically and symbolically linking this "sad land" with the modern republic and demonstrating, in a different context, the links that Lee Grieveson has highlighted between imperial economics, liberal democracy, and the emergence of documentary.[125] And just as *In a New Life* was preceded by a series of "experiments" with visual propaganda and represented one aspect of the military's ongoing development of new uses of cinema, Weiss's film followed the director's earlier experimental films (most prominently the 1935 *People in the Sun* [*Lidé na slunci*]).

The discourse, legislation, and careers that surrounded the Film Group's work illustrate the institutional dimensions of this development. For what materialized at the intersection of Jeníček's organization and theoretical conception, Elbl's financial support, and the work of members of the Czechoslovak avant garde such as Lehovec gave shape to the "alternative" to commercial cinema that Elbl and others had sought to foster and to which the documentary ultimately gave lasting shape. As such, as this chapter discusses above, the Film Group resembled numerous other institutions born elsewhere in this period at a similar nexus of state, industrial, and avant-garde forces.[126] Yet in critical ways, the Film Group's structure and the films that it made also depended on the Czechoslovak

Army itself, with its long history of tactical uses of media (the "deep and fruitful" tradition to which Jeníček referred in 1937), independent budget and production facilities, and the mandatory nature of military service. In keeping with Jeníček's favored use of the term, it was in this institutional sense that the Army was at cinema's vanguard.

POSTSCRIPT

Although Germany's March 15 invasion officially brought about the Czechoslovak Army's dissolution, the Film Group had felt the impact of Munich months earlier, with its budget dwindling by February 1939.[127] As German occupation began, Jeníček, Elbl, and Lehovec scattered, pursuing the work they had begun in the 1930s in different capacities. Lehovec continued to work as a filmmaker. For a time, he remained at AB, as short film production in Czechoslovakia initially felt the pressure of the occupation less acutely than feature film production.[128] After AB was closed in 1940, he moved between various studios, eventually becoming the first head of the postwar documentary studio, Krátký Film.

Elbl was dismissed from the Ministry of Foreign Affairs in March 1939 and went on to work as a commentator and editor for *Aktualita*. He was a member of the underground communist resistance and spent much of the war planning for the postwar film industry; for both this and his outspoken politics, he was arrested by the Gestapo in May 1942. When he was released the following December, he returned to underground activity, helping form the National Assembly of Czech Film Workers (Národní výbor českých filmových pracovníků). After the war, he, too, would be a central force in the newly nationalized film industry, as secretary of the now-officially recognized Assembly and plenipotentiary of import and export. Years later, he would recall the time during which the Film Advisory Board, the Commission for Cultural-Propaganda Films, and the Film Group emerged as the beginning of the long road toward the film industry's nationalization.[129]

Jeníček turned his attention during the war primarily to film theory, publishing *The Short Film* in 1940 and *The ABCs of the Short Film* in 1944, while also making films for AB.[130] When the military was reconstituted in 1945, he returned to his previous position at the head of the Army's film division. While he would remain there only until 1948, the identity that he had fostered in the interwar Film Group nevertheless persisted. Postwar Czechoslovak military cinema, first, remained an institutional exception: Just as the interwar Ministry of Defense was unique in maintaining its own production facilities, postwar Army Film was the only branch of Czechoslovak cinema (beyond amateur film) exempted from the nationalized film industry. Second, postwar Army Film continued to explicitly frame its identity in interwar terms: as a site of sponsored "experimentation" and a training ground for young filmmakers, many of whom had either come from, or would continue on to, careers in "civilian" cinema. Because of both its relative independence and the military's central position within the Czechoslovak government, the studio was able to maintain this identity as a "workshop" through the end of the 1960s. (In contrast, Baťa's studios were liquidated along with other commercial film studios upon nationalization.)

Finally, and as a result of these facts, Army Film remained a key site for innovation in Czechoslovak nonfiction film, which itself maintained similar concerns and goals through the radically different political moments of World War II, the postwar Third Republic, and the post-1948 socialist period. As Jeníček asserted so confidently in his writings, the interwar Film Group's contributions to Czechoslovak nonfiction film were inseparable from its role as a producer of propaganda devoted to making the Czechoslovak state "visible." We might also reverse this formulation: If film and photography's modern, documentary optics made the state (that essential manifestation of Central European modernity) visible, seeing the state also required seeing with a modern, documentary eye. This—the idea that military propaganda must be modern and must be a progressive force for Czechoslovak cinema—would, in turn, reemerge forcefully in Army Film in the late 1960s.

All of Film Is an Experiment:
Army Documentary, Postwar
Reconstruction, and Building Socialism

IN THE INAUGURAL EDITORIAL of the weekly newspaper *Kulturní politika* (*Cultural Politics*)—published on September 14, 1945, four months after Czechoslovakia's liberation—editor-in-chief E. F. Burian wrote that the paper would be of most use to the country, an "avant garde of democracy," if it furnished its readers with information "from both the West and the East." For the postwar state, in Burian's conception, remained as exceptional as it had been in the interwar period, an "experiment" that should borrow from various models as it emerged from the year zero of the war.[1]

Cinema offers another reading of this situation. In 1946, as if gesturing to these models, Czechoslovakia hosted three foreign film festivals: one featuring Soviet films, one British films, and one French films.[2] The film industry, moreover, was at the vanguard of Czechoslovakia's reconstruction: Nationalized on August 11, 1945, it was the country's first to become the property of the state.[3] Short film was to play a particularly important role in postwar Czechoslovakia. As Jiří Weiss wrote in *Kulturní politika*, film, "the art of the quickly changing twentieth century," should not be "afraid of life."[4] Rather, short films should swiftly and effectively respond to the issues facing the state, for "practically every step of the new state film is an experiment," he wrote; "in fact, all of film is an experiment."[5]

If, echoing Jiří Jeníček's applied, practical understanding of "experimentation," Weiss's language linked postwar film to postwar statecraft (itself, in Burian's words, an "experimental" process), it also indicated that interwar conceptions of cinema's "function" remained central to the way that Czechoslovak film was understood in the first years after 1945. Like the government and the Army in films like *In a New Life* and *Song of a Sad Land,* cinema in postwar Czechoslovakia was to be an agent of infrastructural and social change. Czechoslovak military cinema's history in the first postwar decade tells a similar story of continuity: As had been the case since the 1920s, the Army's film institutions remained important analogues to "civilian" film culture: sources for new understandings and uses of cinema, for innovations in film form, and sites for filmmakers' education.

Whether temporal (stretching from the First Republic to the Stalinist period) or geographic (looking both east and west for models), such continuities alter the traditional image of Czechoslovak cinema of the late 1940s and early 1950s. Films of this decade are often read as an exception—a socialist-realist pause between the modernism of the 1930s and the 1960s, produced by a monolithic, hierarchical film industry. Army Film's history, however, asks us to see the period outside such Cold War frameworks. It demonstrates that, despite the Czechoslovak government's pronouncements of nationalized cinema's "newness" and celebration of the "Soviet model," the country's film culture at this moment built on historically deeper, and geographically broader, foundations. The "system" surrounding filmmaking, moreover, was never fully united in purpose and practice, but rather defined by competition, contradictions, and negotiation.

THE THIRD REPUBLIC

The 1946 British and Soviet film festivals were indicative of larger forces, for it had been in these two countries that Czechoslovakia's postwar future had been debated and planned in the years between 1938 and 1945—Edvard Beneš and other politicians fled to London, where the country's government-in-exile was founded, and many of Czechoslovakia's communist leaders spent the war in Moscow. In March 1945, the Londoners joined their compatriots in Moscow to negotiate the shape that the postwar government would take.[6] The body that resulted from these discussions—a coalition of six parties (four Czech, two Slovak, all of them left or left-leaning) known as the National Front—announced its plans for Czechoslovakia's postwar restructuring the following April, in the Slovak city of Košice.

That the Košice Program was heavily influenced by the Communist Party was evident in two of its key provisions: the nationalization of banks and important industries, and the military's reconstruction.[7] In fact, as Condoleezza Rice writes, the Košice Program did not intend simply to reconstruct the Czechoslovak Army; rather, it meant to "establish a new army (*nová armáda*)" whose primary institutional and political point of reference was the Soviet Red Army.[8] This process, however, proved complex and turbulent, for the Czechoslovak Army, like the government itself, had divergent experiences during the war. Czechs in the Protectorate had not been forced to serve in the German Army, but Czechoslovak soldiers—like the Legionnaires before them—had been part of two prestigious exile units: in England, where pilots flew with the Royal Air Force, and in the Red Army, whose Czechoslovak First Army Corps helped liberate its homeland.

The contested nature of Czechoslovak politics during the Third Republic was echoed in the country's social and geographic landscape. Despite the fact that Czechoslovakia escaped much of the physical and infrastructural damage its neighbors suffered during World War II, the period from 1938 to 1948 fundamentally transformed its population, making the once-multinational republic far more ethnically homogeneous than before. Nearly all of Czechoslovakia's Jews (and a large segment of the country's Roma population) were murdered during the war, and in 1945 and 1946, the state expelled a majority of its German-speaking population. The expulsions occurred in two phases. First, in the so-called "Wild Transfer" of the spring and summer of 1945, almost 700,000 were driven out by Czech vigilante groups in "retribution" for the events of the war, and then in the "Organized Transfer," which began in January 1946, two million were moved to Allied-occupied zones of Germany.[9] A population transfer was also initiated between ethnic Magyars living in Slovakia and ethnic Slovaks living in Hungary, although many Magyars remained in Slovakia.[10]

Forced or voluntary, this period's migrations not only created a state that was, in its ethnic makeup, more "Czechoslovak" than before but also left a population ripe for integration into new political identities. The country's western borderlands, which the German expulsions had drained of its population, stand as a striking example of this. In the period between 1945 and 1948, with the Czechoslovak government's encouragement and facilitation, this area was resettled by Czechs, Slovaks, Magyars, and Roma from other parts of Czechoslovakia in search of better economic conditions, as well as by displaced Czechs and Slovaks from elsewhere in Europe. These settlers were at the core of two new identities: On the one hand, as Nancy M. Wingfield has argued, they helped "create a new, entirely Czech postwar history of the area."[11] On the other, they proved a strong source of support for the Communist Party, which was active in helping them find community (in Party organizations), as well as legal rights to confiscated German property.[12] As a result, in part, of dynamics such as this, in Czechoslovakia's 1946 elections, the Communist Party freely won 38 percent of the vote.[13]

Thus, while dramatic, the events of February 1948—when the resignation of several of the coalition government's non-Communist ministers set off a chain of events that included the formation of a Communist-controlled cabinet and purges of non-Party members from most organizations and institutions—did not mark a radical shift in Czechoslovak politics.[14] Nor, however, were they the logical outcome of National Front governance. Rather, they emerged as part of a social, cultural, and political process rooted both in the war and the interwar First Republic. As historian Bradley F. Abrams has demonstrated, moreover, domestic discussions of postwar reconstruction helped establish the groundwork for the events of "February," with communist intellectuals framing a Soviet-oriented form of communism as a natural, logical response to Czechoslovakia's wartime experience, and—building deliberately on the Czechoslovak "myth"—a reflection of national identity itself.[15]

NATIONALIZED CINEMA

Cinema's nationalization, too, had deep roots, with government centralization of Czechoslovakia's private film production, distribution, and exhibition companies representing in one sense the culmination of efforts that Jindřich Elbl and others began during the interwar period and continued during the Protectorate in the National Assembly of Czech Film Workers. The first plans for nationalization, in fact, were approved as early as 1942, in discussion with Czechoslovak politicians in London and Moscow.[16] As had been the case with the founding of the Film Advisory Board and similar organizations, nationalization was understood not only as an institutional achievement but also as the embodiment of a new conception of cinema, whose founding principles—in place of "commerce" and "entertainment"—were "education" and "culture."

As chapter 1 discusses, the short (e.g., cultural-propaganda, documentary, instructional, popular-scientific, etc.) film was central to this "alternative" conception of cinema in the interwar period. Accordingly, the format—whose production and exhibition had expanded worldwide during the war—benefited richly from nationalization.[17] Programs of short films played to sold-out audiences in the first months after Czechoslovakia's liberation, and short filmmakers were given a stable home in the nationalized film industry's new Krátký Film division, led by Film Group veteran Jiří Lehovec.[18] Interwar proponents of the short film, moreover, occupied important positions in the nationalized film industry. In addition to Lehovec, Elbl served as the plenipotentiary of import and export for the newly founded Czechoslovak Film Society (Československá filmová společnost, or ČEFIS), which was, coupled with the Slovak Film Society (Slovenská filmová společnost), nationalized cinema's central institution until 1948. Lubomír Linhart was ČEFIS' director. Jiří Weiss was a member of its Central Dramaturgical Board, as well as a director in one of its production groups.[19] The educational and national-cultural conceptions of cinema critical to Jeníček's theory of the short film were also reflected in the 1946 founding of Czechoslovakia's national film school (FAMU, the Film Faculty of the Prague Academy of Performing Arts [Filmová fakulta Akademie múzických uměni v Praze]).

As had been the case in the interwar years, when in keeping with its distinct needs and uses for cinema, Czechoslovakia's Ministry of Defense maintained an independent budget for cinema, the postwar Army was also uniquely situated with regard to the nationalized film industry. Military

film was one of two fields exempted from the jurisdiction the nationalization decree granted the government over film production, distribution,
and exhibition; the other was amateur film. (In the decree's phrasing, "The
regulation in paragraph one does not apply to the filmic activities of the
Ministry of National Defense and to amateur film.")[20] As such, postwar
military cinema transformed at a different rate, and for different reasons,
than "civilian" cinema. The institutional actors involved in military film
production were largely the same as those of the mid 1930s: The Army's
General Staff served as primary administrator and censor, and the Military Technical and Aviation Institute (Vojenský technický a letecký ústav,
whose film group—still led by Jeníček—was now known as the Ministry
of Defense's Film Division) remained in charge of production itself.[21] The
group continued to produce newsreels and instructional, propaganda,
and technical films, while also employing film professionals during their
military service.[22]

Postwar military filmmaking, however, differed from its interwar pre-
cursor in the presence of a new, third actor: the Main Department of
Education and Enlightenment (Hlavní správa výchovy a osvěty, hereaf-
ter HSVO), the Ministry of Defense's political education division. Modeled on the First Army Corps's wartime education program and largely
a Communist Party organization, the HSVO was formally incorporated
into the Czechoslovak Army by the Košice Program and signaled the
changing political currents in the ministry.[23] Equipped with its own film
group (independent from the one overseen by Jeníček), the HSVO quickly
secured oversight over military cinema, with its members writing screenplays and treatments, approving those written by other military depart-
ments, and choosing films to be distributed to military bases.[24] This, in
turn, presaged a new understanding of cinema's role in the Army, in which
the HSVO's Soviet-influenced approach to military political education
figured prominently.[25]

As an exchange between the HSVO and Jeníček demonstrates, the new
department catalyzed many of the institutional changes to Czechoslovak
military cinema in the immediate postwar period. In October 1946, having been asked by the HSVO to draft new guidelines for instructional film
production (presumably in anticipation of Czechoslovakia's first centralized economic plan, in 1947–1948), Jeníček described his vision of the Film
Division's mission in terms that made clear that he intended military film

to continue in its interwar path. "The Film Division of the Ministry of Defense," he wrote,

> supports the spiritual-cultural, military-professional, training and moral work of the military authorities and all of the units that attend to the defense of Czechoslovakia ... produces high-quality creative films on the basis of its own screenplays, as well as according to those prepared by divisions of the Army, the HSVO, and the General Staff.

He went on to outline the division's tasks and jobs. The division head (Jeníček himself), he wrote, should direct it "from a technical, creative, and dramatic standpoint" and—echoing the pedagogical focus of his conception of both the interwar Film Group and the short film—supervise "the cinematic education of those assigned to the division." Below the head should be an "assistant group," a technical group, a dramaturgical group, two production groups, and employees in charge of the laboratory, editing room, projectors, and film-lending office. Screenplays and treatments should be approved by a military film board.[26]

Having not received a reply, nine days later, Jeníček wrote to the chief of the General Staff, urging a response to his proposal and the resolution of several other pressing issues: for a building to be found to house the Film Division's employees and equipment; for the division to determine whether it would shoot on 16mm, 35mm, or both (films would ultimately be shot primarily on 35mm); for the approval of a production plan for "training, ideological and short films"; and for an interministry commission to decide if any material remaining from the German occupation of Barrandov—cameras, editing and sound equipment, lights, automobiles—could be given to the Army.[27] While the latter points to the lack of resources that was a more general problem in the postwar military, Jeníček's queries about space and production plans are evidence of the political pressure he evidently felt as, with the HSVO's rise, the Film Division was gradually marginalized.[28] He was, for instance, careful to include the new term "ideological film" in his discussion of the Film Division's production plan and to note that the plan should meet not only the military's needs but also those of the two-year plan.

The response that Jeníček received from the HSVO confirmed that the Film Division's marginalization was political in nature. "The proposal," the HSVO's representative, Miloš Staněk, wrote, "suggests that the head of the Film Division wants to concentrate all decisions about military film in his own hands, and that he is attempting to eliminate . . . the influence of other people. This goes against the idea of the collective, which we recognize today as essential to success in any field."[29] In addition to appealing to the notion of the "collective," Staněk noted that Jeníček's proposal was filled with "needless foreign phrases" that ought to be replaced with "Czech phrases." With this, he drew a distinction between Jeníček and the HSVO that mirrored the more general tension in the Czechoslovak Army between soldiers who had spent the war in Britain and those who had spent it in the Soviet Union and that implicitly claimed national identity—and thus legitimacy—only for the latter.

Little documentation remains of the films made by the Third Republic's Film Division.[30] However, K. M. Walló's treatment and screenplay for the 1946 film *We Are Defending the Border* (*Střežíme hranice*) indicates that, institutional tensions notwithstanding, Czechoslovak military film's concerns remained relatively consistent between the interwar and immediate postwar periods.[31] The treatment states that the film's goal was "to capture the life of soldiers in the borderland mountains, and to simultaneously make use of this interesting and attractive subject for moral-political education, in commemoration of our lost borders."[32] It was also to depict "the goals of the soldier as well as the member of the SNB [Sbor národní bezpečnosti; the police] to protect our national property against the infestation of the nation."[33]

Like *Soldiers in the Mountains, We Are Defending the Border* is set in Czechoslovakia's western borderlands in wintertime. But where the 1938 film was an optimistic allegory for multinational coexistence and cooperation within the Czechoslovak state, the latter, inflected with the nationalist discourse of the immediate postwar period (epitomized by the turgid phrase "infestation of the nation"), serves as both an implicit justification for the German expulsions and an explicit justification for the region's new, "Czechoslovak," identity. Here, the border symbolizes not only the Czechoslovak military's postwar strength but also the "betrayal" that occurred at Munich, in which Sudeten Germans are implicated as a fifth column. The film offers an allegory-in-miniature of this idea in a dramatic sequence in which, under the cover of fog, German "trespassers" attempt to cross the border and to "impoverish" the Czechoslovak state—but are stopped by the soldiers.[34]

1948–1950

The events of "victorious" February 1948 unfolded swiftly: On the twentieth of the month, twelve non-Communist ministers resigned from the cabinet in protest of the Communist minister of the interior's purge of non-Communists from the police. President Beneš accepted their resignations, thus allowing the then-majority Communist Party to form its own government. As the government transformed, so, too, did most professional, cultural, and political institutions and organizations, from which, in the last days of the month and the first days of March, "action committees" (*akční výbory*) purged those unsympathetic to the Communist Party. Finally, in June, the Communist prime minister, Klement Gottwald, replaced Beneš as president.

The upheavals in cinema were less pronounced than those in other areas, as the field had been dominated by the Communist Party since 1947.[35] Nevertheless, 1948 brought changes to the film industry as well, with the consolidation of the nationalized (*znárodněný*) ČEFIS and Slovak Film Society into the single, state-owned (*zestátněný*) Czechoslovak State Film (Československý státní film) in April 1948. Leadership changes followed, including Lubomír Linhart's August 1948 removal from his position at the head of ČEFIS and naming as ambassador to Romania (he would return to Czechoslovakia in the 1950s, working as a professor at FAMU and at Charles University).[36]

In the military, the process of creating a "new army" gathered speed. Officers were the primary target of the immediate post-"February" purges, in particular those who had spent the war in the West, many of whom defected immediately.[37] Among those who remained and were purged in the spring of 1948 was Jeníček, whom a military disciplinary board found guilty of "fraternizing throughout the entire occupation with members of the SS," of telling his sister that he believed Germany would win the war, and of allowing his daughter to marry a German military officer. The disciplinary board's report, a simple form with a mere typewritten paragraph, offers evidence neither for nor against these claims and seems to be a prepared "confession," a common strategy in the purges.[38] Jeníček was removed from military service on April 30 and granted a "vacation" that lasted until his forced retirement from the military on November 1, 1948, at the age of fifty-three.[39]

In both Czechoslovakia's military and civilian spheres, the action committees worked quickly, and the result of the purges was dramatic. Nevertheless, the two years after 1948 were chaotic, and it was only in 1950 that, in Jiří Knapík's words, "the fundamental attributes of the Stalinist model of cultural politics" were established.[40] In this year, responding to pressure for ideological conformity from the Soviet Union (made nervous by Yugoslavia's refusal to adhere to Moscow's views), Czechoslovakia began to collectivize its agricultural regions, and the first of the decade's devastating show trials took place. This, known for its most famous defendant, Czechoslovak National Socialist politician Milada Horáková, was followed a year later by the Slánský Trial, so called after the Czechoslovak Communist Party's general secretary, Rudolf Slánský, who was among the fourteen high-ranking members of Czechoslovakia's Communist leadership tried for treason (eleven were executed).[41] A year earlier, as Kimberly Zarecor details, a "change in rhetoric" had occurred, "as the term 'Soviet model' replaced the phrase 'national road to socialism,'" the distinctly Czechoslovak expression through which the Party had previously framed the postwar transformations in politics and culture.[42]

Nineteen fifty was also a watershed year for the Czechoslovak military, witnessing the replacement of Minister of Defense Ludvík Svoboda—a war hero who, in World War I, had served in the Czechoslovak Legions in Russia, led the First Czechoslovak Army Corps in key battles in World War II, and who had served in his position since 1945—with Alexej Čepička. Čepička was Gottwald's son-in-law and had been minister of justice since 1948.[43] In 1950, Čepička's star was rising fast: He played an important role in the show trials and was the member of the Czechoslovak Communist Party's Politburo and Central Committee with the closest connections to the Soviet Union and to Stalin personally.[44]

With Čepička's appointment on April 25, 1950, the Czechoslovak Army began rapidly to grow and centralize, in response to Soviet demands for militarization, in anticipation of a third world war, and in service of the minister's own, often outsized, goals. Between 1949 and 1953, the years of the country's first Five-Year Plan, the Army doubled in size.[45] Simultaneously, it improved conditions for soldiers (housing, rations, uniforms). The Soviet Army was the template for these developments, as Čepička signaled a month after his appointment in a speech unambiguously entitled "To Conform, in Everything, to the Model of the Soviet Army, and to Proceed according to It in Daily Work and in All Tasks," and as Soviet military "advisors" stationed throughout the military helped ensure.[46]

As the military began to demand more of the Czechoslovak economy, it also became a more prominent presence in Czechoslovak culture. Čepička devoted significant resources to establishing military cultural institutions, among them libraries, the Army Opera (Armádní opera), the Army Artistic Corps (Armádní umělecký soubor), the Central House of the Czechoslovak Army (Ústřední dům čs. armády), and the Army Artistic Theater (Armádní umělecké divadlo).[47] Such institutions had a dual objective. On the one hand, they were intended to make the Army a visible part of public life and, through this, legitimize the military to Czechoslovakia's civilian public. On the other hand, they were to assist in soldiers' political education—a major priority for Čepička, as he indicated in 1950 when he reconstituted the HSVO as the Main Political Administration (Hlavní politická správa, or HPS).[48] Like its predecessor, the HPS oversaw all military cultural production, including cinema. In a signal of its importance, the department spanned the military and civilian spheres, operating as a branch of the Ministry of Defense while a representative also sat on the Central Committee of the Communist Party.[49]

Both Čepička's grand intentions for military cultural institutions and the HPS's increasing importance heralded changes for Czechoslovak military filmmaking; in fact, perhaps seeing in film a means of raising both the Army's and his own status in public life, Čepička took a special interest in cinema. Following Jeníček's purge, Czechoslovak Army filmmakers, operating under the auspices of what was then called the Military Film and Photographic Institute (Vojenský filmový a fotografický ústav, or VFFÚ), overseen by the HSVO, had made only a limited number of films.[50] After Čepička's appointment, this number increased, and in 1951, the institute's film group was renamed Czechoslovak Army Film (Československý armádní film, or ČAF).

Simultaneously, the group was restructured. Although in 1946, the HSVO had criticized Jeníček for proposing a vertical (and not "collective") organization for military filmmaking, the new structure closely

resembled the one that Jeníček had suggested. Army Film's 1952 statute
illustrates this: The studio's "chief" (*náčelník*), it states, appointed by the
head of the HPS, was to "decide on all questions of a military, economic,
Party, and organizational nature, with the exception of artistic questions." The studio's second-in-command and its artistic director was its
lead dramaturg (*vedoucí dramaturg,* at times referred to as artistic chief, or
umělecký vedoucí), who "answer[ed] for ČAF in all ideological-artistic matters" and was also appointed by the head of the HPS.[51] The lead dramaturg
oversaw the dramaturgical group, which was responsible for three fields:
documentary films, instructional films, and newsreels. Additional key
positions in the studio were the economic deputy (*ekonomický náměstek*)
and production deputy (*výrobní náměstek*). In place of the Military Film
Board that Jeníček had proposed, two advisory boards consulted on, respectively, "ideological-artistic" matters (the Ideological-Artistic Board;
Ideová-umělecká rada), and matters pertaining to the artistic and technical aspects of films (the Artistic-Technical-Economic Board; Umělecko-
technicko-ekonomická rada).[52]

In part, this organization resembled Czechoslovak State Film's own
new structure, which, after March 1948, included the office of "ideological chief."[53] Yet the ideological-artistic board was also evidence of the
continued influence of the HPS and its vision of political education on
Army filmmaking. The studio's statute also reflected this. Where in 1946,
Jeníček's description of military cinema's mission had emphasized both
professional pedagogy (film was to "support the spiritual-cultural, mil-
itary-professional, training and moral work of the military authorities
and all of the units that attend to the defense of Czechoslovakia") and
"the cinematic education of those assigned to the division," in 1952, the
statute emphasized political education for both the military and civilian
communities. It described the studio's mission as

> to heighten the battle-readiness and political preparedness of the Army
> and the civilian population; to help disseminate ideas of proletarian inter-
> nationalism and socialist patriotism; to instill in them national pride and
> unlimited loyalty to the people, party, and government; to instill in them
> love toward the Soviet Union; to help commanders and political workers
> in their jobs; to heighten the military arts in members of the Army; to lead
> them to perfect command of military technology and masterful control of

weapons; to encourage, in soldiers, discipline, loyalty to the military oath, bravery, and personal responsibility for the defense of their homeland.[54]

FICTION FEATURES, SCALE, AND PRESTIGE

This focus on political education was reflected in new types of films, as the studio began to devote focused attention to fiction features (only three of which it had produced in the interwar years). While this, too, was timely, occurring as Czechoslovak discourse about cinema began to frame the fiction feature as a powerful pedagogical agent, it also signaled that, for Čepička, cinema's role in making the Army as prestigious and "visible" as possible had to do, in part, with format and scale.

In order for the studio to embark on these productions, it needed personnel, laboratories, and studio space beyond those of a short-film studio. The former it found in "civilian" filmmakers—a priority that Čepička described in his 1951 speech, where he noted that, for military cinema to be effective, the Army's filmmakers needed to cooperate with "our civilian elements, artists, cultural workers, and institutions."[55] The number of filmmakers carrying out their military service in Army Film grew accordingly, as did the number of external (contract) employees. Some of these (many of them recent graduates of FAMU) were called up during the Army's expansion in 1950–1951: Directors Ladislav Helge and Zbyněk Brynych entered Army Film in 1950; František Vláčil in 1951.[56] Vojtěch Jasný and Karel Kachyňa joined the studio in 1952, after graduating from FAMU. Although the majority served only during their required years in the military, several filmmakers remained in the studio for longer periods, among them Vláčil, Jasný, and Kachyňa.

Facilities it also found in the "civilian" sphere: at Barrandov, the home of Czechoslovak State Film. On May 1, 1951, Army Film's creative and production teams moved into Barrandov's old color and black-and-white laboratories and gradually requisitioned other space in the studio. (Barrandov's laboratory workers later complained of this move as a "categorical order to hand over the old laboratories without exceptions.")[57]

Čepička's requisition of space at Barrandov was both practical and highly symbolic, for it framed the military studio as a cultural power equal to Czechoslovak State Film—and to Barrandov, a central site in the history of Czechoslovak cinema. This gesture was echoed in the area of exhibition when, in 1953, the Lucerna cinema on Vodičkova Street off Wenceslas Square—the site of Barrandov chief Miloš Havel's former office—became the new Army Cinema, thus freeing the Army's former downtown cinema (at the corner of Jungmannova and Myslíkova streets; the former and current location of the Komedie theater) for the use of the Army Artistic Theater, headed by E. F. Burian.[58]

Eventually Army Film faced more than mere grumbling about its forays into "civilian" cinematic territory: In 1954, Czechoslovak State Film complained to the Politburo (the highest level of Party governance) about Army Film's use of Barrandov property and aspirations to make fiction features. In return, Army Film accused State Film of deliberately marginalizing the military studio. In a memorandum to the Politburo, Army Film noted that all of its productions not intended exclusively for military use were offered to State Film for distribution in civilian cinemas. However, State Film, it argued, "does not distribute ČAF's [Army Film's] productions to such a range and extent as it distributes its own." The memorandum's final paragraphs offer an abrupt solution to this problem, proposing that Army Film ultimately become a part of State Film:

> It would be proper for the time being to deepen and continually improve cooperation between ČAF and ČSF [Czechoslovak State Film] and prepare, according to the experience of the Soviet Army, the conditions for the transfer of Czechoslovak Army Film as a whole (not only the groups for acted film) to Czechoslovak State Film after its consolidation. The transfer can be completed, according to our estimates, in two to three years.[59]

This never came to pass, and in compromise, the Ladislav Novotný–Bedřich Kubala production group was established at Barrandov in 1954, charged with making films with a "military, defense, or similar theme."[60]

Despite Army Film's inability to establish itself as a producer of fiction features, Čepička's interest in the format, requisition of "civilian" property, and recruitment of prominent artists shed light on what the studio's autonomy from the nationalized film industry permitted Army Film during Czechoslovakia's Stalinist period. As had been the case in the interwar years, this autonomy was intended to accommodate the military's distinct needs and uses for cinema, needs and uses that, as chapter 1 discusses, helped crystallize "civilian" understandings of cinema in 1930s Czechoslovakia. Čepička, conversely, whose understanding of prestige envisioned the dissolution of boundaries between the military and civilian spheres, used Army Film's autonomy to disavow the distinctiveness of military cinema. This, in turn, has implications for how we understand media culture in early 1950s Czechoslovakia.

The quarrel between Army Film and State Film is evidence, first, that in the absence of a commercial market for film, competition for cinematic resources and viewers persisted in Czechoslovakia's nationalized film industry, as did alternative forms of capital—in this case, the symbolic currency of prestige (embodied, as it had been in the interwar period, by the fiction feature). This competition was different in nature than the competition that was an omnipresent and often structuring force in socialist Eastern Europe and that was typically accompanied by discourse about "improvement." For the rivalry between Army Film and State Film did not have a common goal—whether producing better films or fostering more effective filmmaking practices. Rather, it centered on the "double task" that, in Vinzenz Hediger's and Patrick Vonderau's words, industrial organizations face: "maintaining their own stability and improving their structure and operations in the face of the competition."[61]

This, finally, suggests that the institutional "polymorphism" that historian Marc Ferro has characterized as "one of the specific traits" of Soviet politics—in which various institutions of state maintained "the capacity to act, to exercise power, to put inter- and micro-institutional changes into practice"—was fundamental to socialist Czechoslovak media culture.[62] Such polymorphism was, moreover, a structural by-product of one of the state's core cultural policies (the nationalization decree, which established separate spheres of film production). As Ferro points out in the Soviet case, the Red Army was the paradigm for such spheres of "micro-autonomy on the inside of the system."[63] This was also the case for the Czechoslovak Army, though the phenomenon extended to the Communist Party itself, as historian Kevin McDermott has observed, writing that "at no time was the 'party' a singular entity; we might even claim that it was more a composite than a homogeneous body."[64] Fragmentation within the Party in fact aided Army Film's forays into the "civilian" cinematic sphere, for the powerful Minister of Culture, Václav Kopecký (also a member of the Central Committee), played a key role in the Lucerna negotiations and advocated for military films to be distributed more widely. Nationalization, in short, neither produced a "total" system for film production nor eliminated competition from this system; instead, it made these dynamics internal.[65]

THE TANK BRIGADE

Although the three fiction features that Army Film produced under Čepička—Vojtěch Jasný and Karel Kachyňa's 1954 *Everything Ends Tonight* (*Dnes večer všechno skončí*), Karel Kachyňa's 1955 *Lost Track* (*Ztracená stopa*), and Ivo Toman's 1955 *The Tank Brigade* (*Tanková brigáda*)—are traces of the minister's failed vision of military cinema, they also reflect the significance of this vision for Army Film. *The Tank Brigade* in particular embodies Čepička's efforts to find a cinematic expression of prestige and to picture the Army as a central force in Czechoslovak culture and politics.

The Tank Brigade must be read in the context of postwar discussions of the fiction feature, which, as this chapter discusses, framed the format in pedagogical terms: as an agent in the ideological and infrastructural tasks of postwar reconstruction. After 1949, as "postwar reconstruction" was recast as "building socialism," the format was increasingly discussed in terms of the "Soviet model." The Communist Party's landmark 1950 "Directive regarding the Creative Tasks of Czechoslovak Film: 'Toward a High Ideological and Artistic Level of Czechoslovak Cinema,'" a blueprint for Party conceptions of the fiction feature at this moment, encapsulates this. "Following the example of great Soviet film," it states,

> Czechoslovak film must play an important role in the education of the
> new, mature citizen of the Republic, the devoted builder of socialism, who
> loves his free country feverishly and will resolutely defend it at any time
> against the attacks of enemies [and who is] wedded by indestructible and

deep bonds of freedom and love with the nations of the Soviet Union, the people's democracies, and progressive powers throughout the world.[66]

The directive also injected a new term into Czechoslovak cinema, establishing socialist realism as its "fundamental creative method," a step that Czechoslovak culture took in other areas this year.[67] Socialist realism was, indeed, Soviet in origin, having been adopted as Soviet literature's central "creative method" at the First Congress of Soviet Writers, held in Moscow in 1934. In his address to the Congress, Soviet Communist Party Secretary Andrei Zhdanov called for writers to "depict reality in its revolutionary development," to combine "the truthfulness and historical concreteness of the artistic portrayal" with "the ideological remoulding and education of the toiling people in the spirit of socialism," and through this, to become "engineers of human souls."[68] The "method" had been discussed in Czechoslovakia since this time, with debates in the 1930s and 1940s focusing on socialist realism's potential to intervene in the "crisis of the avant garde," helping define its social and political utility and engagement with public life.[69]

As Valérie Pozner writes, there is disagreement about whether Soviet socialist realism should be understood in aesthetic terms, "as a system of rules, norms, and restrictions," or as encompassing "any work accepted by the regime and distributed in a space that considered this mode of creation" to be socialist realist.[70] Czechoslovak discourse of the early 1950s largely reflected the latter. Tereza Petišková, for instance, quotes then-Minister of Education Zdeněk Nejedlý telling artists in his 1952 text "On the Graphic Arts, Music, and Poetry" that "you can do everything; yes, socialist art is calling you directly to capture life and art in all its breadth. No one will give you a recipe, or force one on you. . . . In short, be who and what you have to be today, in this time and in this republic. Everything else will follow."[71] Similarly, in his 1950 *Thirty Years of Struggle for Czech Socialist Poetry* (*Třicet let bojů za českou socialistickou poesii*), considered a seminal text for Czechoslovak socialist realism, Ladislav Štoll espoused a largely social understanding of the "method," calling for artists to participate in the process of building socialism, for, as he wrote, "socialism needs poetry just as it needs the strength of . . . locomotives; without it, it is impossible."[72] As such, Czechoslovak discussions of socialist realism in the early 1950s functioned similarly to the phrase "Soviet model," itself constantly repeated throughout the country (and elsewhere in Eastern Europe) in this period, but whose meaning often remained vague. As historian John Connelly writes of educational institutions in the region, this was in part due to Soviet policy itself, which pressured satellite governments to adopt Soviet "models" yet offered little guidance in how to do so.[73]

Czechoslovak socialist realism nevertheless had aesthetic dimensions. Kimberly Zarecor describes these in architecture: first, "the literal copying of Soviet examples," and second, "an attempt to create a national socialist style inspired by Soviet methods but with distinctly Czech and Slovak characteristics."[74] This style, however, was short-lived, for as she writes, when socialist realism was introduced, "the situation on the ground in Czechoslovakia was quantifiably and qualitatively different from that of the Soviet Union." In consequence, "many of the changes to architectural design in the early 1950s were superficial—literally and figuratively."[75]

The same might be said of cinema. The directive did encourage Czechoslovak films to emulate Soviet films, holding that "the model of . . . high idealism, party spirit, and artistic mastery are Soviet films, which demonstrate the richness of socialist life; are a mirror of the sentiments of Soviet man; consolidate the moral-political union of the people; and mobilize them . . . to achieve communism."[76] And post-1950 productions also often follow the parabolic "master narrative" that Katerina Clark has described in the socialist realist novel, which focuses on an exemplary individual (the "positive hero") whose life story "symbolically recapitulate[s] the stages of historical progress as described in Marxist-Leninist theory."[77] These films are frequently marked by distinctive themes and locations: contemporary interpretations of the Czechoslovak "myth," the western border.[78] Many of these, however, had been present in Czechoslovak cinema since 1945 and earlier. Just, then, as post-"February" film culture added new emphases to a social and political project surrounding cinema that remained largely continuous throughout Czechoslovakia's first postwar decade, the adoption of socialist realism did the same for Czechoslovak cinema's aesthetic and thematic concerns.

In Army Film, however, the deployment of these styles and themes also intertwined with institutional needs and aims. *The Tank Brigade* makes this clear. The film tells the story of the First Czechoslovak Army Corps's tank brigade and its role in two key events of World War II: the 1944 Battle of the Dukla Pass and the 1945 liberation of the Silesian city of Ostrava. Its narrative revolves around the Czechoslovak tankists' relationship to their Red Army "teachers" and pits the country's Soviet-based forces (figured as strong and selfless) against those based in London (effete and bourgeois, endlessly pining for Picadilly). In *The Tank Brigade,* echoing contemporary political discourse, Czechoslovakia's liberation is the result of Soviet tutelage, military strength, and self-sacrifice.

The Tank Brigade borrows heavily from Soviet "models"—appropriating aspects, for instance, of Soviet directors Georgi and Sergei Vasilyev's popular 1934 film *Chapayev,* while following Clark's "master narrative" in its structure. Its "positive hero" is the Slovak tank driver Jurko, a rebellious, vain veteran of the Battle of the Dukla Pass. After his brigade is told by their London-based commanders that they will not receive any more tanks for operations in Ostrava, the headstrong Jurko departs for the more active artillery corps. Later, guided by a communist educator and following the example of his Soviet teacher Andrej Pavlovič (who is martyred while liberating Czechoslovakia), Jurko rejoins the unit and drives the first tank into Nazi-occupied Ostrava. Just as Clark interprets the "master narrative" as a surrogate for a larger political narrative, Jurko's education, increasing discipline, and political transformation stand in for those of the Czechoslovak state itself, for which the Soviet Union—represented by Andrej Pavlovič and the educator—is the model.

The Tank Brigade's use of the "master plot" and references to *Chapayev,* however, were not merely political gestures. They also proved effective means to express Čepička's vision of prestige and the integration of the military and civilian spheres. The film is self-consciously extravagant, with its gesture to a classic of Soviet cinema, use of costly color film stock, and dramatic and expensive battle sequences (which employed a staggering three thousand Czechoslovak soldiers as actors).[79] It was designed to be screened in distinguished, centrally located cinemas such as the former Lucerna. Moreover, it draws its subject matter from contemporary events, at times to grotesque ends: The actor playing the recently deceased president Klement Gottwald wore a latex mask reportedly so stiff that he could barely move his face, forcing the camera to remain several meters away

FIGURE 2.1

Liberating Ostrava (*The Tank Brigade*). Film still courtesy of
Národní filmový archiv/National Film Archive, Prague.

to preserve a sense of verisimilitude.[80] With all of this, the film envisions
an unshakeable bond between the military and the statewide project of
"building socialism": Without the First Army Corps, it asserts, socialism
in Czechoslovakia could not have been built.

EXHIBITION AND THE SHORT FILM

Film exhibition was another area in which Čepička's Ministry of Defense pursued prestige, visibility, and links to the civilian sphere. Indeed,
although they were not administered by Czechoslovak State Film, military
cinemas were an integral part of Czechoslovakia's postwar "cinefication"
(*kinofikace*) plan, which—building on the interwar expansion of the 16mm
network and responding to postwar infrastructural challenges—aimed to

construct approximately 2,500 new cinemas in Czechoslovakia.[81] Some of these would be renovations of existing permanent cinemas; some would be new constructions. Others would be located in "everyday" spaces such as factories, hospitals, airports, train stations, and trains themselves.[82] Toward the end of 1946, Czechoslovak State Film also announced the introduction of mobile cinemas, three of which were in operation by 1947, twenty-three and twenty-four by 1948 and 1949, respectively.[83]

Whether fixed or mobile, these cinemas were charged with a similar task: to assist in infrastructural and ideological reconstruction, shaping the postwar state and its "new" citizens by bringing film to new places, contexts, and audiences. The aid that cinefication provided in shaping the postwar state was, at times, quite practical. Consider, for instance, an October 10, 1945, letter from the Local National Committee (Místní národní výbor) in the Sudeten village of Libochovany, which requested a cinema license from the Ministry of Information

> primarily to show educational films (fruit growing, viticulture, etc.), which we consider necessary precisely because quite a number of settlers in our region . . . must acquaint themselves with the specific conditions of local agriculture, with modern methods of rational farming and the special lines of farming in our region.[84]

As this letter signals, cinefication was also entwined with Czechoslovakia's shifting social and ethnic dynamics. In fact, Michal Čarnický dates the first postwar use of mobile cinemas in the country to an early 1946 action in which approximately 72,000 ethnic Slovaks were resettled from Hungary to Czechoslovakia (primarily to its emptied borderlands).[85] Here, cinema was part of an ensemble of mobile media—radios, gramophones, film, and automobiles—presumably intended to encourage enthusiasm for the postwar Czechoslovak project among the settlers, who were volunteers.[86] This event might be read as the apotheosis of cinefication's goals, for while in postwar Czechoslovakia, mobile cinemas were used—as they had long been elsewhere—as a means of integrating the population within a unified state identity, the 1946 resettlement action took the more radical step of using mobile cinemas to help constitute the population itself.[87]

As was the case in other areas of film culture, cinefication took on new significance toward the end of the 1940s, as it became more closely tied to the Communist Party's goals for reconstruction and particularly to its multiple-year economic plans and to the process of agricultural collectivization. In these years, the borderlands retained their centrality to cinefication, as did the agricultural and industrial regions that formed the Plans' backbone.[88] Mobile cinemas—which increased dramatically in number, to 85 in 1950, and 122 in 1955[89]—traveled regularly to these areas, with programs that combined newsreels with Soviet and Czechoslovak short and feature films.[90] At the same time, new events such as the Working People's Film Festival and Film Spring in the Village used cinema both to educate workers in new production methods and tools and as entertainment.[91]

Developments such as mobile cinemas were not novel for the Ministry of Defense, which had long maintained a range of projection and screening facilities and technologies (these included, as Jeníček described in 1936, military cinemas open to civilians, projection facilities in garrisons, and mobile cinemas, all served both by civilian distributors and by the Army's own film-lending office).[92] In fact, the Army played a decisive role in the development of Czechoslovak State Film's postwar mobile cinemas, providing the Ministry of Information with the cargo truck that, equipped with a projector, accompanied the Slovak settlers.[93] Nevertheless, with the Third Republic's eclipse, discourse about military film exhibition also transformed, framing mobile cinemas in particular as a manifestation of cinema's "new," post-"February" social and political role. Mobile cinemas' significance, this discourse held, lay not in the films they showed but rather in their very apparatus: As an article in the Armed Forces daily *Obrana lidu* (*Defense of the People*) remarked in August 1949, "The times are changing, and with them, bourgeois thinking. Take, for example, our soldiers in military training camps. They wouldn't change their field program for anything. It's as simple as hanging a white screen on a cargo truck and placing a projector on an elevated surface."[94]

After his appointment, Čepička actively set about expanding the ministry's exhibition capacity. In 1950, he inaugurated regular courses in film projection open to all members of the Army and, in 1951, called for the improvement of the "network of projection booths for garrisons," as well as for an increased "number of mobile cinemas for training camps."[95] The HPS ensured standardization among the films screened in these venues, initially by distributing lists of "recommended" films (which bases then borrowed from Czechoslovak State Film's lending office) and, on January 15, 1951 (evidently after situations in which inappropriate films had been sent to military bases by State Film), establishing its own film-lending office, Central Film Distribution (Ústřední distribuce filmů).[96] Finally, in August 1952, the first Army Film Festival took place, with a traveling program of films by the military film studios of the "people's democracies" of Czechoslovakia, the Soviet Union, China, Poland, Bulgaria, Hungary, and Korea.[97] The festival was reviewed in the grand terms in which it was conceived: as an integral part of Czechoslovak cinema's postwar development, "effectively carr[ying] out the mission of nationalized cinema, helping this powerful wave to disseminate progressive film art among the people, and with it . . . the ideas of world peace and the building of a higher socialist order."[98]

However, we must once again question such claims of novelty. For not only had interwar military film exhibition practices anticipated "the mission of nationalized cinema," but they had also played a similar functional—or, to borrow Paul Virilio's phrasing, "tactical"—role for the military as an institution.[99] Whether their ostensible goal was instruction, propaganda, or entertainment, moving films to "every corner of the state," as Jeníček wrote in 1936, helped forge a common field of knowledge and institutional culture, as well as a shared understanding of what soldiers were defending—that is, a vision of the state itself.[100] Here, again, the echoes of industrial film in Czechoslovak military cinema are apt, for as Petr Szczepanik writes of the Baťa studio's interwar films, "The internal functions of [the company's] industrial films, circulating on the inner routes within factories and between branches and satellite towns, were above all information, training, and standardization."[101]

If this exhibition network mirrored, in a sense, the shape of the postwar Czechoslovak state, a similar dynamic was visible in the content of the military films (most of them short films) that circulated within this network. While some of these addressed contemporary political or cultural topics (the deaths of Stalin and Gottwald, the Red Army's Alexandrov Ensemble visiting Czechoslovakia) and most, like *The Tank Brigade*, contributed rhetorically to the process of reconstructing and politically reorienting the state, they also played a "tactical" role for the army.[102] Some helped define Czechoslovakia's postwar social dynamics and the critical relationship between the military and civilian spheres. Others were geopolitical in nature, picturing Czechoslovakia's military alliances and its position in the "Eastern bloc," in Europe, and in the world. Such intertwined institutional and geopolitical dynamics, in turn, ask us to read these examples of Stalinist-era cinema in a new light.

THE WESTERN BORDER

A mobile cinema screening at a remote military base features prominently in Zbyněk Brynych and Roman Hlaváč's 1952 short border-guard film *They Shall Not Pass (Neprojdou)*. As its projectionist, who has arrived by car, is busy with preparation, a group of border guards waits in front of the luminous screen. Behind it, a lush pine forest marks the boundary between Czechoslovakia and West Germany (see plate 1). The mobile cinema's location and presence is telling. For if cinefication intended to foster an identity for Czechoslovakia's citizen-spectators that mapped onto the far-flung network of cinemas, *They Shall Not Pass* exemplifies this process, positing the border-guard audience as a model for Czechoslovakia's own social integration, especially that of its border regions.

Brynych and Hlaváč's film was not the only Army production of the early 1950s to draw links between Czechoslovakia's border guards and its social and political identity: Vladimír Sís's *Ironclad Border (Pevný břeh)*, made a year later, depicts a nautical guard unit on the country's fluvial border with Austria (the Danube River). Taken together—it was recommended that the films be screened in a double bill—the two short films offer a variation on the evolving theme of the border in Czechoslovak military film, a theme that had long served as a channel for social reflection.[103] In *Soldiers in the Mountains* (1938), the border served as proxy for interwar Czechoslovakia's multinational nature ("all for one, one for all, all for the greatness of Czechoslovakia"), while the 1946 *We Are Defending the Border*, evoking Munich, implicitly justified the German expulsions. In the early 1950s, Czechoslovakia's western border-guard companies not only exemplified the increasingly ethnically homogenous postwar "Czechoslovak" identity but also, situated on this "border between two worlds," the ideological parameters of the Cold War itself.

They Shall Not Pass establishes this framework in its opening moments, as Jan Čuřík's camera pans over the border landscape, coming to rest on a sign that reads "Warning. Forbidden area." "Our western border," the voice-over announces,

> the forests and mountains that the famous Chods guarded . . . and our soldiers . . . abandoned in 1938. It is through here that Western imperialists send spies, terrorists, and murderers. Against them stands the Border Patrol, the best and bravest sons of the working people. They have their great example, Soviet border guards.

By positing Soviet border guards as successors to the Chods—a community of Czech families in the Bohemian-Bavarian borderlands who, in the sixteenth century, instituted a tradition of civilian border patrols—*They Shall Not Pass* reiterates the Communist Party's postwar interpretation of the "Czechoslovak myth." The Chods had been an important national symbol since their appearance in National Awakening author Alois Jirásek's 1884 novel *The Dogheads* (*Psohlavci*), and they experienced a revival in the mid 1950s, with the 1953 reissue of Jirásek's novel.[104] In these contemporary interpretations, as in *They Shall Not Pass,* the western border was given a new, dual significance, representing both Czechoslovakia's border with West Germany and the frontier of the socialist sphere.

The Chods' national narrative is Czech, as was Jirásek's National Awakening. *They Shall Not Pass* nevertheless applies this narrative to Czechoslovakia as a whole, via the synecdoche of the border-guard company. We meet, for instance, a soldier who is contentedly writing a letter to his wife. The film's release materials describe this scene: "Here, among Czech and Slovak boys, lives Private Ferko. He used to speak only Hungarian, but he learned Slovak quickly in the Army."[105] Ferko, we may infer, is an ethnic Magyar who remained in Czechoslovakia after the war. Thus, if the film positions the Soviet Union at the triumphal endpoint of the age-old conflict between Czechs and Germans, other ethnic and national differences are similarly reconciled within the socialist state—and particularly in its vanguard, the borderlands.

Ironclad Border depicts a similar relationship between the state's outside and inside—its border and its social identity. The film opens on a shot of the Danube under low clouds, threatened (as its soundtrack, Wagner's

"Flight of the Valkyries," signals) by a vaguely Germanic West. Like its inland counterpart, the Danube Border Patrol is a microcosm of postwar Czechoslovakia: Its members hail from different parts of the country, professions, and national groups, but they work together to defend the state and socialism. In *Ironclad Border,* however, Czechoslovakia's new national identity is matched by the new regional identity visible on the Danube: the Hungarian border guards working alongside the Czechoslovaks, and the Bulgarian and Romanian riverboat crews who keep trade moving on the busy river. While these figures communicate through the symbolic, international language of semaphore, the film implies that this internationalism is inconceivable without the overarching figure of the Soviet Union—for as it notes in voice-over, the Danube flows towards the (Soviet) Black Sea.

They Shall Not Pass and *Ironclad Border* each end with a guard silhouetted against the setting sun, rifle visible and eyes trained watchfully on the border. Evoking iconic images of North American cowboys, these images suggest the idea of the frontier embodied by the Western, a genre in which, in Tom Conley's words, "space is the object and *modus vivendi* of narratives that tell of the founding of new political orders or claims staked to new lands."[106] This comparison seems to be historically and locally apt: Eagle Glassheim discusses a "'Wild West' atmosphere in the borderlands" in the years after the war.[107] And Mark Pittaway's quote from a 1948 British Embassy report on the postwar landscape indicates something similar: "A traveler entering Czechoslovakia by road from Germany is struck by the contrast between the rich and well-kept fields and busy villages through which he has just passed and the desolate weed-grown wastes and empty dwellings which are his first sight of Czechoslovakia."[108] Yet these spaces' "emptiness" was their advantage, the Army border-guard films suggest, for it left room for the "new" Czechoslovakia to be built, a process in which the military and its cinema were indispensable.

CHINA

Army Film expanded *Ironclad Border*'s efforts to situate Czechoslovakia geopolitically in another series of early-1950s films, these looking beyond Europe to the East Asian people's democracies. This series was the result of a collaboration between the Czechoslovak and Chinese People's Army film studios that affirmed Czechoslovakia's alliance with Stalin and the Soviet Union in the years before the Sino-Soviet split of 1961–1962. It was anchored by two feature documentaries: Vojtěch Jasný and Karel Kachyňa's 1953 *People of One Heart* (*Lidé jednoho srdce*), a chronicle of Vít Nejedlý's Army Artistic Corps's (Armádní umělecký soubor Víta Nejedlého) 1952 visit to China, and Vladimír Sís's *The Road Leads to Tibet* (*Cesta vede do Tibetu*, 1956), which documents the 1953–1954 construction of the Sikchang-Tibet highway between China and Lhasa, Tibet.[109]

The Chinese-Czechoslovak coproductions were part of a wider program of cultural exchange between the two countries inaugurated in 1950.[110] In addition to the Army Artistic Corps (a song-and-dance troupe), a state theater company traveled to China in 1953, while the Chinese filmmakers who collaborated with Jasný and Kachyňa on *People of One Heart* returned to Czechoslovakia in 1953 (as documented by Ján Lacko in the Army film *Greetings to a Great Land* [*Pozdrav veliké země*], 1955). In 1956, Army cameraman and director Jiří Ployhar traveled to Tibet with the Czechoslovak automobile company Motokov, producing the 1957 documentaries *The Great Trial* (*Velká zkouška*) and *Notebook from Tibet* (*Zápisník z Tibetu*, also about the construction of a road to Tibet), and František Vláčil and Chinese director Chao Kuan made the film *Shooting Competitions in Peking* (*Střelecké závody v Pekingu*), documenting an international riflery competition.[111] These collaborations, in which Czechoslovak and Chinese filmmakers worked side by side, were discussed in the terms of socialist internationalism and "people's friendship." At the same time, the popular productions—which sparked a series of responses in various media (e.g., books and magazines)—served as publicity for military culture, offering intriguing, quasi-ethnographic glimpses of "exotic" places that most filmgoers would have been at pains to visit yet in which the rhetoric of internationalism implicated them.[112] Indeed, the popular and military press framed *The Road Leads to Tibet* as, above all, an adventure story, the tale of the director and cameraman's yearlong trek into faraway and strange lands.

The Army Artistic Corps's visit to China was also epic in scale, beginning in Beijing (Peking), continuing to Nanjing (Nanking), Shanghai,

Guangzhou (Canton), central China, and northeast China, then circling back to Beijing. The film documents the Czechoslovak and Chinese armies' song-and-dance troupes performing and learning each other's songs and dances, as the Czechoslovak artists glimpse, in the film's words, "the new China and its people."[113] As all of the artists on the trip served as official representatives of the Czechoslovak state, the production was highly controlled—Jasný recalls being sequestered in a Beijing hotel room for two weeks while he wrote the film's screenplay and not being permitted to shoot before it was written and approved.[114] Nevertheless, in the press that followed the film's release, Kachyňa and Jasný discussed it as reportage, a prominent literary genre at the moment, writing in the magazine *Československý voják* (*Czechoslovak Soldier*) that the "great reportages of [communist journalists] Julius Fučík and Egon Erwin Kisch" reminded them that "general expositions and reflections interest the viewer much less than reportage."[115]

Despite this, *People of One Heart* is concerned less with documenting local specificity than with the dissolution of national and ethnic differences within socialism. Echoing the visual structure and narrative logic of *They Shall Not Pass*'s opening sequence, its animated first moments establish the film's geopolitical framework, beginning with a slow pan across the cosmos and coming to rest on a long shot of the Earth spinning in space. "It may sound like a dream," says the narrator. "People say a time is coming when there will be no wars, when man will not hound man, when nations all over the world will say, 'We are people of one heart.' And this is not just a dream: In one third of the globe, it has happened." With this, the film affirms its frame of reference as neither China nor Czechoslovakia but as internationalism itself.

Maps, both literal and figurative, continue to structure the film: The opening scene cuts from the globe to a map that depicts the Czechoslovak artists' journey from Prague to Beijing, their plane a moving shadow. The map, like the globe before it, seems small and toylike, trivializing the vast distance the delegation is traveling. The voice-over emphasizes this, stating that "we flew over the powerful Soviet Union, without whose victory there would not have been victory in Czechoslovakia or China. We flew eleven thousand kilometers to the faraway—and yet so close—People's China."

FIGURE 2.2

People of One Heart. Film still courtesy of Národní
filmový archiv/National Film Archive, Prague.

Documentation of the Czechoslovak delegation's visit follows. In keeping with the dialectical relationship between "far" and "near" to which
the opening animations allude, the film is structured by, on the one
hand, touristic images of China (sweeping pans over the Yangzi [Yang-
tze] River; shots of architecture, folk costumes, and music) and, on the
other, evocations of sameness between the country and Czechoslovakia.
Czechoslovak and Chinese soldiers are photographed in pairs, holding
hands, and during a visit by the delegation to the city of Shenyang, the
Chinese coal-mining and steel production center is dubbed the "Chinese
Ostrava," in reference to Czechoslovakia's own center of heavy industry,
a major focus of its economic planning efforts.[116] Through these pairings
and equivalences, *People of One Heart* domesticates the "exotic," just as,
in its exhibition, the film itself did for spectators who could "visit" China
without leaving Czechoslovakia. In a reviewer's words:

The image before your eyes is strangely familiar. You may say—this is in our country, in Czechoslovakia. Long lines of light, modern, inhabitable homes . . . a new settlement, of which there are dozens in our country. But this is a settlement for Shanghai textile workers, and our soldiers are sitting on benches with them and chatting.[117]

In the film's final scene, the co-articulation of Chinese and Czechoslovak cultures (producing the titular "people of one heart") comes to a climax. Onstage at a May Day celebration, the Czechoslovak artists sing military songs for a Chinese audience. Afterward, a "surprise" is announced: a dance entitled "Meeting on the Banks of the Yangzi." Czechoslovak soldiers in Chinese naval dress uniforms reinterpret the Chinese dances we have seen them learning earlier in the film and welcome to the stage a group of Czechoslovak soldiers, dressed in their own brown uniform. The two groups embrace and dance together, hoisting Chinese and Czechoslovak flags aloft. The camera cuts intermittently to the watching Chinese soldiers, who enthusiastically applaud the performance.

"Meeting on the Banks of the Yangzi" reinforces People of One Heart's defining framework of "far but near." In the dance, once again, the "strange" and the familiar are elided—Chinese culture is located in Czechoslovak bodies, just as, we may infer, Czechoslovak culture could be located in Chinese bodies—with the national body thus exemplifying internationalism itself. This internationalism, however, is not uncentered; rather, like national cooperation on the Danube, it cannot exist without the Soviet Union's mediation. For the Army filmmakers can reach Beijing only by flying through Moscow, and Jasný and Kachyňa, in their article in Československý voják, note that they and their "Chinese comrades" "understood each other very well—naturally, through a Russian translator."[118]

The exoticism that runs throughout People of One Heart features more prominently in The Road Leads to Tibet, which the Chinese People's Army commissioned in 1953. Čepička discussed this in a report on the project to the Czechoslovak Communist Party's Central Committee in October of that year, writing that the filmmakers' projected yearlong stay in China would, on the one hand, "further develop the collaboration already begun between Chinese and Czechoslovak Army Film." On the other hand, it would "capture the lives" of the Chinese soldiers constructing the road and those of "the national minorities of southwest China and the nations of Tibet."[119] At the film's core, however, was its function as propaganda for the Chinese government and its imperial assertion of control over Tibet, in which the construction of this highway through the Himalayas played a role.

The Chinese Army had requested Czechoslovakia's aid in documenting the construction.[120] Thus, while a screenplay had been required of Jasný and Kachyňa, in their accounts of the production of *The Road Leads to Tibet,* Sís and Vaniš emphasized the first-person dimension of reportage or adventure stories. In keeping with a convention of literary reportage, the mode of production itself—in this case, the film camera—was central to these accounts. As the filmmakers recalled in *Obrana lidu* in 1955,

> when, in the fall of 1953, we put our cameras into special boxes, we both had the same thought at the same time: Where will we unwrap them for the first time? When will the first meters of film unspool on our journey to Tibet? . . . Mountains. The highest mountains in the world. This was why our cameras were coated with anti-freeze, and why, at first, they were stored in . . . boxes on which white writing noted that they had set off on the long journey from Czechoslovakia.[121]

The "Chinese-Czechoslovak film expedition" in fact proved a genuine—and at times dangerous—adventure, as Sís's son, author Peter Sís, describes in his children's book about his father's journey, *Tibet through the Red Box* (1998).[122] "An act of nature," Sís writes, separated his father "from the project and he was subsequently lost in Tibet, where he lived through unimaginable experiences and met with the Boy-God-King [the Dalai Lama] in the forbidden city of Lhasa."[123] It was not only Tibet, however, that proved "unimaginable" to the filmmakers or their cameras: Echoing a common trope in ethnography, they wrote of their difficulties "filming or photographing these wild people of the mountains."[124]

> The glistening lens inspires mistrust in them, and the unknown man aiming . . . at their faces with it, that's just too many things at once. . . . It usually ends with a brisk escape, the best solution to such an unfamiliar situation. With young Tibetan girls it is definitely better. Their curiosity gets the better of their fear. What is that thing, that black box on long legs, entirely unlike everything they've seen before?[125]

This was all of a piece, however, as the construction of the road itself was both dangerous and difficult. The Chinese soldiers in *The Road Leads to Tibet* toil in snow, wind, and ice and battle through dangerous mountain passes—all, in the film's words, to "modernize" the impoverished mountain region. Indeed, in this film, communication between "nations" is a matter neither of a plane journey from Prague to Moscow to Beijing nor of translation. Rather, it requires the same manual labor that, at home in Czechoslovakia, was at the core of "building socialism"—itself fundamentally a process of modernization—and that, in Sís and Vaniš's telling, the film's production required.

In the end, this labor, physical and visual, pays off, leading to "a new day" in Lhasa, as well as to a triumphant ending to the explorers' film: After the harsh glacial climate in which they had been filming, their cameras thaw to the vision of the

> first signs of the new life that is coming to Tibet.... Kind Chinese doctors
> examining a Tibetan toddler, mothers on horseback... with children
> in their arms that came into the world in the hygienic conditions of a
> maternity hospital, state-owned shops offering cotton fabric and other
> things that for the majority of Tibetans were previously an unattainable
> dream.[126]

Though with sequences such as this, it fulfilled its "documentary" Chinese commission, *The Road Leads to Tibet* was fundamentally neither about Tibet nor about China. Rather, like *People of One Heart,* this military film told the story of Czechoslovakia's *own* modernity and "location"; the roads and routes, metaphorical or real, that linked *it* to the world. In fact, both films resemble Jeníček's *In a New Life* and Weiss's *Song of a Sad Land,* also tales of the entwined labors of "modernizing" and "civilizing" in a colonial context. Where these films are set at home, in the multinational First Republic, Jasný and Kachyňa's film, produced by a much less ethnically diverse state, figures Czechoslovakia's cosmopolitan modernity through its dizzying fusion of the domestic and the "foreign." And in Sís and Vaniš's film, the equated processes of building a road and making a film—both of which hinge on modern technologies—mirror the building of socialism. Through this equation, Czechoslovakia becomes an indirect actor in Tibet's "modernization." As journalist Karel Beba wrote of the film, "The cameras . . . film the arrival of automobile convoys [in Lhasa], the beloved "iron yaks," among which our Pragovkas are not the least."[127]

PUBLIC HOLIDAYS AND THE CIVILIAN SPHERE

In a broad sense, Army Film's Chinese collaborations and border-guard films continued the geopolitical mission that, twenty years earlier, Jeníček had envisioned for military propaganda, using the optical medium of film to visually express the boundaries of state and "nation." At the same time, two other genres of military films—military-parade films and aviation films—took on the equally tactical task of legitimizing the post-1948 Army to the Czechoslovak public. These films commemorated "Liberation Day" (*Den osvobození,* May 9, commemorating German capitulation) and "Czechoslovak Air Force Day" (*Den československého letectva,* celebrated in September), two of the new postwar holidays that were intended to help reorient public culture and memory.[128] Tereza Petišková likens these celebrations to public performances, whose scripts "contained the timeline of events, list of approved appropriate slogans and of the way public buildings should be decorated."[129] Their audiences were equally stage managed: A Central Committee memorandum about Prague's 1952 Liberation Day parade notes that tickets for prominent seated and standing positions at the parade should be given only to active members of Communist Party organizations, who should also have "approved awards" pinned to their clothing.[130]

As befit its importance, Liberation Day was the subject of one of Army Film's first major productions under Čepička, Ivo Toman's feature-length documentary *Military Parade 1951* (*Přehlídka 1951*). This film established the model for the ones that would, in each year of the minister's tenure, follow it—*Triumphant March* (*Vítězný pochod,* 1952, dir. Ivan Frič), *We Are Prepared* (*Jsme připraveni,* 1953, dir. Ján Lacko), *Military Parade 1954* (*Vojenská přehlídka 1954*), and, in 1955, *Unafraid* (*Bez obav,* dir. Vojtěch Jasný)—positioning the Liberation Day parade as the culmination of a narrative about Czechoslovakia's postwar reconstruction that begins with Soviet liberation and continues through the Communist Party's rise to power and the planned economy's establishment.[131]

The film opens with two brief shots from May 1945, of Prague's Old Town Hall in flames.[132] As it cuts to archival footage of Red Army tanks driving, in triumph, through the city's streets, a voice-over intones:

> Six years ago, on the direct order of Generalissimo Stalin . . . the Soviet
> Army liberated the Nazi-occupied city of Prague. Six years ago, a new
> freedom blossomed in our land. Six years ago, all the creative powers of a
> new life were set free.

The action then shifts to shots of contemporary men and women working
in mines and quarries, "the free people of our hardworking nation," who

> started to construct a new home for themselves and their children. They
> had their example in the heroic people of the Soviet Union. They had
> their plan. Their two-year, then their five-year plan for the construction
> and reconstruction of the state. The plan of the Communist Party of
> Czechoslovakia. The plan of Klement Gottwald.

As if in sync with the perpetual forward motion of the "plan," the following section features a train speeding from the countryside toward Prague,
bringing these workers, and soldiers from remote bases, to the military
parade. The parade represents both the bulk of the film and its climax,
symbolizing not only that the Army is defending the "home" that these
workers are building but also that these "builders of socialism" are themselves potential soldiers—the intertwining of the military and civilian
spheres central to Čepička's Ministry of Defense.

Toman's film, like those that followed it, was a major undertaking,
employing sixteen military cameramen (as well as numerous assistant
cameramen and assistant directors) to film the parade alone.[133] The presence of these numerous "eyes" underscores the crucial role that vision
played in military parades, as well as in films about them. For while vision is at the etymologic root of the term *přehlídka* (*review*), the troops in
military-parade films were intended to be seen not only by the officials and
spectators at the parade itself but also by civilians in cinemas. These civilians, in turn, would "see" the military as a central part of their lives.[134] A
review of *Military Parade 1951* made this clear, writing that the film should
"strengthen the bond between working people and the Army. The Czechoslovak people love their army. They are well aware that it is the safeguard
for the creation of peace and the road to socialism."[135]

The Central Committee used similar language to describe Czechoslovak Air Force Day, which was to "show the growing strength of the
Czechoslovak Air Force, and strengthen working people's understanding
of what is being done to safeguard the building of socialism," as well as

FIGURE 2.3

On the parade route (*Military Parade 1951*). Film still courtesy of
Národní filmový archiv/National Film Archive, Prague.

to "help raise interest on the part of the civilian population—especially
youth—in the Air Force."[136] Films documenting Air Force Day were accordingly structured similarly to those documenting the Liberation Day
parade, like them drawing links between the military and the labor of
"building socialism," which the armed forces defended.[137] And as in the
military-parade films, this relationship was figured as fundamentally visual in nature.

Vision is thematized in the first sequence of *Blue Day* (*Modrý den*, 1953),
directed by Vladimír Sís, which opens in a location very far from Air Force
Day in Prague, with a long aerial shot of the Tatra Mountains in Slovakia.
The narrator recites verses by the poet Stanislav Neumann, and a child
dressed in folk costume climbs one of the peaks to watch military glider
pilots as they soar by (see plate 2). As we look out with him on the landscape, the poem suggests his ambition: "[to] unfold my wings and fly like
a bird, a free being, fearless, to touch the clouds. . . . Mother, somewhere

down there, would say, 'My boy, how brave he is!'... To fly and sing and to shout, 'Look, Man can do anything!'"

Departing from the Tatras, *Blue Day* adopts the pilots' point of view, showing the population and spaces over which they fly: riverboat captains at work, lush fields, women harvesting fruit, looking up at the planes as they fly by.[138] Finally, the planes (now, fighter jets) reach Prague, and children gather to watch. In all of these sequences, the film cuts between shots of what the pilots see (the landscape, people on the ground) and shots from the ground of the planes themselves, establishing a sense of mutual visibility through this shot-reverse shot pattern.

In its final scene, *Blue Day*'s action moves to the airfield where Air Force Day is taking place. We see Army mechanics, doctors, and pilots and, as the voice-over announces, "dads and moms ... workers and first-graders." In front of great red stars, children play in airplanes. Pilots (women and men) flip and turn their planes among the clouds, in shots that figure them—as Emma Widdis observes in Stalinist-era Soviet aviation films—as "extraordinary individuals," or heroes.[139] Toward the end, the film extends this figuration to another guest at the air show: President Antonín Zápotocký, whom the camera pictures on the dais, then turns to the sky, where skywriters trace his initials, and finally the word GLORY.[140] Yet this sequence's visual logic departs from the one that *Blue Day* initially establishes, in which vision (depicted through the exchange of glances between pilots and their civilian spectators) forms the legitimating glue between the military and civilian spheres—for the president is attributed the controlling gaze that Widdis ascribes to pilots. Zápotocký, that is—a proxy for the Party, government, and military, inscribed in the sky—is given the capacity that Jeníček attributed to film and photographic propaganda: to see the entirety of, and thereby defend, the Czechoslovak state.

POSTWAR DOCUMENTARY

Military Parade 1951's release materials note that its filmmakers "draw from the long tradition of Soviet documentary film, whose workers succeed ... in capturing on film historic events in political and public life, among them the yearly military parades."[141] And many of the subjects (public celebrations, expeditions), characters (pilots, border guards), and narratives that this chapter discusses were, as scholars such as Widdis have described, also prominent in Stalinist-era Soviet and East European cinema.[142] Soviet influence on Army Film was to be expected, given the Red Army's role in shaping the postwar Czechoslovak military, Čepička's relationship with Stalin, post-1950 rhetoric about the "Soviet model," and the exchange between Soviet and East European cinema cultures that took place in events such as film festivals. Yet as this chapter argues, these similarities should not be interpreted simply as evidence of Soviet centralization of East European media industries, just as pronouncements of post-"February" cinema's revolutionary nature should not be taken at face value. Rather, they should be examined in historical and institutional context.

Indeed, in addition to their links to contemporary Soviet cinema, Army Film's nonfiction productions of the early 1950s followed the trajectory that Czechoslovak documentary established in the 1930s, demonstrating what a reviewer observed of Jeníček's 1938 *In a New Life:* "how the military, even in indirect ways, improves the social standards of the population."[143] They did so using a format associated with the social documentary internationally, one defined by length (generally between ten and fifteen minutes), didactic voice-over, use of "typical" characters (e.g., Ferko), and address to citizens and soldiers-as-citizens.[144] In this, Army Film was not alone: as Lucie Česálková has demonstrated, the Czechoslovak "civilian" short film, too, took similar forms and performed similar functions from the end of the war through the mid-1950s.[145] Czechoslovakia, in fact, was at the center of postwar international efforts to define the documentary, hosting the first and ultimately only congress of the World Union of Documentary in July 1948, in the west Bohemian spa town of Mariánské Lázně. Here, delegates from both sides of the "Iron Curtain" (including—beyond the congress's catalyst, Joris Ivens—Basil Wright, Henri Langlois, Jean Painlevé, George Stoney, Ivan Pyrjev, and Mikhail Romm) established four categories of documentary (social, cultural and educational, scientific, and experimental) and gave the mode a common definition:[146]

> the business of recording on celluloid any aspects of reality, interpreted either by factual shooting or by sincere and justifiable reconstruction, so as to appeal either to reason or emotion, for the purposes of stimulating the desire for and the widening of human knowledge and understanding, and of truthfully posing problems and their solutions in the sphere of economics, culture and human relations.[147]

They also discussed their shared tasks and practical concerns; among them, strengthening copyright protection for documentary films, expanding commercial and non-commercial distribution, and locating funding and assuring salaries for filmmakers.[148] Even at this critical moment in Czechoslovakia's own history, that is—just five months after victorious "February"—its documentary filmmakers understood their work within a fundamentally international context.

In addition to their links to international documentary, Army Film's productions of this period also, and importantly, served institutional goals. Critical among these were garnering prestige, legitimizing the reconstructed military, and ensuring uniform practices and cultures within the Army itself. These goals did not differ significantly from those that the Czechoslovak Army had pursued through cinema in earlier decades, and accordingly, common themes run throughout its films of the 1920s to the 1950s: the state's border (and its guards), military parades (which also featured prominently in interwar films, among them the 1935 *Our Soldiers*), and aviation (the subject of a range of military and "paramilitary" films of the mid-1930s).[149] Furthermore, as Jeníček's writings demonstrate, interwar and postwar films were equally concerned with visualizing the Czechoslovak state in its spatial, social, political, and cultural dimensions and assuring its integrity. In sum, although contemporary politics are unmistakable in Army films made under Čepička—a devoted Stalinist, working at the height of the Cold War—these films also fulfilled the "functional" needs and demands that had allowed Czechoslovak military filmmaking to flourish in previous decades. For propagating or celebrating the Army, defining the space it defends, standardizing its internal operations, and linking it with civilian culture are constant tasks for military media in all states.[150]

The question of the institution, however, is also important to this period in Army Film's history in a second sense, for while the uses and themes of military cinema remained relatively constant from the 1920s to the 1950s, the institutional structure in which military film was produced shifted with Čepička's appointment. Inspired by Grierson's film units, and in the context of the 1930s, Jeníček's Film Group had developed around his relationship with the avant-garde and amateur film and photographic communities, his interest in film and photography's geopolitical function, and a conviction about the short film's uniqueness. Čepička's Army Film, conversely, had ambitions to the prestige of elegant movie palaces and fiction features, of the cultural elite, of Barrandov, and of the concept of a "studio" in place of a "film group." These ambitions were bolstered by his prominent position in the Czechoslovak Communist Party, his marriage to the president's daughter, and the power that the military commanded in the post-1948 period, through which Army Film garnered substantial financial, material, and personnel resources. Ambition was also the minister's downfall: Čepička was the only member of the Czechoslovak Politburo removed from his position in 1956, when, in the wake of the Soviet Union's Twentieth Party Congress, he was "accused of introducing the cult of personality in the army."[151] In one of the criticisms written about the minister, he was accused of demonstrating "megalomania, immodesty and incorrect forms in the areas entrusted to him, for instance, in the areas of Army theater, film, sport, etc."[152]

Even beyond the Central Committee, Čepička's new vision for Army Film was unpopular, as *The Tank Brigade*'s lukewarm critical reception demonstrated.[153] This, too, however, proved productive for Army Film: Not only did the studio's failure to establish itself in fiction-feature production force it to maintain its focus on nonfiction film, but the necessity that the studio's "propaganda" help bridge the gap between the civilian and military spheres also forced it to continue testing the boundaries of this format (which it did with its newly gained resources and talents). As the next chapter discusses, these resources allowed the studio's interwar identity as a "workshop"—an institution concerned simultaneously with education and "experimentation"—to persist. This institutional experimentation is one of the defining aspects of Czechoslovak military cinema's history. Yet though it emerged in the liberal-democratic 1930s and would, in the 1960s, ally Army Film with the "reformist" Czechoslovak New Wave, it was also fostered, in part, by Čepička and his visions of grandeur.

3

The Crooked Mirror: Pedagogy and Art in Army Instructional Films

WHEN, IN MARCH 1955, the Combat Training Directorate (Správa bojové přípravy, SBP) hosted a conference on instructional filmmaking, Army Film's chief, Ludvík Zavřel, spoke second in the program. Following a tribute to Alexej Čepička's vision for military cinema by Deputy Minister of Defense Bohumír Lomský (himself to become minister the following year), Zavřel turned to film itself. "We see in the newsreel, documentary and acted film," he said,

> a powerful means of political education for our soldier, for all the virtues and qualities that the military oath entails of him.
>
> The second of our most important tasks is to help our soldiers in battle readiness. Training films ... teach and help teach our soldiers to become the true masters of their weapons.
>
> These two tasks are impossible to separate from one another: just as a soldier who is politically conscious but cannot master or handle complicated battle technology and the military arts is not useful for us, so a perfectly trained soldier without political or patriotic feelings, without all the positive qualities of a loyal citizen of our people's democracy, has no value.[1]

Zavřel's assertion that military film should play two pedagogical roles—one political, and one having to do with a soldier's technical and professional expertise—was reflected, in the 1950s, in two forms of Army instructional films. Training films taught technique or introduced new equipment, while short narrative films instructed soldiers in behavior, politics, and morality. Using the same terms (*příklad* and *vzor*, respectively) through which Czechoslovakia's political development and relationship to the Soviet Union were charted in the first postwar decade, studio discourse discussed both kinds of films as "examples" or "models." And indeed, just as these terms were used to describe phenomena as wide-ranging as educational policy, governmental structure, and aesthetics, in these films, the notion of the "example" or "model" had numerous resonances, speaking simultaneously to a film's content, its form, its pedagogical effect, and the concept of the "Soviet model" (*sovětský vzor*).

This chapter discusses both these "model" films and their limit cases. For although training films and narrative shorts were intended as "examples" for soldiers and were themselves typically patterned after formal or generic "models," each mode also encompassed films that, via the very rhetoric of the "model," proved exceptions to the rule. Two films produced between the years 1950 (when Čepička was appointed) and 1956 (when he was demoted) epitomize this phenomenon. First, numerous formal and narrative "models" drive František Vláčil's idiosyncratic 1953 training film *Flying Blind Using System OSP* (*Létání bez vidu podle systému OSP*). Second, Karel Kachyňa's 1956 *Crooked Mirror* (*Křivé zrcadlo*), a short narrative film, decisively departs from—and ultimately upends—its predecessors' moral and behavioral codes. These films, in turn, nuance Zavřel's statement about military cinema's pedagogy, highlighting the continuing relevance, in the Stalinist period, of Army Film's interwar identity as a "workshop." And where this book's previous chapter demonstrates the links between Czechoslovak cinema culture of the 1930s and 1950s, this chapter looks ahead, highlighting the connections between the 1950s, the 1960s, and the New Wave.

THE "MODEL"

References to the "model" are scattered throughout Army Film's memoranda, speeches, and reports of the early to mid-1950s. The term *vzor*, for example, appears twice in a 1952 SBP introduction to a screening of Soviet training films:

Our army today has crafted all of its most important rules and regulations according to the invaluable experience of the victorious Soviet
Army....

Chief among these is instructional-methodological preparation, within
which we have lacked a tool that, with living word and image, provides a
model—we have lacked a sufficient number of valuable training films.

Today we will see such tools, and these of the high quality that only
the Soviet people—whether soldiers or film workers—are capable of
creating....

We will respect this new great gift of the Soviet Army and insure that
the working methods in the films we see become a *model* for all of our
work.[2]

"Model," here, is a flexible term. In its first appearance, it refers to a film's
content and form; the "living word and image" that illustrate what the
viewer is to learn. In its second appearance, the term signifies what Soviet
training films themselves represent: the Soviet Army's working methods,
which Czechoslovakia's "new Army" was to use as a political and institutional blueprint.

The term's latter use also speaks to the political changes that chapter 2
discusses, when, circa 1950, the phrase "Soviet model" became prevalent in
Czechoslovak public discourse, replacing the idea of a Czechoslovak "road
to socialism." This rhetoric held that all areas of Czechoslovak life were,
from this point forward, to be shaped according to Soviet experience:
politics and society, the economy, culture. Soviet "advisors" in various
government agencies and institutions were to help facilitate this process.[3]
The military, modeled after the Red Army since the 1945 Košice Program,
followed a similar trajectory, with Soviet advisors ensuring similarities
between the Soviet and Czechoslovak armies that extended from institutional structure to rules and regulations, from munitions to the epaulets
on uniforms.[4]

Although Army Film had no advisors of its own, Soviet influence was
still evident in the studio, and particularly in its training films. In fact, in
the first years after 1950, dubbed or subtitled Soviet films constituted the
majority of the training films shown to the Czechoslovak Army, while
Czechoslovak screenplays for training films were routinely translated into
Russian so that the Soviet advisors in the branch of the military for which
the film was made could approve them.[5] While this had practical advan-

tages for the Czechoslovak Army, which, as one of the "brotherly armies," needed to learn to use Soviet military technology (a process that a dubbed Soviet film could simplify and standardize), it also suggests a third understanding of the term "model": Soviet training films did not only "model" behavior, technique, or political identity; they also represented *formal* models to copy or imitate, much in the way that Soviet uniforms were "models" for Czechoslovak uniforms.[6]

THE TRAINING FILM AND ITS VIEWER

The three genres of training films that Zavřel's speech described—the "exemplary" (*ukázkový*) film, the "instructional" (*instrukční*) film, and the "instructional-methodological" (*instrukčně-metodický*) film—reflected these diverse interpretations of the "model."[7] In turn, the "model" that each genre represented was understood to have a unique pedagogical function and to interact with the viewer in distinct ways. For "when making a training film," Zavřel warned, "its consumer [*konsument*], the viewer, must be fully taken into account."[8]

The question of how film could teach (in contemporary rhetoric, how it could instruct and inspire the population in postwar reconstruction and, later, in "building socialism," how it could help shape socialism's "new man") was, as chapter 2 discusses, a defining concern for Czechoslovak cinema in the first postwar decade. The increased production of explicitly pedagogical (often short) films represented one approach to this project; infrastructure offered another, with cinefication framing the medium and the spaces in which it was projected as, in the words of one journalist, a "people's university."[9]

Other approaches focused on cinema's traditional association with entertainment, attempting, in Pavel Skopal's words, to "redefine the primary frame through which the new, ideologically mature socialist viewer was to understand the event of the film screening."[10] Feature-length fiction films with contemporary political content, such as *The Tank Brigade,* were part of this strategy. However, as Skopal describes, when such films proved unpopular with Czechoslovak audiences, a different approach was used, in which the politically undesirable films that moviegoers would more readily watch (such as domestic interwar productions) were programmed alongside other texts (introductory titles; short films) that "framed" the films, with the intent of helping viewers interpret them "correctly."[11] As an example, Skopal gives Jiří Voskovec and Jan Werich's 1937 *The World Belongs to Us* (*Svět patří nám*), which was introduced "not as a fictional comedy, but rather as 'testimony,' a document of Czech filmmakers' antifascist struggle."[12]

Tactics such as these, in which paratexts formed the core of a pedagogical strategy, drew on the long history of similar devices in cinema. As Tom Gunning has described, lectures that accompanied early twentieth-century film screenings not only "support[ed] claims that film was an educational medium" but also created the "fragmented and possibly dialectic effect" of "discontinuity between a film unfolding on the screen and a lecturer commenting upon it"—that is, the conditions for an active, dual consciousness on the part of the spectator, who would simultaneously be absorbed in and critically engaged with a film.[13] Building on these foundations, Army Film's three genres of training films reflected a variety of approaches to and conceptions of pedagogical "modeling." These included the depiction of behavioral or practical "models" (with "model," here, signifying the technique or technology about which the spectator was to learn), the understanding of spectatorship itself as an experiential "model," and the use of secondary texts (often onscreen lectures or voice-overs) as explanatory "models."

Of these genres, the exemplary film was the simplest: it, in Zavřel's words, "*does not teach directly, but demonstrates*" and was designed to show "things that are, due to their expense, not very easy to demonstrate to soldiers and commanders in individual bases."[14] At times, catalogues of military training films categorized such films differently: as "reportage/exemplary," "reportage," or, if they were short in length, simply "shots." These terms, which frame such films' production and function as essentially documentary in nature, help clarify the "model" that the films offered, which was the action, technology, or behavior they depicted.

In his description of the second genre, the instructional film, Zavřel clarified the distinction between "teaching" and "demonstrating." "As opposed to the exemplary film," he noted," this type of film "attempts to *teach the soldier, to instruct him in the way he must carry out a given exercise.*" He added that these films were "*accompanied by an explanatory voice-over* that explains, complements and emphasizes what the viewer should notice, what he should learn."[15] As such, these films drew on the tradition of the lecturer, whose voice it "internalized," guiding the viewer's attention and emphasizing what he or she was to learn.

The double emphasis on pedagogy in instructional films, which both *showed* behavior and *explained* it, was underscored by their settings (frequently classrooms) and their mise-en-scène and action, which left little room for ambiguity in interpretation—essential when one was instructing a soldier in, to quote the title of Vladimír Horák's 1958 Army instructional film, "what a bazooka can do" (*Co dokáže tarasnice*). Ivan Frič's *Love Your Weapon* (*Miluj svou zbraň*, 1953), for instance, is composed of three sections: the first two live action, the final animated. Its second section is its centerpiece. Here, soldiers demonstrate how to clean and maintain an anti-aircraft gun, a process that the film's animated section explains in more detail. Mise-en-scène is a pivotal part of how this scene "models" technique: the walls of the set are white, with only one piece of décor—a sign emblazoned with the film's title. This reflects the section's formal properties more generally, for the soldiers appear to be "models" for the action that the slogan commands: their faces are expressionless, and they do not speak. The section's integration of montage and sound is similarly economical. Long shots feature soldiers performing the tasks the voice-over describes, while medium shots and close-ups show details of a technique or equipment; each element serves a purpose, and there are no extraneous shots or words.

The film's first sequence, in which an instructor shows the tools for cleaning guns to a classroom of soldier-students, underscores this purposeful economy. This sequence functions as a "framing" device similar to those that Skopal describes in exhibition practices, amplifying the second section's no-risk formal strategies by ensuring that viewers interpret it, like the events in this classroom, as a pedagogical exercise. At the same time, it serves as a point of identification for the off-screen spectator, who would have been sitting in a military classroom that resembled the one in which the onscreen students sit.

The third genre, instructional-methodological films, in Zavřel's words, "[place] the greatest demands on soldiers as well as on Army Film's creative workers." Because they were intended, among other things, to teach commanders how to train their subordinates, Zavřel noted that "this type of film typically cannot avoid using direct speech-dialogue ... demand[ing] ... an almost actorly performance ... that [a soldier] ... perform for the camera a specific scene thought out in advance and written into a screenplay."[16] Nevertheless, he warned, dialogue in such films should be limited—partially because good soldiers were not necessarily good actors and partially in deference to the spectator: "Every useless piece of dialogue ... prolongs a film ... after a while, the viewer stops taking intensive notice, and films of this character that are longer than forty minutes in length tire a viewer."[17]

Pedagogy in instructional-methodological films was thus a different matter than it was in exemplary or instructional films. Here, spectators were not only to learn by observing "examples" (with or without guidance) but were also expected to take cues from their experience watching other kinds of films, particularly narrative films. As Zavřel signaled by discussing performance quality and audience attention spans, as well as by characterizing the training film's spectator as a "consumer," the spectator's pleasure was central to this mode of filmmaking. Indeed, his description of the genre suggests that such films were intended not only to help viewers replicate the behavior they "modeled" but also to encourage them to enter the "world" of the fiction film.[18]

Such films were often filmed on set or location and adopted formal strategies from narrative cinema. Václav Hapl's *De-mining a Passage III* (*Odminování průchodu III*, 1954), for instance, demonstrates its subject via the fictional story of a de-mining unit. The film is acted and scored with orchestral music; its lighting is low-key and dramatic; and its camera movements are planned not for pedagogical economy but for dramatic effect. This is clear in its first scene, set at night, in which an exterior camera tracks toward a field office window through which we see an officer working at a desk.

After we cut inside the office, however, the reason for Zavřel's warning about soldier-actors becomes clear, for it is evident that the film's performances do not "match" the dramatic quality of its visual and sonic dimensions. A soldier enters the office, and the officer explains the de-mining maneuver to him. Their dialogue is shot using a shot-reverse shot pattern and scored, yet the actors deliver their dialogue stiffly and without emotion, recalling the performances in *Love Your Weapon:* they, too, seem to merely be "models" for soldiers' behavior. Similar formal tensions run throughout the rest of the film, where, within the basic framework and style of a narrative drama, the film presents practical subjects: the soldier explaining the task to his de-mining team, the task successfully accomplished. Certain scenes, such as a tense moment in which a soldier crawls under barbed wire to reach a mine, are accompanied by an explanatory voice-over. Explanatory animated sequences occasionally interrupt the diegesis.

De-mining a Passage thus synthesizes the instructional film's bifurcated structure, offering, in place of *Love Your Weapon*'s classroom scenes, an ongoing interpretive commentary on the actions it presents. The form of spectatorship that this promotes is similar to the one that Gunning describes. Here, however, the lecturer's "dialectic effect" is contained within the film itself, whose narrative elements encourage the spectator to identify with the onscreen characters and thus learn from "experience" but whose impassive performances, voice-over, and animations also ask him or her to step outside of this "experience" and understand it reflexively as a pedagogical "model."[19] This active, dialectical mode of spectatorship, in turn, exemplifies the critical consciousness that was an ideal quality of, in Zavřel's words, the "loyal citizen of [the Czechoslovak] people's democracy."

The film's production history, however, offers a different way to interpret this synthesis. Hapl was not satisfied with *De-mining a Passage,* complaining to the SBP in 1954 that after its screenplay had been approved by military and studio officials and its storyboard was complete, SBP officials decided abruptly to change it, which "could not be managed without fundamental encroachment on the dramatic structure as a whole." "Even though," he wrote, "I have reworked the film—especially its visual side— from the very beginning, it will be very difficult to direct."[20] Zavřel, too, mentioned this in his 1953 "Report on the Production of Training Films," explaining that, during the film's production, "military advisors attempted to expand the content of the finished material by adding new elements that were not in the original screenplay."[21]

Complaints such as Hapl's and Zavřel's were common, with Army Film's employees often protesting SBP interference in their films' dramatic structure or visual logic. Just as commonly, however, the SBP criticized Army Film. In December 1952, for instance, its chief, Karel Veger, complained about a film with the working title *The Private in an Attack* (*Vojín při zteči,* dir. Karel Kachyňa and Vojtěch Jasný), writing that after the screenplay was approved, the SBP proceeded with preparation, training the unit slated to act in it "until it could carry out the action in a fully mechanized way."[22] However, the film's production proved anything but "mechanized": poor weather conditions delayed shooting, and Army Film continually changed the crew. These conflicts indicate that the instructional-methodological film's hybrid form was also the residue of a production process that reflected fractures in military understandings of what film, and filmmaking, should be and do.[23] For unlike the films discussed in chapter 2, which were produced solely under the auspices of the Main Political Administration (HPS) (which administered Army Film, military propaganda and culture, and political education), training films were produced in collaboration between the SBP (representing various branches of the military) and Army Film, of whom the SBP commissioned productions. As Veger's use of the word "mechanized" indicates, military training teaches behaviors that will be repeated with precision and is designed to minimize risk and contingency. Film production, however, accounts for contingency and depends on the dynamic interaction between the crew and their subjects. These labor practices, moreover, have divergent temporalities. With its repetitions, retakes, and encounters with the unexpected, its dependence on weather or available light, filmmaking's temporality differs markedly from that of military drills, which can be set to a stopwatch.

FICTION AS MODEL: FRANTIŠEK VLÁČIL

These conflicts, as well as many of the formal "models" used in Czechoslovak Army training films, were resolved in complex and distinctive way in František Vláčil's 1953 *Flying Blind Using System OSP,* an instructional film. Vláčil's film is a self-conscious meditation on the military's pedagogical uses of cinema, as well as on the idea of the "model," of which it posits cinema itself as the consummate example. Ultimately, however, Vláčil's film also calls into question the "model's" very validity as a concept.

Flying Blind begins in black and white, in a slow tracking shot of military trucks parked in a line on an open field. It is pouring. The camera stops to frame an officer in a raincoat, looking worriedly at the sky, and then follows him as he enters a truck where a radio operator is trying to make contact with a plane. The men do not speak, and the soldier's attempts to contact the plane sound less like words and more like a drone, echoing the sound of the rain on the roof and the crackling of the radio. The soldiers progress from radio to flares, but to no avail; the sequence draws to a close as the plane crashes. In a long shot of the rain-soaked field, soldiers emerge from trucks. The film image grows gradually smaller, until we realize that the camera is tracking backward: this has been a film-within-a-film. A light turns on, transforming the image suddenly to color and revealing a classroom of soldier-students watching the screen (see plate 3). The students take out their notebooks as an instructor walks to the front of the room and begins to explain how to avoid the fate of the characters in the film: by using the new Soviet radar system "OSP."

The following section then adopts a form that is in some respects similar to that of other instructional films: the camera is usually aligned with the onscreen students; the voice-over, accompanied by illustrative shots, describes objects or processes; animated sequences explain details and complex procedures; and the instructor provides an interpretive framework. Vláčil, however, also "models" the radar technology for the on- and offscreen students in unique ways. For instance, after the film-within-a-film ends, the instructor hangs a framed photograph of a plane on the blackboard. We cut to the listening students and then back to the photograph, which has, over the course of the cut, transformed into an animated scene, with dynamic lines, measurements, and sketches showing how to land such a plane. He later demonstrates "System OSP" using a three-dimensional model of a green, mountainous area with a runway (see plate 4). This, too, becomes animated, with lines and lights demonstrating the angle of approach and radar signal of a moveable plane on a wire. Finally, the instructor shows OSP's workings on another three-dimensional model, this one a replica of an airplane's navigational instruments.

After these demonstrations, he tells the students to take their seats. The lights turn off, and, in the dark, the camera turns again to the film screen as the instructor tells the students, "This is how it looks in reality."

A series of still images (slides, in the film's diegesis) appear, after which we see a color reprise of the film-within-the-film that opened *Flying Blind,* featuring a successful landing—facilitated, naturally, by the proper use of System OSP. The film ends with a longer live-action sequence in which a pilot demonstrates the system in action (in fact another film-within-a-film, as frequent cutaways to the onscreen audience confirm).

Like *De-mining a Passage,* then, *Flying Blind Using System OSP* is hybrid, moving between pedagogical "framing" and narrative immersion: the film's classroom setting encourages the viewers to identify with the onscreen students, who are their "models" in interpreting the film's practical demonstrations; devices such as the film-within-the film (which uses narrative conventions to reproduce field conditions) encourage viewers to learn through immersive narrative "experience"; the instructor acts as a lecturer, "modeling" a way for the viewer-students to understand what they see. Yet unlike *De-mining a Passage, Flying Blind Using System OSP* seamlessly integrates these modes of spectatorship. The film's animations and relief model are apt examples of this. While numerous Army training films feature animated sequences, they are not typically part of a film's diegesis and are therefore visible only to "offscreen" students (spectators). In *Flying Blind,* conversely, the blackboard and relief model incorporate animation within live-action sequences, thus implying that the animation is visible to both classrooms. These sequences blend expository, pedagogical elements with immersive (and magical) "cinematic" elements, positing an on- and offscreen spectator who is engrossed in the action, taking pleasure from what he sees yet conscious of the fact that he is learning from it.

Flying Blind's initial film-within-the film plays a special role in constructing this mixed mode of spectatorship. When, as offscreen spectators, we first see the film, we are caught in medias res. The full-frame film fills our scope of vision, just as we are immediately swept up in its drama, entering, as we do, midway through the story. At the moment the camera tracks backward and the film is revealed to be part of a larger diegesis, however, the film-within-a-film becomes a different sort of "model," one akin to the relief model or the model of the airplane's controls: something that can be explained, contextualized, or "framed." This shift is effected by cinema's own language and techniques: by the backward tracking shot that situates the screen within the classroom. *Flying Blind* thus figures cinema itself—which simultaneously embodies multiple types of "models" and multiple modes of spectatorship—as flexible and multifaceted, the ideal model.

The notion of cinema as flexible, capacious, and forward-thinking, in turn, characterizes the way in which Army Film's employees worked in the 1950s and 1960s—and in particular František Vláčil, who was called up to the Czechoslovak Army during the mobilization that followed Čepička's appointment.[24] Although he had no formal training in filmmaking (he was a film enthusiast who had studied philosophy and art history while at university in Brno), he was placed in Army Film, where he directed over thirty films before departing in 1958 to work as a director for Czechoslovak State Film.[25] Chronicles of Vláčil's career typically cite his time in Army Film as a crucial professional turning point that "decided his orientation toward the feature-length fiction film" and taught him "the art of cinema"; Antonín Liehm writes that Vláčil "found his way to film through his work at the Army Film Studio."[26]

The clearest link between Vláčil's military and "civilian" careers is the 1958 *Glass Skies* (*Skleněná oblaka*), one of the last films he produced for Army Film. The film, according to its release materials (which classify it as a "short, color film-poem"), "tells the story of three generations of a flying family, and particularly a young boy enchanted by airplanes, whose desire to understand the unknown cannot be broken—even by the tragic death of his father."[27] Two years later, Vláčil made his first fiction feature for State Film, *The White Dove* (*Holubice,* 1960), a film for which the Army short is clearly a study. As in the case of *Glass Skies,* flight is the heart of *The White Dove,* a portrait of a young boy in a wheelchair, anchored in Prague, and his relationship to the titular white dove, who flies all over Europe. Although their milieus differ, in the earlier film's short format, Vláčil introduces themes (metaphysical and political metaphors for flight, father-son relationships, children's psychology) and imagery (model birds, windows, reflections, and water) that he develops further in the feature film.

Glass Skies is the best known of Vláčil's Army films (winning a prize for experimental and avant-garde films at the 1958 Venice Short and Documentary Film Festival) and the only one generally considered part of his oeuvre.[28] Yet *Flying Blind*—and particularly its opening film-within-a film—demonstrates that five years earlier, Vláčil was already developing

FIGURE 3.1

Glass Skies. Film still courtesy of Národní filmový
archiv/National Film Archive, Prague.

elements of the style that *Glass Skies* would reflect and that his later films
would refine: black-and-white cinematography, prominent tracking shots,
and keen attention to sonic and visual atmosphere. The latter is central
to *Flying Blind*'s opening sequence, whose soundtrack is composed of
the ambient crackling radio, falling rain, and drone-like military commands—sounds whose visual analogue is a haziness borne out by the fog
and rain.

In fact, despite its rather technical topic, this opening section has the
otherworldly, dream-like quality characteristic of many of Vláčil's later
films, where—as is the case here—it is signaled by sound. Among these
is the 1961 *Devil's Trap* (*Ďáblova past*), which chronicles the intertwining
of the supernatural and natural worlds in a medieval farming community.

In a sequence where a mystic dowses for an underground spring, for instance, the soundtrack is suffused with a faint, eerie buzzing, and horses spook seemingly without reason, suggesting that not only the audience but also some of the onscreen characters hear it—that is, that these mystical dimensions are in fact quite concrete. Sound plays a similar role in *Marketa Lazarová*, Vláčil's adaptation of Vladislav Vančura's 1931 novel of doomed love between the young son and daughter of two warring clansmen in medieval Bohemia. Here, dialogue seems overheard rather than directly spoken, and choral music features prominently, forming an auditory counterpart to the film's ever-present frost and snow (its answer to *Flying Blind*'s fog and rain).

Weather, indeed, transcends both the visual and physical world in many of Vláčil's films, reaching into the levels of sound and subjectivity. In *Marketa Lazarová*, there is a sense of a "thick" and enveloping meteorological environment that derives in part from the film's source novel, where it is encapsulated by the narrator's recurring exclamation, "frost, frost, frost!"—spoken as if in frustration at the bleak landscape that surrounds his story.[29] This environment seems to make it difficult both for the characters to see and for the narrator to grasp the story he is telling: after Marketa has been abducted and raped, he asks—seemingly trying to glimpse her through the fog—"Is she crying? She is crying!"[30] Befitting this atmospheric "thickness," time in the novel moves slowly. While Marketa is held in the camp of her family's rival, time is likened to fog, "rolling": "The unhappy girl cries again. He embraces her, and the third night rolls on like the first night."[31]

Flying Blind anticipates this atmospheric occlusion of vision. While in *Marketa Lazarová*, the concept is abstract (as it is in the novel, where the narrator is unnamed and unplaced—and thus we do not know if, were the skies clear, he in fact *could* see Marketa), in the instructional film, its meaning is more literal: the Army plane crashes because its pilot cannot see through the fog. Nevertheless, the fact that the "atmospheric" trope was present in Vláčil's work in 1953 suggests that *Marketa Lazarová*'s sonic and visual dimensions are not only a skilled interpretation of Vančura's prose but also elements with which the director was working long before 1967.[32] More crucial is the fact that these elements manifested themselves in training films, which are and were—as the SBP's complaints demonstrate—not typically conceived as a site of reflection, abstraction, or ambiguity, in part because of their very reliance on mimicry and repetition.

This, however, also indicates that the conflicts between Army Film and the SBP around the notion of film-as-military-pedagogy and film-as-art were inconsequential. For the content-based, strictly pedagogical approach to cinema that the SBP advocated was not at odds with the formal, "artistic" understanding of cinema that filmmakers like Hapl defended. This was in keeping with Czechoslovak military filmmaking's long affinity with industrial film, a mode in which, as Yvonne Zimmermann writes, "the actual use of a film [can] change its basic function and generic character," be it "advertising, information, instruction [or] education."[33] *Flying Blind Using System OSP* functioned similarly. As a tool for military pedagogy, it had a vitally important logic for the SBP and the Army—it taught Czechoslovak soldiers about Soviet technology, it ensured that soldiers trained at different bases were fluent in the same methods and techniques, and it "modeled" a relationship to cinema for the soldier. At the same time, the film illustrates the institutional form of pedagogy that Czechoslovak military film institutions had practiced since Jiří Jeníček's days, and that was still a priority for Army Film, as a 1954 memorandum observed, asking "whether young, talented filmmakers will be able to achieve self-realization in the Army, whether it will allow them to grow in their filmmaking skills, and on the whole, whether an environment and atmosphere will be created that permits the production of good films."[34] *Flying Blind*, finally, reflects the ways in which the military film studio, although no longer part of the Army's Investigative and Experimental division, continued in this tradition, mapping out new forms, techniques, and uses of that most advanced cultural phenomenon, cinema—which, like System OSP, embraced multiple, and novel, modes of vision.

SHORT NARRATIVE FILMS AND SOLDIERLY BEHAVIOR

The critical spectatorship that Army training films encouraged—which prompted viewers to both learn and analyze behavior in the process of becoming a soldier-"citizen"—were even more central to Army Film's short narrative films, whose moral and political concerns hewed closer to those of "citizenship." Indeed, produced under the auspices of the HPS, these films' focus echoed that of Army Film's border-guard, military-parade, and aviation films: the political and social transformation of postwar Czechoslovakia and its population.

The films had a standard structure and narrative. All were approximately fifteen minutes long, and all told the story of a soldier who erred, politically, behaviorally, or morally, and subsequently learned the lesson of his ways—a transformation that, as in the socialist realist "master plot," usually involved learning "correct" political values and behaviors. Among their precursors was the *agitka*, a type of short propaganda film that emerged in Russia during its Civil War and that traced a narrative of redemption through political conversion. Peter Kenez describes Soviet *agitki* as "short films, between five and thirty minutes long, with extremely didactic content, aimed at an uneducated audience," whose form varied from simple "living posters" composed primarily of slogans and images to short narratives.[35] The term, indeed, was the namesake for these short narrative films, which were often called *agitky*, as well as for other types of Czechoslovak short films designed to encourage particular behaviors.[36]

More fundamentally, the films followed a common convention in instructional filmmaking (military and otherwise) in which narrative strategies presented negative and positive "models" for behavior—what Brian Larkin describes, in reference to British colonial "educational documentaries" in Nigeria, as "Manichean divisions."[37] One of Jeníček's interwar instructional films, the 1936 *Practical Examples of Guard Duty* (*Praktické příklady ze strážní služby*), follows this format. The film begins with the intertitle "When a soldier on guard does not properly carry out his duties." A man wanders through a sunlit field toward a military base, where he encounters a sentry on duty. "What do you want here?" asks the soldier. "Simply to walk around," responds the man. He turns to leave; we then cut to a close-up of his face, on which a sly expression appears. "Soldier," he says, turning and offering the guard a flask, "it is so hot—have a bit of lemonade; quench your thirst. You are standing in the hot sun." "I can't," says the soldier, "it's against the rules." "Don't be afraid!" responds the man, and as the soldier acquiesces and puts down his gun, the man overpowers him, then sets the base on fire. This melodramatic narrative is followed by a second that begins with the telling intertitle "The proper execution of guard duty." Once again, we see the man creeping through the field, looking stealthier and more villainous than before. A vigilant soldier in a guardhouse catches sight of him. In a series of quick cuts, we see the visual exchange between the man and the soldier. "Stop! Hands up!" shouts the soldier, and the man stops. The soldier summons two infantrymen, who capture the man and lead him offscreen.

With this negative-positive structure (in which an instance of incorrect behavior is "framed" by one of correct behavior) and emphasis on personal responsibility for military security, such films were prototypes for the short narrative films that Army Film produced in the 1950s. Like the later films, they present soldiers as human, and thus fallible and improvable, and encourage the spectator to learn both from the "model" of the behavior presented onscreen and by seeing himself reflected in its characters. In the 1950s, however, these films had an additional political logic. Not only did they speak to Czechoslovak cinema's grander citizen- and state-shaping pedagogical mission; they also, like the HPS's short films, staged an encounter between the military and civilian spheres, encouraging soldiers to be responsible members of both communities ("loyal citizens of our people's democracy"). Accordingly, furloughs, in which soldiers bridged these two spheres, were a frequent topic for such films. Some depicted the threats to the military that could occur when a soldier left his base, emphasizing personal responsibility for defense and security. Others depicted the personal and moral stakes of moving from regimented life on base to "uncontrolled" life off base.

The former is the topic of Zbyněk Brynych's 1951 *The Enemy Is Listening to You* (*Slyší tě nepřítel*), which tells the story of two friends, Jindřich and Jirka, during a weekend furlough from their base near the town of Cheb, situated on the border with West Germany. During their train ride home, they meet a gregarious man whom Jirka quickly befriends and in whom he confides that a military exercise is occurring that day. Over the course of the film Jindřich realizes that the man is a spy, and as the spy flees with Jirka's military secrets, Jindřich pursues and captures him. Jirka is court-martialed; the spy is jailed.

The Enemy Is Listening to You is narrated in the first person, by Jindřich. His reflections are probing and personal, presented in a voice that seems to both observe the moment in its immediacy and comprehend its mean-

FIGURE 3.2

Court-martial (*The Enemy Is Listening to You*). Source: Vojenský
historický ústav/Military History Institute, Prague.

ing in retrospect, thus functioning as an interpretive device similar to
the lecturer. As we see Jirka and the spy conversing in the train, we hear
Jindřich's voice-over: "None of us had any idea that the man with Jirka in
the hallway was a spy: neither this woman knitting, nor the man who only
had eyes for his newspaper." These words are followed by close-ups of each
of the characters in the train compartment, underscoring the links the film
draws between the civilian and military spheres: Jirka's words, they imply,
affect every one of these individuals.

With its first-person perspective, however, Jindřich's voice-over also
suggests that he or any other of the people in the train could have prevented Jirka's security breach—and thus that they, too, are responsible for
the conversation's outcome. As the film's final scene, Jirka's court-martial,
makes clear, the viewer is implicated in these moral questions and judg-
ments. Here, a military commander lectures the audience on the impor-

FIGURE 3.3

Escape. Source: Vojenský historický ústav/Military History Institute, Prague.

tance of keeping military secrets. For much of this scene, the camera is situated at the back of the courtroom, positioning the viewer (who, we should remember, would have always been a soldier) as a member of the audience: like Jindřich, the viewer has something to learn.

The manner in which *The Enemy Is Listening to You* frames the collective guilt behind Jirka's error echoes the emphasis on mutual visibility in Army Film's aviation and military-parade films. Soldiers or not, the film implies, citizens must constantly watch one another—and must be aware that they are constantly being watched. The duality of this awareness is also the duality of self-criticism, a ritual act at all levels of public culture in Stalinist Czechoslovakia, one that, in Marci Shore's words, enabled the "[exorcism of] all lingering demons of bourgeois thought within oneself, thereby rendering 'the enemy' both internal and external."[38] *The Enemy Is Listening to You* follows this "model" precisely, for its titular "enemy" is not only the spy but also, potentially, each of the characters in the film, as well

FIGURE 3.4

Opportunity. Source: Vojenský historický ústav/
Military History Institute, Prague.

as the viewer. Thus, seeing and being seen become moral acts, in which
surveillance is balanced by privately monitoring one's own thoughts and
actions.

Vojtěch Jasný's 1956 *Opportunity* (*Příležitost*)—a tale of marital infi-
delity in which furloughs pose danger not only to the Army but also to
a soldier's family—frames the moral aspects of a soldier's responsibility
to the military community differently. *Opportunity* begins as a group of
soldiers leaves their base for an evening in Prague. "You know neither my
voice nor my face," says the anonymous narrator (played by actor Vlastimil Brodský; as in *The Enemy Is Listening to You,* this film's voice-over is
that of an unnamed friend of the wayward soldier, František), "but I know
you because I am one of you." Scenes of the soldiers exploring the city and
visiting a nightclub are intercut with a scene introducing František's wife
Věrka. Alone in the countryside with their child, Věrka is "deciding," as

FIGURE 3.5

Loves of a Blonde. Film still courtesy of Národní filmový
archiv/National Film Archive, Prague.

the narrator tells us, "whether to write to František, or whether to visit
him in Prague with the money that she was just barely scraping together."
František goes home with a woman from the club (a prostitute, the film
implies). The next morning, Věrka travels to the base to visit him, and his
friend, the narrator, encounters her at the base's gates, looking in vain for
her husband. "When I saw her and realized who she was," he says, "I felt
sorry for her. I wanted to at least say something to her, but what should I
say? There was nothing I could say."

Over the course of the decade, unsettled, nearly existential endings
such as this one—which offers neither reprimand nor solution—became
increasingly common in the Army's short behavioral films, as Václav
Hapl's *Escape* (*Útěk*), produced a year later, confirms. *Escape* tells the story
of a medic at a rural military hospital whose weekend leave is canceled
when his supervisor is unexpectedly called away. The weekend begins un-
eventfully, the medic longs to see his girlfriend—to whom he had planned

to propose during his leave—and thus he escapes, leaving the hospital in the care of a nurse. While he is gone, a patient becomes gravely ill with typhus, while at the same time, soldiers from the base are in a car wreck, stretching the hospital's capabilities. *Escape* cuts between scenes of the developing crisis in the hospital and those of the medic in the city, enjoying his stolen time with his now-fiancée. The film ends without commentary as the medic, arriving at the hospital early the next morning, watches an ambulance pull away with the typhus patient, posing the question of whether the entire hospital is infected.

Although both *Opportunity* and *Escape* are nominally moral tales about a soldier's duties to the army and his family, the true substance of each is elsewhere. In *Escape,* it is in cinematography and the glowing early-morning mist through which the medic returns to the base. In *Opportunity,* it is in the film's scenes in Prague. Accompanied by a syncopated, discordant orchestral soundtrack, the city here does not appear menacing or dangerous, as one might expect in a tale of temptation and downfall, but rather energetic and intoxicating. In fact, the film's nightclub scene is nearly seven minutes long, occupying almost half of the fourteen-minute film. This scene is not only essential to the film, however, representing the core of its moral quandary. It also marks a shift in the short narrative film as a genre and speaks to Army Film's position within the history of postwar Czechoslovak fiction film.

In the scene, the narrator, František, and their friends flirt with women at an adjacent table. The camera follows the interplay between the two groups of friends, capturing the humorous way in which, in the busy nightclub, dancing couples cross their field of vision. This scene is highly referential, from its nightclub echoes of British Free Cinema to the tune the band plays, borrowed from Nicholas Ray's *Johnny Guitar* (perhaps in tribute to the bartender, a Joan Crawford look-alike).[39] It also anticipates a nearly identical scene in Miloš Forman's 1965 *Loves of a Blonde* (*Lásky jedné plavovlásky*), in which a group of aging soldiers on furlough are brought—an intended diversion—to a factory town populated primarily by bored, beautiful young women.[40] In Forman's film, just as in *Opportunity,* a table of soldiers flirts with a table of women across a crowded dance floor.

Opportunity's nightclub scene thus positions the film as the unexpected midpoint of a familiar cinematic genealogy, one that begins with realist movements such as British Free Cinema and Italian Neorealism and ends with the Czechoslovak New Wave. Jasný's own films, indeed, follow this trajectory—*Opportunity* was a turning point within the New Wave director's career, for the year after the film was completed, he left the Army and directed his feature debut for Czechoslovak State Film (in the Kubala-Novotný military production group), *September Nights* (*Zářijové noci*). *September Nights* is also a tale of love and furloughs and draws both on *Opportunity* and on Jasný and Kachyňa's earlier Army feature, the 1954 *Everything Ends Tonight*. But its moral overtones are markedly different from those in *Opportunity*: in *September Nights,* a young soldier who sneaks away to be with his pregnant wife before her delivery is first threatened with punishment but is later defended by a commander who recognizes the absurdity of the military rules.

In all of these films—Army Film's three short narratives and *September Nights*—the border between military and civilian spaces represents a site of potential danger, one at which the military community risks losing control over its members and at which soldiers can put both the Army and their personal and moral lives in jeopardy. The films' explicit or implicit interpretive devices are intended to help the viewer "frame" and correctly understand this border. In *The Enemy Is Listening to You*—produced in the year of the Slánský trial—interpretation and control are represented, on the one hand, by the court-martial scene, in which the soldier (and by extension the viewer) is reprimanded and instructed and thereby brought back to the military fold. On the other hand, they are represented by self-criticism's interpretation and control. In *Escape,* interpretation is purely internal: while its protagonist understands his *own* behavior as errant, he is, in the film's existential ending, left standing in front of the military hospital; we never see him re-enter it. *Opportunity,* too, sidesteps public moments of instruction, leaving the narrator (the viewer's surrogate conscience) to interpret František's actions—but even then, only indirectly. *September Nights,* however, makes a bolder move by discarding these interpretive frameworks in favor of a new one, which openly posits Army regulations as inappropriate.

This new interpretive framework, and the series of films that led to it, must be read in light of its political context. Stalin had died in 1953, and *September Nights, Opportunity,* and *Escape* all appeared in the aftermath of the Soviet Union's Twentieth Party Congress of February 1956, at which First Secretary of the Communist Party Nikita Khrushchev publicly criticized Stalin's crimes, opening the door for other reckonings with the past. Although, like their East German comrades, Czechoslovak workers had staged a series of protests (swiftly quelled) following Stalin's death, the Twentieth Party Congress's political effects in Czechoslovakia were minor compared with those in neighboring Poland or Hungary. There were numerous reasons for this. Among them was the fact that Klement Gottwald had died less than two weeks after Stalin himself, allowing the government in power to claim that the main perpetrator of its own "cult of personality" was already out of office and erroneously hold itself up as an agent of reform (Čepička, the country's only political casualty of the period, nevertheless served as scapegoat). High-ranking members of the government, furthermore, had been closely involved in the show trials of the early 1950s, and revelations about this period could threaten their own political positions. Finally, there were simply fewer public calls for reform in Czechoslovakia, where standards of living were comparatively good, and the Communist Party thus had a higher degree of popular support.[41]

The Congress's effects were, instead, felt in Czechoslovakia's intellectual and cultural life—in the critical speeches at the Second Czechoslovak Writers' Congress in 1956 and in the films that, from the middle of the decade, increasingly focused on everyday life and its problems.[42] The consequences that this had for the idea of the "model" in Army films were multiple. As Stalinism, with its strict binaries, was critiqued, Army's short narrative films, too, began to call clear-cut behavioral "models" into question. With this new uncertainty, the films' formal "model" changed— trading its strict negative/positive structure for one that was more ambiguous and complex.

THE CROOKED MIRROR OF THE THAW

The "model's" collapse as a distinct political, behavioral, and formal paradigm is most clearly expressed—in topic, form, and even title—in a film from 1956, Karel Kachyňa's *Crooked Mirror* (*Křivé zrcadlo*). Indebted to predecessors such as Jeníček's 1934 *Morning in the Barracks,* which instructs soldiers in proper dress and behavior, *Crooked Mirror*, like *Opportunity* and *Escape*, transposes this topic to the space beyond the barracks.[43] Unlike these films, however, *Crooked Mirror* is structured not as a single exemplary story, but rather as a series of episodes united within the overarching narrative of a military "fashion show," whose host, glamorous actress Stella Zázvorková, introduces each sequence in front of a red velvet curtain (see plate 5).

At each appearance, Zázvorková describes, in an unmistakably satirical tone, the way a soldier should dress, while the majority of the scenes that follow depict men dressed in an opposite manner, and humorously inappropriately. "What an original, refreshing, and unconventional impression this leisure model makes! Such elegance!"[44] exclaims Zázvorková in an early scene, after which we cut to a shot of young actor (and rising star) Vladimír Menšík leaning lazily against a fence on the banks of the Vltava River in Prague, grooming himself with the help of a hand mirror, and grinning lasciviously at women. Menšík cuts quite the opposite of an "elegant" figure; nevertheless, Zázvorková's narration holds up each element of his wardrobe as "exemplary": "The knotting of the tie must be appreciated for its time efficiency," she observes, while Menšík unhurriedly adjusts his cravat. At the end of the scene, as she tells the viewer that "individual accessories can be worn in various ways," Menšík threads his hat through one epaulette and his belt through the other, grinning goofily and ogling a passerby (see plate 6).

This pattern, in which a soldier does the reverse of what Zázvorková describes—or in which her recommendations clearly defy military regulations—is repeated throughout the film. "As far as footwear is concerned, few comrades have so far grasped its real potential," she observes, as a soldier reaches for a spoon stowed in his boot. "Your return to the barracks in this state will guarantee you many weeks of popularity" (Menšík staggers, drunk, toward the barracks gates, belt still duly hanging from his shoulder). One section is more sinister: a very drunk, very dirty soldier emerges from a grim-looking urban pub (see plate 7). Zázvorková introduces him: "And now, dear friends, the next tremendously popular model. Best suited here is surely the label [she pauses for effect] 'casual elegance.'" The soldier eyes women, picks his teeth, rummages for food in a trash can, and smokes a cigarette that he finds there, as the camera hovers over his grimy, frayed uniform, full of halfheartedly repaired holes. Midway through the section, like Menšík, he looks at himself in a hand mirror. As he groggily adjusts his coif, he spies the reflection of two (properly dressed) military officials approaching. He hides behind an open door as they pass, emerges, thinking he is safe, only to be "caught" by another soldier, whom he sheepishly salutes.

Given scenes such as these, *Crooked Mirror* might be read as instruction by negative example—a common trope in Army training films. Yet its mode is satire, and as such, the film can be interpreted in various ways: as a comedy or as a serious-minded example of how or how not to dress. This is encapsulated in its title, which plays with the concepts of the "model" or "mirror." If, following both the 1950 directive and the rhetoric of instructional films, the viewer of such a film was meant to learn from, or "mirror," the behavior he saw onscreen, in this film's "crooked mirror," it is less clear what he or she was meant to do. Alongside this lack of pedagogical clarity is a more obvious political critique. *Crooked Mirror* presents a markedly dim view of the military in civilian life: parading about the city in their "fashionable" uniforms, leering and loitering, these soldiers look like buffoons or, worse, derelicts. At the same time, in their inability to correctly follow military rules and regulations, and in doing precisely the *opposite* of what Zázvorková's voice-over describes, they are also exemplars of a deeply rooted tradition in Czech culture: they are quintessential "Švejks," characters based on the protagonist of Jaroslav Hašek's 1921 novel *The Good Soldier Švejk and His Fortunes in the World War*.

Švejk, in Hašek's novel, is a "half-witted" denizen of Prague, a man who makes his living selling mutts as purebreds and passes his days swilling beer at a local pub. When called up to World War I, Švejk manages, time and again, to land himself and his fellow soldiers in trouble—and to avoid being sent to the front—usually by following, to a word, the orders given to him. Thus, while ostensibly proving himself the ideal imperial subject, Švejk, wittingly or not (and a key to Švejk is that one never knows whether he is cunning or stupid, pro- or anti-Austrian, etc.), becomes the ultimate Czech patriot. Much like their literary predecessor, *Crooked Mirror*'s characters are hardly warriors and perhaps also half-wits.

This reference to Švejk is not only oblique but direct and textual. Near the end of the novel, Švejk, lost in the Polish countryside while attempting to return to his unit (but in fact veering away from it), comes across a lake in which a Russian prisoner is bathing. Frightened by the sight of a soldier, the naked prisoner flees, and the story continues:

> His Russian uniform was lying underneath the willows and Švejk was curious to know how it would suit him, so he took off his own and put on the uniform worn by the unfortunate naked prisoner. . . . Švejk wanted to see his reflection in the water and so he walked such a long way along the dam of the lake that he was caught by a patrol of field gendarmerie, who were looking for the escaped Russian prisoner. They were Hungarians and in spite of his protests they dragged him off to the staff command at Chyrów where they put him among a transport of Russian prisoners. . . .
>
> Everything happened so quickly that it was only the next day that Švejk realized the situation and wrote with a piece of charcoal on the white wall of the schoolroom where the detachment of prisoners was billeted: "*Here slept Josef Švejk of Prague, company orderly of the 11th march company of the 91st regiment, who as a member of a billeting party was taken prisoner in error by the Austrians near Felsztyn.*"[45]

In short, by putting on a foreign uniform and looking for a mirror in which to see himself, Švejk is captured by his own men, once more inadvertently assuring that he cannot go to the front. When read alongside Crooked Mirror's own figuration of mirrors, this chapter in Švejk's misadventures, whose politics center on Czech national identity in the Austro-Hungarian Empire, imbues Kachyňa's film with new political dimensions. Here we must recall the multiple resonances of the "model" in Army pedagogical films: not only was a soldier meant to "mirror" the behavior a film demonstrated, but the Soviet Union was a "model" for the postwar Czechoslovak military. Crooked Mirror turns these ideas on their head. With its soldiers in uniforms that they think are attractive but in fact are awkward or in tatters, the film embodies the Army's reckoning with its own history in the first part of the decade. As the Czechoslovak Army's uniforms were, on Čepička's orders, modeled after the Soviet Army's own uniforms, these resonances would have been clear to a military audience.[46]

Yet in keeping with Švejk's own Sphinx-like character, his evocation is also the most complex aspect of Crooked Mirror—a film whose title, after all, is the same as that of an 1883 story by Anton Chekhov. On the one hand, as the Soviet-Czechoslovak/Austrian-Czech parallel that the film's focus on uniforms suggests, Švejk's appearance might be read as a national, anti-Soviet statement. On the other hand, Švejk did not automatically imply national sovereignty, for the bumbling soldier was a common figure in military rhetoric even at the height of Soviet influence in the Czechoslovak Army, when he was used to critique the First Republic.[47] However, it is through this very indeterminacy that *Crooked Mirror* offers such a decisive articulation of 1956's resonances, signaling through its restoration of Švejk's inscrutability that the clear-cut, legible "models" reflected in earlier military pedagogical films were no longer valid.

We must nevertheless be cautious of relying on Švejk to explain the culture of Army filmmaking in the 1950s. For unlike what is known as *švejkovství*, an activity with a hint of subversion, the studio's support of experiments with film language and narrative was not the lucky by-product of, or a side activity to, the routine work that one might imagine making instructional films (some of which were, in point of fact, deeply formulaic) to be. Rather, it was a stated goal of the studio, as the 1954 memorandum indicates with its unmistakably auteurist question of "whether young, talented filmmakers will be able to achieve self-realization in the Army."[48]

As chapter 1 shows, this was not a novel way of framing the studio's mission. Rather, it reflected both the military's institutional mandates to develop new media (from radar systems to film and its attendant technologies) and train its members, and the further development of a studio culture that had emerged in the interwar period, when Jeníček shaped the Film Group as an institution that would educate young filmmakers and give them the resources to "experiment" and develop new uses for cinema. Čepička, envisioning in the grandest terms a rapprochement between the military and civilian spheres, changed the framework for these ambitions, trading the short film for the fiction feature. But despite the minister's ambitions, it was, curiously, the military sphere that was gradually left behind, criticized, or mocked by the Army's own productions, whether in films that pictured soldiers primarily in night clubs, left a medic standing in front of his military base, or pointedly condemned military regulations. Army Film's institutional mandate thus led to questioning of the military as an institution, just as the "model," that most Stalinist of terms, ultimately provided the terms within which Stalinism was rejected.

This was, in fact, the case for much cultural production of the Thaw in Eastern Europe and the Soviet Union: as Katerina Clark writes of Soviet fiction of this period, when writers "produced fiction containing critiques of Stalinism, they often used the ready-made code or system of signs of the Socialist Realist tradition," with changes arising "from within the tradition the writers were opposing."[49] Marci Shore observes the same in the speeches at the Second Czechoslovak Writers' Congress, in which writers criticized Stalinism using its own language.[50] Army Film, however, suggests that in Czechoslovak cinema, this story extends beyond the Thaw to the 1960s and the New Wave. For not only did many of the filmmakers who passed through Army Film go on to be mainstays of Czechoslovak popular cinema (Vláčil, Jasný, Kachyňa, and Brynych all became major figures at Barrandov soon after their departures from the Army studio), but Vladimír Menšík was a hapless, romantic soldier in both *Crooked Mirror* and *Loves of a Blonde,* and Vlastimil Brodský played similar roles in *Opportunity* and *September Nights.* Moreover, as the links between *Opportunity* and *Loves of a Blonde* and between *Glass Skies* and *The White Dove* demonstrate, many of the films that the Army studio produced were integral precursors to the canon that these filmmakers, and others like them, would go on to create. When read in this institutional light, that is, the New Wave is linked not only to the period of destalinization but also to what came before it: the rhetoric and form of the Stalinist period.

PLATE 1

Mobile cinema (*They Shall Not Pass*). Source: Vojenský historický ústav / Military History Institute, Prague.

PLATE 3

Film-within-a-film (*Flying Blind Using System OSP*). 35mm frame enlargement
courtesy of Národní filmový archiv/National Film Archive, Prague.

PLATE 4

Models (*Flying Blind Using System OSP*). 35mm frame enlargement
courtesy of Národní filmový archiv/National Film Archive, Prague.

PLATE 5

Stella Zázvorková introduces the "military fashion show"
(*Crooked Mirror*). 35mm frame enlargement courtesy of
Národní filmový archiv/National Film Archive, Prague.

PLATE 6

"Individual accessories can be worn in various ways." Vladimír
Menšík in *Crooked Mirror*. 35mm frame enlargement courtesy of
Národní filmový archiv/National Film Archive, Prague.

PLATE 7

"Casual elegance." *Crooked Mirror.* 35mm frame enlargement courtesy of Národní filmový archiv/National Film Archive, Prague.

PLATE 8

Color Wheel. 35mm frame enlargement courtesy of Národní
filmový archiv/National Film Archive, Prague.

4

Every Young Man: Reinventing Army Film

BEDŘICH BENDA, WHO SUCCEEDED Ludvík Zavřel as Army Film's chief, had been in office for five years when, at the end of November 1965, he sent an unusual proposal to the Main Political Administration (HPS). "With the increasingly wide distribution of our films to cinemas and television, both domestically and abroad," he wrote, "we are encountering difficulties when the studio's full name [Czechoslovak Army Film] is used. . . . In 1951, the abbreviation ČAF was established. There is no point in changing this brand; rather, we should emphasize it." He requested that from January 1, 1966, the studio's name be changed to STUDIO ČAF (succinct, catchy, and accompanied by a "well-designed logo").[1]

Benda's self-conscious "branding" of Army Film encapsulates the way in which the studio developed after Alexej Čepička's departure. Although the late 1950s found Army Film at loose ends, from 1960 to 1966 its leaders undertook a savvy, deliberate process of self-refashioning. In place of fiction features, the studio once again highlighted its innovations in nonfiction filmmaking. In place of asserting the military's links with the civilian sphere, its films spoke to a public that saw the Army as an institution out of step with contemporary life—even if this meant that their themes circumvented the military or critiqued it. Distance between the studio and its parent organization was also evident in the new cast of characters that, by 1965, populated Army films. Departing from the heroic border guards and pilots of the previous decade, this ensemble was diverse and decidedly everyday: a local hockey team, juvenile delinquents, a reluctant reservist. And unlike *The Tank Brigade,* with its explosions, battlefields, and cast of thousands of soldiers, in the two fiction features that Army Film made in this period—Karel Kachyňa's 1965 *Long Live the Republic (Me and Julina and the End of the Great War) (Ať žije republika [Já, Julina a konec velké války]),* a coproduction with Czechoslovak State Film, and Jan Schmidt's 1966 *The End of August at the Hotel Ozone (Konec srpna v hotelu Ozon)*—war is merely the pretext for very different kinds of stories.

As their thematic range expanded, Army Film also abandoned the redemptive narratives, high-key lighting, and epic scale of many of its 1950s productions in favor of modes of filmmaking influenced by the difficult questions and answers of the social sciences (anthropology and the newly resurgent field of sociology), by literary reportage, and by lightweight, portable camera and sound-recording technologies. Such influences and techniques were also crucial to the Czechoslovak New Wave, which emerged concurrently with Army Film's renaissance, and in histories of which Kachyňa's and Schmidt's films became standard entries. At times, the studio encouraged comparisons between itself and the New Wave: Kachyňa, interviewed in 1966 by *Film a doba's (Film and Time's)* editors (along with Army Film's lead dramaturg Roman Hlaváč, its lead director, Pavel Háša, and cameramen Jan Čuřík and Josef Illík), argued that the difference between Czechoslovakia's military and "civilian" studios had become negligible. "As for dramaturgy, creative conception or philosophy," he asserted, "there fundamentally isn't anything [in Army Film] that isn't in Czechoslovak State Film, which means that the Army studio is simply one of its dramaturgical groups, albeit a small one."[2] Háša echoed this: "There used to be a definite isolation to our studio. Now it has changed: we have practically become a part of Czechoslovak [State] Film."[3]

Although, as this book argues, Army Film's history allows us to critically revisit the New Wave, it would be an error to follow Háša or Kachyňa and consider the studio, in the 1960s, to have been simply a branch of State Film. For Army Film's metamorphosis in this period was, on the one hand, the result of the Czechoslovak Army's own transformation, an internal process of reform that reached its apex with the Prague Spring of 1968. On the other hand, for Benda and Hlaváč—along with Háša, the engineers of Army Film's reinvention—engaging with the public entailed not only making new kinds of films but also finding a way to speak to the public *about* these films and the studio that made them. Benda's request to the HPS is telling in this respect, for throughout this period, Hlaváč and he worked to craft a public identity for Army Film, one whose outlines would be as neat and recognizable as those of the studio's new logo. Drawing on Army Film's postwar and—in acknowledgment of Jiří Jeníček's work—interwar histories, this identity saw an institution that was a premier site for nonfiction film production; that was, precisely *because* of its military nature, socially engaged, particularly with Czechoslovakia's youth; that nurtured young filmmakers' artistic development; and whose institutional structure and "purposeful" nature provided a structural impetus for experimentation with film's form and uses. And while, as Benda noted, Army films themselves circulated more extensively than ever before—to domestic and international documentary film festivals, to special programs in "civilian" cinemas, and on television—this narrative, too, was widely disseminated, through press conferences, interviews, and articles.

"GENERATIONS"

These changes, in fact, began two years before Benda became studio chief, in 1958. In this year, František Vláčil, after directing *Glass Skies,* moved from Army Film to Barrandov, his long military apprenticeship over. Kachyňa and Vojtěch Jasný had already departed for Czechoslovak State Film, where Jasný had directed *September Nights.* With this, Army Film's first postwar "generation"—the group of filmmakers who had entered the studio with Čepička's 1950 call-up—was gone. Within two years, a second generation would begin to arrive, one that included directors such as Schmidt, Pavel Juráček, Jiří Menzel, Jan Němec, Karel Vachek, Ivan Balaďa, Juraj Šajmovič, Rudolf Adler, and others: the generation of the New Wave.

Between the two generations, the studio found itself in a holding pattern. In this, it reflected the state of Czechoslovak cinema as a whole, which was at a crossroads at the end of the 1950s. As chapter 3 describes,

Czechoslovakia, unlike its neighbors, had not experienced dramatic social upheaval or political change in the wake of Stalin's death or the 1956 Twentieth Party Congress, but the Congress's effects rippled through the country's intellectual and cultural life. In cinema, films began to draw themes from private and everyday life and to look to realist trends in Western cinema (British Free Cinema; Italian Neorealism) for stylistic inspiration. Films like these, Ivan Klimeš writes, made it clear to the Central Committee—whose Ideological Commission still adhered to the conception of cinema outlined in the 1950 directive—that "their initial notion of socialist art as an aid to communist education was simply not accepted by a large and influential part of the artistic community."[4]

Instead of accommodating these shifts, the Central Committee went on the offensive. At the First Festival of Czechoslovak Film, held in the Slovak town of Banská Bystrica in February 1959, Party officials sharply criticized "Twentieth Party Congress" films such as Ján Kadár and Elmar Klos's *Three Wishes* (*Tři přání*), Oldřich Lipský's *A Star Goes South* (*Hvězda jede na jih*), and Václav Krška's *Hic sunt leones* (*Zde jsou lvi*) for, among other things, using contemporary subjects to criticize contemporary society "not from a Party position, but rather from a petit-bourgeois standpoint."[5] In the festival's aftermath, filmmakers such as these were censured, personnel changes were made in State Film—whose Artistic Board was renamed the "Ideological-Artistic Board"—and the Ministry of Education and Culture assumed a more prominent role in censorship. Yet, Klimeš provocatively argues, Banská Bystrica had another, unexpected, result: With its faith in the "older generation" who had made these films shaken, the Party threw its weight behind the younger generation of filmmakers who would, in time, form the core of the New Wave, entrusting them to "fulfill its post-February ideal of socialist cinema."[6]

The short film, too, was at a crossroads at the end of the 1950s. Although it was still, for some, one of nationalized cinema's great hopes—an agent that, as critic Jiří Struska wrote in April 1960, could "help society move forward"—critics wrung their hands over the fact that the developments in production and exhibition heralded so enthusiastically in the late 1940s had not had their intended effects.[7] The short film was "an important tool for cultural revolution," wrote Ladislav Janžura, and the "cinefication network, including portable projectors and cultural facilities ... is so widespread that film can be fully used to ... disseminate a range of ideas and emotions."[8] But short films cycled primarily through the specialized Time (Čas) cinemas, and newspapers and magazines reported on them only when they won awards at foreign film festivals. "We find out about them," Ivan Soeldner complained, "only at Venice or Oberhausen."[9] If film distribution was to fault for this, so, in Antonín Navrátil's view, was a production system that expected too much from these films: the short film, intended to help create a new society, was overworked, forced into an unmanageable pace of production that left the films themselves mechanically produced and uninspiring. "As was later said with bitter irony," he wrote, "that bakers didn't bake bread so that people would have something to eat, but rather to fulfill the plan, short film studios stopped being creative centers and became factories."[10]

FROM THE ARCHIVES OUT

Army Film was somewhat sheltered from the upheaval that followed Banská Bystrica: it was not a part of State Film and therefore escaped the conference's critical spotlight. It was nevertheless at the double focus of two crises: the crisis in the short film, and the institutional crisis caused by the departure of its best and most experienced directors. Hlaváč described this in the *Film a doba* interview: "Understandably, after the first group of people left for Barrandov, the studio weakened and had to gradually build up new powers." "It got [these powers] back," he recalls, "from a group of young people."[11]

Army Film's regeneration thus mirrored the process that Klimeš observes in State Film, where young filmmakers—with the Party's blessing—took the studio's reins. In the Army, however, this happened not for political reasons, but because of the studio's natural function as a professional way station for filmmakers, an institution to which only some were expected to devote full careers and whose population was, on the whole, the young age of soldiers fulfilling their basic service. This new set of "young people"—most of them recent graduates of FAMU—began to arrive in 1959, with documentarian Rudolf Krejčík; in 1961, camera-man Juraj Šajmovič and director Ivan Balaďa joined him.[12] Within three years, most of the male members of the New Wave had also entered the studio.

The military studio's transformation, however, was also the work of its leadership. When Benda was appointed chief in 1960, he wasted no time in setting out a new program for Army Film, writing in *Obrana lidu* that "the current conception of film as a matter simply of projectionists and projecting belongs to the past."[13] The Army would, instead, deepen and expand its use of film. Soldiers would take a more active role in military film culture, organizing film clubs, improving cinemas on bases, and mak-ing amateur films. And in place of a previous regulation that soldiers watch only one film per week, they should now watch two films per week. Bases themselves (not the military's Central Film Distribution office) should select these films, thus allowing them to tailor screenings to the "current tasks and life of their base."[14] The day before this article appeared, the HPS had announced that, effective January 1, 1961, Central Film Distribution would be removed from its direct purview and made an internal part of Czechoslovak Army Film.[15]

Another crucial development of the early decade was Roman Hlaváč's promotion to lead dramaturg. Hlaváč was the scion of an established Czech film family—his father, Josef, had been a screenwriter and promi-nent Prague cinema owner in the interwar years—and had himself worked in cinema since 1947, when, at age 22, he joined ČEFIS.[16] When he was called up to the Army in 1951, Hlaváč was assigned to Army Film, where he stayed, as a dramaturg and screenwriter, until the late 1960s. Where Benda was responsible for Army Film's organization, Hlaváč was responsible for the films that it made. His emerging dramaturgical line became clear in August 1961, when *Obrana lidu* published an interview with Hlaváč that established the studio's thematic trajectory for the first years of the new decade.

The article appeared just nine days after construction began on the Berlin Wall and indicated how Army Film would position itself vis-à-vis the geopolitics of the early 1960s. "We are," Hlaváč told the newspaper,

carefully following the growth of West German militarism and revan-chism, and we are also following foreign film materials. We include every

film about the Bundeswehr's training and goals, or about revanchist meetings, in our newsreels.... We have also put out a number of movies about
the work of foreign agents. All of them are based in West Germany or West
Berlin.[17]

Among the Army films on this theme that Hlaváč mentioned were Jiří
Ployhar's 1960 spy drama *Agent K Talks* (*Agent K vypovídá*), a coproduc-
tion with East Germany's DEFA studio, and the compilation films *The
Fifth Column* (*Pátá kolona*, dir. Rudolf Krejčík, 1962), *Battleships of the
Twentieth Century* (*Křižáci XX. století*, dir. Vladimír Horák, 1960), and
Witness (*Svědectví*, dir. Pavel Háša and Ivo Toman, 1961). In their topics, all
of these films reflected the political climate in Eastern Europe during the
"Berlin crisis," which began in 1958, sparked by Soviet fears of American-
aided West German rearmament, and culminated with the construction
of the Berlin Wall.[18]

Just as their content reflected regional geopolitical priorities, these
films' form was equally rooted in regional developments, for compilation
filmmaking was undergoing a revival in Eastern Europe and the Soviet
Union at this moment.[19] Although the films were part of a broader postwar
trend in which archival film and photographs were used to investigate the
history of World War II, in East European compilation documentaries,
newly unearthed Nazi material had a specific political function, legitimizing postwar communist governments by emphasizing their antifascist
nature.[20] These films typically followed a standard political narrative that
positioned communism as the endpoint of a political teleology that began with capitalism's ills, the Great Depression, and the trauma of World
War II—all of which archival footage indexed as the past.[21]

The use of archival footage as both evidence and an anchor for progressive historical narratives was not new to Army Film, and was founda-
tional to military-parade films of the 1950s. In Ivo Toman's *Military Parade
1951*, for instance, shots of Prague's Old Town Hall in flames, followed by
footage of Red Army tanks driving through the city's streets, form the
background to contemporary footage of "building socialism." The film's
archival images offer incontrovertible proof of the Soviet Union's role in
liberating Czechoslovakia, while also grounding a confident historical
movement from past to present: from Nazi occupation to Soviet liberation
to the postwar socialist state.

If this was an orthodox historical narrative, "orthodoxy" might also characterize *Military Parade 1951*'s formal approach to archival footage, for this was reiterated throughout Czechoslovak nonfiction film of the same period. Navrátil described this polemically in a March 1964 essay in *Film a doba,* in which he noted that, during the early and mid-1950s, specific clips of "jubilee" historical moments "moved from editing room to editing room," among them the footage of the Red Army's liberation of Prague used in *Military Parade 1951.* He compares restrictions on the use of archival material in the early 1950s to those on scholarship, writing that, at this time, "a great deal of authentic footage was, due to . . . its topics, made top-secret. . . . This was just as it was in historiography. . . . scholars and artists could only study materials about chirping sparrows, so to speak."[22] These familiar clips, then, constantly repeated, offered a visual shorthand for a set of canonical historical events that the public was meant to recognize and to know how to interpret.

When compilation filmmaking regained popularity at the end of the 1950s, this understanding of film archives as a source of evidence was little changed. However, the notion of how archival material became evidentiary shifted radically. In place of the controlled "shorthand" use of historical footage, filmmakers sought out ever greater amounts of material; in place of an understanding of meaning as immanent, literally visible in historical footage, it was seen as arising through editing. Jan Hořejší characterized this shift in a September 1961 article on compilation film, where he wrote that "a clear answer to the question 'how could that have happened?' or 'how was it really?' cannot always be given by a shot alone. . . . The camera captures a certain reality. Editing offers the *sense* of this reality and its *interpretation.* . . ."[23]

Although Hořejší begins this passage with Vsevolod Pudovkin's famous axiom "the foundation of film art is editing," the model for Czechoslovak films of this period was not only the seminal work of Soviet filmmakers but also—and more importantly—that of East German filmmakers, who were uniquely positioned to explore the history of Nazi Germany from the perspective of its own audiovisual productions, as when Germany was divided, numerous film archives found themselves located in the German Democratic Republic.[24] (As Jay Leyda writes, "The division of Germany made it possible for the first accusations against Germany to come from Germany.")²⁵ Andrew and Annelie Thorndike were prominent among these. In the couple's films (such as *You and Many a Comrade* [*Du und mancher Kamerad,* 1956] and the suggestively titled series *The Archives Testify* ... [*Archive sagen aus* ...]), extensive and carefully researched archival material is used as, in Leyda's words, a "devastating weapon of accusation," frequently against West German figures and organizations with ties to the Nazi past.²⁶ The archives thus do "testify," not only to political crimes, but also, by extension, to the necessity of the East German state.

Geopolitical questions such as these were brought more sharply to the fore with the Berlin crisis and, in these years, reflected in compilation films produced throughout the region, many of which followed the "Thorndike model." In East Germany, for instance, Karl Gass's 1962 *Look at this City!* (*Schaut auf diese Stadt!*) historically justified the Berlin Wall's construction, while in Czechoslovakia, which shared a border with both East and West Germany, compilation films framed the latter state as a revanchist threat and thereby justified the Cold War's geopolitical divisions. Among the earliest Czechoslovak compilation films to do so was Emanuel Kaněra and Jiří Mrázek's 1958 *A Small Unknown Land* (*Malá neznámá země*), which, according to its release details, "shows ... that the end of the Third Reich did not mean the end of fascism, which, under Adenauer's leadership in West Germany, is raising its head again."²⁷ Later films produced, like Kaněra and Mrázek's, by Krátký Film's Documentary Film division included Josef Kořán's 1961 *Guardians* (*Ochránci*), which "reminds us of ... the voices of those in West Germany who are calling for the same kind of European society that Hitler and his followers established in Czechoslovakia on March 15, 1939."²⁸ Contemporaneous essays about compilation filmmaking echoed the language in these descriptions, emphasizing the urgency of the West German threat. Jiří Hrbas, in a 1962 issue of *Kino,* wrote:

> In thinking about ... political documentaries today, in 1962, it seems to me that their importance is exceptionally great, especially at this time. ... These films ... WARN us against the repetition of disastrous events. ... MOBILIZE all progressive powers against fascism, which, although damaged during the last war, was decidedly not wiped out!²⁹

»Svědectví« Hákové kříže měly skrýt nápis na pomníku:
Vláda tvých věcí se do tvých rukou navrátí,
ó lide český!

FIGURE 4.1

Witness: "The swastikas covered the writing on the memorial: The
government will return your belongings to you, O Czech people!" Publicity
still courtesy of Národní filmový archiv/National Film Archive, Prague.

Not only was Army Film's early 1960s series of compilation films part of
this movement; it also ultimately became the most celebrated Czechoslovak contribution to the format.[30] The magnum opus of the studio's compilation films was *Witness,* on which filmmakers worked for nearly three
years and whose two parts total three hours. The film won the East German Film Critics' Prize at the 1961 Leipzig Film Festival (Internationale
Leipziger Dokumentar- und Kurzfilmwoche) and, according to Benda,
was the most successful Czechoslovak film abroad in that year, having
been screened in "more than sixty countries of the world, sometimes even
on television, as in the Soviet Union and Cuba."[31]

Witness might be seen as the *Why We Fight* of Czechoslovak cinema, offering an exhaustive overview of the history of the Czech and Slovak lands
from the interwar period to the present. Part 1 (*Betrayal* [*Zrada*]) begins
on the brink of the Great Depression and continues through the Spanish

Civil War, the Anschluss, and the titular "betrayal," the Munich Agreement. Throughout, the film emphasizes that "betrayal" signifies both the events at Munich and the West's neglect of Eastern Europe thereafter, a familiar rhetorical gesture that allowed Munich to legitimize the region's communist government and Soviet influence. Part 2 (*Victory* [*Vítězství*]) focuses on World War II. It begins in occupied Prague in 1941 and continues through the 1942 assassination (by British-trained Czechoslovak paratroopers) of Reinhardt Heydrich, the *Reichsprotektor* of the Protectorate of Bohemia and Moravia; the 1943 execution of the Czech communist journalist Julius Fučík by the Nazis; and the 1944 Battle of the Dukla Pass. It ends with the proclamation that "history will never repeat itself; the world is changing. The Communist Party has decided this; we have decided this."

This concluding statement is intriguingly reflexive, for despite its orthodox vision of recent history, *Witness,* in fact, represents a more detailed engagement with the past than had yet been seen in postwar Czechoslovak documentary. The footage from which the film was composed was gathered not only from the Czechoslovak Film Archive but also from East Germany's film archive, the Gosfilmofond archive in Moscow, and collections in Kiev and Bratislava.[32] In response to advertisements that they placed in newspapers, the filmmakers also collected a vast amount of privately owned and home-movie footage. The result was a compilation of material that few viewers had seen before, including UFA newsreels, amateur films, Depression-era footage shot by the Left Front, previously unknown interwar images of Gottwald, and material from the Spanish Civil War.[33] Though the breadth of the filmmakers' discoveries dazzled critics, it also sparked complaints: Navrátil, in his essay in *Film a doba,* complained that "Army filmmakers could make *Witness* and wonder at its unknown material *only because* 'civilian' filmmakers did not have access to it."[34] Hlaváč, who wrote the film's screenplay, repudiated this in a letter to the editor in June, writing that "the filmmaking team for *Witness* found the material for this film primarily in the 'civilian' Czechoslovak Film Archive, where they worked under the same conditions as numerous filmmakers before and after."[35]

Navrátil's critique was, however, prescient, for apart from its ambitious scale and breadth, what distinguished *Witness* was the Army studio's institutional relationship to the material that constituted the film, a relationship that, with this production, began to shift from a simple equation between historical footage and "evidence" to a more complex engagement with the material's temporal and formal dimensions. This is legible in the history of the film's production: While *Witness* was in preparation, its assistant director, Rudolf Krejčík, was assigned to choose footage for the film at the Czechoslovak Film Archive. During this process, Krejčík arranged with Miloslav Jílovec, *Witness*'s production manager, to designate a certain amount of material for his own use. He ultimately earmarked approximately five thousand meters of footage, most of it German or Czechoslovak collaborationist material (newsreels, home movies, and amateur films) that showed the wartime years and the development of the Sudeten German Party through its own eyes.[36] When his Army service was over and Krejčík moved on to a career at Czechoslovak State Film's documentary studio, this material became the foundation for his compilation film *Every Day in the Great Reich* (*Všední dny velké říše*, 1963).[37]

Despite the fact that *Every Day in the Great Reich*'s politics and narrative in certain ways reiterate *Witness*'s, the film's approach to historiography is considerably different. This is clear both in its title, with its invocation of the "everyday," and in parts of its narrative that address cinema's own temporal and historical properties.[38] Early in the film, for instance, the voice-over—speaking from a present-day perspective—describes what we see, amateur footage of a Sudeten German cultural celebration in 1927:

> This was all a very long time ago. But it hasn't been forgotten.... The greatest attraction was the film camera.... That was something for us.... Yes, it was something, to celebrate our national past as if it were alive ... at that moment, everything was in the present ... everyone tried to look like people looked in the biograph.... But film is such an uncanny witness— film, which, with an impersonal precision, records a moment, a likeness, a gesture at an insignificant event in the past ... a moment that, simply in the fact that it was captured and can be repeated, is given a certain hidden meaning. But then—then it was only the present.

The film does not fully incorporate these initial explorations of the links between past and present: It ends with a depiction of Germans being expelled from Czechoslovakia. As they walk away from the camera, the voice-over (again, suggesting the thoughts of the figures onscreen) concludes, "This can probably never happen again ... we have left forever."

Nevertheless, Krejčík's film disavows the conclusiveness of this final statement, framing its constituent footage as more than merely "evidence" for
the historical teleology within which, in *Witness,* similar material is inscribed. The voice-over, moreover, recalls Jeffrey Skoller's observation—
in reference to archival material in contemporary experimental films—of
the ways in which, "by being recorded and stored in one moment in time
and then experienced at another," "a moment" is "turned into an object."[39]
This is appropriate to *Every Day in the Great Reich,* for the film's treatment
of archival films and photographs not as "facts" but as "objects" presaged
the more explicitly experimental approaches that would define later Army
productions, whose logics of assembly are markedly different.

Every Day in the Great Reich's departure from *Witness*'s conception of
archival material was nonetheless rooted in the earlier film. For though
Krejčík's film was not officially an Army production, it was made because
Army Film allowed the director—who, as a soldier performing his basic
service, was paid very little—to use "studio time" to work on a personal
project.[40] This instance of a secondary, unofficial economy in Army Film,
in which "surplus" footage represented an alternative form of compensa-
tion, is significant in two ways. First, the notion of archival footage as, in a
sense, a commodity underscores *Every Day in the Great Reich*'s treatment
of such material as "objects" and not transparent evidence of history—
objects that are moveable, transferrable, easily reorganized. Second, it
reflects a crucial dimension of Army Film's development in this period,
when Benda and Hlaváč decentralized not only Army Film's distribution
and exhibition systems but also its production processes, allowing the
young "generation" who entered the studio in these years a considerable
degree of latitude in making films.

Witness was a resounding success—after its victory at Leipzig, the
film went on to Czechoslovakia's own Karlovy Vary Short Film Festival
(Dny krátkého filmu v Karlových Varech), where, along with three other
Army productions (František Karásek's *Illusion of Flight* [*Iluze za letu*],
Jozef Sedláček's *Yesterday Was Sunday* [*Včera neděle byla*], and Krejčík's
own *Fairy-Tale about a Castle, Children, and Justice* [*Pohádka o zámečku,
dětech, a spravedlnosti*]), it shared first prize—and inspired by this, Army
Film continued with the compilation format.[41] Some of the studio's films,
like their predecessors, addressed topics having to do with World War II

(e.g., Háša's 1965 *Lidice,* about the Bohemian village destroyed by German troops in retaliation for Heydrich's assassination). Others followed *Every Day in the Great Reich* in their unorthodox approach to historiography and archival material, among them Hlaváč and Háša's *Nine Chapters from Ancient History* (*Devět kapitol ze starého dějepisu*), on which the filmmakers began work in 1963 but did not complete until 1969. These films, in turn, became the backbone of Benda and Hlaváč's attempts to expand Army Film's activities and widen its appeal to civilian audiences—plans within which not only archival filmmaking but archival material more broadly figured prominently. The minutes of a 1962 meeting of Warsaw Pact filmmakers in Prague reflect this.[42] During this meeting, the studios—which had met before but had, to date, rarely discussed their artistic and military goals—agreed to begin a collaboration, important components of which (encouraged by the Czechoslovak delegation, Hlaváč and Benda) were to be the "regular exchange" of newsreel footage, "collaboration between the archives of individual studios," and "mutual aid in negotiating access to the state film archives of individual countries."[43]

The footage garnered by the Warsaw Pact exchange would play a central role not only in Army Film's compilation films but also in the studio's newsreel division, which Benda and Hlaváč radically altered in early 1962, firing its editorial board and bringing in, as Benda reflected later, "young comrades who succeeded in removing [the newsreel's] formulaic elements and energizing it with new and fresh ideas."[44] From 1962 to 1965, the studio produced two newsreels. One, *Army Bulletin* (*Armádní zpravodaj*), was distributed within Army cinemas, while the second, *Army Newsreel* (*Armádní filmový měsíčník*), addressed topics of civilian interest and was shown on Czechoslovak Television (Československá televize). "We are trying to give [the newsreel] wider applicability," Hlaváč noted during the Warsaw Pact meeting. "Young people work on it, among them soldiers during their years of basic military service. We want the newsreel to be young, a vibrant platform, a school for viewers and filmmakers."[45] While Warsaw Pact footage was an integral part of this newsreel, Benda was careful to note that it was to be used by the young directors any way they wished.[46] At the same time, the footage could be used in future compilation films and would help build up Army Film's own archival collection.[47]

EVERY YOUNG MAN

Benda and Hlaváč's emphasis on the newsreel's appeal to youth, its "freshness" and novelty, reflected a more general crisis in the Czechoslovak Army, which by the late 1950s had developed what Condoleezza Rice terms a "serious image problem." The abuses and excesses of Čepička's tenure as minister of defense, compounded with traditional Czech pacifism, had made the military, for much of society, an unpopular, untrustworthy institution. Young, educated professionals, moreover, were reluctant to join the officer corps, whose promotion system remained largely political, yet which needed them sorely.[48] Such disaffection was captured neatly in Juráček's 1964 diptych *Every Young Man* (*Každý mladý muž*), produced by the Novotný-Kubala production group at Barrandov, whose first section, "Achilles' Heel," follows a young and old soldier as the duo loaf about Prague on furlough, drinking beer and being kicked out of parks.

This intertwined institutional crisis and crisis in legitimacy was evidence of broader demographic issues in Czechoslovakia. At the cusp of the 1950s and 1960s, the country was home to a large number of young, well-educated professionals who had lived most, and in some cases all, of their lives under wartime occupation or socialism. Although they had thus grown up surrounded by early socialism's promises of equality, liberation, and transformation, at the beginning of their adult lives, they found their professional and personal possibilities circumscribed by an ossified system. Political scientist Kieran Williams summarizes this situation: "Half the population had no experience of the capitalist system but had not benefited from the socialist one."[49]

Like other "new course" policies in Eastern Europe, Czechoslovakia's reforms of the 1960s represented, in part, an attempt to address such generational alienation and to establish legitimacy among Czechoslovak youth. For while generational discontent was widespread in this period, "youth" was also, as Susan E. Reid writes, "one of the most valorised terms in the symbolic system of the Thaw, cogently embodying the party's promises of rejuvenation of the socialist project, of social and scientific progress and of the imminent advent of Communism."[50] Nevertheless, the reforms were primarily spurred by the economy, whose foundations were growing shaky. Even as Czechoslovakia's 1960 constitution proclaimed that the country had reached the final stage of socialism—thereby allowing it to change its name to the Czechoslovak Socialist Republic[51]—in this year and the next, Czechoslovakia faced an economic recession, and its Third Five-Year Plan (1961–1965) failed in its second year.[52] Economics were accordingly a primary topic at the Twelfth Czechoslovak Party Congress of December 1962, during which economists proposed solutions that looked beyond central management. At the end of the 1960s, reformers such as economist Ota Šik would elaborate these ideas further.[53]

It was at the Twelfth Party Congress that a second major departure in Czechoslovak politics occurred, with the exoneration of the victims of the 1950s show trials. Although this was only the first step toward the victims' full rehabilitation and the government's acknowledgment of its complicity in the trials (which would not occur until 1968), its effects extended outward, as culture and society started to engage with topics that had previously been taboo.[54] Rehabilitations took place in the military as well, with the increasingly reformist HPS—and particularly its chief, Václav Prchlík—spearheading a movement to address the fate of Slovak officials who had been purged and imprisoned (and in some cases subjected to forced labor and torture) in 1951.[55]

Among the formerly restricted topics to be revived in the Congress's aftermath was Franz Kafka, on whom, led by literature scholar Eduard Goldstücker—himself a victim of the political trials of the 1950s, imprisoned from 1951 to 1955—Czechoslovak writers held a conference in May 1963 in the town of Liblice. Vladimír V. Kusin describes Kafka's rehabilitation as part of a larger shift in discourse about "reality" and "realism": Whereas Soviet theorist Dmitri Zatonsky had, in 1959, argued that Kafka was "all that was most reactionary and most hostile to realism in contemporary bourgeois literature," Czechoslovak journalist Alexej Kusák observed at the Kafka conference that "*The Trial* is for me a basic probe into the social reality of the modern world."[56]

Indeed, in concert with the country's belated reforms, Czechoslovak writers, intellectuals, and artists began to think anew about the concept and politics of realism in the early 1960s. An essential part of this process was the translation of books and essays by two influential Western Marxist critics, the Austrian Ernst Fischer and the French Roger Garaudy, both of whom broadened the categories of "realism" and "socialist art" to encompass figures such as Kafka and Václav Havel (whose absurdist 1963 play "The Garden Party" Fischer described, in "The Deformation of Man," as "an attempt to give artistic form to an essential aspect of our age").[57] These writers and their texts were discussed extensively and impassionedly in the Writers' Union journal *Literární noviny* and elsewhere, and these discussions had ramifications in other spheres of cultural production.

Cinema—and particularly the emerging New Wave—was one of them. The decade's shift in discourse about cinematic realism can be contextualized by examining similar discourse in 1948. In an essay written this year, critic Jiří Sequens had summarized the Communist Party's official assessment of various cinematic "realisms," concluding that contemporary West European cinema's interest in the common man's "life and problems" was "not enough." The only form of realism that was "morally and socially responsible" was Soviet (or socialist) realism. "It could not be otherwise," he wrote, for

> the realism of the socialist state, which is built solely and above all on true and firm values, gives Soviet film a foundation on which its best and most sensitive talents have created . . . their great works, which discover and celebrate the simple greatness of man, his ability to transform the world, to create a new socialist society. The most fundamental characteristic of Soviet realism is its revolutionary nature. . . . It is a realism that is true, deep, and above all educational.[58]

With this, Sequens described the pedagogical—state-building and citizen-making—charge of Czechoslovak cinema culture of the 1950s. However, after events such as the Third Five-Year Plan's collapse made it clear that "building socialism" had not yet produced its desired results, this understanding of realism seemed insufficient to critics and filmmakers. The critical and creative engagement with realism that followed mirrored a process that had recently occurred elsewhere in Eastern Europe—for instance, Poland, whose "new cinema" of the mid-1950s (the "Polish School" films of Andrzej Wajda, Andrzej Munk, and others) represented, in French film critic André Bazin's words, a mode of filmmaking "in real harmony with socialist society," and an alternative to socialist realism, which he described ironically as "the time when the famous Chiaourelli taught Polish filmmakers a lesson by explaining to them that it was neither decent nor sensible to show Julius Caesar blowing his nose."[59]

Many Czechoslovak critics interpreted the New Wave—whose arrival was marked by a series of films in 1962–1963—as a search for precisely such a "new cinema in real harmony with socialist society." The New Wave's approaches to this varied. Some films (among them Kadár and Klos's World War II partisan tale *Death Is Called Engelchen* [*Smrt si říká Engelchen*]), in the model of the Kafka conference, looked backward, examining ideas and histories that had not previously "fit" into public discourse—a characteristic aspect of Thaw films throughout Eastern Europe.[60] Others (Věra Chytilová's *Something Different* [*O něčem jiném*], Miloš Forman's *Competition* [*Konkurs*]) borrowed from the approaches of cinéma vérité, offering, in critic Miloš Fiala's words, "new contacts with the present, the discovery of the mentality and psychology of today's people . . . the attempt to look at the present from new viewpoints."[61] Still others, like Jasný's *Cassandra Cat* (*Až přijde kocour*), were abstract and fanciful, or, like Štefan Uher's *The Sun in a Net* (*Slnko v sieti*), adopted their protagonists' subjective perspectives on the world. Critic Galina Kopaněvová, in 1967, wrote of these films, too, as fundamentally realist: "The Czechoslovak film avant-garde has arrived at the domain of a new visualization of reality, one that exists in the world of the consciousness, ideas, and fantasies of the creator."[62]

As some fiction filmmakers began to use techniques drawn from nonfiction film, Czechoslovak nonfiction itself was undergoing a renaissance. This had, in fact, begun in 1960, when the Karlovy Vary Short Film Festival took place for the first time. Modeled after the Leipzig Film Festival in East Germany, what was known as the "little" (*malý*) or "winter" (*zimní*) Karlovy Vary promised to remedy the problems that documentary critics had bemoaned at the end of the last decade. The festival swiftly became the Czechoslovak short film's center of gravity, and its energy was channeled into other developments: in June, the dedicated short-film Time Cinema on Wenceslas Square was reopened as the Prague Cinema, promising revamped nonstop programs of domestic and foreign popular-science, sports, nature, animation and puppet films, and documentaries.[63]

Nineteen sixty, as Army Film's compilation films demonstrate, also marked the appearance of new formal approaches to nonfiction; in Jiří Struska's words, it was at this moment that Czechoslovak documentary "began to attempt a deeper film language, a heightened emotiveness, etc."[64] While *Witness* and other Czechoslovak compilation films of the "Berlin Crisis" looked to the example of East German documentary, other strands of Czechoslovak documentary developed in reaction to works that filmmakers saw at festivals abroad. Filmmakers were inspired by the Polish "Black Series," socially critical documentaries that had, as part of the larger changes in Polish cinema to which Bazin refers, begun to emerge during the Thaw, by British Free Cinema, by—in documentarian Václav Táborský's words—"quick cutting, hidden cameras, sounds, synchronous sounds, simple people, gripping moments."[65] Most popular, however, was cinéma vérité, with its alluring promise of "truth," that long-standing foundation of the Czechoslovak "myth."[66]

A YOUNG WORKSHOP

The role that Army Film would play in the short film's renaissance was confirmed in January 1962, when the studio first participated in the Karlovy Vary Short Film Festival.[67] The series of films that the studio entered into the competition—*Illusion of Flight, Yesterday Was Sunday,* and *A Fairy-Tale about a Castle, Children, and Justice,* crowned by its masterwork, *Witness*—was awarded first prize (an honor it shared with Krátký Film's Gottwaldov branch), and the jury praised Army Film as a "'young workshop' for Czechoslovak film."[68] Journalists were amazed at the studio's sudden "appearance": Army Film's contribution to the festival, in Ivan Soeldner's words, was a "revelation."[69]

This recognition confirmed that Benda and Hlaváč's re-envisioning of the studio was working as they had hoped: Army Film was becoming known for its inventive films and for its relevance to the concerns of civilian audiences and "civilian" cinema. In response, they intensified their efforts at shaping the studio's public identity. From March 22 to March 28, 1963, Army Film held the first ever retrospective of its work, exhibiting twenty-four films, in rotating programs, at the Prague Cinema.[70] The March program was followed, in October, by a series of thirteen Army films exhibited in cinemas across Prague.[71]

Discussions of these retrospectives in the Czechoslovak press became the foundation for a narrative about Army Film that would evolve over the following years, and whose outlines the studio's leadership, in large part, determined. On the first day of the March retrospective, a journalist with the initials "dv"—presumably Ivan Dvořák, one of Army Film's dramaturgs—wrote in the daily Večerní Praha (Evening Prague) that the program "represents the first opportunity for viewers to see the best works from this studio, which has given an entire generation of creative workers to Czechoslovak fiction film."[72] At the start of the October program, he wrote that it represented "a cross section of the oeuvre of a studio that has recently achieved wide cultural and artistic renown."[73] The characterization of Army Film as both a training ground for Czechoslovak fiction film and an emerging "cultural and artistic" force in its own right became fundamental to the studio's descriptions of itself, as did the notion that the Army, as an institution that intersected with the lives of nearly all Czechoslovak youth, was fundamentally in touch with society as a whole. "After all," wrote Dvořák in an August 1963 article about the studio in the journal Kino (Cinema), "everyone who enthusiastically plays sports today, or is sustained by a particular hobby, or those mastering the military arts during their Army service will soon create the material and spiritual values of the society of tomorrow."[74]

Benda and Hlaváč attempted a new publicity strategy the following January, holding a combined press screening and conference that featured the 1963 productions Reporter (Reportér, dir. Pavel Háša), A Little Winter Music (Malá zimní hudba, dir. Milan Růžička), Unnamed Cemetery: Requiem Aeternam (Cintorín bez mena: Requiem aeternam, dir. Ivan Baladʼa), and Heroes for Whom No Time Remained (Hrdinové, na které nezbyl čas, dir. Ivo Toman). The critical responses to this event in turn became part of the studio's narrative, establishing new explanations for both Army Film's formal and institutional distinctiveness and its proximity to Czechoslovak "civilian" culture. These explanations focused on the studio's organizational character: as Jaroslav Boček argued in Kulturní tvorba (Cultural Production), reporting on the press conference, Army Film's innovations in film language were rooted, above all, in its "purposeful [*účelový*]" nature and similarity to industrial film. Army Film, he wrote,

> has the strong tradition of being an experimental studio. Young people come to it bearing ideas and impulses, and it is not for nothing that the studio is proud of the fact that Jasný and Kachyňa, František Vláčil, Štefan Uher, Stanislav Barabáš and quite a few others got their start here—for these filmmakers, it is precisely the industrial, experimental character of work in the studio that gave them the first opportunity to apply themselves in film.[75]

These experiments were, he argued, further made possible by the studio's dramaturgy, which limited its films' topics to those with links to the military but did not limit *how* it approached these topics—in contrast to Krátký Film, which was not limited in topic but was required to follow strict generic categories (e.g., the popular-scientific division made popular-scientific films; the animated and puppet film division made animated and puppet films).[76] Army Film was thus free to look at the military through various lenses, the creative results of which, Boček concluded, were evidence "of Czechoslovakia's developing film culture." Ivan Soeldner echoed this idea eleven months later in the same publication, writing that "Army Film's unique position among other short film studios does not mean that it should be 'on the margins' of Czechoslovak cinema. We have been following its attempts at an idiosyncratic dramaturgical approach for some time now. The soldiers are traversing the boundaries of conventional military themes."[77]

Although there are no extant transcripts of the 1964 press conference, an interview with Benda that appeared in the Party daily *Rudé právo* (*Red Right*) on March 3, 1964, suggests that this narrative originated with the studio itself. Asked by the interviewer what Army Film's "thematic" (versus Krátký Film's "generic") limitation meant in practice, Benda responded that "we try to make full use of every possibility to develop all kinds and genres of film, from reportage and documentary to popular scientific and instructional films, to short stories and film novellas." This dramaturgical strategy, he argued, was necessarily broad, for the Army was required to speak to society as a whole, and particularly to youth. Thus, while "defense" was, naturally, Army Film's primary thematic interest, the studio was, at present, interpreting this theme "much more broadly" than before, making films not only "about soldiers, for soldiers," but also for civilians.

According to Benda, the studio's "open" approach to dramaturgy also had another goal: "The principle of allowing everyone to concern himself with what is closest to him, and to try out various things." "We do not only rely," said Benda, "on the so-called old cadre, but equally, if not more, on the young. In this way, we try to preserve the character of a creative workshop for young talents, which is part of the studio's tradition." With this phrase—deliberately reiterating the language with which the 1962 Karlovy Vary Festival had praised Army Film—Benda underscored what *Opportunity* and *Flying Blind Using System OSP* demonstrate: the studio's history of cinematic pedagogy. The "tradition" to which he referred, however, did not only date to the 1950s, when Jasný and Vláčil worked in Army Film. Rather, in the first postwar reference to the studio's interwar roots, Benda made clear that Army Film's identity as a "workshop" dated to the interwar years. "It is important to recognize this," he added, "for nothing, no new 'workshop,' is created just like that, either within days, or in a single year."[78]

Writing after an Army Film press conference in November 1965, critic Jiří Tvrzník synthesized Benda's and Boček's arguments. The studio, he wrote,

> has a markedly wide thematic view. Its dramaturgs wisely offer its directors subjects that are not, strictly speaking, about military themes or "obvious" needs for the Army, but subjects that also have considerable meaning for society as a whole. The artists contribute to this, and so does the studio itself, which offers them not only the possibility to experiment, but also the creative means to formulate a position, to develop their artistic personality. These auteurs are seeking—and finding—their place in contemporary film, and are thus maintaining an important connection with Czechoslovak cinema as it develops.[79]

That this—defining Army Film as a studio that, in its administrative dimensions, its orientation toward the widest swaths of civilian society, and its institutional mandate to train young men, was *structurally* conditioned to experiment with film form—appeared in the same month that Benda proposed a new name for the studio is perhaps not accidental. By late 1965,

Army Film's identity, like this name and its logo, had been tested, shaped, and refined.[80]

REPORTERS AND REPORTAGE

Army Film's second major success of this period, Háša's *Reporter*—among a series of Czechoslovak documentaries to collectively win the second-place Silver Dove at the 1963 Leipzig Film Festival—exemplifies Tvrzník's "wide thematic view." Narrated by legendary actor Jan Werich—co-founder, with Jiří Voskovec, of the popular interwar Liberated Theater (Osvobozené divadlo), and himself a sometime author of reportage—*Reporter* captures a day in the life of the photojournalist Karel Hájek.[81] Hájek was an uncontroversial, popular figure, and *Reporter* follows its subject's lead. It is a portrait of, in the film's own words, "a reporter who loves his work, and loves people" that ends with Hájek photographing ecstatic crowds at a May Day parade. Yet the film is also resolutely nonmilitary—there is nothing in *Reporter* that refers to defense, nor to war.

Reporter, however, is not only about Hájek but also about reportage itself, one of the genres that Benda mentioned in his March 1964 interview, which the film represents in Hájek's personal photographic archive. Dating to 1920, this archive is a virtual catalogue of Czechoslovakia's interwar and postwar history, and Háša pays considerable attention to it, reviewing its moments of life under occupation; its portraits of famous actors and political figures. Other Army films of this period adopted a similarly "wide," journalistic view. In Milan Růžička's *Cecoslovacco buono* (1967), Army filmmakers traveled to Italy to investigate the history of Czechoslovak soldiers who worked with the famous Garibaldi partisans during World War II. And to make the 1967 television documentary *The Story of Kalevi Liiva* (*Vyprávění o Kalevi Liiva*), Ivan Balaďa and Juraj Šajmovič journeyed to Tallinn with Czech Holocaust survivor Erna Weissnerová, who was serving as a witness in the trial of her former jailors at a World War II labor camp.[82]

For Balaďa, reportage was also a question of literary genre. Earlier in the decade, the director had made two films for Army Film—*Unnamed Cem-*

FIGURE 4.2

Reporter. Publicity still courtesy of Národní filmový
archiv/National Film Archive, Prague.

etery: Requiem Aeternam (1963) and the 1964 *Man in a Great Hall* (*Človek
vo veľkej hale*)—that adapted short reportages from Slovak author Ladislav
Mňačko's 1962 collection *Where Dirt Roads End* (*Kde končia prašné cesty*),
a book that Miloslav Vojtech describes as a series of "sociological studies
of 'godforsaken corners' of Slovakia."[83] Mňačko, whom Balaďa had known
since childhood, was a journalist by profession and had been at the Communist Party cultural vanguard since 1945, when he began writing for the
Party dailies *Rudé právo* and *Pravda* (*Truth*).[84] He was also an active voice
for reform from the late 1950s through the 1960s: Marci Shore describes
Mňačko's speech at the Third Czechoslovak Writers' Congress in 1963—in
which he called for his colleagues to acknowledge their own guilt in the
crimes of the 1950s—as, for the Union, "an irrevocable point of departure
in confronting Stalinism."[85]

  Delayed Reportages (*Oneskorené reportáže*), a book that Mňačko published in the same year as the Third Congress, was similarly consequential.

A series of stories about people unjustly persecuted during the Stalinist period, the book is as much about these figures as it is a reflection on the history of journalism itself, for, during the early 1950s, Mňačko reflected in a January 1964 interview, "Journalists couldn't . . . point out serious problems in Czechoslovak life.'"[86] Indeed, in its very title—with its indication of belatedness—the book cut to the heart of destalinization in Czechoslovakia. It also did so in its form, which reflected contemporary interest in "reality," truth, and revelations, as well as reportage's current popularity as a literary genre. Long an important mode of cultural production on the left, reportage had been central to Czechoslovak literature immediately after the war, when, quickly written and disseminated, it was a useful aid in reconstruction (much like the short film, which Jiří Weiss praised in 1945 for precisely these qualities).[87] It remained so in the early 1950s, becoming resurgent again in the 1960s.

Mňačko's style is distinct: in an echo of his speech to the Writers' Congress, his reportages of the 1960s use the genre's first-person voice (not always the author's own) as a mode of investigation and existential questioning, producing what Jelena Paštéková describes as a "distanced subject position vis-à-vis facts," and a mode of writing on the "border between the literature of fact and fiction."[88] Mňačko's narrators often describe a scene, an image, or an object and subsequently deconstruct or cross-examine it through a series of questions or hypotheses. *Unnamed Cemetery,* for instance—adapted from the bluntly titled first piece in the collection, "Cemetery of Dead Germans" (*Cintorín mrtvých Nemcov*)—is set in the Slovak mountain village of Hunkovce, not far from the site of the Battle of the Dukla Pass. In the reportage, a man walks through a cemetery hastily erected by retreating German troops, ruminating on the war through the objects he encounters, from flowers laid on a grave ("Several days must have passed since it was laid there. A relative? Probably a relative. Even here, even to Dukla, Čedok brings German tourists.")[89] to the grave markers ("The crosses made the strongest impression on me. All of them straight and ornamentally rounded at the ends. . . . How did they get this uniformity? Did each division make their own in workshops behind the front lines, or were they made in bulk, in a factory?").[90]

While in Mňačko's reportage, each object sparks a question, and each question is the starting point for numerous reflective threads, in Balad'a's adaptation, the multiple layers of the narrator's voice-over are eclipsed by the film's simpler visual register, which moves between sequences in the cemetery and a series of documentary photographs from World War II that depict Nazi officials, ceremonies, and atrocities.[91] In this, the film both fails to grasp the complexity of its source text and falls back on the evidentiary understanding of archival material that propelled films like *Witness,* and that the events of 1956 and 1963 had begun to deconstruct.

Man in a Great Hall, made a year later, was more successful in its attempt at, in Navrátil's words, "filming literary reportage," in particular in adapting Mňačko's form of "artistic reportage."[92] Mňačko's text captures the meditations on life and labor of a man observing another man monitoring a nuclear reactor, meditations that become critiques of labor practices and discourse in late socialism. The narrator begins by observing how the factory's automation produces a mechanized form of labor for the "man in a great hall":

> His working hours are eight, he is paid for an eight-hour work day, he survives eight hours daily in this hall, and sixteen times every five or six minutes he circles the pea-green control board and writes down a few numbers. For the rest of the time he stands, like an unmoving statue, except that he is a man and not a bronze sculpture; his nerves are constantly working.[93]

He follows this with a mocking imitation of how this labor might be publicly discussed:

> This man alone in a great hall is the adumbration of the man of the future; he is the hero of the atomic age, the age of cybernetics and automation. The factory we are speaking of, the factory that is the muscle of our five-year plans, has a tiny staff. With four guards, two cleaning women, an assistant and the office staff, there are thirty people altogether. The labor productivity here may be the highest possible in our current stage of social production.[94]

The reportage ends by emphasizing the dehumanizing nature of labor that makes a man's body superfluous; simply a "bronze sculpture":

> Just imagine—it is night, the machine is screeching, this man stands in the hall and has time, has a great deal of time, to think deeply. Might it not sometimes occur to him to ask what his young wife is doing? . . . And on New Year's Eve, when his friends come by, drinking, saying that this is

FIGURE 4.3

Man in a Great Hall. 35mm frame enlargement courtesy of
Národní filmový archiv/National Film Archive, Prague.

only once a year, but he can't drink, he's on his way to the night shift—and
he can't drink even when he goes to the day shift. He must come to work
with a clear head, ventilated. Just imagine a drunk or a lazeabout in this
job—all day working in front of an atomic reactor.

I looked for a long time, for an entire hour at the man alone in the hall. I
considered going to him and confessing, but maybe it would be better if he
didn't find out that two watchful eyes were following him.[95]

Here, finally, as the narrator implicates himself—a "watching" presence
who should, but does not, "confess"—in maintaining (and not critiquing)
these dehumanizing structures, the reportage's autobiographical dimensions become clear, for it was in these same terms that Mňačko had casti-
gated the Czechoslovak Writers' Union.

Balaďa's adaptation of this story amplifies the incipient fragmentari-
ness in *Unnamed Cemetery;* by necessity, the film includes only sections
and images from Mňačko's reportage. In dreamlike, fractured sequences

accompanied by motifs from J. S. Bach, we see the man observing the machinery; the glass wall through which the narrator watches him; moments from his life at home. Yet in other sections, the film reaches beyond these concrete "things." For instance, where Mňačko's narrator reflects on what the "man in a great hall" might be thinking ("About his wife? . . . About his paycheck? But maybe . . . about winning a sprinter's race with a new, if not world, then European record? About what was, what will be, or what should be, what is?"),[96] Baláda figures a footrace—shot, first, from a helicopter, then on street level, as the protagonist holds high a golden apple of illusory triumph.

It is in scenes such as this that *Man in a Great Hall* finds the cinematic language with which to express the questions of the Thaw that Mňačko's prose so concisely embodies. This language, crucially, abandons documentary "reality" for impressionistic, at times surrealist, imagery: the golden apple; a baby carriage on a grappling hook, dangling precariously above the reactor. By eliding the literary reportage's two registers (fact and fiction, the observed and the imagined) the film moves beyond *Unnamed Cemetery*'s dualism and, like the reform process itself, penetrates below the evident surface of things.

SOCIAL SCIENCE AND THE MILITARY-CIVILIAN DIVIDE

If *Man in a Great Hall* grasped the contemporary moment by abandoning documentary strategies for fiction, the opposite was true for a number of other Army films of this period. These embraced the social scientific methods that became central in the 1960s not only to documentary film worldwide, but also to Czechoslovakia's academic community, as sociology, having lain fallow during the early years of socialism, itself underwent a revival.[97] Cinéma vérité, popular since the decade's beginning, was the basis for these documentary investigations, but by the late winter of 1964, Czechoslovak filmmakers and critics—like those elsewhere in the world—had started to question vérité's efficacy and rigor in investigating the present. Accordingly, they organized one of the Karlovy Vary Short Film Festival's "Free Tribune" discussions around the theme "Cinéma Vérité and After." Navrátil, writing after the festival in *Rudé právo,* described the rationale behind the discussion: "The technical ability to authentically record life phenomena and popular opinion can no longer satisfy the demand for concrete, evaluating, sociological research into reality, such as we should require of documentary film if it is to become an active social power."[98]

While films such as Baláda's represented one attempt to come to terms with cinéma vérité's "after," numerous other Army films of the mid to late 1960s attempted the same by combining observational style with interviews. Though the latter were a cornerstone of both television journalism and, ultimately, documentary, they were also central to the sociological methods that the Army had begun to use to shape military cinema culture itself, in a continued attempt to define political education for a disaffected generation. As the director of the Central Film Distribution office, Ladislav Čtverák, wrote in his "Plan for 1965," "One of the office's "main goals" for that year was to "work from the analysis and conclusions of the sociological research that was carried out over the past few months into how soldiers spend their free time, and into military culture."[99]

Among Army Film's most successful uses of these methods was Jan Schmidt's 1965 *Life after Ninety Minutes* (*Život po devadesáti minutách*), which documented the Real Madrid soccer team's visit to Prague and won an honorable mention at the 1965 Leipzig Film Festival and first prize for documentary film at the 1966 Karlovy Vary Short Film Festival. Interspersed with game footage, the film's man-on-the-street polls probe issues that extend beyond sports—in Jiří Tvrzník's words, Schmidt "compares divergent social conditions" (i.e., life in Eastern and Western Europe) and "asks questions about people's relationships to sports and within sports." However, he noted, "[the film] does not aim to solve problems . . . but rather to give voice to them."[100]

In the context of the Army's crisis in legitimacy among Czechoslovakia's civilian population, and particularly its youth, *Life after Ninety Minutes'* topic was strategic. Since the 1920s, athletics had been a common theme in Czechoslovak military films, serving as a bridge to the civilian sphere (a function that sports—a paramilitary activity—had in the Army more generally).[101] Youth were another such bridge and were the subject of another "sociological" Army film, Ivo Toman's 1963 *Heroes for Whom No Time Remained* (*Hrdinové, na které nezbyl čas*), which uses interviews and observational camerawork to investigate the social phenomenon of juvenile delinquency. Yet in publicity for the film, the studio leadership took an unexpected tack: where journalist Ladislav Tunys had described *Heroes* as "related to men in military uniform," for "in time, these 'heroes' will enter the Army," Hlaváč, in the *Film a doba* interview, clarified that the film "has very much to do with all the moral problems young people have with the Army."[102] Like Tvrzník's interpretation of Schmidt's film, then, Hlaváč's statement signaled that Army Film did not intend to "solve" these "moral problems"; rather, by "giving voice" to them, it intended to ally itself with this critical "generation."[103]

Milan Růžička captured a different sort of generational disaffection with the military in his 1962 *Old Codgers (Tatíci)*, which follows a group of reservists—all of them, as the voice-over remarks with sociological specificity, thirty-three years old, married, and with "between one and four children"—on a mandatory training weekend.[104] The group is somewhat round around the edges, more at home in the pub than with push-ups and sprints, and as we become privy to the reflections of a single character (a man named Laco, whose narration replaces the film's initial, omniscient voice-over), it becomes clear that the men's ambivalence about the Army has to do precisely with the demographic details that the voice-over has announced: with these "wives and children." The reservists spend the weekend practicing for a parachute jump, but in the film's final sequence, as his cohort dutifully leaps from a plane, Laco panics, reflecting on his life at home—all, Růžička implies, that he would lose if the jump went awry. Just as Hlaváč suggested Army Film's desire to reveal, but not solve, social problems in an effort to connect with its young primary constituency, *Old Codgers* does the same for middle-aged reservists, offering no corrective to Laco's apparent error. He rides down in the plane, and his commander pats him amiably on the back as he descends its steps, parachute unopened on his back.

The most pointed and critical treatment of the "generation" came in 1968, with Rudolf Adler's *They Took Me for a Soldier (Za vojáčka mňa vzali)*. Following a group of young men in a Moravian-Slovakian village—those born in 1949 and, thus, the first generation to have lived all of their lives in state-socialist Czechoslovakia—as they are conscripted, the film comes directly to terms with the age cohort at the heart of the Army's crisis in

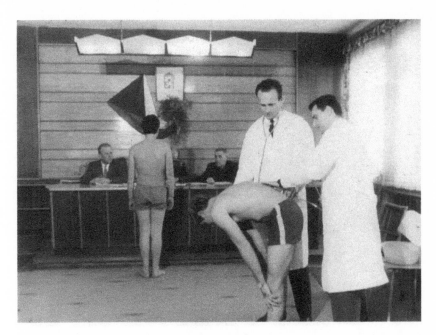

FIGURE 4.4

Echoes of Švejk (*They Took Me for a Soldier*). 35mm frame enlargement
courtesy of Národní filmový archiv/National Film Archive, Prague.

legitimacy.[105] For Adler, however, primarily an ethnographic filmmaker,
the question of the generation was anthropological instead of sociological,
and by framing conscription as a social ritual or coming-of-age process, he
empties it of its traditional ideological significance and opens it to analysis
and critique.

The film, indeed, approaches the question of the "generation" from a
broad perspective, opening with a group of old men, their days as soldiers
long past, singing a folk song about conscription. The men's reminiscences
about their time in the Army and the song's suggestion of timeless tradition set the tone for the vérité-style scenes that follow, in which we watch
women preparing food and decorations, villagers buying celebratory pea-
cock feathers, and the recruits being driven around the village in a gar-
landed horse cart, quite drunk. Alongside these ritual social and cultural
practices and objects, however, is a colder bureaucratic ritual—and it is in
scenes of the young recruits, shivering in their underwear as they swear

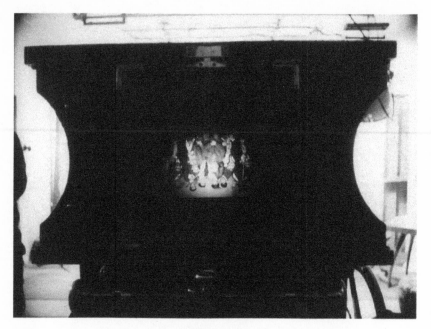

FIGURE 4.5

Upside-down in the photographer's camera (*They Took Me for a Soldier*). 35mm frame enlargement courtesy of Národní filmový archiv/National Film Archive, Prague.

allegiance to an officer in full dress uniform, that Adler's critique becomes evident. Here, the military is not a benign, avuncular force that airs critical moral questions; rather, it is a source of fear and danger.

The scene also seems to be yet another reference to *The Good Soldier Švejk,* evoking a scene in which Švejk, examined by Austrian doctors, is determined to be "a patent imbecile and idiot according to all the natural laws invented by the luminaries of psychiatry" (see figure 4.4).[106] Švejk, in fact, appears in *They Took Me for a Soldier,* whose recruits paint a life-sized portrait of Hašek's antihero and carry it with them throughout the day. He is fastened to the back of their horse cart; he sits with them at dinner, where they offer him a swig of slivovice. As he did in *Crooked Mirror,* Švejk offers these men a model for "saying one thing and doing another," for participating in rituals but simultaneously mocking them. The film adopts this attitude as a structural characteristic, as we see in a scene in which the recruits sit for a group portrait. The photographer tells them to smile and to try to avoid looking like they are in a "conscription mood" (which is to say drunk, as they are). As he does so, Ivan Koudelka's film camera captures the posing recruits in the still camera's medium-format lens, which reflects them upside down. The ritual formality of recruitment, this image suggests, is just that: a formality. For war and battle are notions far removed from this small village and these young, vulnerable men.

NEW MODES OF EXHIBITION

It took until the end of May 1968 for *They Took Me for a Soldier* to work its way through the bureaucracy surrounding civilian film exhibition, and by that moment, with the Prague Spring in full swing, the critical film was approved for screening both in short film cinemas like the Prague and as a short before feature films.[107] Theaters were only a minor aspect of Army Film's civilian exhibition strategy in this decade, however; more important were a wide variety of film festivals and the fast-growing medium of television.

Although Army Film had participated in festivals since the early 1950s (among them the Mariánské Lázně, and later Karlovy Vary, International Film Festival; the Venice Short and Documentary Film Festival; its own Army Film Festival), the number and types of festivals to which the studio sent its films shifted and expanded in the 1960s. Military festivals are one index of these changes. In place of the grandly conceived Army Film Festivals of the early 1950s, in the later decade, the Warsaw Pact film studios initiated a series of new events. Some of these were practical in nature, involving professional seminars and workshops as well as screenings.[108] Among them was the September 1964 "International Meeting of Army Film Workers" in Warsaw, organized by the Polish Army film studio Czołówka, to which Benda sent a series of films drawn from Army Film's most successful recent productions: *Reporter, Heroes for Whom No Time Remained, Unnamed Cemetery, Man in a Great Hall, A Little Winter Music,* and Jozef Sedláček and Bruno Šefranka's *Legend* (*Legenda*, 1963).[109]

Others were film festivals proper. The first official Warsaw Pact military film festival took place in Varna, Bulgaria, in October 1966, and from

Bulgarian film critic Christo Kirkov's review, it is clear that Army Film was well received at it: Kirkov described the studio's films as harbingers of the success that Czechoslovak cinema had recently achieved with the New Wave. "Czechoslovak film," he wrote, "does not only ask to be seen, but it also asks the viewer to think. It is laudable that the high level of Czechoslovak film production is visible even in the work of the Army studio."[110] Similarly, reflecting on Warsaw Pact film culture in the *Film a doba* interview, Háša compared Army Film favorably with its counterparts, noting that "the others either don't have such a long history behind them, or are more purposeful organs." Compared with non-socialist Army film studios, Hlaváč added, Army Film was also unique. Recounting a conversation with Western army filmmakers at a military film festival in France, he noted that "they were very surprised at the films we make, and when we told them that among the things we want to show with these films is that we do not want war, they responded: We could never do that."[111] Here, Hlaváč highlighted the strategic nature of much of Army Film's antimilitarism, which, in an international context, offered proof of the socialist armies' superiority.

Short film festivals, however, and in particular the Karlovy Vary and Leipzig festivals, were the heart of Benda and Hlaváč's festival strategy, for it was at these festivals that Army Film took part in international conversations about nonfiction film form and politics and that the studio was, in turn, discussed as part of Czechoslovakia's resurgent short-film culture. Army Film won numerous prizes at Karlovy Vary, whose location alone was a statement of the short film's growing importance: by 1960, when the festival first took place, the spa town had been home to the larger International Film Festival for fourteen years. Karlovy Vary was preceded each fall by Leipzig, to which Army Film sent films regularly throughout the 1960s, winning four of the festival's top prizes between 1963 and 1967: the second-place Silver Dove in 1963 (for *Reporter*), 1965 (for *Lidice*), and 1966 (for Milan Růžička's 1966 *Front Cameraman* [*Frontový kameraman*]), and the first-prize Golden Dove in 1967 for Háša's military music documentary *Tin Sunday* (*Plechová neděle*). This number was high, given the studio's size: the much larger Krátký Film won six prizes (one Golden Dove and five Silver Doves) in the same period of time.[112]

Festivals like these not only articulated a distinct sphere for nonfiction film, signaling its increasing importance over the course of the decade, but as the slogan ("The Path to Neighbors" ["Weg zum Nachbarn"]) of Leipzig's West German counterpart in Oberhausen (Westdeutsche Kurz-filmtage) suggested, also served the cultural-diplomatic purposes that defined prominent international festivals such as Berlin and Karlovy Vary.[113] Leipzig, too, was understood in these terms, as a space for "dialogue"—in its first two years (1956–1957), between filmmakers from the "two Germanies," and from its third year (1960), among progressive filmmakers from across the globe.[114] Even when this "dialogue" failed, Cold War politics were prominent in these festivals. On the eve of the 1962 Oberhausen festival, for instance, the West German government prevented East Germany from participating, which, as the Czechoslovak embassy in Berlin recounted in February 1963, required "the other countries of the socialist camp to cancel their participation."[115] As such, the festivals followed the path to which "international documentary" was destined after the failure of the World Union of Documentary—which, as Huub Jansen writes, "fell victim to the Cold War" after the 1948 Mariánské Lázně congress.[116]

The World Union of Documentary's vision of a nonfiction film culture that, united by professional concerns and practical goals, spanned "East" and "West," seems nevertheless to have lived on in specialized events such as the French military film festival. Army Film participated in, and won awards at, numerous such festivals across Europe in the 1960s. Balaďa's *Man in a Great Hall*, for instance, won first prize in the category "Sociology of Human Relationships" at the 1966 Labor and Industrial Film Triennial in Antwerp, Belgium; Schmidt's *Courage* was awarded a prize at the 1968 Oberhausen Sports Film Festival; and Růžička's documentary about Croatian fishermen *A Rather Different Night* (*Docela jiná noc,* 1967) played at a 1967 festival of maritime films in Riga.[117] In these festivals, a film's professional or pedagogical "function" seems to have been more important than the bloc politics of festivals such as Oberhausen, as well as those of Western festivals that, in Dorota Ostrowska's words, "were interested in the pictures which showed some signs of dissent from the Socialist dogma."[118] Thus, just as the military's unique uses for cinema allowed Army Film's tasks and concerns to remain relatively constant from the 1920s through the 1960s, in the process challenging the temporal divisions of the Cold War, the movement of its films did the same, revealing the other geographies that existed in parallel to the period's binary geopolitics.

Television was Benda and Hlaváč's second area of focus for exhibition and the medium that brought the studio into closest dialogue with Czechoslovakia's civilian population. As Benda remarked in his 1964 interview, Army Film offered many of its productions to Czechoslovak Television, including the regularly programmed *Army Newsreel,* in which, he said, "we talk about soldiers to their relatives at home, as well as to soldiers themselves."[119] The studio had occasionally shown its films on television since the 1950s, and over the course of the 1960s, coproduced films with Czechoslovak Television.[120] Yet just as Army Film was transforming in the early 1960s, so was television, becoming, in Paulina Bren's words, "a gathering place for those wishing to push existing boundaries," a site for conversations that had, to date, rarely occurred in the socialist Czechoslovak public sphere.[121]

During the years that it was screened weekly on television (1962 to 1965) *Army Newsreel* became an unlikely home for such conversations. This newsreel was one of Hlaváč's innovations and, as he announced at the 1962 Warsaw Pact conference, the format that he intended to make a "vibrant platform, a school for viewers and filmmakers."[122] Indeed, many members of the New Wave worked on *Army Newsreel,* making it—the Army production with perhaps the widest distribution—a site in which the studio's ambition to "nurture talents" became publicly evident.[123]

Director Karel Vachek's time in Army Film speaks to this fact. Vachek had graduated from FAMU in 1963 with the thesis film *Moravian Hellas* (*Moravská Hellas*), a bitingly satirical view of "official" folk culture in communist Czechoslovakia that landed him in trouble, and was not screened publicly until after August 1968.[124] *Moravian Hellas* is a jarring, disjunctive film encompassing observed and staged sequences shot at the folk festival in the Czechoslovak village of Strážnice; periodic (nearly surrealist) narration by the twins Jan and Karel Saudek, who, dressed in military uniforms, interrogate the film's subjects using heavy recording equipment; and abrupt sonic elements (drumbeats, gongs). When, in Army Film, Vachek was assigned to work primarily on newsreels, the editing-

FIGURE 4.6

Plankton (*Hundred-Year Flood*). Source: Vojenský historický
ústav/Military History Institute, Prague.

heavy assignments not only lent themselves naturally to his interests and
skills, but also gave him an unexpected opportunity to extend *Moravian
Hellas'* political critique.

Vachek's segment of *Army Newsreel 5/1965* (*Armádní filmový měsíčník
5/1965*), for example, is composed entirely of Warsaw Pact military footage
and takes, in Vachek biographer Martin Švoma's words, "its militaristic
dimensions ad absurdum, so that it bec[omes] a parody."[125] Although
Vachek recalls being praised by his Army superiors for this episode, we
also see, here, the effects of Benda's 1962 stipulation that Warsaw Pact
material be used any way filmmakers chose: in his film, Vachek disregards
the context and intended "meaning" of this material.[126] Instead, he treats
it as found footage, in a way that corresponds with William C. Wees's
characterization of found-footage filmmakers as "artist-archeologists of

the film world ... sift[ing] through the accumulated audio-visual detritus of modern culture in search of artifacts that will reveal more about their origins and uses than their original makers consciously intended."[127]

An approach to archival material as found footage is also visible in the director's 1965 *Hundred-Year Flood* (*Stoletá voda*), which documents the Czechoslovak Army's rescue efforts during catastrophic floods in Slovakia in June of that year.[128] Although Vachek and Ivan Koudelka are credited as co-directors, Koudelka was primarily responsible for shooting the material, and Vachek (who did not partake in the filming) with editing it.[129] In this sense, the film, like Vachek's work with the Warsaw Pact material, might also be thought of as an archival project. Indeed, the strategies of collage and counterpoint that Vachek employed in his newsreel segment are fundamental to *Hundred-Year Flood*, in which he sets extraneous "objects" against (and superimposes "objects" on) the documentary images of the floods. These are, most frequently, text pulled at random from newspaper stories about the flood: the title YES is superimposed over the film's opening image of the river and over a statue caught in the flood, the title PLANKTON over the image of a flooded toy castle (see figure 4.6). The meta-title REAL AND NOT-REAL—critiquing, as *Moravian Hellas* had, Czechoslovak documentary's then-current fascination with realism and "reality"—appears elsewhere. In addition to the film's voice-over commentary, nondiegetic sounds are also interjected as "objects," seemingly arbitrarily, throughout the film: a dog barking, a cow mooing, church bells. The sum effect is that of a collage rather than a report on the disaster, an idea that is confirmed by Navrátil, who reported unfavorably on the film from the 1966 Karlovy Vary Short Festival: "Vachek isn't trying to make a reportage or an exposé, but his film ... attempts to support its concreteness by pulling authentic quotes from print—which, in their chronological and thematic disorder, achieve just the opposite effect."[130]

This near-total disregard for archival material's "meaning" and emphasis on images and sounds as "objects," finally, defined another of Vachek's newsreel segments, in *Army Newsreel 3/1965* (*Armádní filmový měsíčník 3/1965*), an ostensible celebration of the twentieth anniversary of Ostrava's 1945 liberation. Like *Hundred-Year Flood*, this segment was not composed of archival material, but collage strategies were central to its critique; in this case, a decisive rejection of the historical myths that propelled many of the Army studio's earlier uses of archival footage.

Army Newsreel 3/1965 is structured similarly to *Hundred-Year Flood,* with "found" sounds and images integrated into what appear, at first glance, to be straightforward narratives. The opening voice-over announces that the viewer will see five "notes about war and life" from "Ostrava soldiers," the first of which begins with a young, bored-looking miner. Leaning against a wall and looking occasionally at the camera, he recites a seemingly memorized monologue about his life in the Army and then his life in Ostrava, where in addition to mining, he is an amateur boxer. His wife stands next to him, looking equally bored, and eventually takes the microphone and recites her addition to this story. The characters look screen right, and the camera, on cue, pans swiftly in the same direction to focus on a boxer training with a punching bag.

The flattening effect this scene's construction and camera movement have on space is emblematic of the film as a whole. Vachek frames *Army Newsreel 3/1965* in straight, two-dimensional shots in which characters recite dialogue in emotionless voices and in which actual two-dimensional images (magazine clippings, horticultural sketches, family photographs of the subjects) figure prominently. He also frequently cuts away from his interviews to zoom in on another two dimensional, "found" image: a crumbling concrete building in a snowy field, the cracks in whose walls approximate the shape of a tree. This two-dimensionality is central to the film's collage effect (which, as a structuring concept, effectively makes the film *itself* a two-dimensional object), as well as to a broader distancing strategy that, as the superimposed text in *Hundred-Year Flood* does, asks the viewer to question the import of what he or she is seeing.

As the film gravitates toward progressively absurd stories, this sense of distance increases. The second "note" introduces a former soldier who is assembling a ball of aluminum foil; the third introduces a tank driver who escaped to the Soviet Union to work with the Czechoslovak troops in World War II and now works for the forestry department. The fourth note introduces "artists" who worked in circus troupes and now perform an acrobatics-and-juggling show at the Palace Hotel in Ostrava. Their performance is overlaid with contemporary Czechoslovak pop music and

FIGURE 4.7

Interview about the Battle of the Dukla Pass (*Army Newsreel 3/65*).
Source: Vojenský historický ústav/Military History Institute, Prague.

intercut with fan photographs of Henry Fonda and Brigitte Bardot, Beatles album covers, and book covers for the popular German author Karl May's American western adventure stories.

In contrast to these "notes," whose absurdity amplifies the film's distancing effects—showing not war's gravity and heroics, but its bizarre or banal underbelly—the film's final "note" is more sober, both in terms of the story its characters tell and in terms of the parallel story the film's form tells. Here, a couple sits in their parlor, two meters from the stationary camera, and recounts their experiences fighting in the Battle of the Dukla Pass. The pair recite their narratives in the same laconic tone evident in the film's other sections, but instead of stale or humorous, their stories are harrowing: The woman recalls working in a Red Army unit alongside her first husband, who was killed during the battle, and recounts seeing his colleagues "torn to pieces." The flatness with which she delivers this memorized passage and the camera's impassivity sit uneasily with her story's drama, forming an internal contradiction that suggests the inhumanity of both war and its commemoration—a clear antimilitary statement that is supported by *Army Newsreel 3/1965*'s earlier smaller, absurd stories. At the same time, the film refutes the historical narrative visible in films like *Witness,* in which the end of World War II is a legitimizing moment for the postwar communist government. Crucially, it does so both in its narrative and in its collage dimensions, which, in their flatness and disjunction, deny the very possibility of progressive historical development.

The importance of the fact that Vachek's film was produced for *Army Newsreel* cannot be overstated, given the newsreel's large television audience—and *Moravian Hellas*'s ban puts this in context, for *Army Newsreel 3/1965* is, in many ways, more directly condemning of certain founding myths in communist Czechoslovakia than Vachek's thesis film. Although Vachek recalls it being banned, the newsreel segment, in fact, was seen widely enough to merit mention in an extensive article on the New Wave in *Film a doba,* where its meaning was not lost on Jaroslav Boček: "Vachek does not restrain his pointed sense of absurdity: in the Ostrava episode of the Army newsreel he allows a man to speak who passed through the front, survived a difficult battle, and after all that, all that is left to him is a pile of medals."[131]

THE NEW WAVE

Boček was right: it is the New Wave that forms the background to this story, for while Benda and Hlaváč were organizing Army Film's revival, something big was happening in Czechoslovak fiction film. After the successes of 1962–1963, the country's cinema had continued to grow, and so swiftly that critics at home and abroad were caught off guard. "Somehow we still can't get our wits about us," wrote critic Antonín Liehm in 1964. "We rub our eyes, we pinch our hands to convince ourselves that this isn't only a dream. But no, we are more or less conscious, fully aware, and the entirely unexpected ascent of our cinema in the last two years is an undisputable reality."[132] Although it would maintain its momentum through 1969, by 1967, the New Wave had produced many of its key works: Jan

FIGURE 4.8

Long Live the Republic. Film still courtesy of Národní
filmový archiv/National Film Archive, Prague.

Němec's *Diamonds of the Night* (*Démanty noci*) was released in 1964 (the
year after his Army short *Memory of Our Day* [*Paměť našeho dne*], also an
adaptation of an Arnošt Lustig story). The omnibus film *Pearls of the Deep*
(*Perličky na dně*) was released in 1966, the same year that saw the release
of Věra Chytilová's *Daisies* (*Sedmikrásky*). In 1968, Jiří Menzel's *Closely
Watched Trains* (*Ostře sledované vlaky*) would win an Oscar.

Short works such as Balad's reportages, Vachek's newsreels, and
Adler's ethnographic films, however, demonstrate that the "Czechoslovak film miracle" was not only the province of fiction features—that it
encompassed numerous genres and production contexts, some of whose
films paralleled, and at times exceeded, the New Wave in their formal
innovation and their political and social critique (the qualities for which
the New Wave is typically praised). Army Film's employees, moreover,
routinely moved between the studio and Barrandov.[133] Yet Army Film

also never quite gave up on Čepička's dream of fiction features. Thus, twice in the 1960s, the studio departed from its role as a "source of talents," a training ground for the New Wave, and joined it directly.

Army Film became involved in the first production because of its subject matter (a young boy in Moravia coming of age during the end of World War II) and director: *Long Live the Republic* (1965), a coproduction between Army Film and State Film, was directed by Kachyňa, who returned, with it, to the studio in which he had begun his career. Its second involvement in the format, however—the only fiction feature after 1956 of which Army Film was the sole producer[134]—was sparked not only by subject but also by the concerns about institutional relevance and prestige that had driven the studio since its earliest postwar days.

The film, *The End of August at the Hotel Ozone* (1966), was directed by Jan Schmidt and written by Pavel Juráček while the two were serving in Army Film. Based on a science-fiction short story by Juráček, *Ozone* tells the story of a band of women (six young and one, their leader, old) who roam a version of Earth ravaged by nuclear war, foraging to survive and seeking men with whom to procreate.[135] The women stumble upon an abandoned-looking hotel in the wilderness that, miraculously, is home to perhaps the last man on earth—a man who is far too old to father children. The man and the older woman recall the civility of the prewar era, teaching the "feral" girls the lost arts of dancing, of dining, of using a television set. After the woman dies of exhaustion, the girls kill him and walk off toward what seems an almost certain doom.

Schmidt recounts what happened after Army dramaturgs submitted the script to a military approval commission:

> I was suddenly called to the Ministry of National Defense, where there was an uproar. . . . They began to lecture me that we were allowing for the possibility of a third world war and the destruction of the world and that this was not only entirely contradictory to the code of conduct for a citizen of a socialist state but also for a soldier of the People's Socialist Army. Our army should be battling for peace! That with this film, we were disturbing the moral education of the citizens. It looked like a disaster. It seemed that they would cancel the production.
>
> Only, we were living in a moment that was quite a lively era. In our hands, we had several testimonials that we had asked various important people to write for us. I pulled these out at one meeting at the Ministry

when it looked like they would forbid the film to be made. I also pulled out a document in which Jan Procházka's creative team at Barrandov declared that if the army didn't want to make this film, Barrandov would take over all the liabilities. The soldiers then waved their hands and said, "So let it be shot, after all. We're not going to give it to that Procházka just like that."[136]

Jaromír Kallista, who worked as a production manager on the film, corroborates the story. "We worked on the film for a long time," he recalls, "but they stopped production, because even at that time, it didn't fit ideologically. This was because the film shows the end of the world after a war, and there was the notion at that time that all wars had been won in the Eastern Bloc."[137]

Despite these difficulties, the fact that *Ozone* was ultimately made says a great deal about institutional priorities in both Army Film and the Czechoslovak Ministry of Defense at this moment. The studio's censorship practices were central here. While Benda was in office, censorship in Army Film was typically an internal affair: each screenplay was reviewed by the studio's dramaturgs and by Benda himself, who could decide whether or not to refer it to Army Film's Ideological-Artistic Board. In films that dealt with "particularly weighty, contentious, or difficult material," Benda could ask for the HPS's approval. However, the only censorship that every film was required to undergo was upon completion, when the General Staff decided the venues and audiences (military or civilian) to which they would be released, and their level of secrecy.[138] Kallista recalls that censors did not typically impede films that the studio wanted to produce: it was "easy to explain things to them. . . . Moreover, it was such a progressive time that they sensed that something was going on, but couldn't quite orient themselves in it."[139]

Schmidt and Juráček's screenplay seems to have been one of the rare cases that Benda sent to the HPS for approval, presumably because of its risky topic (according to studio policies, Army Film's chief was held personally responsible for the "ideological-artistic level" of the studio's productions).[140] And while the fact that the HPS agreed to produce *Ozone* simply because Czechoslovak State Film had offered to do so indicates that Army Film's paradoxical antimilitarism was tolerated by the highest levels of military administration (the HPS, which had representation on the Central Committee), it also underscores that this toleration did not

FIGURE 4.9

In a ruined church (*The End of August at the Hotel Ozone*). Film still
courtesy of Národní filmový archiv/National Film Archive, Prague.

necessarily signal agreement with the studio's practices. Rather, it had to
do with continued competition between Army Film and State Film—
the kind of competition that, as chapter 2 discusses, nationalization had
promised to eliminate from Czechoslovak cinema. *Ozone* is evidence not
simply that competition remained, but that it remained at the highest
levels of power. This military-made antiwar film, that is, not only reflected
a studio devoted to supporting auteurist experimentation as a means of
rapprochement with the civilian population. It also reflected a military
administration that continued to see culture as a source of prestige and
prestige as symbolic currency.

Ozone is unrelentingly violent: throughout its hour and a half, the
women ravage their surroundings, escalating from throwing live ammuni-
tion into a bonfire to killing a snake, then a dog, then a cow, then the man.
At the same time, it flouts the stalemate of the arms race by implying in its

first scene—where four voices (Russian, English, Chinese, French) count from ten to the zero of a nuclear explosion—that members of the international community bear equal responsibility for the Cold War. It is hard not to read *Ozone*'s narrative as an allegory: the nuclear war as a stand-in for World War II; the girls' savageness as an index of lost First Republic civility and refinement. Its setting only emphasizes these allegorical readings. *Ozone* was shot in three locations: an old mill in southern Moravia (the location for the "Hotel Ozone"); the ruins of the northwest Bohemian border town of Doupov, emptied by the German expulsions and, at the time, a military training zone; and other restricted military zones along the Western border—spaces where only Army Film had permission to shoot. Schmidt recalls these as "villages that had been destroyed and houses that were overgrown with grass and ruined churches. For our vision of a destroyed world, it was quite appropriate."[141]

With this film, then, Army Film returned to the Western border. Here, as in Brynych and Hlaváč's 1952 *They Shall Not Pass,* the border is a frontier; *The End of August at the Hotel Ozone* might be read as a science-fiction western. The frontier, however, has new significance in this film. It is not a utopic multinational space; neither is it the site for "the founding of a new political order" or a "border between two worlds." In fact, *Ozone*'s location shooting makes it visibly evident that the frontier is a site of ruin—of Baroque churches, once elegant, now crumbling, of military debris, of untamable wildness. If one is not killed here, one's blood will eventually be poisoned by the radiation permeating the world. This border eats away at the center, through which the Army critiques not only itself but also postwar Czechoslovak history more generally: for the borderlands, once conceived as a site of social possibility, harbingers of a bright future, are now plainly a failed space.

Ozone's production history, however, demonstrates that this film's criticism was not accidental or underhanded. Like the narrative experiments in Army training films, it was not simply a matter of permissive censors, metaphors, or the coded language that is often observed in postwar East European cinema. Rather, it was self-conscious, supported not only by Army Film—to whom sensitivity to the desires and critiques of Czechoslovak youth was institutionally vital—but also by the HPS, with its ties to the Central Committee. While the HPS's involvement in the film's production foreshadowed that department's increasing reformism, it also makes clear that, at times, "reform" had other motives, and that the New Wave's politics—often read in terms of conflict between artists and the "system"—had deeply "systemic" dimensions. Indeed, for the HPS, *Ozone* was a matter of nothing more lofty than competing with another ministry and fostering prestige, while for Army Film, it was, in part, a matter of maintaining legitimacy.

Such other motives in many ways define this period in Army Film's history, which witnessed the studio's leadership consciously building an institution—and a narrative about an institution—whose dialogue with "modern" cinema and search for a new relationship to contemporary life, programmatic experimentation with film language, and criticism of both the Army and Czechoslovak politics were practical ways to reach the "generational" demographic to which it was bound. "We work," Hlaváč said to the *Film a doba* editors, "from the idea that the primary viewer of our films is a young man, about twenty years old. One can speak to such a man about a whole range of things." In this sociological age, Novák added statistics: the military's principal population was between eighteen and twenty-four years old, and the approximately two million people in this age cohort in Czechoslovakia formed eighty percent of the country's film-going public.[142] But this was also the "generation" of the Czechoslovak New Wave, nearly all of whose central figures—many of them, briefly, soldiers themselves—passed through the studio's doors en route to Barrandov.

5

A Military Avant Garde:
Documentary and the Prague Spring

WHEN CZECHOSLOVAKIA hosted joint Warsaw Pact military maneuvers in late September 1966, Army filmmakers—among them, Rudolf Adler, Ivan Balaďa, Karel Vachek, Juraj Šajmovič, Ivan Koudelka, Jaromír Kallista, Hynek Bočan, Jaromír Šofr, Tomáš Škrdlant, and Karel Slach—were sent to south Bohemia to document the war games. Kallista remembers the Vltava Maneuvers as a "Švejkish" event. On their last day, he recalls, the filmmakers, wearing the blue jeans and striped sailor's T-shirts in fashion at the time, were placed in an Army transporter painted repeatedly with the word FILM ("so they wouldn't confuse us") and driven in front of the dais waving like "hooligans" at President Antonín Novotný and the military commanders in chief. Moreover, the exercises took place in a "symbolic" location: "in the area of Putim, Švejk's Putim."[1]

These Švejkish dimensions inflected the three films that Army Film produced to document the Vltava Maneuvers (and with the maneuvers, the concept of Warsaw Pact unity). The first and second, both entitled *Vltava 1966*, and variations on one another, frame the exercises for civilians and military officials, respectively. The third film, however, *Memory of Three Mornings in a Czech Meadow* (*Vzpomínka na tři rána v českém lese*), alternates the polished color images that make up the first two films with black-and-white documentation of the exercises' less dignified underbelly: Soviet soldiers, drunk, singing and playing the accordion; Hungarian soldiers playing poker with a deck of pinup-girl cards. In counterposing black-and-white and color, the public face of the exercises and their private face—and in constituting an alternative to the first two "official" films—*Three Mornings* does just what the Army filmmakers did when they waved at Novotný, underscoring the farcical nature of the ostensibly deadly serious exercises.

As Antonín Liehm observed in his speech to the Fourth Czechoslovak Writers' Congress, held nine months after the Vltava Maneuvers, by the late 1960s, *švejkovství* had become a tolerated aspect of intellectual life in Czechoslovakia. We have, he reflected, "achieved a fairly extensive, if not very intensive, freedom to criticize. Whenever we disagree, reject, ridicule or expose, we are greatly encouraged in our efforts by the authorities— provided, of course, we know when to stop. As a result, our critics live in a state of happy irresponsibility."[2] Such Švejkish criticism had, indeed, been present in Army Film, and many Army *films*, in years and decades previous: in the 1956 *Crooked Mirror*, which not only evokes Švejk's misadventures with proper military dress but questions the "Soviet model" using its own rhetoric, and in the 1968 *They Took Me for a Soldier*, in which the hapless Švejk's image is the emblem for a new generation of conscripts.

Yet from late 1967 through 1969—a period that encompassed the height of the Prague Spring, the August 1968 Warsaw Pact invasion of Czechoslovakia, and its aftermath—Švejkish jokes and paradoxes gave way to a new attitude in the Army and its productions. This replaced implicit criticism with direct criticism, antimilitarism (for in *Švejk*, there is always the sense that the Army must be avoided—whether through South Bohemian anabasis, capture by enemy forces, or exile in the psychiatric ward of an imperial hospital) with expressions of solidarity with the Ministry of Defense. If the latter sentiment was unexpected in the cinema of the Czechoslovak People's Army—whose short films had, for most of the 1960s, been marked by their critique of their sponsoring institution—the former went further, articulating an alternative sense of what Army Film was and could be as an institution, a sense in which, to borrow Liehm's words, the studio became fundamentally responsible.

Alternatives, Liehm's speech suggested, were precisely what the Novotný government did not want. And alternatives, in many ways, were the story of 1968 in Czechoslovakia, when politics and culture buzzed with the possibilities of the new model for society that the reforms were building.

In this sense, Army Film's late-sixties productions—whether works that situated Czechoslovakia not in the Eastern Bloc or the Warsaw Pact but in "Europe," or a series of experimental films that offered a sober vision of post-invasion reality—continued to be a product of their time. But once again, and most fundamentally, they were also a product of the Army studio as an institution in society.

1968

The meeting at which Liehm made his speech was one of the prime instigating events of the Prague Spring, a moment that, Paulina Bren writes, belonged to "the intellectuals, the students, and the intelligentsia" of Czechoslovakia.[3] Liehm's calls for responsibility, his critiques of the Communist Party and government, were echoed by his peers (among them Milan Kundera, who in the same year published his novel *The Joke*) and resulted in the Writers' Union publication *Literární noviny* (*Literary News*) being wrested from their control and in Ludvík Vaculík's, Ivan Klíma's, and Liehm's own expulsions from the Party. But criticism was already visible in other areas of culture: in philosophy (where thinkers like Karel Kosík and Ivan Sviták laid the theoretical groundwork for a new form of socialism), in history (where scholars began to critically examine the postwar period), and in the arts, including cinema, where the New Wave had been in full swing for a half decade.[4]

This criticism had as its goal neither the market nor the West—in Liehm's words, its intent was to describe and foster a "true democratic socialism"—and it found its political answer in January 1968.[5] In this month, Novotný resigned as first secretary of the Communist Party and was replaced by reformist Alexander Dubček. When Novotný relinquished the more symbolic office of president in late March, Ludvík Svoboda was elected in his stead, placing Czechoslovakia's government fully under the control of reformist politicians. Over the course of the almost nine months between early January and late August, as they gradually distanced themselves from Moscow, the reformers reversed many of the previous two decades' policies: the victims of the 1950s show trials were rehabilitated, censorship was abolished, and a diverse set of national voices began to be heard, most notably that of Slovakia.[6] The reforms that economist Ota Šik had discussed in 1963 had been in progress since 1966; by 1967, the planned economy had been scaled back, with "targets" replaced by "suggestions." In 1968, plans were done away with entirely, replaced by "guidelines."[7]

For Czechoslovaks, the reforms' effect was a profound shift in everyday life: citizens were able to travel, even to the West, and to openly discuss books and films that had until recently been censored. In Czechoslovak State Film, the abolition of censorship had important resonances throughout 1968, as did the work of FITES, the Union of Cinema and Television Artists, which, like other workers' associations, increasingly moved cinema's labor force toward self-determination.[8] Among the fiction features released in this year were Jiří Menzel's *Capricious Summer* (*Rozmarné léto*) and František Vláčil's *Valley of the Bees* (*Údolí včel*). Among those in production in 1968—and released in 1969—were Juraj Herz's *The Cremator* (*Spalovač mrtvol*), Evald Schorm's *The End of a Priest* (*Farářův konec*), Jaromil Jireš's *The Joke* (*Žert*), and Vojtěch Jasný's *All My Good Countrymen* (*Všichni dobří rodáci*).

A SMALL COUNTRY AT THE HEART OF EUROPE

At the same time, the Army was transforming. Military reforms clustered around the generational problems and issues of legitimacy that had come to the fore earlier in the 1960s, as well as several new ones: national questions, rapprochement with the West, and Communist Party influence on the Armed Forces.[9] Václav Prchlík's Main Political Administration (HPS) continued to lead these reforms; when, in February 1968, Prchlík was appointed to the Central Committee, they continued under the new HPS chief, Major-General Egyd Pepich. Pepich's appointment, as well as that of another Slovak, Martin Dzúr, as minister of defense (replacing Bohumír Lomský), occurred in the context of the rehabilitation of the Slovak officers who had borne the brunt of military purges in the post-1948 period.[10] Pro-Western generals who had been persecuted after 1948 were also exonerated. General Karel Kultvašr, accused of plotting to overthrow the government, was the most prominent of these, and his rehabilitation (on May 16, 1968) indicated a rapprochement with the West that was echoed by the publication, in the same month, of the "Gottwald Memorandum."[11]

The Memorandum, written by the elite Klement Gottwald Military Academy, called the military politics and policies of the preceding twenty years into question. Dismissing the notion of West German revanchism (as chapter 4 details, a focus of Czechoslovak compilation filmmaking during and after the Berlin Crisis) as a political tool designed to foster solidarity within the "Eastern Bloc," its authors wrote that the bonds between the Warsaw Pact countries were weak and largely rhetorical:

> In reality . . . the threat of German aggression increasingly acted as an added external factor designed to reinforce the cohesion of the socialist community. The military factor was meant to compensate for inadequate economic cooperation and the lack of development of other ties between the socialist countries.[12]

Moreover, they argued that "the generally valid model of a socialist military system" fundamentally misunderstood foreign policy by framing it within "a stereotyped notion of the class struggle, dividing subjects into friendly and hostile . . . reduc[ing] the essential political differences between sovereign States to the fundamental class antagonism."[13] War, the Memorandum concluded, could be prevented only with "an active foreign policy designed to normalize relations between Czechoslovakia and the Federal Republic of Germany."[14] And Czechoslovakia—still discussed as a small state that, bordering the West on two sides, would be "physically liquidated" in a nuclear war—ought to be sovereign in its military affairs, its military policy "a policy of European security, a policy promoting the process of lessening international tension in Europe, of all-European cooperation and the cooperation of European progressive forces."[15]

With this, the Memorandum pronounced two of the cornerstones of postwar Czechoslovak military policy invalid: the notion that the country's western borders were the last line of defense in a war between "two worlds," and that the Soviet Union not only offered the ultimate "model" (*vzor*) for the Czechoslovak Army but also guaranteed the smaller country's security. It thus did away rhetorically with the "bloc" politics that defined films like *They Shall Not Pass*. In its place, it offered the idea of

Europe, an abiding dimension of the Czechoslovak "myth" that coursed throughout the discussions and debates of the Prague Spring.[16]

The growing distance between the Czechoslovak Army and the Soviet Union—as well as between the reformist HPS and more conservative sectors of the Army such as the General Staff—reached a tipping point with another series of joint Warsaw Pact maneuvers on Czechoslovak territory, in July 1968. The maneuvers took place without incident, but after they ended, Soviet troops did not leave the country. During a press conference on July 15, Prchlík admitted that the Czechoslovak Army had not been told when they would depart: "Tomorrow," he said, "one will be wiser than today."[17] This statement's sarcastic tone and political undercurrents (laying bare, as the Gottwald Memorandum had, the illusory nature of Warsaw Pact unity) resulted in Soviet intervention in the HPS, whose critical culture Prchlík had helped develop: on July 17, its chief, Pepich, was replaced by the conservative František Bedřich.[18] In early August, Prchlík himself was recalled from the Central Committee.[19] Soon after, early in the morning of August 21, Warsaw Pact tanks rolled across Czechoslovakia's borders, with the goal of finally putting the Prague Spring, which had made Moscow so anxious, to rest.

The tumult of the summer of 1968 had relatively little effect upon Army Film. Indeed, just as, during the Prague Spring, *Obrana lidu* and other HPS-administered cultural organs became outspoken sites for criticism of the military status quo, the films that the studio produced after August 21 continued their support of the now-imperiled reform process, adding to it unambiguous opposition to the invasion.[20] In some films, the Gottwald Memorandum's evocation of "Europe" was a central trope, allowing Czechoslovak military propaganda to fulfill the geopolitical role with which it, since Jiří Jeníček, had been charged—this time, in light of the invasion. Roman Hlaváč, for instance, referred to Czechoslovakia's identity as a "small country at the heart of Europe" to whose existence international propaganda was critical in a November 1968 interview about Pavel Háša's *Nine Chapters from Ancient History* (*Devět kapitol ze starého dějepisu*), a feature-length compilation film for which he wrote the screenplay.[21] Although the film is historical in its scope, narrating the history of the Czech and Slovak lands from the late nineteenth century to the First Republic, its concerns, he told journalist Ladislav Tunys, were in fact contemporary, for when they were part of the Austro-Hungarian Empire, the Czech and Slovak lands faced the same problem that they did at that very moment: "sovereignty.... the problem of the relationship between a great power and a small country, the problem of the freedom of a nation."[22]

Nine Chapters, indeed, reworks the Czechoslovak "myth" for the late 1960s and revives subjects common to interwar military films, such as the Czechoslovak Legions (much of its footage was drawn from the Army's Legionnaire Film Archive) and Tomáš Garrigue Masaryk, whose First Republic it frames as the solution to the "problem of the freedom of a nation."[23] Simultaneously, it revises the geopolitics of early- and mid-1960s compilation films. Where *Witness* had posited a divide between Eastern and Western Europe, *Nine Chapters*'s on-screen narrator opens the film by welcoming the viewer to "the twentieth century in Europe" and, over actuality footage of Paris and Vienna at the turn of the century, rhetorically asks in which city life is most beautiful.[24] These new geopolitics were equally visible in the film's production—which took place in archives in the United Kingdom, Poland, Paris, the Soviet Union, and Yugoslavia—and in its makers' plans for distribution.[25] *Nine Chapters*, Hlaváč remarked, would likely "interest the world":

> Many people have found out about our country in the past stormy months, but they know little or nothing about the broader historical and international political context of this country in the center of Europe. Perhaps it would help them understand our standpoints and positions.... If we could manage in this way to make use of the world public's heightened interest in our country, it would only be for the best.[26]

In *The Crown Jewels of the Czech Kingdom* (*Korunovační klenoty Královstí českého*), a short promotional film about the October 1968 exhibition of the Czech crown jewels, commissioned by the Government Tourism Board, Jiří Ployhar recast the "myth" through an engagement with film genre. Ployhar was known for such commissions, which promoted Czechoslovakia as destination for foreign visitors, and in *The Crown Jewels*, he makes use of the lush aerial shots, bright colors, and informational voice-over that defined these productions. He also, however, draws connections between the jewels' history (which dates to Charles IV and the fourteenth-century "Golden Age" of the Czech lands) and current events: at the end of the film's ten minutes, as Alexander Dubček, Ludvík Svoboda, Josef Smrkovský, and other prominent reformers examine the treasures, the voice-over proclaims that "the kings have disappeared, but the symbols of Czech statehood"—the reformers, it is implied—"remain." "Millions of Czechs," it concludes, "see more than just the past in [the jewels]. They have become the symbol of the sovereignty we have never relinquished."[27]

In a 1970 report, Army Film's economic deputy, Stanislav Čeřovský, highlighted *The Crown Jewels'* "double function" as both military propaganda, "helping foster pride in members of the Czechoslovak People's Army in the beauty of the country they are preparing to defend," and advertising, "propagating Czechoslovakia abroad."[28] The Czechoslovakia that tourists, government officials, and soldiers would see in the film, however, differed markedly from the one that appeared in Army films of the 1950s and early 1960s. This was not lost on post-invasion censors: Although *The Crown Jewels* was approved for public screening, like *Nine Chapters*, it was eventually banned.[29] Censors concluded that the film, an "alleged reportage about the crown jewels," "manifests a clear tendency toward national nihilism . . . and a sort of messianic gigantism of the Czech nation, which, with its 'spring' (read: 1968) is influencing the entire world."[30]

OUTSIDE THE PLAN

If films like *The Crown Jewels* and *Nine Chapters* indicated the HPS's continued engagement with the Prague Spring—as well as the reform process' own intensification—after August 1968, they also reflected the persistence of the institutional identity that Army Film's leaders had carefully managed over the course of the 1960s.[31] Kallista, indeed, remembers the end of the decade as a moment at which, in Army Film, "the terrain was better than it was in Czechoslovak State Film."[32] Not only did the studio continue to be a uniquely fertile sphere for film production, but the culture of film-watching that Bedřich Benda had sought to energize in 1961, when the Central Film Distribution office was incorporated into Army Film, had grown increasingly dynamic. Journalist Luděk Čermák estimated that by 1968, the number of film clubs in Army barracks exceeded that of film clubs in the civilian sphere, and these clubs were vibrant and progressive, featuring films such as Ingmar Bergman's *Wild Strawberries* (*Smultronstället,* 1957), Alain Resnais's *Hiroshima mon amour* (1959), and Michelangelo Antonioni's *La notte* (1961).[33] If earlier in the decade, when the Army was viewed as conservative and out of touch with Czechoslovak society, programming like this might have seemed surprising or paradoxical to critics, by this point, seven years after Benda and Hlaváč began their reinvention of Army Film, it was entirely in keeping with the studio's public image. And while such "paradoxes" had become central to the themes of Army Film's antimilitary productions, in the months surrounding the invasion, this concept became central to the form that the studio's most critical films took.

This was legible for the first time in the 1967 film *Metrum,* which, intended as a documentary about mass transportation in Moscow, was commissioned by the Czechoslovak-Soviet Friendship Society (Svaz československo-sovětského přátelství) and assigned to Balaďa and Šajmovič. The filmmakers departed for Moscow, yet, as Šajmovič recounts in a 2003 interview, when they arrived, they were disappointed by what they encountered: "We looked over the depots [and] were shocked that the transportation system was functioning at all . . . it was a boring environment with no inspiration. The people . . . spoke to the camera in agitational catch-phrases." However,

> one day . . . we went down into the Metro. We stiffened. We became silent, we were shocked. What an experience! It was really something. It had power. Rhythm. It really worked! . . . Suddenly and simultaneously we decided that this was it. We decided that we simply must shoot the film here. Is it transportation? Yes![34]

The filmmakers thus abandoned the subject they had been assigned and made a film that is largely defined by this encounter with the Metro, with its crowds flowing up and down great escalators and through hallways, the chiaroscuro faces and bodies of its passengers, and its cathedral-like architecture. Šajmovič's handheld cinematography is a central partner in constructing the film's atmosphere, and itself relies on location for its aesthetics: escalators become the basis for ersatz tracking shots, and, in the film's final shot, the camera travels on a train from the darkness of the subway to the light outside, with the combination of location lighting and a fixed aperture creating an in-camera fade to white.

FIGURE 5.1

Metrum. 35mm frame enlargement courtesy of Národní
filmový archiv/National Film Archive, Prague.

Such location-based techniques produced what was, on one level, precisely what the Friendship Society was looking for: rather pure documentation of transportation in Moscow, insofar as the location of the Metro is
integral to the film's form and texture. On another level, however, *Metrum*
engages dimensions that extend beyond the Metro itself: Šajmovič's use of
light, the linearity and direction of the up-and-down-moving escalators,
and the film's final shot all suggest a messianic dimension to the space that
is emphasized on a sonic level by the liturgical music—a *panychida,* or
Orthodox requiem, recorded secretly in a Moscow church—that the film
superimposes on the everyday murmuring, clicking and rumbling of the
subway.[35] (As Mikhail Ryklin and Boris Groys note, this spiritual dimension, the notion that it represented a utopia on earth, had been crucial to
the Metro since its design and construction in the 1930s.)[36]

The formal duality that *Metrum* embodies was also reflected in its reception. "After the approval screening," Šajmovič recalls, "the military
bigwigs in Prague tore out their hair and immediately sent another team

to shoot the correct film about Moscow transportation."[37] But this—presumably the final, mandatory screening for the General Staff—was not the end of *Metrum*. Army Film's dramaturgs sent the film to the 1969 Karlovy Vary Short Film Festival, where it shared first prize for documentary film. The festival jury wrote of *Metrum* as a "breakthrough authorial achievement that, through the image of a major city's underground railway, gives rise to a suggestive representation of the fate of modern man, who is seen as alienated and powerless."[38]

And hence, in a sense, *Metrum* became two separate projects. One, the original assignment—a new film presumably delivered to the Czechoslovak-Soviet Friendship Society without a word about its secret twin—served the original purpose of solidifying cultural relations between Czechoslovakia and the Soviet Union. The second film, still called *Metrum*, was briefly canonized by Czechoslovakia's short-film community. Thus, from the duality embodied by its form (a subjective, abstracted form of reportage) to the doubling of films ultimately produced (one for military purposes, one for civilian; one "official," one "unofficial"), we may see how *Metrum* was a product of the institution that made it: both the Ministry of Defense, with its divisions between the conservative General Staff and the reformist HPS, and Army Film, with its capacity to do, and be, multiple and at times contradictory things at once.

We may, however, also read *Metrum* as the product of this institution in a second sense, by examining the language studio officials used to describe the film's economic dimensions. *Metrum* is mentioned for the first time in Army Film's "Report on the Fulfillment of the Plan" for the first quarter of 1968, where it is described by a unique phrase, "outside the plan" (*mimo plán*).[39] While this phrase, on a basic level, designates that *Metrum* had not been written into Army Film's annual budget, production schedule, or dramaturgical outline, it would become an institutional descriptor for a series of innovative Army films made this year and the next.

Quarterly reports such as this were central to Army Film's operation and accounted for the thematic and economic "plans" and production schedules that governed the studio's work in a given year. These were a small reflection of the numerous multiple-year "plans" that had driven and defined Czechoslovakia's nationalized economy since 1947 and that were, in the studio as elsewhere, accompanied by discourse revolving around the syntactical similarity between the phrases "fulfilling the plan" and "building socialism." Both phrases refer to the construction of something whose outcome is already known: communism is the end-point of the Marxist vision of history, while, in the state-socialist economies of Eastern Europe, the issuing of an economic plan also rhetorically mandated that it be completed. Both, moreover, share an inherently progressive temporality: "Building socialism" might be read as embodying, in Svetlana Boym's words, "the teleological, forward-looking time of Marxist-Leninist progress toward the bright future," while Martin Sabrow observes, in postwar East Germany, an "amalgamation of progress and plan."[40]

As, in Emma Widdis's words, planning was, "in a sense, a conceptual rather than practical or pragmatic activity," when discussions about reforming Czechoslovakia's planned economy began in 1963, they opened the door to criticism in other areas.[41] Among these was documentary film production. In an article published in *Film a doba* in 1965, three years before Army Film first used the term "outside the plan," Antonín Navrátil skewered planning practices in Krátký Film. "The fact that in a field as specific as documentary everything will not go according to plan is plain enough," he wrote.

> It is time for these matters, the economic conditions of documentary work, to be given a reasonable and acceptable limit determined by the *specific character* of film production. . . . In film production, four-year planning is nonsense that only complicates the work of artists while demonstrating its indispensability to bureaucrats.[42]

With this, Navrátil pinpointed a critical disjuncture between the discourses and practices of economic planning and those of documentary production. Documentary, he argued, is a mode of production whose temporality is defined by spontaneity and contingency and is thus fundamentally incompatible with the steady forward progress of the "plan."

Similar language appeared in Army Film's second "Report on the Fulfillment of the Plan" for 1968, issued on July 26—ten days after Prchlík's press conference and less than a month before the Warsaw Pact invasion. Where the year's first report had merely mentioned that *Metrum* was produced "outside the plan," in the second, Benda ruminated on the practice of planning in the studio. Noting that the first half of 1968 saw

considerably more planned films "diverg[ing] from their real fulfillment,"
he, like Navrátil, reflected on the difficulty in matching economic planning's standard half- or quarter-year timeframes to those of filmmaking:
"In film production, the fact has always been that a plan cannot do justice
to its realization, as is the case in common . . . manufacturing, because at
the time it is assembled . . . very little . . . is perfectly known."

Later in the report, Benda discussed the ways in which 1968 itself had
affected film production:

> The process of renewal has extended into the film business—film pro-
> duction is trying to be a core part of it—this has expressed itself both in
> finished works, and above all in works in progress.[43] These realities were
> further made possible by the common knowledge that it is not possible to
> convincingly capture the real development of a half-year in film produc-
> tion, as is possible in the case of economic results.[44]

The term "works in progress," here, emphasizes the temporal basis of
Benda's and Navrátil's calls for a new mode of economic organization for
filmmaking, underscoring the need for film institutions to be tuned more
closely to the present and contingent—or what, following Navrátil, we
might call "documentary time."

A CONFLICT BETWEEN REALITY AND THE PLAN

As Benda indicates, however, in its very contingency, "documentary
time" was also the temporality of Czechoslovakia, 1968. In the sixteen
months between January 1968 (when Alexander Dubček came into office)
and April 1969 (when he resigned), the situation in the country changed
dramatically from day to day—and during the invasion, hour to hour,
second to second. In keeping with this, chronicles of this period are frequently structured as lists of dates (such as in Zdeněk Hejzlar and Vladimír Kusin's *Czechoslovakia, 1968–1969: Chronology, Bibliography, Annotation*) or even specific moments: *The Czech Black Book* narrates, minute
by minute, the events taking place around Czechoslovakia during the
invasion.

Benda's report for the third quarter of 1968 (filed on October 29) reflects
this dramatic temporal condensation and disruption. In the report, Benda

continues to critique the centralized planning of filmmaking, beginning, as he had his previous report, by underscoring "the exceptionality of the year 1968 with regard to film production" and pointing to the invasion as a particularly unsettling moment (difficulties fulfilling the plan in the year's third quarter were "even more due to . . . the occurrences of . . . the twenty-first of August," which forced the studio to stop work for a period). If, here, we again see the close connections between Army films made "outside the plan" and the unpredictable events of 1968, later in the report, Benda introduced a new way to reflect on the interplay between economic planning and nonfiction filmmaking, writing of a fundamental "conflict between reality and the plan."[45]

With this, Benda continued the debate about documentary's engagement with reality that, as chapter 4 discusses, had occupied Czechoslovak filmmakers and critics throughout the decade. During the Prague Spring, however, a moment at which rhetoric about "reality" and its corollary, "truth," were omnipresent, this discussion took on new dimensions.[46] Questions of medium were central to this, for as Czechoslovak Television had continued its rapid transformation from a conservative voice to, in Bren's words, a site of "freewheeling live debates, unscripted interviews, uncensored confessions, and startling political revelations," it seemed to have inherited the mantle of "truth" that, earlier in the decade, cinéma vérité had promised.[47]

This situation sparked a number of critical responses. One came in August 1968 from the tireless Navrátil. "Is Documentary Dead?," a response to the question of whether television had "dug documentary's grave," characterizes the history of nonfiction film in postwar Czechoslovakia as a long journey toward "truth," one undertaken in opposition to what Navrátil terms "power." In the 1950s, Navrátil argues, the "documentary image of reality was replaced with the constructed image of dreamed-up 'typical examples.'" Circa 1963, inspired by the Thaw and by the ethical and formal impulses of "film truth," documentarians "rose from their own ashes, and approached truth."[48] In doing so, they helped "blaze the trail toward January [1968]," becoming "not only the educator of the nation in the best sense of the word, the corrector of public opinion, but also the serious disputant of official politics."[49] In highlighting this public, corrective role, Navrátil answers the question that his article's title poses:

documentary is not threatened by television. Rather, it is through television—which he sees primarily as a technology for transmission, not as a medium with its own characteristics—that documentary's "truth" can reach an even wider audience.

In addition to its instrumental understanding of television, Navrátil's argument hinges on two convictions: first, that the film camera's mechanical vision of the world automatically reveals "truth." Here, it echoes contemporary American rhetoric about cinéma vérité that held that, in Jonathan Kahana's words, "social space might contain unconscious or invisible truths, but you could reveal them if you just knew where to point your camera," a concept, Kahana observes, "consistent with the ideology of Cold War liberalism, which maintained that free societies had nothing to hide."[50] Early in the article, for instance, Navrátil discusses the 1954 Czechoslovak documentary *The Hockey Players' Christmas* (*Vánoce hokejistů*, dir. Jindřich Ferenc), shot during a Czechoslovak-Swedish hockey match in Stockholm. The cameramen, Alois Jiráček and Josef Pešek, Navrátil writes,

> did not have blinders on, and looked beyond the rink. They looked around Stockholm with their camera. And they did so with Czech eyes, the eyes of people to whom the Western world had been closed for a number of years, painted as the hotbed of all injustice, as a world in which workers starve in destitute slums, while fat capitalists lounge about in their easy chairs, smoking thick cigars. Only that Czech camera didn't discover any such decay. It showed an orderly, clean and beautiful city, pleasant and orderly people. . . . The comparison of slogans and propaganda with [this] concrete image did not end well.[51]

Second, working from the popular understanding of the Prague Spring as a moment of revelation, Navrátil argues that, until this point, "truth" had existed outside of, and in opposition to, the socialist state—but that in 1968, the possibility existed for them to merge. This is reflected in the contrast he draws between "slogans and propaganda" and the "concrete image" and in a more direct statement later in the article, where he says, "I don't need to point out how, and how many times, Czech and Slovak documentarians have come to blows with state power."[52]

Such perspectives were relatively new for Navrátil. As chapter 4 discusses, writing four years earlier about the 1964 Karlovy Vary Short Film

Festival's Free Tribune ("Cinéma Vérité and After"), the critic had called the idea of a technologically mediated "truth" or "reality" into question.[53] Yet Navrátil was not the only figure in Czechoslovak documentary to consider cinéma vérité, in 1968, as no longer needing an "after," but rather as an entirely appropriate mode of representation—a trend skewered by Karel Vachek in his 1968 feature-length *Elective Affinities* (*Spříznění volbou*), produced by Krátký Film. In this film, Vachek uses cinéma vérité's technologies and techniques—those that he derides in his 1964 *Moravian Hellas*—to simultaneously offer, and call into question the very possibility of, an intimate view of the presidential election (here, the Drew Associates's 1960 *Primary* is a key point of reference).[54] The film chronicles, in the ironic words of its opening titles,

> Ten filmed days with Dubček, Šik, Smrkovský, Goldstücker, Císař, Černík, Svoboda and others—between March 15th and 30th, 1968. With an Éclair camera (16mm) and a Nagra [tape recorder], 6 hours and 20 minutes of rough synchronized footage were shot, out of which was assembled the "image" of the fourteen days that preceded the elections of the president of the Czechoslovak Socialist Republic.

The ideal of a pure "image" that Vachek's film satirizes (and Navrátil's article describes) is in one sense the "reality" to which Benda refers—vital and changeable, it is impossible to foresee in budgets or schedules. But Benda's complaint about a "conflict between reality and the plan" was in its nature very different from Navrátil's essentially liberal argument that, until 1968, "truth" (rooted in a mechanically captured "reality") and "the socialist state" (embodied by "the plan") were incompatible. Benda was writing from the perspective of two military institutions, Army Film and the HPS, that had become distinctly permissive over the past five years. His concern was thus not the restrictions placed on filmmakers by "state power" but rather the strictures of bureaucratic language itself: the fact that the rhetoric of planning left no way to account for the new mode of film production that 1968, in its disorder, required, and that *Metrum* exemplified. For Benda, this did not mean that filmmakers should throw off the shackles of the state but rather that novel institutional language and processes were necessary to encompass this mode of production— implicit in which was a critique of earlier Czechoslovak media politics.

"Truth," that is, was not alien to the socialist state, nor did the camera suffice to capture "reality." And it is precisely this that the term "outside the plan" addressed, on the one hand describing a mode of filmmaking whose dual, hybrid aesthetic, like *Metrum's*, was particularly well suited to Czechoslovakia in 1968, and on the other, creating the rhetorical and institutional space for films like this to exist.

LOOKING AHEAD

Nineteen sixty-eight's unpredictable, turbulent nature was at the core of a second film produced "outside the plan" by Baláda, the 1969 *Forest* (*Les*). Like *Metrum*, the film documents an "unplanned" encounter with "reality," in this case the funeral procession of Jan Palach, a philosophy student at Charles University in Prague who immolated himself in January 1969 in protest of the consequences of the invasion and died a few days later. The students with whom he attended university organized a funeral procession that was attended by thousands and that represented the last major spontaneous protest of the Warsaw Pact invasion before the post-invasion period of normalization began in earnest.[55] Palach's funeral also highlighted the changes that had occurred in Czechoslovak media culture since the invasion and underscored documentary's continued relevance within it. For while, as Bren reports, television and radio were forbidden from "broadcasting programs or segments on Palach," according to Baláda, during the funeral procession, "everyone who had a camera" was in the streets, filming.[56] *Forest*, however, shot by a collective of cameramen with instructions from Baláda and Šajmovič, was a different sort of film. "I looked for a metaphorical means of expression," Baláda says. "I remembered Gorky's prose-poem, 'Danko's Burning Heart.' A cantata had been composed on the text, and we knew in advance we wanted to use it in this way. So the reportage details of the funeral procession are not there."[57]

Indeed, almost nothing in *Forest* is expository, and like *Metrum*, the film is made up primarily of crowd shots. These impart an overwhelming impression of the mass: the camera rarely allows anything other than

FIGURE 5.2

Honor guard (*Forest*). 35mm frame enlargement courtesy of
Národní filmový archiv/National Film Archive, Prague.

human faces and bodies to enter the frame, and we are never given any
visual clues to the reason behind the gathering, beyond a brief sequence
in which we glimpse, through the crowds, a student honor guard. Thus, as
in *Metrum,* the viewer has the sense of being part of the crowd, glimpsing
what one can, from an embodied point of view.

This lack of explanatory detail is matched by spatial indeterminacy. *Forest* begins, as *Metrum* does, with a series of tracking shots. Some of these
sketch barely visible figures standing in line in the pre-dawn darkness;
others are tilted upward, showing streetlights and the outlines of rooftops
against the sky. Yet unlike *Metrum's* tracking shots, these do not orient the
viewer in a particular space—in fact, they do the opposite. Just as in the
crowd shots, where the viewer has no sense of where he or she stands, in
Forest's opening moments, which should logically serve as establishing
shots for the entire film, location is implied to be indeterminate. This sense

FIGURE 5.3

Forest. 35mm frame enlargement courtesy of Národní
filmový archiv/National Film Archive, Prague.

of dislocation is heightened by the film's frequent use of frontal shots of
faces and bodies and extreme high-angle shots, which eliminate spatial
and historical context.

For Baláda, this decontextualization is part of the film's metaphoric
charge and works in dialogue with its soundtrack. Gorky's story is that
of a young man, Danko, who leads an enslaved people out of a dark, dangerous forest by holding his own burning heart aloft as a beacon. When
they emerge from the forest, Danko dies, a martyr, unthanked. The use of
this metaphor in *Forest* is complex. On one level, the film posits a simple
equivalence between the figures of Danko and Palach. Within this, however, is a broader critique of post-invasion Czechoslovakia. Kieran Williams argues that Palach's actions reflected the ultimate refusal by most
of Czechoslovak society to resist the invasion:

> In his effort to stir the nation he opted for self-destruction rather than ter-
> rorism; he chose the morally superior route of defiance, just as the entire
> country had in August [1968] when it renounced violent resistance to the

invasion. Though stunning in its dignity, this approach brought no political rewards. What he had not counted on was the symbolic power of the martyr in Czech constructs of identity; he became another member in a pantheon that Masaryk had denounced as an unhealthy distraction from genuine action.[58]

Baladʼa, in his discussion of *Forest*, seems to critique post-invasion Czechoslovakia in a similar way. He notes that his film's static dimensions were intended partially to emphasize a lack of action, an idea that *Forest*'s ending underscores, picturing the assembled masses as they scatter: "The sadness was real and big," says Baladʼa,

> but afterward, when the funeral procession ended, people went home quickly, as if from a football match.... So I put that at the end, because I sensed what would come, that people would really forget.... Where *Metrum* ends with the light, here, they split apart, they disperse.[59]

Although its style is similar to *Metrum*'s, *Forest* diverges from its predecessor not only in its engagement with space (location) but also in its engagement with time. At the level of mise-en-scène, *Forest* operates entirely in the static present of the actions we see on screen; there is no kinetic logic to "move" the narrative forward. Simultaneously, in suggesting a lack of resistance, the film stretches forward in time to the socially and politically atomized period of normalization. Unlike *Metrum*, however, whose messianic time might be read as a guarantee of a redemptive future, no such redemption is legible in *Forest*, whose crowds disperse but whose cameras remain at the site of the funeral procession—and in 1968's perpetual present tense.

Forest was not the only Army production to look ahead in this way: Tomáš Škrdlant and Angelika Hannauerová's *The Descendants* (*Potomci,* 1969, a coproduction with Czechoslovak Television) anticipates the "underground" culture that would develop in the following years. Army Film's economic deputy, Stanislav Čeřovský, justified the film in the familiar terms of youth: it is, in his words, "a probe of the world of hippies, whose exterior often disturbs us more than some of their positions toward life and society do. An understanding of this 'world of hippies,' even if they represent only a fragment of the young generation, is useful for education in the Army."[60] The "world of hippies" the film shows us is in fact the community that would drop out of mainstream society after the invasion:

the figures hanging around, using drugs, playing harmonicas and guitars, and explaining their philosophies of life and art include musicians Vlasta Třešňák and Jaroslav Hutka, both of whom would later sign the central dissident text of the post-1968 period, Charter 77. Despite these unproductive activities, *The Descendants'* filmmakers do not pass judgment on these figures but, rather, give voice to their critique of contemporary society—even, in the film's closing scene (where the four friends run Beatles-like through the streets of Prague, accompanied by sitar and drums), framing them as misunderstood celebrities.[61]

If *The Descendants* thus offered continued evidence of Czechoslovak Television's radical dramaturgy and social criticism during the Prague Spring, another Army film made for television, Rudolf Adler, Bohuslav Blažek and Pentti Riuttu's *Quieting (Jurmo)* (*Ztišení [Jurmo]*, 1969, coproduced by the Finnish broadcasting company Yleisradio), did the same, this time through the medium of television itself.[62] Again capitalizing on Adler's expertise in ethnographic filmmaking, *Quieting* captures the lives of the last seven inhabitants of Jurmo, which the credits note is one of the northernmost inhabited spaces in the chain of wild islands that make up the Finnish archipelago. The film is composed primarily of observational scenes: fishermen sharpening axes on a hand-spun lathe and repairing nets by hand, women baking traditional bread, families listening to waltzes on a hand-cranked gramophone. It is appropriately quiet, with almost no dialogue either between the subjects or between them and the filmmakers; instead, the soundtrack is made up of the diegetic sounds that fill daily life on the island: bleating lambs, a church organ, a bubbling spring, the gramophone music.

An exception to this is a scene in which five of the island's inhabitants gather for dinner, watching, as they eat, a subtitled television broadcast of a fashion show. The men and women are silent, and as the program's pop music clashes with the clicking of silverware against plates, the directors' cutaways to full-screen images of bespangled, shimmying bodies on the monitor appear radically out of place—except for the fact that the silver components of the models' dresses resemble the tiny fish on the dinner plates. The superficial, consumerist world in which this fashion show exists—and that the television itself represents—the scene indicates, is Jurmo's inevitable fate: the destination for most of its young residents. Nevertheless, as a cut to a scene of ice fishing accompanied by a woman's reedy folk song makes clear, Jurmo is an alternative, and perhaps an idyll. As such, this film, too, seems to look ahead, prefiguring the post-1968 phenomenon of "inner immigration."

A MILITARY AVANT GARDE

While *Forest* documented the effects of the invasion on Czechoslovakia's civilian sphere, a series of "unplanned" Army Films from 1969 shed light on something less widely discussed: its ramifications for the rank-and-file Czechoslovak soldier. These ramifications were substantial: the invasion and occupation fully disempowered the Czechoslovak Army on its own soil, and soldiers were ordered to the barracks as Warsaw Pact troops entered the country. Films on the topic accordingly abandoned both the antimilitarism and civilian concerns of earlier in the decade and began to see the military—traditionally a bastion of order and routine— as a site of confusion and indeterminacy equaling that of the civilian sphere.

Some films did so by reinterpreting longstanding military film genres.[63] Milan Růžička's *On That Green Meadow* (*Na tý louce zelený*, 1968), for instance, followed in Army Film's aviation film tradition and documented the first air show to take place in Czechoslovakia after August 21. The military base is depicted as wholly engaged with the reforms—its walls are scrawled with graffiti reading "Dubček/Svoboda"—and the narrator's pride is evident as he announces that the first plane "with the sign of the Czechoslovak Socialist Republic" will take off. *On That Green Meadow* was, according to Petr Zvoníček,

> a hit ... [that met] with ... salvos of laughter. The Czechoslovak military pilots' Soviet guard was accompanied by the Russian song "I Wander the Streets"... as interpreted by [popular singers] Eva Pilarová and Waldemar Matuška. The film was congenially played before the West German gangster film *Dynamite in Green,* and many viewers came to see the short film a second time.[64]

The commission that banned the film had a different estimation of it, which Zvoníček also recorded: "An alleged documentary. . . . Shot with a hidden camera. Pokes fun at Soviet soldiers and their wives. . . . It is an anti-Soviet and anti-Party film."[65] The ban on the film, in fact, evidently originated in the Soviet Union: a letter from the Representative of the Government of the USSR for the Affairs of the Temporary Arrival of Soviet Forces in Czechoslovakia, Major-General D. Litovstev, described the film as a mocking portrayal of Soviet troops.[66] The Soviet embassy in Prague also watched *On That Green Meadow*, after which no one saw it played in military or civilian theaters.[67]

Other films echoed *Metrum* and *Forest*'s aesthetic. Most significant among these was an "unplanned" tetralogy by director Vladimír Drha and cameraman Karel Hložek that reacts to the September 1968 transfer of Czechoslovak military units from bases in central Bohemia, near Prague, to eastern Slovakia.[68] The transfers ostensibly took place to make room for occupying soldiers, but it was generally understood that they were intended to prevent resistance to the occupation by the reformist Army. Accordingly, they sparked considerable conflict between Soviet and Czechoslovak forces: according to Condoleezza Rice, "occasionally, CLA [Czechoslovak People's Army] soldiers would just refuse to move."[69] The "transfer tetralogy" begins with *Lesson* (*Lekce*, 1969), a sometimes sarcastic, sometimes mournful documentary of soldiers packing up a central Bohemian base and "welcoming" its new residents, and it continues with *34 Women* (*34 ženy*, 1969) and *Color Wheel* (*Barvotisk*; in Slovak, *Farbotlač*, 1969), the first following thirty-four transferred officers' wives on a weekend visit from Prague to their potential new home in Humenné, Slovakia, and the second documenting the first "military marriage," in February 1969, between a transferred soldier and a local textile worker.

Lesson is sharply ironic from its first moments, in which, over the jaunty opening notes of a military march, two title cards appear. The first reads, "The Minister of Defense issued an order this year for the transfer of soldiers from several bases around Prague to eastern Slovakia. The goal was to free up military buildings." The second card reads, simply and caustically, "The order was carried out." To the strains of the military march and from the point of view of a moving tank, *Lesson* then shows residents of the town waving to soldiers as they drive through the streets and soldiers going about the work of moving their base's furnishings across the country. The march stops abruptly and symbolically as the tank, its barrel draped with the Czechoslovak flag, halts in front of a concrete wall. There is nowhere further for it to go.

In place of the march, a mournful, at times eerie, electronic soundtrack accompanies the following section. We see naked soldiers showering and shaving, and Hložek wanders with his handheld camera throughout the soon-to-be-abandoned barracks, capturing their half-disassembled spaces in very long takes. He focuses on evocative "found" images: a book with the ironic title *The World and Its Problems* abandoned on a bed, a soldier asleep on a pile of mattresses, soldiers (presumably the base's new Soviet residents) hanging a collage of pornographic photographs on a wall. This section is again bracketed by sound. As the drumbeats of another march begin, we see a repetition of a trope that has run throughout the film: huge socialist realist tableaux being carried out of the barracks and into storage. In the film's final shot, we watch from outside the storage room's broken window as a painting of female peasants is leaned against the window, the women seemingly imprisoned behind its bars (see figure 5.4). After the last strains of the march fade away, the painting falls from the window, leaving its fractured panes black and empty.

This ending is described in the film's release details: "Four soldiers carry the 'cult' images into a little courtyard. . . . Through a barred little window, the image we have seen with the *kolkhozi* falls and disappears. Through the bars, there remains only darkness."[70] If, in its mournful tone, *Lesson's* depiction of the move displays opposition to the occupation, this sequence is the film's most explicitly political, encapsulating 1968's resonance for most Czechoslovaks: disillusionment with the promises of early socialism, for which the paintings offer a simple metaphor. However, in the blank window from which socialist realism has, it seems, permanently departed, Drha and Hložek suggest that space remains for new modes of representation, among which, perhaps, is that which *Lesson* and other "unplanned" films represent.

Drha and Hložek's subsequent films, 34 *Women* and *Color Wheel,* use a similar style to depict the transfer's aftermath. The black-and-white 34 *Women* follows officers' wives on a Ministry of Defense–sponsored junket to eastern Slovakia, where military commanders try to convince them to join their transferred husbands. Yet between the overnight train trip and interminable "friendly gatherings" in which the women seem mostly to drink and smoke, they barely have a moment alone with their husbands (see figure 5.5). In suggesting the invasion's collateral social damage, 34

FIGURE 5.4

Lesson. 35mm frame enlargement courtesy of Národní
filmový archiv/National Film Archive, Prague.

Women is linked thematically to *Color Wheel,* whose wedding Drha documents from its preparations to its church ceremony, ending with a raucous
party in a pub. The first film evokes this collateral damage in juxtaposition:
in the extreme distance between central Bohemia and eastern Slovakia,
captured in lengthy handheld sequences in the train; in the disjuncture
between military officials' optimism and Humenné's grim surroundings;
in the film's sarcastic intertitles. Conversely, *Color Wheel*'s grotesque, car-
nivalesque images (captured in the garish palette from which the film
takes its name) *themselves* signify this damage, which is emphasized by the
film's opening and closing images: a live rooster by a chopping block, and
the dead animal, its fresh blood red on the snow (see plate 8).[71]

The tetralogy ends with the film *Village* (*Ves*), a portrait of Milovice, one
of the central Bohemian Army towns from which Czechoslovak soldiers
were transferred and which the film depicts during its occupation.[72] *Village,* however, only alludes to these details—as in *Forest,* the viewer has no

FIGURE 5.5

Thirty-Four Women. 35mm frame enlargement courtesy of
Národní filmový archiv/National Film Archive, Prague.

information about where and when it is set. This lack of context seems to
hinge on *Village*'s point of view, which is implied to be that of a child seen
in its opening and closing sequences (see figure 5.6). The film begins with a
close-up of the back of the child's head, accompanied by a harpsichord lullaby. As in *Lesson,* music is essential to establishing *Village*'s atmosphere:
When the child turns to face the camera, the score shifts to a minimalist
electronic composition that recalls *Lesson*'s soundtrack. There follows a
series of still shots of wintry village life, filmed parallel to the camera and
at eye level: a family in a courtyard, a man riding a hand-powered recum-
bent tricycle, children sledding. We see agricultural tools—a scarecrow,
the seat of a tractor; and images from the natural world—a dog playing
with a kitten, a duck and a rabbit wandering in a snowy marsh, horses feed-
ing, chickens roosting. We see still shots of houses, stores, statues, walls,
boarded-up windows, and graves, seemingly abandoned. Three progressively magnified images of a relief bust on a pub's exterior wall follow; the

FIGURE 5.6

Village. Source: Vojenský historický ústav/Military History Institute, Prague.

last is bisected by a broad, deliberate, vertical scratch on the celluloid. Soviet soldiers walk intermittently through the frame, and in one shot a child appears to mimic them, patrolling in front of a building with a stick strapped military-style to his back (see figure 5.7). The film concludes with the lullaby with which it began, as the first child turns its back again to the camera.

The idea that this is a child's perspective explains *Village*'s associative structure as well as its content. In the child's gaze, everyday items such as the tractor seat or scarecrow are interpreted as abstract objects (as communicated to the viewer through their decontextualization and the film's flat compositions) while the film's logic of assembly refuses narrative context for shots such as those of the patrolling soldiers. These strategies of estrangement, in which everyday objects and occurrences are made to look peculiar, encourage the viewer, by extension, to see the transfer and the occupation, which have left this village empty, as themselves strange and

FIGURE 5.7

Children patrolling (*Village*). Source: Vojenský historický
ústav/Military History Institute, Prague.

unnatural. *Village,* then, is at once a documentary film and an estrangement of its own documentary images, a form that not only recalls the one
pioneered by *Metrum* but moves it squarely into the military realm, which
it frames as a world out of joint.[73]

Lesson, 34 Women, and *Village* were screened at the 1969 Karlovy Vary
Short Film Festival.[74] While the festival—which took place from March
15 to 21, just weeks before Dubček stepped down—effectively marked the
end of these films' public life, it was also there that Army Film's work over
the period 1968–1969 was recognized, with the Czechoslovak Journalists'
Club awarding the studio a prize "for its work [over the period of the in-
vasion]," praising "the way [its artists] gave shape to the problems of the
time with an expressive social engagement and artistic responsibility."[75]

Another contemporary appraisal of the "transfer tetralogy" elaborated
on these comments, characterizing the films' unique form and its relation

to its social and media context. In an article in *Kino,* Ivan Dvořák discussed the three films by Drha that had been made by that point—*Lesson, 34 Women,* and *Village*—as well as Adler's Army films. His observations, however, can be extended to the rest of the studio's "unplanned" films:

> It would seem that reporting on real events is above all a matter of facts. But Drha, just like his slightly older comrade Adler, is a child of the age of television, which chased facts from the film screen to the television monitor. And thus his film reportages use objective reality only as an excuse to catch the atmosphere of the "great move." This connects small, individual human problems with great ones; from making sure one has a roof over one's head and a comfortable bed under him, to solving the problems of family life, of moving wives and children, and all of the many simple life needs and feelings that for many viewers are not, precisely in connection with soldiers, entirely clear. Just like Adler, he does not seek an answer to the questions "what" and "why," but rather "how."[76]

This text thus captures the aesthetic this chapter describes—one balanced between the visible and the invisible, the concrete and "atmospheric." It also offers a response to the same question that, eight months earlier, Navrátil attempted to answer in his *Film a doba* article: that of documentary's relationship to "reality" and "truth" in 1968, a moment at which television had come to the forefront of the reform movement. However, where Navrátil wrote of television as a new venue for documentary—one that would allow it to thrive and reach a wide audience—in Dvořák's estimation, television has *freed* documentary from journalistic, "factual" demands, allowing it to reveal other "realities" and "truths." It is these critical realities that films such as Drha's and Baláda's uncovered in their encounter with 1968.

Dvořák's description of Army Film's "unplanned" aesthetic as a new, probing lens primed to make contemporary life visible evokes the interwar debates about film's engagement with reality that chapter 1 discusses. On the one hand, the description recalls Jeníček's belief in film and photography's medium-specific modern, documentary nature. On the other hand, like fi-fo, it rejects the notion of a purely optical "truth." Regardless, perhaps better than other postwar Army films, the "transfer tetralogy" "sees the state" as Jeníček had intended military propaganda to do. For although in place of vérité's claims to a self-evident truth, films such as

Drha's call into question the very images from which they are constructed, it is through this that they offer such a lucid vision of Czechoslovakia circa 1968: a place and time defined by its fast-moving chronology, unpredictable changes, and volatility.

The Czechoslovak state is also where these films, and the studio that produced them, emerged—for as this book chronicles, Jeníček's "workshop" persisted through the 1950s and 1960s, becoming, by the latter decade's end, a space in which "experiments" with film's language and uses were uniquely possible. In fact, by late 1969, Army Film may have been the only such space in Czechoslovakia, as State Film was normalized earlier than Army Film. Yet what emerged in Army Film as a result of both its interwar and postwar histories was also remarkably similar to a reformed model for Czechoslovakia's nationalized cinema that Liehm proposed in a 1968 speech to FITES. In his speech, Liehm excoriated "centralized power" for its boorish, uncultured nature, arguing that it was as detrimental to art as the market was.[77] He proposed that the industry be decentralized and that filmmakers be ensured "the right to work," as well as "creative freedom."[78]

These tenets largely describe Army Film in the 1960s: the studio was, on account of its exclusion from the nationalization decree, inherently decentralized and thus largely autonomous; producing commissioned works for the Army or other clients, its employees could count on steady work, either for their two or three years of military service or for long decades. And by 1968, by virtue of its almost nonexistent censorship, extensive financial resources, and supportive administration, it offered filmmakers nearly complete "creative freedom." The alternative system that Liehm sought, in short, was already there: in an echo of the "unplanned" films' own form, a persistent alternative *within* the "system."

Coda

NORMALIZATION

Alexander Dubček resigned in April 1969. That summer, under his replacement, First Secretary Gustáv Husák, the prolonged process of "cleansing" Czechoslovak society of its reformist elements began. In spite of this, Army Film remained confident in its late-1960s course. Stanislav Čeřovský, in his summary report for 1969, continued to emphasize the social and military relevance of the studio's critical films, particularly to Czechoslovakia's youth. "The living environment, free time or 'moral profile' of [military] youth," he wrote,

> is connected with ... these issues in [soldiers'] civilian lives, both before and after their time in the Army, which, in turn, strongly influence their time in the Army.... We can therefore demonstrate and confirm that these two spheres of Czechoslovak society cannot be separated, that they interpenetrate each other—and thus they must be interwoven in the Army studio's work. It is true that this issue is a very difficult one—not only from an artistic standpoint, but also from an ideological standpoint. However, this difficulty does not mean we should disregard it; on the contrary, we must consider it with intensive attention and approach it with a very thoughtful, long-term philosophy and with serious, scholarly preparation of each treatment and screenplay.[1]

While this paragraph echoed justifications for Army Film's dramaturgy that had been made since the middle of the decade, the report's final lines suggested something different. "The technical knowledge of Studio ČAF's artists and other workers," Čeřovský wrote, "ensures that they can continue, without any structural or party changes, to increase the ideological and political engagement of [the studio's] work."[2] Here, the report on the fulfillment of the plan—previously malleable, shaped to justify the studio's practices—became an appeal for survival.

It was ultimately unheeded. In early October 1970, the Main Political Administration (HPS), under its new leadership, ordered Army Film to conduct "party screenings" (*stranické prověrky*)—purges—by the end of the month. Bedřich Benda, protesting illness, delayed the screenings by several weeks.[3] When they finally took place, they followed the format they did elsewhere in Czechoslovakia. Each employee was interviewed on a set of specified themes, in order to evaluate "the scope, activity, and social consequences of [his or her] political positions and actions" during the "exceptional" period of 1968–1969.[4] Employees could retain their Party membership, have their membership canceled, or be expelled from the Party. They risked being transferred, demoted, or losing their jobs.[5]

The purges and their aftermath decimated the institution that Benda and Hlaváč had built during the preceding decade, particularly its dramaturgical and artistic branches.[6] Among the studio's leadership, Benda and Čeřovský were expelled from the Party, with Benda—like Jiří Jeníček before him—receiving a gentleman's release to the reserves.[7] Roman Hlaváč had already departed for Czechoslovak Television at the end of 1968.[8]

At the same time, the archive of Army Film's Central Film Distribution office underwent its own "screening," which removed hundreds of now ideologically problematic films—primarily Czechoslovak productions from 1960 to 1969—from circulation.[9] These included Army Film's short nonfiction films of the period, most of which were not shown publicly again until after 1989.[10] Some productions appear to have met a more severe fate: Jan Schmidt recounts receiving an anonymous phone call in 1969, warning him that *The End of August at the Hotel Ozone* was on a pile of Army films that were slated to be burned. The voice on the line said: "'Mr. Director, the Army Studio is going to burn films. *Hotel Ozone* is in the line for tomorrow. It will be ready to be burned at 10 o'clock. Another, the best copy of the film, will be on the top of the second pile.' So I went there and saved the film."[11]

It was thus that another period in the history of Czechoslovak military cinema came to a close. And as was, by now, customary, the ascendant era began with proclamations of its novelty. In 1972, Jiří Lelek, the studio's new chief, denounced the late 1960s as a period during which Army Film's productions were "permeated with liberalism, pacifism, nationalism, anti-Sovietism, and anti-Soviet positions." The period of normalization would represent an "attempt to rehabilitate [the studio] from previous years' deviation from its proper calling and [from the] politically incorrect and damaging creative deformations that led to the misuse of Army Film's facilities and to right-wing opportunism." It would be characterized by "a strengthened central direction . . . both from the side of the new leadership and from the side of the [military], and a fundamental reconstruction of film content," emphasizing the "military and defense politics of the KSČ [the Czechoslovak Communist Party], and the education of soldiers in proletarian internationalism, class consciousness, and socialist internationalism." Political education in the studio, "which from 1968 and even several years before then was practically nonexistent," would be reinstated.[12]

METAPHOR, ARCHIVE, HISTORY

During the screening of the Central Film Distribution's archive, it was noted that "practically all" of the "political documentaries" and newsreels produced by Army Film in 1968 were removed from circulation to military and civilian audiences. Of those produced in 1969, just thirteen—most of them newsreels—were permitted to circulate, while twenty-one films were removed from distribution. In 1970, production was stopped on eleven films, and thirty-four went into distribution.[13] Even among these, however, the 1960s' legacy was still palpable. Václav Hapl's *Man Will Not Die of Thirst* (*Člověk neumírá žízní*, 1970), for instance, followed Czech psychiatrist Stanislav Grof—a founder of the field of transpersonal psychology, soon to emigrate to the United States—as he administered LSD to psychiatric patients, to whose verbally described hallucinations Hapl gave cinematic form. From these sequences, Hapl built an essay on modern human consciousness, interweaving scenes in a mental institution with iconic images of the twentieth century: New York city skyscrapers, enraptured fans at Beatles concerts, nuclear explosions, footage from Nazi concentration camps.

Yet as the archive's screening signaled, the 1960s of LSD and the Beatles were of less concern to Army Film's normalizers than the 1960s of Dubček and the Gottwald Memorandum. And thus, while the new studio officials tolerated metaphysical questions in films such as Hapl's, Juraj Šajmovič's proposal to document the construction of Prague's Nusle Bridge (which spans the New Town and Vyšehrad neighborhoods and opened in 1973) was immediately rejected. Šajmovič explains that, while the bridge was being built,

> they put tanks [on it] to test its strength.... When I read about it in the news, I immediately went to František Řička [the studio's new lead dramaturg] and said, "I'd like to make a documentary about that." He said, "You'd like those Russian tanks again, eh?" I wanted that.... I wanted to make a documentary analogy with the tanks ... everyone would have understood that we were looking for an analogy with the Russian tanks. [Řička] understood it immediately. I said no, I want to make a documentary, a pure documentary. But he said no. Because it was strongly metaphorical.[14]

Šajmovič's recollection of this conversation aptly summarizes Army Film's own transformation in the years immediately after the Prague Spring, which was marked by a shift in the way that the institution understood films—both those it produced and those it held in its archives. Indeed, in denying the possibility for documentary material to have metaphoric dimensions, the studio took a decisive step away from the dynamics that had defined its late-60s productions: *Metrum*'s evocations of life and death, the intimation of stasis in *Forest*'s crowd shots, the dead rooster with which *Color Wheel* ends. This occurred in tandem with a departure from the institutional identity that Benda and Hlaváč had fostered in the 1960s, its studied antimilitarism and focus on cinematic pedagogy and form.

A letter written by Benda a month before the 1968 invasion puts this in context. In June of that year, the Czechoslovak military was preparing for the fiftieth anniversary of Czechoslovakia's founding. The HPS had, in connection with this, assembled an "advisory board of military history offices, military editors and publishers, military cultural and artistic institutions, Army Film, and the editorial boards of Army radio and Army television" to help shape foreign propaganda that would express the "current internal and external political developments"—that is, Czechoslovakia of the Prague Spring.[15] Benda responded to a request for topics for the board to address in a curious way, excoriating Czechoslovak diplomats, who, he wrote, "have seen our films primarily as a means for social meetings with their foreign colleagues . . . often, 'they went to the Army for a lecture,' and used our film as an accompaniment." "These functionaries," he concluded, see "these actions as a success. We consider them luxurious primitivism."[16] For Army films, in his view, should always be screened in the "presence of our artists," in a "well-prepared screening linked with a press conference." Military films, in other words, were not only a means to an end—instruction in a process or a maneuver, demonstrations of a geopolitically important alliance, or simply excuses to socialize. Instead, even as tools for public diplomacy, military films should be taken on their own terms, given proper, focused attention, introduced by their makers, and discussed afterward.

Benda's protests were, of course, nothing new, for similar questions about the nature and use of military films had been present in the studio since its inception. They were reflected in Army Film's exclusion from the nationalized film industry in 1945 and in Čepička's resistance to this exclusion. They were expressed in the conflicts between Army Film and the Combat Training Directorate (SBP) over instructional filmmaking in the early 1950s. And they were even visible in the 1930s, when the regimented nature of Jeníček's production process alienated his collaborators. As I have argued in this book, these tensions often reverberated in the civilian sphere, where they sparked broader questions about cinema—what films should look and sound like, how they should be made, what they should signify and do.

If, as Řička's refusal of Šajmovič's bridge documentary suggested, the studio's new production policies sought, in part, to minimize these close and often provocative links between the military and civilian spheres, archival practices, too, aimed to diminish film's potential energy. The Central Film Distribution archive's screening accomplished this by framing its content as numbered objects that could be burned or put into storage and, ideally, forgotten, along with the past they so richly evoked. It is perhaps for this reason that these films' "rediscovery" after Czechoslovakia's 1989 "Velvet Revolution" was the subject of such wonder in an August 1990 article by journalist Petr Zvoníček. For beyond their evocation of 1968 and all its promise, their emergence from a "vault"—a pregnant metaphor in the history of postwar East European cinema—may have encapsulated the hope that 1989 would make good on this promise.

By the time I researched this book, the metaphors by which, in the Czech Republic, communist-era archives such as Army Film's own were understood had shifted. At the heart of this transformation were the country's Secret Police files, which were made available to the public in 2007 under the auspices of the government-sponsored Institute for the Study of Totalitarian Regimes (Ústav pro studium totalitních režimů). As was the case elsewhere in Eastern Europe, the opening of the Secret Police archives in the Czech Republic was a fraught event, at whose public face stood the files of, in Cristina Vatulescu's words, "public figures famous for their resistance to the Soviet regime."[17] In 2008, debate was raging over one such case: the publication, in October of that year, of an article in the magazine *Respekt* (*Respect*) alleging that in 1951, novelist Milan Kundera had informed on a Western émigré agent. The "Kundera affair," precipitated by a document found in the Institute for the Study of Totalitarian Regimes, triggered a flurry of discussions about archives, historical argument, and the government's role in supporting organizations such as the institute.[18] In this context, state-sponsored productions like the Army's became vulnerable to interpretation as similar kinds of "incriminating" documents.[19]

What is striking about these interpretations is not only how they echo, in Vatulescu's words, "the ways that the police devised for writing and reading . . . files—to assign guilt . . . to turn art into incriminating evidence, and to pass quick judgment."[20] It is also how they suggest what Benda, back in 1968, might have been complaining about. For in broadly equating films such as the Army's with the institution that produced them, these interpretations continue to see the studio's films instrumentally, and not as complex formal, political, and social objects, a characteristic I argue was the very product of their institutional charge. This complexity is the heart of Army Film's history, as it is of similar institutions. Yet it, too, is revealed by the archive. For when we examine the reams of paper that accompanied the films' production, distribution, and exhibition, the stories of those who made them, and the films' multifaceted aesthetic dimensions, simple assignations of meaning become impossible and, with them, the reductive terms of the Cold War. Here, the archive does not offer clear "evidence"; rather, it troubles and refines established concepts, categories, and frameworks: the concept of the avant garde and its institutional context; the categories of the governmental actor, institutional actor, and individual actor.[21] And as the most sophisticated example of this stand the films themselves: at times poignant, at times routine; intricate and irreducibly detailed.

NOTES

INTRODUCTION

1. Navrátil, *Cesty k pravdě či lži*, 67.

2. Muriel Blaive writes that Čepička cultivated "a cult of his own personality" (Blaive, *Une déstalinisation manquée*, 62).

3. Jiras and Mareš, *František Vláčil: Zápasy*, 5.

4. Skilling, *Czechoslovakia's Interrupted Revolution*, 33.

5. "Studio ČAF—tendence a tvůrci," 1.

6. Navrátil, *Cesty k pravdě či lži*, 68.

7. Šmidrkal, *Armáda a stříbrné plátno; Obraz vojenského prostředí.*

8. Hames, *The Czechoslovak New Wave*; Liehm and Liehm, *The Most Important Art*; Liehm, *Closely Watched Films*; Škvorecký, *All the Bright Young Men and Women*.

9. Biller, "Wenn der Kater kommt," in *Bernsteintage*.

10. Army film archivists, in discussion with the author, March 2012.

11. "Useful cinema" is defined by Charles R. Acland and Haidee Wasson in their introduction to *Useful Cinema*, 4. The term, they write, "overlaps with, but is not equivalent to, similar terms such as 'functional film,' 'educational film,' 'non-fictional film,' and 'non-theatrical film.' We define useful cinema to include experimen-tal films and a variety of didactic films that are fictional as well as non-fictional, narra-tive as well as non-narrative. The concept of useful cinema does not so much name a mode of production, a genre, or an exhibi-tion venue as it identifies a disposition, an outlook, and an approach toward a medium on the part of institutions and institutional agents. In this way, useful cinema has a much to do with the maintenance and lon-gevity of institutions seemingly unrelated to cinema as it does with cinema per se."

12. This phrasing is Michal Bregant's; I thank him for discussing this concept with me.

13. Kopaněvová, Novák, and Svoboda, "Hovoříme v přítomném čase," 434.

14. On the Czechoslovak military as "foreign," see Rice, *The Soviet Union and the Czechoslovak Army*, 106.

15. Horak is writing of industrial films, "products of corporate public relations" that, he argues, have historically been "totally uninteresting as either aesthetic or socio-historical objects" (Horak, "A Neglected Genre," 36). For an overview of the archival politics surrounding such "marginal" film practices, see Frick, *Saving Cinema*.

16. See Kovács, *Screening Modernism.* The problem of what to call the region with which this book is concerned is central to work in this field. (See, e.g., Imre, *East European Cinemas,* xv–xvii; Coates, *The Red and the White,* 2–3; and Hames, *The Cinema of Central Europe,* 1–13.) In chapter 1, I use the terms "Central Europe" and "East Central Europe," in keeping with the cultural and intellectual interactions this book traces between Czechoslovakia, Germany, and Austria. In chapters 2–5, I refer to "Eastern Europe," in reference to the Cold War. I do so, however, with an understanding of these terms' limitations.

17. For a review of recent work in the field, see Anikó Imre's introduction to *Companion to Eastern European Cinemas,* as well as the texts in this volume. In English, see also Coates, *The Red and the White;* Cunningham, *Hungarian Cinema;* Imre, *East European Cinemas;* Imre, Havens, and Lustyik, *Popular Television in Eastern Europe;* Levi, *Disintegration in Frames;* Owen, *Avant-Garde to New Wave;* Trumpener, "*La guerre est finie*" and *The Divided Screen;* Marsha Siefert, "East European Cold War Culture(s)"; and Vatulescu, *Police Aesthetics.* Czech film scholarship has been a vibrant area for historical reassessments, particularly the Department of Film Studies and Audiovisual Culture at Masaryk University and the National Film Archive's journal *Iluminace.* On the related field of postwar Soviet cinema, see, e.g., Valerie Pozner's "Le « réalisme socialiste »"; and Vinogradova, "Between the State and the Kino."

18. Imre, ed., *East European Cinemas,* xiii. For an example of scholarship in production studies in postwar East European cinema, see Petr Szczepanik, "'Machři' a 'diletanti.'"

19. Antonín and Mira Liehm's *The Most Important Art,* with its chapter on the period 1945–1955, stands as an exception in the classic literature, while scholars have

recently begun to systematically investigate Czechoslovak cinema culture of the 1950s. For an overview of these studies, see Skopal, *Naplánovaná kinematografie.*

20. Škvorecký, *All the Bright Young Men and Women,* 28. Among the areas of film and media history from which this book draws are the study of "useful," "orphan," and particularly institutional cinema, and media industry studies. For an overview of key concerns in the latter field, see Jennifer Holt and Alisa Perren's introduction to their volume *Media Industries.*

21. Škvorecký, *All the Bright Young Men and Women,* 28–30.

22. Liehm, *Closely Watched Films,* 3.

23. Hames, *The Czechoslovak New Wave,* 2.

24. Ibid., 6.

25. Wasson, *Museum Movies,* 191.

26. Gunning, *D. W. Griffith,* 49.

27. For a recent example of such characterizations of postwar East European media industries, see Applebaum, *Iron Curtain.* These characterizations map onto the "totalitarian model," which, since the 1970s, scholars have critiqued, offering evidence that Soviet and East European Communist Parties and governments were not monolithic and that the region's societies, cultural producers, and institutions at times possessed more agency than has traditionally been thought. On the history and stakes of such critiques, see, e.g., Geyer and Fitzpatrick, *Beyond Totalitarianism;* Fitzpatrick, "Revisionism in Retrospect"; and Katherine Verdery's introduction to her *What Was Socialism?* On the nonmonolithic nature of Party and state power in the Soviet Union, see, e.g., Ferro, "Y a-t-il 'trop de démocratie.'" On the negotiated relationships between the state and society/culture in state-socialist Eastern Europe, see Blaive, *Une déstalinisation manquée;* Bren, *The Greengrocer and His TV;* Clybor, "Laughter and Hatred Are Neighbors"; Giustino, "Industrial Design

and the Czechoslovak Pavilion"; Kalinová, *Společenské proměny;* Pullmann, *Konec experimentu;* Reid and Crowley, *Style and Socialism;* and Zarecor, *Manufacturing a Socialist Modernity.* Similarly, comparative studies of postwar Eastern Europe have demonstrated that the experience of state socialism was not uniform throughout the region, thus disproving one of the totalitarian model's corollaries—that Soviet power in Eastern Europe was itself "total." A crucial work in this area is John Connelly's comparative study of higher education, *Captive University.*

28. Generic terms in this book (e.g., "documentary," "nonfiction," and "short" film) are typically used in correspondence with original sources. Generic categorization, however, was inconsistent over the years the book examines.

29. Nichols, "Documentary Film," 582. On the intersection of governmental and avant-garde forces in documentary's emergence, see also Hagener, *Moving Forward, Looking Back.* Zoë Druick, Lee Grieveson, and Jonathan Kahana have recently demonstrated the interwar liberal state's central role in shaping documentary's formal and ideological dimensions. See Kahana, *Intelligence Work;* Grieveson, "The Cinema and the (Common) Wealth"; and Druick, *Projecting Canada,* and "'Reaching the Multimillions.'"

30. Druick, "'Reaching the Multimillions,'" 86–87.

31. Nichols, "Documentary Film."

32. Nichols, "Documentary Film," 603.

33. Boček, "Studio, o kterém se málo ví," 4.

34. On this intertwining, see Malitsky, *Post-revolution Nonfiction Film,* 32; and Elsaesser, "Archives and Archaeologies." Vinzenz Hediger and Patrick Vonderau write that "few if any scholars at this point have developed a sustained interest in the archival holdings of industrial films in the former Sovjet [*sic*] republics and former so-

cialist countries of central Europe beyond the auteurist canon" (*Films That Work,* 13). Excellent scholarship nevertheless exists on interwar "useful" and industrial cinema in the region. In the Czechoslovak case, see, e.g., Česálková, "*Film před tabulí*"; and Szczepanik, "Modernism, Industry, Film." On police films in the Soviet Union and postwar Romania, see Vatulescu, *Police Aesthetics.*

35. According to Havelka's *Čs. krátké filmy,* vol. 1, in 1954, Krátký Film produced 160 films in its three Prague branches (Artistic film studio [Studio uměleckého filmu], News film [Zpravodajský film], Documentary film [Dokumentární film], and Popular-scientific film [Populárně-vědecký film]), while Army Film produced only 11 films, approximately the same number as each of Krátký Film's popular-scientific film branches in Brno and Gottwaldov (now Zlín). In 1963, Army Film produced 12 films, compared with the 144 films produced by Krátký Film's Prague-based Documentary Film and Popular-Scientific Film studios together. Havelka's lists are nonetheless incomplete, not accounting, e.g., for the dozens of films produced yearly for internal military purposes. For a broader (but still partial) account of the studio's production, see this book's filmography.

36. Writing of the "new social history that dominated Anglo-American historical studies in the 1960s and 1970s," Kafka describes "a certain ambivalence toward the state among the radical academics who pioneered the field. E. P. Thompson's poor stockingers or Joan Wallach Scott's militant glassmakers were members of the working class in a way that clerks never had been" (Kafka, "Paperwork," 341). In cinema, scholarship on John Grierson, to whom some credit the suppression of nonfiction film's radical potential, is an instructive example. See Nichols, "Documentary Film"; and Winston, *Claiming the Real.* This picture is nevertheless changing, as

scholars examine the multiple dimensions of the state's relationship to cinema. For an important reconsideration of the relationship between American documentary and the state, see Kahana, *Intelligence Work*. See also Bloom, *French Colonial Documentary;* Druick, *Projecting Canada;* Grieveson, *Policing Cinema;* Grieveson and MacCabe, *Empire and Film* and *Film and the End of Empire;* Horne, "Experiments in Propaganda"; and Larkin, *Signal and Noise*.

37. For a recent discussion of Weber's conception of the state, violence, and cinema, see Rosen, "Border Times and Geopolitical Frames."

38. Hull, "Documents and Bureaucracy," 253, 260. Other examples of the literature on bureaucracy, documents, and the anthropology of the state include Gupta, *Red Tape;* Hull, *Government of Paper;* Kafka, *The Demon of Writing;* and Sharma and Gupta, *The Anthropology of the State*.

39. As the anthropological literature makes clear, the meaning of states for their populations are internally produced. (See Sharma and Gupta, "Introduction, 10–11.)

40. I thus refer to Czechoslovakia as a "state" instead of a "nation": not only did the state encompass multiple national groups, but within it, the boundaries of national identity were fluid. On the question of the nation in Czechoslovakia, see, e.g., Bryant, "Either German or Czech"; King, *Budweisers into Czechs and Germans;* Wingfield, *Flag Wars and Stone Saints;* Zahra, *Kidnapped Souls*.

41. Kittler, *Gramophone, Film, Typewriter,* xxxix. Virilio writes: "*The history of battle is primarily the history of radically changing fields of perception.* In other words, war consists not so much in scoring territorial, economic or other material victories as in appropriating the 'immateriality' of perceptual fields" (Virilio, *War and Cinema,* 7; emphasis in original). On this concept, see also Shell, *Hide and Seek*.

42. Virilio, *War and Cinema,* 2. During the period this book examines, indeed, the Czechoslovak Army was not actively involved in any major conflict except the Korean War.

43. Elsaesser, "Archives and Archaeologies," 23. On military film production units elsewhere in the world, see, e.g., Richard Koszarski's discussion of the U.S. Signal Corps Photographic Center, "Subway Commandos"; Gladstone, "The APFU" (on the British Army Film and Photographic Unit); and Darret, "Le cinéma au service de l'armée," on the French Army.

44. See, e.g., Jeníček, "Národní pomoc a propaganda," 74.

45. Boček, "Studio, o kterém se málo ví," 4.

46. On the U.S. military's role in the development of postwar cinema exhibition and culture, see Wasson, "Protocols of Portability"; and Waller, "Projecting the Promise of 16mm." See also Streible, Roepke, and Mebold, "Introduction: Nontheatrical Film."

47. Ostrowska, "An Alternative Model," 463.

48. Some of these critiques were relatively benign accusations of formalism. "Here, we must explain the calling of avant-garde cinema today," stated an April 1948 editorial in the film magazine *Kino.* "In the time between the two wars, the old avant garde worked primarily in the field of formal and technical research, and tested various filmic elements. . . . Thanks to them, today's generation has a firm foundation on which to conquer further fields—those of an ideological nature" (Kinos, "O novou avantgardu," 302). Others had tragic consequences: accused of Trotskyism, Záviš Kalandra, an intellectual with ties to Surrealism, was executed in the 1950 show trial that also killed Czechoslovak National Socialist politician Milada Horáková. The tragedy of Kalandra's fate resonates beyond Czechoslovakia, for Paul Éluard, asked by

André Breton to intervene on his friend's behalf, refused (Sayer, *The Coasts of Bohemia*, 255–256). The question of a postwar "post-avant-garde" in Czechoslovakia is explored in depth in Langerová, Vojvodík, Tippnerová, and Hrdlička, *Symboly obludnosti*. On the postwar governmental careers of formers members of the avant garde, see Clybor, "Laughter and Hatred are Neighbors."

49. As Zryd writes, this counters "a romanticized notion of the avant garde as an anti-institutional, revolutionary political praxis." (Zryd, "The Academy and the Avant-Garde," 17). See also Zryd, "Experimental Film"; and Jan-Christopher Horak's argument, in *Lovers of Cinema*, that while "valorization of the independent filmmaker, with the romantic image of the artist that such an inscription entails" has been common in studies of avant-garde cinema, such films should be examined "not only according to their aesthetic achievements, but also in terms of the myriad contexts of their institutional frameworks and reception" (Horak, *Lovers of Cinema*, 4–5).

1. A DEEP AND FRUITFUL TRADITION

1. Balázs, "Three Addresses," 4.
2. Jeníček, "O cílech a úkolech."
3. Navrátil, *Cesty k pravdě či lži*, 68.
4. Orzoff, *Battle for the Castle*, 8.
5. Rothschild, *East Central Europe*, 86.
6. These statistics are recorded by Joseph Rothschild in *East Central Europe*, 89.
7. Such conflicts were common throughout the region. As Joseph Rothschild and Nancy M. Wingfield explain, "An important, often the main, component of the several revisionist-irredentist territorial disputes in interwar East Central Europe was the ethnic one—specifically, one state's interest in politically 'redeeming,' or at least culturally sustaining, a minority of its own nationality that happened to live in another state, and the 'host' state's indignant repudiation of what it regarded

as illicit pressures on its territorial integrity or internal sovereignty." (Rothschild and Wingfield, *Return to Diversity*, 8).

8. Rothschild, *East Central Europe*, 100. Peter Demetz has argued that Czechoslovakia's political survival in the interwar period can be, in part, attributed to the high level of *civic* loyalty among its population, and in particular to German "activists," who "tried to do their best to transform the Czechoslovak state ... into a republic of nationalities." (Demetz, *Prague in Black and Gold*, 342.)

9. For more on the Czechoslovak "myth," see, among others, Abrams, *Struggle for the Soul*; Orzoff, *Battle for the Castle*; and Rak, *Bývalí Čechové*. On myth's role in modern nation building, see, e.g., Anderson, *Imagined Communities*.

10. For more on these themes, see Rak, *Bývalí Čechové*.

11. Orzoff, *Battle for the Castle*, 75.

12. Zeman, "Stát a filmová propaganda," 85.

13. "Film a kinematografie ve státním rozpočtu na rok 1931," 3. On other interwar liberal democracies' engagements with cinema, see Grieveson, "The Cinema and the (Common) Wealth."

14. On film and military secrecy in interwar Czechoslovakia, see the two letters from the Ministry of Defense reproduced in Lucie Česálková's "Žánrové varianty."

15. On filmmaking in the Legions, see Zabloudilová, "Film a fotografie v čs. vojsku."

16. In Zdeněk Štabla's words, the group participated in the "national education of Slovaks" (Štabla, *Data a fakta*, 70). The division's first film to be exhibited theatrically was the actuality film *At the Slovak Government in Žilina* (*U slovenské vlády v Žilině*), which played in the Prague cinemas Lucerna, Invalidů, and Konvikt from January 31 to February 6, 1920 (Štabla, *Data a fakta*, 70 and 84). In Tom Gunning's definition, actuality films were largely produced

before World War I and, as opposed to documentary's "rhetorical and discursive form inserting images into a broader argument or dramatic form," are defined by the *"view,* a descriptive mode based on the act of looking and display" (Gunning, "Before Documentary," 22).

17. Štabla, *Data a fakta,* 85; K. J. V., "Kino: Znamenité pokroky vojenského filmu."

18. The Military Technical Institute would, on January 1, 1933, become the Military Technical and Aviation Institute. See Fidler and Sluka, "Vojenský technický a letecký ústav," 703.

19. For more on *For the Czechoslovak State,* see Rak, "Úvodem k synopsi legionářského filmu"; and Urbanová et al., *Český hraný film I,* 228. On *Slavia-L Brox,* see Urbanová et al., *Český hraný film I,* 183. On *Mountain Calling SOS,* see Urbanová et al., *Český hraný film I,* 71–72.

20. Jeníček describes these modes in his essay "Armáda a film."

21. The quote is an excerpt from Borovský's "Vojsko" (*The Army*), which the journalist—also a key figure in the National Awakening (and, for a time, Němcová's lover)—wrote for the journal *Slovan* between 1850 and 1851.

22. Wingfield, *Flag Wars and Stone Saints.* Petr Szczepanik lists some of the telling titles of articles about film sound published in this period: "The Czech Language in Film," "Film Began to Speak Czech" (Szczepanik, *Konzervy se slovy,* 15). According to Szczepanik, the first Prague screening of a "sound film in the full sense of the term" occurred on August 13, 1929, with the American musical *Show Boat* (ibid., 27).

23. For discussion and analysis of the "contingent" and quota systems implemented throughout Europe in the late 1920s and 1930s, see Higson and Maltby, *"Film Europe" and "Film America."* On the broader cultural and historical issues underlying U.S.-European cinematic relations in this period, see De Grazia, "Mass Culture and Sovereignty."

24. Szczepanik analyzes the Czechoslovak "contingent system" at length in *Konzervy se slovy,* 285–286. See also Klimeš, "Stát a filmová kultura"; and Zeman, "Stát a filmová propaganda ve třicátých letech."

25. Szczepanik, *Konzervy se slovy,* 285. RKO was the only American studio that did not join the boycott.

26. Adolf Hitler was appointed German chancellor in January 1933, and Joseph Goebbels the country's minister of propaganda on March 13 of that year. For a detailed timeline of events in Germany related to cinema and its politics, see Eric Rentschler, "Appendix A." Petr Szczepanik discusses the mechanics by which German films came to dominate the Czechoslovak market (Szczepanik, *Konzervy se slovy,* 285–286); see also Elbl, "Patnáct let filmové politiky."

27. Glassheim, *Noble Nationalists,* 162.

28. As Nancy M. Wingfield notes, the SdP was not "Nazi from the outset." Rather, "it was to the large German community created by the Nazis that the Sudeten German activists looked for support. The Sudeten German community progressively adopted the rhetoric and appearance of the Nazis, including racist language that was virulently anti-Czech/anti-Slav, anti-Semitic, and anti-Communist" (Wingfield, *Flag Wars and Stone Saints,* 233).

29. For more on cultural-propaganda films in this period, see Česálková, "Oběť ve státním zájmu."

30. A MZV Prague, fond III. sekce, 1918–1939, k. 407, Letter from Dr. Papoušek to Jindřich Elbl, October 30, 1933. Elbl, thirty-two years later, recounted the letter's contents in more pointedly nationalist terms, as claiming that the Ministry of Trade's policies were "creating a bastion of Nazi film propaganda in the 350 to 400 cinemas in the Sudeten German region," in "every village in which nary a German

word had been spoken for decades." (Elbl, "Patnáct let filmové politiky," 341.)

31. Elbl, "Patnáct let filmové politiky," 341.

32. Ibid.

33. The text of the agreement between the American studios and the Czechoslovak government included a gesture to concerns about nationality and language, permitting "one American feature film dubbed into the German language" to be distributed to Czechoslovakia" for every eight films imported under the registration system. German-dubbed films, however, were allowed to be screened only in predominantly German-speaking cities (A MZV Prague, fond III. sekce, 1918–1939, k. 400, "Filmy: dovoz amerických filmů—dohoda," January 14, 1935).

34. Klimeš, "Stát a filmová kultura."

35. The Commission's name was shortened, in March 1937, to the Commission for Cultural Propaganda Films (Komise pro kulturně-propagační filmy). For a detailed history of the Commission, its origins, and its activities, see Česálková, "Oběť ve státním zájmu."

36. Pavel Zeman gives some indication of the subjects of Czechoslovak "cultural-propaganda films" at the time, noting that "nature films and advertisements for tourism" were the primary kinds of films funded by the Commission (Zeman, "Stát a filmová propaganda," 85).

37. Another, nongovernmental, instantiation of this idea came with the 1936 founding of the Czechoslovak Film Association, which, as Jaroslav Anděl and Petr Szczepanik write, "support[ed] the production of 'cultural' and educational films, establishing film schools and archives" (Anděl and Szczepanik, "Czech Film Thought—An Introduction," 45.)

38. As Petr Zusi describes, the ideas of function and functionalism can be traced to the National Awakening, when linguistic, literary, artistic and historical projects

helped differentiate Czech culture within the Austro-Hungarian Empire. On this, he quotes Alexej Kusák: "Czech culture inherited a value system that placed functional value … above immanent value. The criterion for this evaluation thus could not be the greatness or originality of a cultural act … but rather its utility, its usefulness in the political struggle of the nation" (Zusi, "Tendentious Modernism," 822, quoted and translated from Kusák, *Kultura a politika v Československu*, 23).

39. Wasson, *Museum Movies*, 12.

40. On the links between national questions and the development of film culture—particularly its institutions (e.g., film archives, schools, and museums; national film histories; etc.)—in the 1930s, see, among others, Hagener, *Moving Forward, Looking Back*; and Wasson, *Museum Movies*. For a detailed discussion of the Czechoslovak case, see Szczepanik, *Konzervy se slovy*.

41. Stašek, "Stát a kinematografie," 5.

42. Elbl, "Hrajte domácí dodatky," 1.

43. Kuba, "Propaganda jako zbraň," 24.

44. Ibid. These arguments echoed justifications for state propaganda made in other democracies during and after World War I, following particularly closely British writings on the subject (exemplified by writings by Stephen Tallents and John Grierson, among others)—as this chapter discusses, a critical model for interwar Czechoslovak propaganda policy and practice.

45. Jeníček, "Národní pomoc a propaganda," 74.

46. Jeníček, "Fotografie a film ve službách."

47. VÚA-VHA Prague, fond MNO Hlavní štáb, Oddělení branné výchovy, k. 215 (1937), sign. 18 5/6–3, J. Elbl to Generální štáb, February 11, 1937. Perhaps not coincidentally, in the same month that Elbl wrote this letter, a representative of the Ministry of Defense, Jiří Letov, was named to the board of the FPS (VÚA-VHA

Prague, fond MNO Hlavní štáb, Oddělení branné výchovy, k. 215 [1937], sign. 18 5/6-74, "Propagační činnost MNO 1937-38").

48. A MZV Prague, fond III. sekce, 1918-1939, k. 402, "Propag. film o naší armádě," April 10, 1937.

49. VÚA-VHA Prague, fond MNO Hlavní štáb, Oddělení branné výchovy, k. 215 (1937), sign. 18 5/6-3, "Propag. film o naší armádě," March 17, 1937.

50. This scene was shot primarily in the military town of Milovice (ibid.).

51. VÚA-VHA Prague, fond MNO Hlavní štáb, Oddělení branné výchovy, k. 215 (1937), sign. 18 5/6-48, "Exploitace filmu 'Naše armada,'" October 20, 1937.

52. VÚA-VHA Prague, fond MNO Hlavní štáb, Oddělení branné výchovy, k. 404 (1939), sign. 18 5/15-5, "Filmy—hlášení nákladů a příjmů," January 31, 1939.

53. VÚA-VHA Prague, fond MNO Hlavní štáb, Oddělení branné výchovy, k. 215 (1937), sign. 18 5/6 85, "Čs. propagační filmy v Německu," November 27, 1937.

54. VÚA-VHA Prague, fond MNO Hlavní štáb, Oddělení branné výchovy, k. 215 (1937), sign. 18 5/6-101, "Československá armada—exploitace v Německu," December 21, 1937.

55. Jeníček is presumably referring to the production of Bedřich Smetana's opera *Prodaná nevěsta* that premiered at Prague's National Theater on October 24, 1936, and ran until October 4, 1938. The costumes and sets for the opera were both designed by Josef Lada, the famed illustrator of Jaroslav Hašek's *The Good Soldier Švejk,* and had the same somewhat caricatured folk elements visible in Lada's illustrations. For the full credits of the production, as well as examples of Lada's costumes, see "Národní divadlo, 'Prodaná nevěsta (Opera).'"

56. VÚA-VHA Prague, Kvalifikační listina (KVL), Jiří Jeníček, nar. 8.3.1895, Beroun.

57. The roots of Czechoslovak amateur photography lie in the Hapsburg period;

as Matthew S. Witkovsky explains, the first club, the Vienna Camera-Club, was founded in the Austrian capital in 1887 (Witkovsky, *Foto,* 13).

58. The "new photography" is explored in depth in Witkovsky's *Foto.* On cultural exchange in interwar Central Europe, see Benson, *Central European Avant-Gardes.*

59. Fárová, *Jiří Jeníček,* 15.

60. Witkovsky, *Foto,* 11.

61. Jeníček, "Něco o nové fotografii," 16.

62. Quoted in Jeníček, *Fotografie jako zření,* 104-105.

63. Jeníček, "Nové proudy v naší fotografii."

64. See Witkovsky, *Foto,* 15-16. The links between modernity and photography's technical dimensions also defined the 1936 International Exhibition of Photography in Prague, of which Jeníček was a co-organizer, and which—like its predecessors elsewhere in the region (e.g., the 1925 Kino- und Photoausstellung [Kipho] exhibit in Berlin)—brought together images from diverse institutional and aesthetic contexts (medical and scientific photographs, reportage, photomontage, etc.). As Jeníček himself recalled about the exhibition, its goal was "only one": "to show decisively what modern photography is!" (Jeníček, *Fotografie jako zření,* 146).

65. Quoted in Jeníček, *Fotografie jako zření,* 106.

66. See, e.g., Teige, "Photo Cinema Film" (1922), Nezval, "*Photogénie*" (1925), and Voskovec, "*Photogénie* and Suprareality" (1925).

67. Jeníček, "Nové proudy v naší fotografii."

68. Jeníček, *Fotografie jako zření,* 124.

69. Jeníček, "Vojáci hrají do filmu." The article builds on ideas developed in Pudovkin's 1929 "*Naturschchik* instead of the Actor." Anděl and Szczepanik date the arrival of Soviet films into Czechoslovak theaters to 1926-1927 (Anděl and Szcze-

panik, "Czech Film Thought: An Introduction," 41).

70. I have been unable to determine Jeníček's political party affiliation, if any. He is described as "leftist" by Antonín Dufek, but given his support of Czechoslovak parliamentary democracy, he was likely not a member of the country's legal Communist Party. Rather, if he was a member of a political party, he probably belonged either to the Social Democratic or National Socialist Party, both of which had strong representation among the interwar political elite (see Dufek, "Fotografie, 1939–1948," 208.)

71. Mansbach, "Methodology and Meaning," 298.

72. Mansbach writes that "allusions to historical myth, events, heroes, and folk styles are as common in Eastern avant-garde designs as they are rare in Western progressive art" (ibid., 296.)

73. Balázs, "Three Addresses," 4.

74. Carter, Introduction, xviii.

75. Ibid.

76. See Carter, "Introduction," xxii–xxiii.

77. Jeníček, Fotografie jako zření, 164–170.

78. Navrátil, Cesty k pravdě či lži, 67.

79. On the Kulturfilm as exhibition category, see, e.g., Hediger and Vonderau, "Record, Rhetoric, Rationalization," 44. For more on the short film in interwar Czechoslovakia, see work by Lucie Česálková, e.g., Film před tabulí, "Oběť ve státním zájmu," and "Žánrové varianty."

80. Uricchio, "The Kulturfilm," 356.

81. Jeníček, Krátký film, 5.

82. Jeníček, "Vojenský film," 165. In this, once again, Jeníček's writings echoed Balázs's, in which Mattias Frey observes a "tension between the universal and the nationally specific," the notion that cinema, while universally legible, is also capable of expressing national identity (Frey, "Cultural Problems of Classical Film Theory," 325).

83. Jeníček, "Národní pomoc a propaganda," 74.

84. Ibid.

85. Jeníček, Krátký film, 27; 30–31.

86. Ibid., 26.

87. Jeníček, Krátký film, 25.

88. VÚA-VHA Prague, fond MNO Hlavní štáb, Oddělení branné výchovy, k. 332 (1938), sign. 18 5/11–4, "Propag. film 'Vojáci v horách,'" January 19, 1938. Emphasis in original.

89. Ibid.

90. Georges Sadoul was a film critic for Regards. See Abel, French Film Theory and Criticism, 147.

91. Jeníček, "Anglický příklad."

92. For more on fi-fo, see Anděl and Szczepanik, Cinema All the Time, 46. For more on the Workers Film and Photo League, see Kahana, Intelligence Work, 69–71.

93. Benjamin, "The Author as Producer," 95.

94. Witkovsky, Foto, 157.

95. Anděl and Szczepanik, Cinema All the Time, 46; Linhart, "The Proletarian Film Struggle in Czechoslovakia," 188.

96. Elsaesser, "Archives and Archaeologies," 22.

97. Jeníček, "Anglický příklad."

98. Cavalcanti, "The Neo-Realist Movement in England," 236–237.

99. Much has been written about the Baťa studio. See, e.g., Szczepanik, "Modernism, Industry, Film." On the concept of "function" in industrial film, see Zimmermann, "What Hollywood Is to America," 110; and Szczepanik, "Modernism, Industry, Film," 362.

100. Kučera, "Advertising and Cinematic Art," 182. Aktualita was founded in 1937 with Ministry of Foreign Affairs support. For more on Aktualita, see Margry, "Newsreels in Nazi-Occupied Czechoslovakia."

101. Jeníček, Krátký film, 27,

102. Bajkay, "Dessau," 224.

103. VÚA-VHA Prague, fond MNO Hlavní štáb, Oddělení branné výchovy, k. 404 (1939), sign. 18 5/23, "Personál pro filmovou skupinu," March 11, 1939.

104. Navrátil, *Jiří Lehovec*, 14–16.

105. VÚA-VHA Prague, fond MNO Hlavní štáb, Oddělení branné výchovy, k. 332 (1938), sign. 18 5/11, "Výrobní podpora filmu Armáda v horách," January 25, 1938.

106. VÚA-VHA Prague, fond MNO Hlavní štáb, Oddělení branné výchovy, k. 332 (1938), sign. 18 5/11–4, "Propag. film 'Vojáci v horách,'" January 19, 1938. Emphasis in the original.

107. Ibid.; emphasis in the original. Sound was so important to Jeníček's conception of the film that he refused to let the Czechoslovak Red Cross reduce it to 16mm for nontheatrical distribution, as the loss of sound on the silent 16mm versions would damage the film's effect (VÚA-VHA Prague, fond MNO Hlavní štáb, Oddělení branné výchovy, k. 332 [1938], sign. 18 5/11–27, "'Vojáci v horách,' redukce na 16mm film," January 3, 1939).

108. VÚA-VHA Prague, fond MNO Hlavní štáb, Oddělení branné výchovy, k. 332 (1938), sign. 18 5/11–4, "Propag. film 'Vojáci v horách,'" January 19, 1938.

109. Srnka was a well-known composer for short films.

110. VÚA-VHA Prague, fond MNO Hlavní štáb, Oddělení branné výchovy, k. 332 (1938), sign. 18 5/11–4, "Propag. film 'Vojáci v horách,'" January 19, 1938.

111. VÚA-VHA Prague, fond MNO Hlavní štáb, Oddělení branné výchovy, k. 332 (1938), sign. 18 5/11–6, "Film '"Vojáci v horách,' pracovní deník," May 31, 1938.

112. Navrátil, "Jiří Lehovec: Portrét dokumentaristy," 384–385. Headquartered at the Barrandov film studios—which were founded in 1933 in Prague by Václav Havel (grandfather of Czechoslovakia's first post-1989 president)—AB's short film studio was formed in 1936 and led by filmmaker Jiří Weiss until 1938.

113. VÚA-VHA Prague, fond MNO Hlavní štáb, Oddělení branné výchovy, k. 332 (1938), sign. 18 5/11–15, "'Vojáci v horách' upozornění [illeg.] tisku."

114. Jeníček's use of the term "Czechness" in a film ostensibly about multinationalism nevertheless speaks to the persistent national biases in interwar Czechoslovakia.

115. jr, title unknown, *Národní listy*, October 14, 1938, quoted in Navrátil, *Cesty k pravdě či lži*, 68.

116. "Naše filmy do New Yorku," 2. On cinema at the 1939 World's Fair, see Wasson, "The Other Small Screen."

117. VÚA-VHA Prague, fond MNO Hlavní štáb, Oddělení branné výchovy, k. 215 (1937), sign. 18 5/7–6, "Návrh na zavedení registr. poplatku na cizí dodatky," May 12, 1937.

118. VÚA-VHA Prague, fond MNO Hlavní štáb, Oddělení branné výchovy, k. 332 (1938), sign. 18 5/21–3, "Čsl. aktuality v německých zvukových týdenících," June 27, 1938.

119. VÚA-VHA Prague, fond MNO Hlavní štáb, Oddělení branné výchovy, k. 332 (1938), sign. 18 5/28, Letter from Kinotechnica, June 2, 1938. Beneš had been elected in 1937, after Masaryk's death.

120. Jeníček discusses the film's production in "Herci filmové reportáže,'" 8.

121. For more on the rhetorical structure of the "argument" in propaganda and documentary, see Gunning, "Before Documentary."

122. Navrátil, *Jiří Lehovec*, 14.

123. Kahana, *Intelligence Work*, 7.

124. ts, "V nový život," 4.

125. Grieveson, "The Cinema and the (Common) Wealth."

126. In the United States, for instance, Jonathan Kahana describes the collaboration between "radical and experimental artists, liberals working in both policy and publicity capacities in state institutions, and the owners and operators of

the communications industry" (Kahana, *Intelligence Work*, 67). Malte Hagener discusses other national cases, including "Stalinist cinema of the 1930s . . . the British documentary movement . . . the French front populaire and the fascist avant-gardes in Germany, Portugal and Italy" with the American and British cases (Hagener, *Moving Forward, Looking Back*, 165).

127. VÚA-VHA Prague, fond MNO Hlavní štáb, Oddělení branné výchovy, k. 404 (1939), sign. 18 5/15–4, "Vojenské filmy—otázka rozpočtová," February 14, 1939.

128. Navrátil, *Jiří Lehovec*, 21. See Demetz, *Prague in Danger*, 192–208, for a detailed discussion of film institutions during this period.

129. Elbl, "Patnáct let filmové politiky 1933–1948."

130. Havelka, *Kdo byl kdo*, 107.

2. ALL OF FILM IS AN EXPERIMENT

1. E. F. B., Untitled.

2. The French film festival took place in Prague from March 22 to April 5; the Soviet from May 17 to 31 in Prague and from June 3 to 5 in Bratislava; and the British from September 27 to October 13 in Prague, continuing afterward in Bratislava and Brno (Havelka, *Čs. filmové hospodářství, 1945–1950*, 57–58).

3. Kusák, *Kultura a politika v Československu*, 188.

4. Weiss, "Film se rodí."

5. Weiss, "Krátký film."

6. The Soviet Army liberated most of Czechoslovakia in May 1945, although the U.S. Army had liberated part of western Bohemia the previous month.

7. Historian Bradley F. Abrams writes that the Košice Program represented an only slightly modified version of the Communist Party's "blueprint for immediate structural changes in the republic" (Abrams, *Struggle for the Soul*, 55).

8. Rice, *The Soviet Union and the Czechoslovak Army*, 39.

9. Frommer, *National Cleansing*, 33–34.

10. Abrams, *Struggle for the Soul*, 181; Wingfield, "Politics of Memory," 253.

11. Wingfield, *Flag Wars and Stone Saints*, 266.

12. Glassheim, "Ethnic Cleansing."

13. Shore, *The Taste of Ashes*, 109.

14. For a detailed account of these events, see, e.g., Bryant, *Prague in Black*, 263.

15. Abrams, *Struggle for the Soul*, 181.

16. Havelka, *Kronika našeho filmu*, 21.

17. On the expansion of informational and educational film production and exhibition during the war, see, e.g., Acland, "Celluloid Classrooms and Everyday Projectionists"; Waller, "Projecting the Promise of 16mm"; and Wasson, "Protocols of Portability."

18. O.K., "Současnost a budoucnost krátkého filmu," 7. For a detailed history of Krátký Film's first fifteen years, see Česálková, "Nedostižné tempo růstu a zbrzděná avantgarda," 228.

19. NAČR Prague, fond KSČ-ÚV-02/04: KSČ-Ústřední vybor, 1945–1989, Praha—sekretariat, 1945–1951, sv. 11, a.j. 115, bod. 1, "Otazky filmu," April 12, 1950. Weiss's activities as a documentarian for the Czechoslovak state had in fact continued almost uninterrupted since 1939, when he fled the country. In London exile, Weiss worked for various state-administered documentary enterprises, making films for the Czechoslovak government and British Crown Film Unit and newsreels for the Soviet government.

20. *Dekret presidenta republiky.*

21. VÚA-VHA Prague, fond MNO 1945, Hl. št., 1 odděl., k. 27, čj. 11125, "Výcvikové filmy—zatímní směrnice," September 7, 1945.

22. VÚA-VHA Prague, fond MNO 1946, Hl. št., 1 odděl., k. 87, čj. 24/13/5, 9, 17, "Návrh směrnic pro výrobu vojenských filmů," October 17, 1946.

23. Rice, *The Soviet Union and the Czechoslovak Army*, 47.

24. VÚA-VHA Prague, fond MNO 1945, Hl. št., 1 odděl., k. 27, čj. 11125, "Výcvikové filmy—zatímní směrnice," September 7, 1945.

25. Jeníček, "O cílech a úkolech."

26. VÚA-VHA Prague, fond MNO 1946, Hl. št., 1 odděl., k. 87, čj. 24/13/5, 9, 17, "Návrh směrnic pro výrobu vojenských filmů," October 17, 1946.

27. Ibid.

28. Rice, *The Soviet Union and the Czechoslovak Army,* 49.

29. VÚA-VHA Prague, fond MNO 1946, Hl. št., 1 odděl., k. 87, čj. 24/13/5, 9, 17, "Návrh směrnic pro výrobu vojenských filmů," October 17, 1946.

30. This book's filmography includes the titles of Ministry of Defense productions that I have been able to locate in various sources, but the list may not be complete.

31. In its finished form, the film was directed by Jaroslav Váchal. See filmography for details.

32. In 1945, Czechoslovakia ceded Subcarpathian Ruthenia to the Soviet Union.

33. VÚA-VHA Prague, fond MNO 1946, Hl. št., 1 odděl., k. 87, čj. 24/13/5, 9, 17, "Natáčení krátkého filmu—předložení námětu," January 7, 1946.

34. Ibid.

35. Knapík, *Únor a kultura,* 33.

36. Ibid., 47–48.

37. Rice, *The Soviet Union and the Czechoslovak Army,* 59.

38. I thank Paul Lenormand for discussing the Army's postwar purges with me.

39. VÚA-VHA Prague, Kvalifikační listina (KVL), Jiří Jeníček, nar. 8.3.1895, Beroun.

40. Knapík, *V zajetí moci,* 46. On 1950's significance, see also Zarecor, *Manufacturing a Socialist Modernity,* 120.

41. The Czechoslovak National Socialist Party was center-left and had no relationship to the Nazi Party.

42. Zarecor, *Manufacturing a Socialist Modernity,* 24.

43. Svoboda was briefly imprisoned in 1951 yet had returned to public life by the mid-1950s. In 1968, he would be elected president.

44. Karel Kaplan discusses Čepička's relationship to Stalin in his *Kronika komunistického Československa;* see, e.g., 120.

45. On the military's growth in this period, see Pernes, Pospíšil, and Lukáš, *Alexej Čepička,* 225–226.

46. Ibid., 218, 223; Kaplan, *Sovětští poradci v Československu,* 82.

47. Pernes, Pospíšil, Lukáš, *Alexej Čepička,* 231–232; Petišková, *Československý socialistický realismus,* 61. These institutions were themselves the subject of Army films of the 1950s, among them *The Army Artistic Theater (Armádní umělecké divadlo), The Czechoslovak Army Theater (Divadlo čs. armády),* and *The Army Theater in Martin (Armádní divadlo Martin).*

48. Rice, *The Soviet Union and the Czechoslovak Army,* 75.

49. Ibid., 76.

50. VÚA-VHA Prague, fond MNO 1954, k. 54, sign. 22 5/4, "Zpráva o činnosti ČAF." For details, see the filmography to this book, although this list may also be incomplete.

51. SA AČR Olomouc, fond 397, k. 1, sv. 38/5 (Tajné spisy 1955), "Statut Československého armádního filmu—předložení ke schválení," April 23, 1955.

52. Šmidrkal, *Armáda a stříbrné plátno,* 9.

53. Knapík, *Únor a kultura,* 48.

54. SA AČR Olomouc, fond 397, k. 1, sv. 38/5 (Tajné spisy 1955), "Statut Československého armádního filmu—předložení ke schválení," April 23, 1955.

55. Čepička, "Dokonalejším využitím."

56. Hanuš, *Podoby Františka Vláčila,* 4.

57. VÚA-VHA Prague, fond MNO 1955, k. 41, sign. 24/19/1, "Dohoda mezi ministerstvem kultury a ministerstvem národní obrany o vytvoření tvůrčí skupiny ve Studiu hraných uměleckých filmů

Československého státního filmu"; Rubáš, "O nové organisaci v laboratořích," 5.

58. VÚA-VHA Prague, fond MNO 1954, k. 74, sign. 18/11, "Výměna armádního kina—výsledek jednání," February 24, 1954; VÚA-VHA Prague, fond MNO 1954, k. 634, sign. 77, "Kino Lucerna—převzetí," July 16, 1954. The Army had received the Divadlo komedie space from the Ministry of Information in 1946 (NAČR Prague, fond MI 1945–1953, k. 201, sv. Praha-MNO, i.č. 246, "Zřízení oblastních kin pro účely MNO," August 15, 1946). The 1953 transfer thus effectively restored the theater—originally that of interwar director Vlasta Burian—to the Burian family.

59. VÚA-VHA Prague, fond MNO 1954, k. 34–35, sign. 24 19/1, "Rozbor situace ve výrobě uměleckého hraného filmu—připomínky."

60. VÚA-VHA Prague, fond MNO 1955, k. 41, sign. 24/19/1, "Dohoda mezi ministerstvem kultury a ministerstvem národní obrany o vytvoření tvůrčí skupiny ve Studiu hraných uměleckých filmů Československého státního filmu." Petr Szczepanik discusses this production group in "'Machři' a 'diletanti,'" 64–65.

61. Hediger and Vonderau, Films That Work, 39.

62. Ferro, "Y a-t-il 'trop de démocratie,'" 817, 821–822.

63. Ibid., 817.

64. McDermott, "A 'Polyphony of Voices'?," 864. Infighting, factionalism, and competition within the Czechoslovak Communist Party is a well-documented phenomenon. Czech cultural historian Jiří Knapík (Únor a kultura) and film historians such as Pavel Skopal ("Filmy z nouze") have analyzed this phenomenon with regard to cinema.

65. On Kopecky, see VÚA-VHA Prague, fond MNO 1954, k. 34–35, sign. 24 19/1, "Rozbor situace ve výrobě uměleckého hraného filmu—připomínky." The description of state-socialist "government intervention" in cinema as "totalizing" in

fact echoes the common understanding of Hollywood as a "monolithic media industry" that Jennifer Holt and Alisa Perren critique. In Hollywood, too, they write, "even during the 1930s and 1940s there were numerous stakeholders within the industries that had different agendas" (Holt and Perren, "Introduction," 4).

66. Purš, Obrysy vývoje československé znárodněné kinematografie, 193–194.

67. Ibid., 196. On the adoption of socialist realism in Czechoslovak architecture, see Zarecor, Manufacturing a Socialist Modernity, 113–176. On music, see Knapík, V zajetí moci, 50. On the visual arts, see Petišková, Československý socialistický realismus.

68. Zhdanov, "Speech to the Congress," 427–428.

69. Petišková, Československý socialistický realismus, 17.

70. Pozner, "Le 'réalisme socialiste,'" 12. The interplay between form and social context that Pozner raises is fundamental to studies of socialist realism. Some recent examples include Evgeny Dobrenko's Political Economy of Socialist Realism, in which he argues that socialist realism was "one of the most significant social institutions of Stalinism—an institution for the production of socialism" (xii); Katerina Clark's "Socialist Realism with Shores," where she writes that "socialist realism is not to any marked degree performing an aesthetic function" (27); and Leonid Heller's "A World of Prettiness," which describes the "categories" in which socialist realism is typically discussed as "in essence deeply ideological and not simply 'aesthetic'" (51).

71. Quoted from "O výtvarnictví, hudbě a poezii," in Petišková, Československý socialistický realismus, 25.

72. Štoll, 30 let bojů. On Štoll, see Abrams, Struggle for the Soul, 59.

73. Connelly, Captive University, 55.

74. Zarecor, Manufacturing a Socialist Modernity, 131.

75. Ibid., 119.

76. Purš, *Obrysy vývoje československé znárodněné kinematografie*, 194.

77. Clark, *The Soviet Novel*, 10.

78. These included, as Ivan Klimeš notes, a series of biographical films about National Awakening figures and key national artists of the twentieth century (Smetana, Jirásek, Němcová, Neruda, Dvořák, etc.; see Klimeš, "K povaze historismu," 83). For more on these themes, see Kouba, "Průvodce po krajinách sorely." Army Film's *Master Jan Hus* (*Mistr Jan Hus*) was a similar film.

79. Urbanová et al., *Český hraný film III*, 314.

80. Zvoníček, "O filmu 'Tanková brigada,'" 523.

81. Čarnický, "'Zítra se bude promítat všude'," 363. As Anna Batistová details, the number of permanent cinemas in the Czech lands increased from 1,418 in 1945 to 2,545 in 1950; by 1955, it had fallen to 2,396 (Batistová, "Cesta k soběstačnosti," 462). Batistová's essay also lists the types of cinemas within the cinefication plan (435n12). On the expansion in small-gauge film, particularly 16mm, and its use in educational settings in interwar Czechoslovakia, see Česálková, "Film před tabulí"; and Horníček, "The Institutionalization of Classroom Films."

82. Batistová, "Cesta k soběstačnosti," 435n12; Česálková, "Film v místech 'nevyužitého času'"; *Filmové informace* no. 28 (July 10, 1952): 7.

83. By, "Putovní kina v našem kinofikačním plánu." The numbers cited here are drawn from Batistová, "Cesta k soběstačnosti," 462.

84. NAČR Prague, fond MI 1945–1953, k. 227, sv. "Libochovany," "Předvádění normálních filmů v Libochovanech u Litoměřic, žádost místního národního výboru," October 10, 1945.

85. Čarnický, "Zítra se bude promítat všude," 361–362.

86. NAČR Prague, fond MI 1945–1953, k. 228, sv. Maďarsko—různé, "Směrnice pro

provedení Dohody o výměně obyvatelstva mezi ČSR a Maďarskem," March 6, 1946. Leslie Waters discusses the Hungarian-Slovak population exchange in "National Displacement."

87. On this function in mobile cinemas elsewhere, see, e.g., Emma Widdis's *Visions of a New Land*, where she writes that Soviet mobile cinemas "brought national 'news' to the village, seeking to transform peasants and workers into participants, or citizens, of the new state" (14). Similarly, Lee Grieveson describes 1920s British mobile cinema vans' role in "making government mobile and capable of circulating among the new electorate" (Grieveson, "The Cinema and the [Common] Wealth," 83). On mobility in postwar cinema culture more broadly, see Acland, "Curtains, Carts, and the Mobile Screen"; and Wasson, "Protocols of Portability."

88. Žalman, "Venkove, dočkal ses!," 71.

89. Batistová, "Cesta k soběstačnosti," 462.

90. "Vítězná posádka," 262.

91. On the Working People's Film Festival, see Havel, "'O nového člověka." On Film Spring in the Village, see Květová, "Filmové jaro na vesnici."

92. Jeníček, "Armáda a film."

93. NAČR Prague, fond MI 1945–1953, k. 228, sv. Maďarsko—různé, "Vyžiadanie automobilov pre pojazdné kina k akcii presídlovania Slovákov z Maďarska," July 1, 1946.

94. kt, "Vojenské kino ve VVT." Screenings by mobile military cinemas typically accommodated between three and four hundred spectators and were managed by specially trained soldiers who transported films and projectors (typically two 16mm Alma projectors and one 35mm Prometa M. 1000 projector) between bases, where they set up a 2.5 × 2-meter screen outside, or in specially adapted barns ("Pojízdné kino u vojáků").

95. VÚA-VHA Prague, *Věcní věstník Ministerstva národní obrany*, no. 69, Octo-

ber 27, 1950, čj. 15 064-HPS z 23/10 1950; Čepička, "Dokonalejším využitím."

96. VÚA-VHA Prague, Ministerstvo národní obrany, Sbírka výnosů z oboru výchovy a osvěty. Rok 1949, no. 37, December 24, 1949, "Závady ve výběru filmů pro VZ seznam doporučených filmů."

97. NAČR Prague, fond KSČ-ÚV-02/5, KSČ-Ústřední výbor, 1945–1989, Praha— politický sekretariát, 1951–1954, sv. 15, aj. 80, bod. 1, "Zpráva o přípravách na I. čs. armádní filmový festival," January 26, 1952. The studio made a film about the festival in 1952 (see filmography).

98. Věstník Československého státního filmu no. 10 (October 25, 1952): 57

99. Virilio, War and Cinema, 2.

100. Jeníček, "Armáda a film."

101. Szczepanik, "Modernism, Industry, Film," 359.

102. Such films also included Song-Hardened Steel (Ocel písní kalená), about military song and its Soviet "example," The Alexandrov Ensemble in Czechoslovakia (Alexandrovci u nás), JVS (Josef V. Stalin), and the paeans to Gottwald Farewell to Klement Gottwald (Rozloučení s Klementem Gottwaldem) and Memory (Vzpomínka). Science Goes with the People (Věda jde s lidem) adapted Party intellectuals Zdeněk Nejedlý and Ladislav Štoll's 1952 text of the same title.

103. Filmový přehled, no. 9 (March 6, 1954): 9–10.

104. The novel was re-released in a children's version by the State Editions of Children's Books, with an introduction by Minister of Education Zdeněk Nejedlý ("our best expert on Alois Jirásek"; see Jirásek, Psohlavci).

105. Filmový přehled, no. 9 (March 6, 1954): 9. Ferko's story followed a common trope in East European documentary of the 1950s. In Polish director Andrzej Munk's 1951 Destination Nowa Huta! (Kierunek—Nowa Huta!), e.g., we are introduced to young workers constructing the grand

Nowa Huta housing estate, who are framed as both young builders of socialism and as individuals whose personal development (as in Ferko's case) maps neatly onto the city's development.

106. Conley, Cartographic Cinema, 209.

107. See Glassheim, "Ethnic Cleansing," 70.

108. Public Records Office (PRO), Foreign Office (FO) 371/71352, "Confidential Report, British Embassy, Prague, 5th August 1948," p. 1, quoted in Pittaway, Brief Histories: Eastern Europe, 43.

109. Jasný and Kachyňa's Chinese counterparts in People of One Heart are listed in this book's filmography. Other short films made as part of the Czechoslovak-Chinese alliance were Old Chinese Opera (Stará čínská opera), From a Chinese Notebook (Z čínského zápisníku), Long Live Mao Tse-Tung (Ať žije Mao Ce-tung), The Monkey Emperor Receives a Weapon in the Palace of the Dragon Emperor (Opičí císař dostává zbraň v paláci Dracího císaře), and Greetings to a Great Land (Pozdrav veliké země).

110. Knapik, V zajetí moci, 56.

111. Vláčil also made Czechoslovak Sport Shooters in China (Naši sportovní střelci v Číně) and Svazarm in China (Svazarm v Číně) during this trip. Army Film's collaboration with China was not its only engagement with East Asia; Korea and the Korean War were also favored topics. Films on Korea included They Shall Not Pass (Korea) (Neprojdou [Korea]), Building Korea (Budující Korea), The Czechoslovak Hospital in Korea (Čs. nemocnice v Koreji), Divided Land (Rozdělená země), The Korean Military Delegation's Visit to Czechoslovakia (Návštěva korejské vojenské delegace v Československu), Bloodless Battle (Nekrvavá bitva), The Good Will Mission (Mise dobré vůle), and 650 Million (650 milionů).

112. In addition to articles about Sís and Vaniš's expedition, for instance, the filmmakers' own travelogue was published in eight illustrated installments

in *Československý voják* (No. 15 [8-9], no. 16 [20-22], no. 17 [24-25], no. 18 [24-25], no. 19 [22-23], no. 20 [24-26], no. 21 [28-29], and no. 22 [29]). In this, Soviet ethnographic documentaries of the late 1920s were presumably a model: As Emma Widdis writes, these frequently had print counterparts that "describ[ed] in detail the daily trials and adventures the travelers encounter[ed]" (Widdis, *Visions of a New Land*, 115). See also Čech, Jasný, and Kachyňa, *Byli jsme v zemi květů*.

113. *Filmový přehled*, no. 37 (September 19, 1953): 4.

114. Vojtěch Jasný, interview with the author, Prague, January 15, 2008.

115. Jasný, Kachyňa, and Ling, "Rodí se společné dílo," 24. Czechoslovak literary reportage of the 1950s paid considerable attention to China; see Janoušek, *Dějiny české literatury*, 2:265-269.

116. Ostrava was also a focal point for cultural productions in the 1950s, among them the military-parade film *Triumphant March*, discussed later in this chapter. For an in-depth examination of Ostrava's built environment and its position in postwar Czechoslovakia's cultural and political landscape, see Zarecor, *Manufacturing a Socialist Modernity*.

117. i.š., "Lidé jednoho srdce," 20.

118. Jasný, Kachyňa, and Ling, "Rodí se společné dílo." The trip to Moscow was nevertheless a watershed moment for Jasný, who recalls it as the moment when he gained full awareness of Stalin's terror (Jasný, interview with the author, Prague, January 15, 2008).

119. NAČR Prague, fond KSČ-ÚV-02/5, KSČ-Ústřední výbor, 1945-1989, Praha—politický sekretariát, 1951-1954, sv. 67, aj. 183, bod. 13, "Vyslání dvoučlenné skupiny pracovníků ČAF do Číny," October 29, 1953.

120. It is unclear how much the filmmakers themselves knew about the project at the outset. Čepička's report to the Central

Committee describes the road as "strategic," while Sís's son, author Peter Sís, writes that his "father found himself in the highest mountain range in the world, in what was described to him as a remote western province of China. Gradually, he learned that this 'western province' was actually Tibet and that he had been sent to film a military operation—the construction of a highway that would open Tibet to China" (Sís, "The Story behind the Book").

121. Sís and Vaniš, "Natáčeli jsme v Tibetu."

122. Beyond their cameras and boxes, the filmmakers were outfitted with a range of special equipment, including a generator, a mobile laboratory, sound materials, and mountaineering gear (Beba, "Cesta čs. filmařů").

123. Sís, "The Story behind the Book."

124. On such tropes, see, e.g., Griffiths, *Wondrous Difference*, 105; and Widdis, *Visions of a New Land*, 115.

125. Sís and Vaniš, "Natáčeli jsme v Tibetu."

126. Beba, "Cesta čs. filmařů."

127. Ibid. The "Pragovka" was a military truck.

128. Many of these were borrowed from Soviet traditions (e.g., International Women's Day and the yearly commemoration of the Great October Revolution).

129. Petišková, *Československý socialistický realismus*, 73.

130. NAČR Prague, fond KSČ-ÚV-02/5, KSČ-Ústřední výbor, 1945-1989, Praha—politický sekretariát, 1951-1954, sv. 24, aj. 94, bod. 34, "Návrh na některá organisační opatření související i civilní části přehlídky čsl. armády, SNB a milic v Praze dne 9. V. 1952," May 5, 1952.

131. This narrative model was particular to military-parade films of this period, though such films continued to be made throughout the studio's history. See this book's filmography for more details.

132. The Old Town Hall (Staroměstská radnice) was damaged during the Prague Uprising of this month.

133. "Lidová armáda pochoduje," 328.

134. *Military Parade 1951* premiered at that year's Karlovy Vary Film Festival (ibid.).

135. Ibid.

136. NAČR Prague, fond KSČ-ÚV-02/5, KSČ-Ústřední výbor, 1945–1989, Praha—politický sekretariát, 1951–1954, sv. 36, aj. 110, bod. 16, "Návrh na uspořádání leteckých dnů v září 1952 v rámci 'Dne československého letectva,'" August 13, 1952. The youth paramilitary organization Svazarm (Svaz pro spolupráci s armádou) played an important role in these holidays, as it did in the films about them.

137. See this book's filmography for a more detailed accounting of such films, which, like military-parade films, were produced throughout the studio's history.

138. This sequence is, in fact, a near-replica of the opening sequence in British director Humphrey Jennings and Stewart McAllister's 1943 film *Listen to Britain*, underscoring British cinema's lasting influence on Czechoslovak cinema.

139. Widdis, *Visions of a New Land*, 135.

140. Zápotocký, previously prime minister, was elected president in March 1953 upon Klement Gottwald's death.

141. *Filmový přehled*, no. 40 (October 5, 1951): 8. In fact, the caption for a full-page illustration in the May 6, 1951, issue of *Obrana lidu* announced that it was not just the films but the parades themselves that were modeled after the Soviet "genre": "The Soviet Army's military parades," it proclaimed, "are our model."

142. On Soviet documentary of the Stalinist period, see Widdis, *Visions of a New Land*.

143. ts, "V nový život," 4.

144. On this format, see Druick, *Projecting Canada*.

145. Česálková, "Noví noví lidé."

146. "Světová unie filmových dokumentaristů." At the time, Ivens was based in Prague, working on his film about postwar reconstruction in Eastern Europe, *The First Years* (*Pierwse lata*).

147. BFI National Archive Special Collections, BCW/3/23, Basil Wright Files, "First Congress of the World Union of Documentary," "Appendix 'B': Constitution of the World Union of Documentary."

148. BFI National Archive Special Collections, BCW/3/23, Basil Wright Files, "First Congress of the World Union of Documentary." Plans for the World Union of Documentary had been made the previous year at a meeting of documentarians at the Brussels Film Festival (see Lehovec, "Dokumentaristé sněmovali," 1).

149. Two of the interwar paramilitary aviation films were directed by Jiří Weiss at AB: *Give Us Wings* (*Dejte nám křídla*, 1936) and *Harbor in a Sea of Air* (*Přístav vzdušného moře*, 1937), both of which were included in a 1938 "List of films and illustrated lectures for the promotion of defense." (VÚA-VHA Prague, fond MNO Hlavní štáb, Oddělení branné výchovy, k. 330 [1938], sign. 18 5/2–22, "Seznam filmů a přednášek s diapositivy k propagaci brannosti," April 12, 1938.)

150. On similar issues in the U.S. case, see, e.g., Wasson, "Protocols of Portability."

151. Taborsky, *Communism in Czechoslovakia*, 117.

152. NAČR Prague, fond KSČ-ÚV-02/2, KSČ-Ústřední výbor, 1945–1989, Praha—politické byro, 1954–1962, sv. 180, aj. 244, bod 15.

153. See, e.g., Liehm, "Nad Tankovou brigádou."

3. THE CROOKED MIRROR

1. VÚA-VHA Prague, fond MNO 1955, k. 376, sign. 24/4/1, "Projev zástupce armádního filmu," March 31, 1955.

2. VÚA-VHA Prague, fond MNO 1952, k. 16, sign. 24 4/2–4, "Komentář

k sovětským vojenským výcvikovým
filmům." Emphasis added.

3. On Soviet advisors in Czechoslovakia, see Kaplan, *Sovětští poradci v
Československu.*

4. Pernes, Pospíšil, and Lukáš, *Alexej
Čepička,* 218, 223.

5. Twenty-five Soviet training films
were subtitled in Czech in 1953, and seventeen were dubbed into Czech. (VÚA-VHA
Prague, fond MNO 1955, k. 74, sign. 24/4/1,
"Zpráva o výrobě výcvikových filmů," December 23, 1953.)

6. As chapter 2 discusses, this formal
definition of the "model" was reflected in
the Communist Party's 1950 directive on
cinema.

7. These were the primary categories
of instructional film produced by Army
Film during the 1950s and 1960s, although
other terms, such as "school" (*školní*),
educational, popular-scientific, reportage,
and "shot" were also used. For more on the
educational or school film, see Česálková,
Film před tabulí.

8. VÚA-VHA Prague, fond MNO 1955,
k. 376, sign. 24/4/1, "Projev zástupce armádního filmu," March 31, 1955.

9. "Film jako lidová universita."

10. Skopal, "Filmy z nouze," 79.

11. Ibid., 81.

12. Ibid. Skopal describes this practice
as existing between 1951 and 1953.

13. Gunning, *D.W. Griffith,* 91–93. On
the film lecturer, see also Musser, *High-
Class Moving Pictures.* In a broader sense,
this active, dual mode of spectatorship is
central to pedagogical media practices.
See, e.g., Acland, "Celluloid Classrooms
and Everyday Projectionists"; McCarthy,
"Screen Culture and Group Discussion";
and Waller, "Cornering *The Wheat Farmer.*"
McCarthy's essay offers a particularly
provocative analogue to Army Film's 1950s
productions, demonstrating that, at the
height of the Cold War, approaches to

"modeling" liberal and socialist citizenship
were similar.

14. VÚA-VHA Prague, fond MNO 1955,
k. 376, sign. 24/4/1, "Projev zástupce armádního filmu," March 31, 1955. Emphasis
in the original.

15. Ibid. Emphasis in the original.

16. Ibid.

17. Ibid. Zavřel's statement recalls
Jeníček's contradictory praise of soldiers as
actors—written, however, in reference to
silent film: "Our soldiers are good film in-
terpreters; they are not shy, and have all the
characteristics of the figures we know from
Russian silent cinema" (Jeníček, "Vojáci
hrají do filmu").

18. Such expectations are common to
certain types of training films, as Stephen
Groening details in an essay on films produced by the Western Union telegraph
company in the 1920s. While, he writes,
"the discipline of film studies has resisted
... portrayals of film audiences as en-
thralled, hypnotized, and easily influenced
... training films *depend* on their audiences
imitating the characters, actions, and habits
portrayed in film" (Groening, "'We Can
See Ourselves,'" 40).

19. Anna McCarthy reaches a similar
conclusion about "antinaturalistic" acting
in postwar American race relations films in
"Screen Culture and Group Discussion,"
writing that "part of [these films'] educational value lay in the manifestly antinaturalistic performances they contained. Role-
play's wooden acting provided viewers with
a tangible reminder of the valued sociological distinction between individuals and
their social roles" (404).

20. VÚA-VHA Prague, fond MNO
1954, k. 249, sign. 24/4/1–2, "Odminování
průchodů: Literární scénář."

21. VÚA-VHA Prague, fond MNO
1955, k. 74, sign. 24/4/1, "Zpráva o výrobě
výcvikových filmů," December 23, 1953.
"Advisors," here, does not refer to Soviet

advisors but, rather, to the professional military advisors assigned to the film.

22. VÚA-VHA Prague, fond MNO 1951, sign. 24/4/2, "Plán na výrobu vojenských výcvikových filmů v roce 1953: Vojín při zteči." It is unclear if this film was ever completed; in its finished version, it may have been Kachyňa and Jasný's 1953 *Na stráži* (*On Guard*).

23. Such fractures were evidently common to other military film studios that employed filmmakers with "civilian" filmmaking backgrounds. On the U.S. case, see Koszarski, "Subway Commandos."

24. Jiras and Mareš, *František Vláčil: Zápasy*, 5.

25. Ibid.

26. Ibid.; Liehm, *Closely Watched Films*, 170.

27. *Filmový přehled*, no. 29 (July 26, 1958): 10.

28. *Filmový přehled*, no. 52 (December 27, 1958): 12.

29. Vančura, *Marketa Lazarová*, 14.

30. Ibid., 59.

31. Ibid., 48.

32. Further proof of this may lie in another of Vláčil's Army Films of the period, the 1956 *Crew on the Peak* (*Posádka na štítě*), about a meteorological team on the Lomnický peak in Slovakia's Tatra Mountains.

33. Zimmermann, "What Hollywood Is to America," 110.

34. VÚA-VHA Prague, fond MNO 1954, k. 54, sign. 22 5/4,"Zpráva o činnosti ČAF."

35. Kenez, *Cinema and Soviet Society*, 31–32. I have preserved Kenez's use of the Russian plural *agitki* here, using the Czech plural *agitky* to describe the Czechoslovak version of the mode.

36. Šmidrkal, *Armáda a stříbrné plátno*, 41–45. Jiří Weiss, e.g., uses the term in his article "Krátký film." Agitation, in these films, follows Georgi Plekhanov's definition, as discussed by Vladimir Lenin: "A propagandist presents many ideas to one or a few persons; an agitator presents only

one or a few ideas, but he presents them to a mass of people" (Lenin, *What Is to Be Done*, in *Collected Works*, 5:409). See this book's filmography for the titles of other *agitky* produced by Army Film.

37. Larkin, *Signal and Noise*, 99.

38. Shore, "Engineering in the Age of Innocence," 402.

39. I thank Tom Gunning for making this remarkable identification.

40. The links between *Opportunity* and *Loves of a Blonde* may be explained by what Jasný recalls as his role as mentor to Forman on both this film and *Black Peter* (*Černý Petr*), both produced when Jasný and Forman were working for Czechoslovak State Film (Vojtěch Jasný, telephone interview with the author, October 1, 2008).

41. For analysis of these issues, see Blaive, *Une déstalinisation manquée.*

42. *September Nights* was among these: Antonín and Mira Liehm refer to it as the "first open attack on functionary dogmatism, insensitivity, pettiness and despotism" (Liehm and Liehm, *The Most Important Art*, 220–221). On the thematic and stylistic shifts in Czechoslovak films of the second half of the 1950s, see Klimeš, "Edice a materiály." On the Writers' Congress, see Shore, "Engineering in the Age of Innocence."

43. Another satirical take on this genre came in 1964, with the film *Good Advice Is Worth Its Weight in Gold* (*Dobrá rada je nad zlato*).

44. All translations from *Crooked Mirror* are by Nataša Ďurovičová.

45. Hašek, *The Good Soldier Švejk*, 666–667.

46. Pernes, Pospíšil, and Lukáš, *Alexej Čepička*, 223. According to Šmidrkal, after 1956, Army filmmakers themselves were no longer required to wear uniforms, although regular soldiers were (Šmidrkal, *Armáda a stříbrné plátno*, 9).

47. A 1954 review of a military performance of a play about Švejk, e.g., writes

that "most successful were military scenes showing 'švejkoviny' as a weapon against an inhuman social system.... Everyone realizes that the spirit of Austro-Hungarian militarism far outlived its 'decrepit sovereigns,' to the time of the First Republic, and in its final remnants even further. Truly only a new system, a new order would... rid us of... that at which Hašek takes aim" (Daneš, "Švejk na cestách").

48. VÚA-VHA Prague, fond MNO 1954, k. 54, sign. 22 5/4, "Zpráva o činnosti ČAF."

49. Clark, *The Soviet Novel*, 13. Similarly, in cinema, András Bálint Kovács writes that the "Polish School" "did not break entirely with the heroic tradition.... All the films did was to emphasize the everydayness of their heroes, who at the same time remained heroes in one way or another.... their strength was precisely to introduce ambiguity into heroic drama" (Kovács, *Screening Modernism*, 284).

50. Shore, "Engineering in the Age of Innocence."

4. EVERY YOUNG MAN

1. VÚA-VHA Prague, fond MNO 1965, k. 56, sign. 13/3, "Příspěvek do Sbírky nařízení a směrnic MNO o změně názvu Čs. armádního filmu na STUDIO ČAF," November 29, 1965.

2. Kopaněvová, Novák, and Svoboda, "Hovoříme v přítomném čase," 436.

3. Ibid., 437.

4. Klimeš, "Edice a materiály," 133.

5. "Zpráva pro ideologickou komisi ÚV KSČ o současné situaci v hraném filmu," in Klimeš, "Edice a materiály," 201. As Klimeš writes, the choice to criticize these films had been made well before the conference began.

6. Klimeš, "Edice a materiály," 137.

7. Struska, "Československý krátký film," 231.

8. Janžura, "Kam s ním?," 92.

9. Ibid.; Soeldner, "Mělo by se něco stát," 354.

10. Navrátil, *Cesty k pravdě či lži*, 216.

11. Kopaněvová, Novák, and Svoboda, "Hovoříme v přítomném čase," 436.

12. SA AČR Olomouc, fond 397, k. 11, Vnitřní rozkazy (1961), č. 6, 7, 20.

13. Benda, "Větší pozornost filmu v armádě."

14. Ibid.

15. SA AČR Olomouc, fond 397, k. 2, sv. 15/1 (Obyčejné spisy 1960), "Začlenění Ústřední distribuce filmů do ČAFS—opatření," August 18, 1960. The weekly screenings to which Benda refers were for entertainment, not training.

16. Szczepanik, "'Machři' a 'dile-tanti,'" 37.

17. "Obrana lidu volá Čs. armádní film." The studio had made films about Berlin and Germany previously; e.g., *Divided City* (*Rozdělené město*) and *Notebook from West Germany* (*Zápisník z NDR*).

18. For more on the "Berlin crisis," see Judt, *Postwar*, 250–253.

19. Compilation filmmaking had long had a distinguished history in the Soviet Union, beginning with the films of Esfir Shub. For more on Shub, see, among others, Leyda, *Films Beget Films*; Malitsky, "Esfir Shub"; and Sarkisova, "Building the Past."

20. This broader trend was reflected in, among many others, Erwin Leiser's 1960 *Mein Kampf* and Paul Rotha's 1961 *The Life of Adolf Hitler* (*Das Leben Adolf Hitlers*). See Barnouw, *Documentary*, 199.

21. Ibid., 198.

22. Navrátil, "Krátkařské aktuality" (March 1964), 154.

23. Hořejší, "Korunní svědek," 3.

24. Barnouw, *Documentary*, 175.

25. Leyda, *Films Beget Films*, 82.

26. Ibid.

27. *Filmový přehled*, no. 40 (1958): 3

28. *Filmový přehled*, no. 43 (1961): 13.

29. Hrbas, "Filmový dokument varuje," 5.

30. In addition to those mentioned by Hlaváč, this series included *Bundeswehr on the March* (*Bundeswehr pochoduje*)—which

was revised as *That Is the Bundeswehr (To je Bundeswehr)* in 1967—and *The General's Sword (Generálův meč)*. Compilation films were a mainstay of the studio's production throughout its existence. See this book's filmography for details.

31. SA AČR Olomouc, fond 397, k. 2, sv. 15/15-N (Obyčejné spisy 1963), "Splnění plánu ČAF za rok 1961," June 12, 1963. This was the name of the Leipzig festival between 1961 and 1967.

32. Hlaváč, "Dopisy," 333; Homuta, "Svědectví."

33. Pavel Štingl, "Lidstvo se nikdy nepoučí," 337; JC, "Svědectví, které žaluje i soudí"; Homuta, "Svědectví"; Strusková, "Svědectví."

34. Navrátil, "Krátkařské aktuality" (March 1964), 154.

35. Hlaváč, "Dopisy," 333.

36. Rudolf Krejčík, interview with the author, Prague, February 18, 2008.

37. Ibid.

38. The film's title, indeed, is similar to that of Soviet director Mikhail Romm's 1965 *Ordinary Fascism (Obyknovennyi fashizm)*.

39. Skoller, *Shadows, Specters, Shards*, 2.

40. Throughout his career, Krejčík specialized in archival films.

41. "Studio ČAF—tendence a tvůrci," 1.

42. The treaty founding the Warsaw Pact was signed in 1955. Its member states included Bulgaria, Czechoslovakia, East Germany, Hungary, Poland, Romania, the Soviet Union, and Albania.

43. SA AČR Olomouc, fond 397, k. 2, sv. 15/12 (Obyčejné spisy 1962), "Teze k jednání s vojenskými filmovými pracovníky spřátelených armád." Warsaw Pact military film studios had, however, collaborated earlier both with one another and with "civilian" film studios in the Pact.

44. SA AČR Olomouc, fond 397, k. 2, sv. 15/12 (Obyčejné spisy 1962), "Hlavní obsahové zaměření ČAF v roce 1963–1964," October 4, 1962.

45. SA AČR Olomouc, fond 397, k. 2, sv. 15/12 (Obyčejné spisy 1962), "Zápis z jednání dne 1.9.1962."

46. SA AČR Olomouc, fond 397, k. 2, sv. 15/12 (Obyčejné spisy 1962), "Protokol ze závěrečného jednání dne 5. září 1962."

47. SA AČR Olomouc, fond 397, k. 2, sv. 15/12 (Obyčejné spisy 1962), "Hlavní obsahové zaměření ČAF v roce 1963–1964," October 4, 1962.

48. For a detailed explanation of these problems, see Rice, *The Soviet Union and the Czechoslovak Army*, 105–106.

49. Williams, *The Prague Spring*, 6.

50. Reid, "The Soviet Art World," 164. For more on youth alienation, and anxieties about youth, in this period, see Katherine Lebow, "Kontra Kultura," 71–92.

51. Leff, *The Czech and Slovak Republics*, 56.

52. Kusin, *Intellectual Origins*, 87–88.

53. On the reforms, see Judt, *Postwar*, 437; and Kusin, *Intellectual Origins*, 87.

54. Skilling, *Czechoslovakia's Interrupted Revolution*, 49.

55. Rice, *The Soviet Union and the Czechoslovak Army*, 68.

56. Kusin, *Intellectual Origins*, 64 (quoted from F. Kautman, "Kafka a česká literatura") and 66 (quoted from Alexej Kusák, "Poznámky k marxistické interpretaci Franze Kafky"), both in *Franz Kafka: liblická konference 1963*, a symposium of speeches from the Liblice conference, 175.

57. Fischer, "The Deformation of Man," 115. On Kafka, see, e.g., Fischer's "Jaro, vlaštovky a Franz Kafka." Garaudy's *D'un réalisme sans rivages*, the French original of which was published in 1963, appeared in Czech in 1964 (Garaudy, *Realismus bez břehů*). Peter Hames notes that Fischer and Garaudy both attended the Kafka conference. (Hames, *The Czechoslovak New Wave*, 139.)

58. Sequens, "O poslání a odpovědnosti," 324.

59. Bazin, "Ils aiment la vie." For more on Eastern European engagements with Bazin, see Lovejoy, "From Ripples to Waves."

60. Among the other Eastern European Thaw films to participate in such re-examinations of history and the present were those of the Polish School (i.e., Andrzej Wajda's war trilogy) and films of the Soviet Thaw, which Josephine Woll demarcates as the period between 1954 and 1967. See Woll, *Real Images,* x.

61. Fiala, "Jaro československého filmu?," 281.

62. Kopaněvová, "Kontexty nového československého filmu," 396.

63. Soeldner, "K současnému stavu krátkého filmu," 113; *Filmové informace,* no. 24 (June 15, 1960): 11.

64. Struska, "Hledání těžiště," 6.

65. Navrátil, *Cesty k pravdě či lži,* 219n44.

66. Ibid., 221.

67. It was only in 1962 that the festival began to encompass productions not only by Krátký Film's main branches but also by other short film studios in Czechoslovakia (Krátký Film's branch in Gottwaldov; Army Film), as well as international productions. Short filmmakers from Poland and the German Democratic Republic participated in that year's festival, as did representatives of television studios in Berlin, Budapest, and London ("Dny ve znamení krátkého filmu").

68. "Studio ČAF—tendence a tvůrci," 1.

69. Soeldner, "K současnému stavu krátkého filmu."

70. dv, "Vojenská přehlídka—tentokrát filmová." I have been unable to locate the titles in this program.

71. dv, "Armádní film přehlíží," 5.

72. dv, "Vojenská přehlídka—tentokrát filmová."

73. dv, "Armádní film přehlíží."

74. Dvořák, "Filmy nejen o vojně."

75. Boček, "Studio, o kterém se málo ví," 4.

76. Ibid.

77. Soeldner, "Vojáci se tuží," 12.

78. "Armádní film na nové cesty."

79. Tvrzník, "Hledají a nalézají," 613.

80. Films also contributed to this process of self-historicizing; among them, *On the Wave of ČAF (Na vlně ČAF), 15 Years of Studio ČAF (15 let Studia ČAF),* and *He Stood by the Pantry (U komory Stál).*

81. Werich published the travelogue *Italské prázdniny* (Prague: Československý spisovatel) in 1960.

82. Weissnerová was one of a handful of Czechoslovak Jews who survived the 1942 transports from Terezín to the Baltic states; of the more than one thousand people on her transport alone, only one hundred were deemed capable of working and were sent to labor camps. The rest of the prisoners were shot and buried in mass graves in the sand dunes of Kalevi Liiva, outside Tallinn. For more on these transports, see "Since then I have believed in fate. . . ."

83. Vojtech, "Ladislav Mňačko," 45.

84. Ivan Balaďa, interview with the author, Prague, September 15, 2008.

85. Shore, "Engineering in the Age of Innocence," 424.

86. "O publicistice a dogmatismu," 7.

87. See Weiss, "Krátký film."

88. Paštéková, "Reportáž ako pokus," 151.

89. Mňačko, *Kde končia prašné cesty,* 10. Čedok was the Czechoslovak state tourism agency.

90. Ibid., 12.

91. The film's credits indicate that at least some of these photographs were taken from an East German book entitled *Der Zweite Weltkrieg—Eine Chronik in Bildern (The Second World War—A Chronicle in Images).*

92. Navrátil, "Krátkařské aktuality" (April 1964), 205. On Mňačko's writing as

"artistic reportage," see Janoušek, *Dějiny české literatury*, 3:307.

93. Mňačko, *Kde končia prašné cesty*, 114.

94. Ibid., 116.

95. Ibid., 116–117.

96. Ibid., 110.

97. On the history of sociology in communist Czechoslovakia, see Musil, "Poznámky o české sociologii."

98. Navrátil, "Dny krátkého filmu." Though chronologically earlier, the Free Tribune's critiques of vérité are similar to those Thomas Waugh discusses in his essay "Beyond Verité": that by the 1970s, it was clear that vérité had "failed to meet the increasing need for explicit sociopolitical analysis to support the momentum of the alternate politics."

99. SA AČR Olomouc, fond 1068, k. (Obyčejné spisy 1965), "Plán ÚDF na r. 1965—zaslání," January 29, 1965. The problem of soldiers' free time was the subject of other films of the 1960s, among them *Our Daily Time* (*Čas náš vezdejší*), *We Move on Friday* (*V pátek se stěhujeme*), and *Kenneled Dog* (*Pes u boudy*), all about soldiers' families, and *Waiting for a Train That Comes according to Schedule* (*Čekání na vlak, který přijede podle jízdního řádu*), which captures soldiers traveling home from their bases, which were often across the country. Vladimír Drha adopted a more impressionistic perspective on the subject in his 1969 *Dream Scenes* (*Snové scény*).

100. Tvrzník, "Hledají a nalézají."

101. During his time in Army Film, Schmidt made three more sports films: *A Game for Men* (*Hra pro chlapy*, 1966), on the city of Jihlava's hockey team; *Courage* (*Odvaha*, 1967), about ski jumping; and the 1964 *New York Cup* (*Pohár z New Yorku*), for which he followed the Czechoslovak national soccer team to the World Cup in New York. For titles of more sports films produced by Army Film—some of them documenting the yearly Spartakiáda—see this book's filmography.

102. Tunys, "Kdyby těch schodů nebylo"; Kopaněvová, Novák, and Svoboda, "Hovoříme v přítomném čase," 436. Czech documentarian Kurt Goldberger had explored a similar subject a year earlier in his award-winning State Film production *Unloved Children* (*Děti bez lásky*).

103. Similar "moral problems" were explored by Miroslav Burger in his 1966 *Questions (About the Army)* (*Otázky [O armádě]*), a film intended for television that polled people on "the meaning of the Army and its mission." (SA AČR Olomouc, fond 397, k. 1, sv. 15/19 [Obyčejné spisy 1966], "Zpráva Studia ČAF o tvorbě za II. čtvrtletí 1966," July 30, 1966.)

104. Růžička made two other films on the topic of reservists: *Seventeen Hours* and *Flyers* (*Letci*).

105. This region was also the subject of Adler's 1969 *Drapte, drapte, drapulenky*.

106. "...že je Švejk notorický blb a idiot podle všech přírodních zákonů vynalezených psychiatrickými vědátory" (Hašek, *The Good Soldier Švejk*, 30; *Osudy dobrého vojáka Švejka za světové války*, 25).

107. *Filmový přehled*, no. 30–31 (July 31, 1968): 15.

108. Kopaněvová, Novák, and Svoboda, "Hovoříme v přítomném čase," 437.

109. A MZV Prague, fond TO-O, Polsko 1960–1964, k. 3, "PLR-festival armádních filmů ve Varšavě," August 17, 1964.

110. VÚA-VHA Prague, fond MNO 1966, k. 167, sign. 31/3–40, i.č. 37524.

111. Kopaněvová, Novák, and Svoboda, "Hovoříme v přítomném čase," 437.

112. See "Hauptpreise in Leipzig (1955–1996)," in Leipziger DOK Filmwochen GmbH, *Weiße Taube auf dunklem Grund*, 216–219.

113. The links between film festivals and Cold War politics have been explored in, among others, Fehrenbach, *Cinema in Democratizing Germany*; and Iordanova, "Showdown of the Festivals." On the history of the Karlovy Vary film festival, see Bláhová, "Národní, mezinárodní, globální."

114. Leipzig's Free Forum (Freie Forum), a site for this dialogue, was presumably the model for Karlovy Vary's Free Tribune (Volná tribuna). For a history of the Leipzig festival, see Mückenburger, "Zur Geschichte des Leipziger Festivals."

115. A MZV Prague, fond TO-O, NSR 1960–64, k. 3, ič. 103940/12, "Účast NDR na festivalu krátkých a dokumentárních filmů v Oberhausenu—NSR," February 13, 1963.

116. Jansen, "Inventory."

117. On *Courage*, see Havelka, *Čs. filmové hospodářství, 1966–1970*, 123. The domestic counterparts to these festivals—at which Army productions were regular features—were numerous: the Review of Sport and Gymnastics Films and TECHFILM in Pardubice, the Review of Technical Films in Hradec Králové, TOURFILM in Špindlerův Mlýn, the venerable popular-science film festival ACADEMIAFILM in Olomouc, and others.

118. Ostrowska, "An Alternative Model," 453.

119. "Armádní film na nové cesty."

120. Czechoslovak Television had been broadcasting since 1953. For more on its history, see Bauer, "Televize jako prostředek." The Czechoslovak Army also had its own television station and programming.

121. Bren, *The Greengrocer and His TV*, 21.

122. This pedagogical role was common to television. On the case of Poland, see Ostrowska, "An Alternative Model," 459.

123. Future members of the New Wave even performed in the newsreel: Its *Little Christmas Present* (*Malá vojenská nadílka*) for 1965 features a young Jiří Menzel—a known heartthrob—in a uniform, winking at popular singer Marta Kubišová, whose performance of her "Even d'Artagnan Would Not Want More" is cut into the newsreel.

124. Švoma, *Karel Vachek, etc.*, 40.

125. Ibid., 49.

126. Karel Vachek, interview with the author, Prague, May 2, 2008.

127. Wees, "From Compilation to Collage," 4.

128. Švoma, *Karel Vachek, etc.*, 50.

129. Ibid.

130. Navrátil, "Na závěr dnů krátkého filmu."

131. Boček, "Nová vlna z odstupu," 633.

132. Liehm, "Argument."

133. Two important examples of this are composer Jiří Šust, who worked on many of the central films of the New Wave, and editors such as Jiřina Lukešová and Jiřina Skalská. See this book's filmography for details.

134. *Filmový přehled*, no. 17 (May 1, 1967): 5.

135. The eponymous short story was published in 1965 in the magazine *Mladý svět* (Ibid.).

136. Holub, "An Interview with Director Jan Schmidt."

137. Jaromír Kallista, interview with the author, Prague, January 28, 2008.

138. VÚA-VHA Prague, fond MNO 1965, k. 56, sign. 14/5, "Zásady pro tvorbu filmů v ČAF," February 13, 1965.

139. Kallista, interview with the author, January 28, 2008.

140. VÚA-VHA Prague, fond MNO 1965, k. 56, sign. 14/5, "Zásady pro tvorbu filmů v ČAF," February 13, 1965.

141. Holub, "An Interview with Director Jan Schmidt."

142. Kopaněvová, Novák, and Svoboda, "Hovoříme v přítomném čase," 436.

5. A MILITARY AVANT GARDE

1. Jaromír Kallista, interview with the author, Prague, January 28, 2008.

2. Liehm, "Author's Foreword," 62–63.

3. Bren, *The Greengrocer and His TV*, 20.

4. For a discussion of these areas of reform, see Kusin, *Intellectual Origins*.

5. Liehm, "Author's Foreword," 60.

6. For a personal account of the rehabilitations, see Kovaly, *Under a Cruel Star*. In addition to the Slovaks, whose national

grievances played a key role in the events of 1968, national groups in Czechoslovakia that began calling for greater self-determination during this period included Germans, Silesians, Moravians, Ruthenians, Roma, and Poles. On this, see Hejzlar and Kusin, *Czechoslovakia, 1968–1969*. On censorship, see Williams, *The Prague Spring*, 67–69.

7. Kýn, "Market and Price Mechanism," 302.

8. Antonín and Mira Liehm describe FITES, which was founded in 1965, as operating as an "a partner, and, when necessary, an opponent, to the state in establishing conditions for artistic film work" (Liehm and Liehm, *The Most Important Art*, 293).

9. On these issues, see Rice, *The Soviet Union and the Czechoslovak Army*, 105–110.

10. Hejzlar and Kusin, *Czechoslovakia, 1968–1969*, 19; Rice, *The Soviet Union and the Czechoslovak Army*, 127.

11. Rice, "The Problem of Military Elite Cohesion."

12. Gottwald Memorandum, 25.

13. Ibid., 26–27.

14. Ibid., 29.

15. Ibid., 30–31, 26.

16. Bren writes of Ludvik Vaculik's speech at the Writers' Congress, in which the novelist confessed to "fear that our republic has lost its good name," as a "serious blow" to "the Czechs especially, who saw their place both geographically and symbolically as very much in the center of Europe" (Bren, *The Greengrocer and His TV*, 17).

17. Quoted in Rice, *The Soviet Union and the Czechoslovak Army*, 140.

18. Ibid., 154.

19. In a signal of the degree to which the public recognized the Army as an ally in the reform process (and of Prchlík's personal popularity), Prchlík's recall was the topic of heated debate in the civilian press (Hejzlar and Kusin, *Czechoslovakia, 1968–1969*, 70–71).

20. Rice, *The Soviet Union and the Czechoslovak Army*, 112.

21. This was legible in the title and subject of *The Legacy of 38 (Pozůstalost 38)*, which depicts a group of former soldiers reuniting in a subterranean fortress in northeast Bohemia, near the town of Náchod. These men, we learn, defended the fortress in 1938, when Czechoslovakia's borderlands were annexed by Germany. In the period after the 1968 invasion, their story takes on added symbolic weight.

22. Tunys, "S Romanem Hlaváčem," 598.

23. Ibid. The Legions themselves were rehabilitated in 1968, marching in a May Day parade for the first time in this year. On symbolism and history in military parades of the 1960s, see Rice, *The Soviet Union and the Czechoslovak Army*, 110 and 131.

24. All of this did not go unnoticed by censors, who eventually banned the film, stating that it showed the "abnormality of capitalist society and documents the aggression of imperialism. In [its chapters about "Masaryk's republic"] it manifests anti-Party and anti-revolutionary (anti-Soviet) tendencies that are all the worse for their purported substantiation by authentic footage. An entirely incorrect interpretation of the role of our Legions in Russia" (quoted in Zvoníček, "Dokumenty jako řemen").

25. Tunys, "S Romanem Hlaváčem," 599.

26. Ibid.

27. Among the other films by Ployhar commissioned by the Government Tourist Board were *Music in the Center of Europe (Hudba v srdci Evropy*, 1967); *Prague Decameron (Pražský dekameron*, 1968); and *Through the Land of Silver Waters (Krajem stříbrných vod*, 1968), about South Bohemia.

28. SA AČR Olomouc, fond 397, k. 2, sv. 59/3-N 1970, "Zpráva o činnosti ČAF," February 16, 1970.

29. Zvoníček, "Dokumenty jako řemen."

30. Ibid.

31. Kieran Williams notes that "the period from the invasion to Dubcek's resignation . . . marked the greatest liberty experienced in Czechoslovakia between 1948 and 1989" (Williams, *The Prague Spring*, 144).

32. Kallista, interviews with the author, Prague, January 28, 2008, and February 11, 2008.

33. Čermák, "Filmové kluby v armádě," 6.

34. Šajmovič, *Duch času*, 8.

35. *Zlatá šedesátá: Ivan Balaďa*. The film's original title, in fact, was *Panychida 36*, a reference both to the Orthodox requiem and to the year of Balaďa's birth.

36. Ryklin, "'The Best in the World,'" 118; and Groys, "The Art of Totality," 264.

37. Šajmovič, *Duch času*, 9.

38. *Filmový přehled*, no. 13 (1969): 2.

39. SA AČR Olomouc, fond 397, k. 2, sv. 59/1-N, "Zpráva o plnění plánu HOZS za I. čtvrtletí 1968," April 26, 1968.

40. Boym, *The Future of Nostalgia*, 231; Sabrow, "Time and Legitimacy," 360.

41. Widdis, *Visions of a New Land*, 31.

42. Navrátil, "Prokleté měsíce," 162–163.

43. "Renewal," here, refers to the Prague Spring and the process of reform.

44. SA AČR Olomouc, fond 397, k. 2, sv. 59/1-N, "Zpráva o plnění plánu u HOZS za II. čtvrtletí 1968," July 26, 1968.

45. SA AČR Olomouc, fond 397, k. 2, sv. 59/1-N, "Zpráva o plnění plánu u HOZS za III. čtvrtletí 1968," October 29, 1968.

46. As Liehm recalled in 1972: "The action taken by the Czechoslovak intellectual opposition was based on the following unformulated assumption: If the Novotný regime proved unwilling to allow true democratization, if it refused to permit alternative methods for dealing with the country's problems, then the regime must be thoroughly unmasked. Its false liberal front, put on mainly to deceive the outside world, must be ripped off" (Liehm, "Author's Foreword," 71).

47. Bren, *The Greengrocer and His TV*, 21, 119.

48. I have translated Navrátil's Czech term *film-pravda* as "film truth," although it is possible that he is referring to cinéma vérité. However, in other writings, Navrátil maintains the latter in the original French; see, e.g., Navrátil, *Cesty k pravdě či lži*, 219.

49. Navrátil, "Je dokumentarismus mrtev?," 398.

50. Kahana, *Intelligence Work*, 295.

51. Navrátil, "Je dokumentarismus mrtev?," 396.

52. Ibid., 397.

53. Navrátil, "Dny krátkého filmu."

54. *Elective Affinities* won several important domestic and international prizes: FITES's 1968 Trilobite, prizes at the 1969 Oberhausen Short Film festival, first prize at the 1969 Karlovy Vary Short Film Festival, and belatedly, in 1990, a Berlinale Camera (*Filmový přehled*, no. 13 [April 11, 1969]: 2; Švoma, *Karel Vachek, etc.*, 70; *Filmový přehled*, no. 40 [October 23, 1968]: 7).

55. Williams, *The Prague Spring*, 188–191.

56. Bren, *The Greengrocer and His TV*, 31; Ivan Balaďa, interview with the author, Prague, September 15, 2008. In addition to these filmmakers, Kieran Williams reports that Palach's funeral procession was attended by "five hundred StB [secret police] officers" (Williams, *The Prague Spring*, 189n152). This statistic—which symbolically pits the Czechoslovak security apparatus against Palach's act—underscores the exceptionality of Army Film within the Czechoslovak military, for *Forest* is very much allied with Palach.

57. Balaďa, interview with the author, September 15, 2008.

58. Williams, *The Prague Spring*, 190.

59. Balaďa, interview with the author, September 15, 2008. Beyond the equation between Danko and Palach is the more complex relationship to the Soviet Union signaled by the fact that it is a work by Maxim Gorky that the film adapts. Balaďa, however, has an affection for Russian literature; his feature film for Czechoslovak

State Film *Ark of Fools* (*Archa bláznů*, 1970) is an adaptation of the Chekhov story "Ward No. 6."

60. SA AČR Olomouc, fond 397, k. 2, sv. 59/3-N 1970, "Zpráva o činnosti ČAF," February 16, 1970.

61. Škrdlant revisited *The Descendants* in 1994, with his film *Long-Haired State in the Middle of a Bareheaded Republic* (*Vlasatý stát uprostřed holohlavé republiky*).

62. Another film that Army Film co-produced with this organization in the same year was *Vïsit (Helsinki)* (*Návštěva [Helsinki]*).

63. These films include *Meeting with the Commander-in-Chief* (*Setkání s vrchním velitelem*, 1969), in which we see President Svoboda inspecting the troops.

64. Zvoníček, "Dokumenty jako řemen." Pilarová and Matuška were popular singers at the time, and, as Zvoníček describes it, their music was clearly used to mock the Soviet soldiers.

65. Ibid.

66. AV PRF, Moscow, f. 198, op. 50, p. 120, d. 17, l. 48. I thank Rachel Applebaum for this and the following reference.

67. AV PRF, Moscow, f. 198, op. 50, p. 120, d. 17, l. 49.

68. Another Army film on the same topic was Milan Růžička's 1968 *Order* (*Rozkaz*).

69. Rice, *The Soviet Union and the Czechoslovak Army*, 166.

70. *Filmový přehled*, no. 4 (1969): 16. Here, "cult" refers to Stalinism, and to socialist realism, which was associated with the Stalinist period.

71. *Color Wheel* was banned before its release. Zvoníček, "Dokumenty jako řemen," quotes the censors' statement:

A naturalistic film with strong formalist tendencies. Play with camera and color. The marriage takes place in a church; the camera, in long takes, follows the church ceremonies, the kissing of Christ on the cross, etc. The marriage banquet, which was shot without

any thought at all, simply shows human "gluttony," the results of "libation"—simply: disgusting. The question is why such a film was ever even shot, moreover on expensive color stock.

72. Šmidrkal, *Armáda a stříbrné plátno*, 93.

73. The commission charged with censoring these films observed: "Soviet soldiers buy out shops, and then an old woman cannot buy anything. It is an anti-Soviet documentary" (quoted in ibid.).

74. Havelka, *Čs. filmové hospodářství, 1966–1970*, 75.

75. *Filmový přehled*, no. 13 (1969): 2.

76. Dvořák, "Dvě generace pod jednou střechou," 10.

77. Liehm, "Author's Foreword," 78.

78. Ibid., 80.

CODA

1. SA AČR Olomouc, fond 397, k. 2, sv. 59/3-N 1970, "Zpráva o činnosti ČAF," February 16, 1970.

2. Ibid.

3. SA AČR Olomouc, fond 397, k. 1, sv. 10/20 (Tajné spisy 1970), "Průběžná zpráva"; SA AČR Olomouc, fond 397, k. 1, sv. 12/1 (Tajné spisy 1971), "Protokol o předání funkce."

4. SA AČR Olomouc, fond 397, k. 1, sv. 10/20 (Tajné spisy 1970), "Zabezpečení vl. usnesení čís. 202/1970 z 27.8.1970," October 5, 1970.

5. For more on the purges, see Williams, *The Prague Spring*, 231–232; and Bren, *The Greengrocer and His TV*, 35–37.

6. For details on Army Film's purges, see Šmidrkal, *Armáda a stříbrné plátno*.

7. SA AČR Olomouc, fond 397, k. 8 (Tajné spisy 1980), "Kádrová řešení související s výsledky stranické prověrky a stav ČAF," August 15, 1971.

8. Šmidrkal, *Armáda a stříbrné plátno*, 89.

9. SA AČR Olomouc, fond 1068, k. 1, sv. 7/11 (Obyčejné spisy 1971), "Podklad pro

jednání o obsahu činnosti ÚDF ČSLA," to
náčelník odd. kulturně výchovné činnosti
HPS ČSLA František Spilka from Miroslav
Koucký, náčelník ÚDF-ČSLA, April 13,
1971.

10. Zvoníček, "Dokumenty jako řemen."

11. Holub, "An Interview with Director
Jan Schmidt."

12. SA AČR Olomouc, fond 397, k. 1,
sl. 12/2 (Tajné spisy 1972), "Rozbor práce
ČSAF z hlediska říjnového pléna," December 7, 1972.

13. Ibid.

14. Juraj Šajmovič, interview with the
author, Prague, September 11, 2008.

15. SA AČR Olomouc, fond 397, k. 1, sv.
10/18 (Tajné spisy 1968), "Vyžádání námětů
pro zkvalitnění propagandy do zahraničí,"
June 10, 1968.

16. SA AČR Olomouc, fond 397, k. 1, sv.
10/18 (Tajné spisy 1968), "Zkvalitnění propagandy do zahraničí," July 3, 1968.

17. Vatulescu, *Police Aesthetics*, 191. On
the opening of Secret Police archives in
East Germany, see Garton Ash, *The File*. On
the Czech Republic and Poland, see Shore,
The Taste of Ashes.

18. Blaive, "L'ouverture des archives,"
209–210.

19. Paul Coates elegantly describes the
tensions that surround these interpretations, writing that the "reluctance to install
oneself in the archive is partly understand-
able, as the informational mine can indeed
by cramped and navigable only in a sweaty,
laborious half-light. Moreover, prolonged
immersion in Stalinist and post-Stalinist
Newspeak can indeed seem to offer one's
own sustaining blood to the hungry ghosts
of a system most Poles are happy to have
escaped" (*The Red and the White*, viii).

20. Vatulescu, *Police Aesthetics*, 191. See
also Blaive, "L'ouverture des archives," 211.

21. Vatulescu suggests something
similar: "The fact that subversion and complicity are so thoroughly entangled does
not mean that we should renounce these
distinctions but that we should look closer
and sharpen our discernment. Thus, we can
nuance these distinctions and create others, opening to the possibility that besides
subversion and complicity there were many
other nodal points in this entangled relationship between the police and art, points
such as mimicry, parody, appropriation,
and estrangements of many shades" (*Police
Aesthetics*, 197).

BIBLIOGRAPHY

Primary Sources

ARCHIVES AND PRIMARY ARCHIVAL COLLECTIONS

Archiv Ministerstva zahraničních věcí, Prague (A MZV)
    III. sekce, 1918–1939
    Teritoriální obory (TO)
Arkhiv Vneshnei Politiki Rossisskoi Federatsii, Moscow (AV PRF)
British Film Institute Special Collections, London (BFI)
    Basil Wright Collection
Národní archiv České republiky, Prague (NAČR)
    KSČ-Ústřední výbor, 1945–1989 (KSČ-ÚV)
    Ministerstvo informací, 1945–1953 (MI)
Správní archiv Armády České republiky, Olomouc (SA AČR)
    Československý armádní film (fond 397)
    Ústřední distribuce filmu (fond 1068)
Vojenský ústřední archiv–Vojenský historický archiv, Prague (VÚA-VHA)
    Ministerstvo národní obrany (MNO)
    Ministerstvo národní obrany (MNO) Hlavní štáb, oddělení branné výchovy
    Ministerstvo národní obrany (MNO) Prezidium

INTERVIEWS

Ivan Balaďa
Vojtěch Jasný
Jaromír Kallista
Rudolf Krejčík
Juraj Šajmovič
Karel Vachek

PERIODICALS

Filmové informace
Filmový přehled
Obrana lidu
Věstník Československého státního filmu

ARTICLES AND BOOKS

"Armádní film na nové cesty: Rozhovor s náčelníkem ČAF Bedřichem Bendou." *Rudé právo*, March 3, 1964.
Bazin, André. "Ils aiment la vie." *France Observateur*, no. 410 (March 20, 1958).
Beba, Karel. "Cesta čs. filmařů za sikansko-tibetskou magistrálou." *Rudé právo*, March 6, 1955.
Benda, Bedřich. "Větší pozornost filmu v armádě." *Obrana lidu*, August 19, 1960.

Boček, Jaroslav. "Nová vlna z odstupu." *Film a doba,* no. 12 (December 1966): 622–635.

———. "Studio, o kterém se málo ví." *Kulturní tvorba,* January 30, 1964, 4.

By. "Putovní kina v našem kinofikačním plánu." *Filmová práce,* no. 43 (October 26, 1946), 1.

Cavalcanti, Alberto. "The Neo-Realist Movement in England." In Abel, *French Film Theory and Criticism,* 233–238.

Čech, Jaroslav, Vojtěch Jasný, and Karel Kachyňa. *Byli jsme v zemi květů.* Prague: Naše vojsko, 1954.

Čepička, Alexej. "Dokonalejším využitím všech forem kulturní činnosti k prohloubení politické práce v armádě: Projev na aktivu kulturně osvětových pracovníků československé armády v Praze." *Obrana lidu,* September 2, 1951.

Čermák, Luděk. "Filmové kluby v armádě." *Záběr,* no. 21 (1968): 6.

Daneš, Ladislav. "Švejk na cestách." *Obrana lidu,* September 11, 1954.

Darret, Commandant. "Le cinéma au service de l'armée." *Revue historique de l'Armée* 18, no. 2 (1962): 121–131.

Dekret presidenta republiky ze dne 11. srpna 1945 o opatřeních v oblasti filmu. www .totalita.cz/txt/txt_zakon_1945-050.pdf (accessed April 10, 2014).

"Dny ve znamení krátkého filmu." *Lázeňský časopis* 1 (1962): 3.

dv. "Armádní film přehlíží." *Večerní Praha,* October 5, 1963, 5.

———. "Vojenská přehlídka—tentokrát filmová." *Večerní Praha,* March 22, 1963, 3.

Dvořák, Ivan. "Dvě generace pod jednou střechou." *Kino,* no. 4 (1969): 10.

———. "Filmy nejen o vojně." *Kino,* no. 8 (1963): 4.

E. F. B. Untitled. *Kulturní politika,* September 14, 1945.

Elbl, Jindřich. "Hrajte domácí dodatky." *Filmový kurýr,* no. 26 (June 25, 1937): 1.

———. "Patnáct let filmové politiky, 1933– 1948: Jak byl znárodněn československý film." *Film a doba,* no. 7 (July 1965): 340–354.

Fárová, Anna. *Jiří Jeníček.* Prague: Státní nakladatelství krásné literatury a umění, 1962.

Fiala, Miloš. "Jaro československého filmu?" *Film a doba,* no. 6 (June 1963): 281–287.

"Film a kinematografie ve státním rozpočtu na rok 1931." *Filmový kurýr,* no. 52 (December 24, 1930): 3.

"Film jako lidová universita." *Zemědělské noviny,* January 14, 1949.

Fischer, Ernst. "The Deformation of Man." In *Art against Ideology,* translated by Anna Bostock, 77–134. London: Allen Lane, Penguin Press, 1969.

———. "Jaro, vlaštovky a Franz Kafka." Translated by Ludvík Kundera. *Literární noviny,* no. 41 (October 12, 1963): 9.

Franz Kafka: liblická konference 1963. Prague: Nakladatelství Československé akademie věd, 1963.

Garaudy, Roger. *Realismus bez břehů.* Translated by Eva Janovcová, Jiří Kolář, and Alena Šabatková. Prague: Československý spisovatel, 1964.

Gottwald Memorandum. In *Military Political Views Prevalent in the Czechoslovak Army, 1948–1968,* edited by Josef Hodič. The Experience of the Prague Spring 1968, Working Study no. 5, 1979.

Hašek, Jaroslav. *Osudy dobrého vojáka Švejka za světové války, 1.–4. díl.* With illustrations by Josef Lada. Praha: Cesty, 2000.

———. *The Good Soldier Švejk and His Fortunes in the World War.* Translated by Cecil Parrott. New York: Penguin, 1973.

Hlaváč, Roman. "Dopisy." *Film a doba,* no. 6 (1964): 333.

Holub, Radovan. "An Interview with Director Jan Schmidt." Translated by Miloš Stehlík. *The End of August at Hotel*

Ozone. DVD. Dir. Jan Schmidt. Chicago: Facets.

Homuta, J. "*Svědectví.*" *Obrana lidu,* October 24, 1961.

Hořejší, Jan. "Korunní svědek." *Kultura* 38 (1961): 3.

Hrbas, Jiří. "Filmový dokument varuje." *Kino,* no. 17 (1962): 5.

i.š. "Lidé jednoho srdce." *Československý voják,* no. 22 (1953): 20.

Janžura, Ladislav. "Kam s ním?" *Film a doba,* no. 2 (February 1961): 92–93.

Jasný, Vojtěch, Karel Kachyňa, and Liu Ling. "Rodí se společné dílo." *Československý voják,* no. 11 (1953): 24.

JC. "Svědectví, které žaluje i soudí." *Jihočeská pravda,* November 11, 1961.

Jeníček, Jiří. *Abeceda krátkého filmu.* Prague: Knihovna Filmového kurýru, 1944.

———. "Anglický přiklad." *Lidové noviny,* September 22, 1934, afternoon ed.

———. "Armáda a film." *Lidové noviny,* February 28, 1936.

———. "Fotografie a film ve službách politické propagandy." *Národní politika,* November 15, 1932.

———. *Fotografie jako zření světa a života.* Prague: Československé filmové nakladatelství, 1947.

———. "Herci filmové reportáže 'V nový život.'" *Pestrý týden* 14, no. 3 (January 21, 1939): 8.

———. *Krátký film.* Prague: Nakladatelství Václav Petr, 1940.

———. "Národní pomoc a propaganda." *Branná politika* 2, no. 5 (February 4, 1939): 72–74.

———. "Něco o nové fotografii." *Pestrý týden* 4, no. 33 (August 17, 1929): 16.

———. "Nové proudy v naší fotografii." *Národní politika,* March 18, 1934, 4.

———. "O cílech a úkolech vojenského filmu." *Venkov,* no. 45, 1937.

———. "Vojáci hrají do filmu." *Lidové noviny,* March 20, 1937.

———. "Vojenský film." In *Vojenský kalendář na rok 1935.* Prague: Svaz čs. rotmistrů, 1934, 165.

Jirásek, Alois. *Psohlavci: Historický obraz.* With illustrations by Mikolaš Aleš. Prague: Státní nakladatelství dětské knihy, 1953.

Kinos. "O novou avantgardu." *Kino,* no. 18 (1948): 302.

K. J. V. "Kino: Znamenité pokroky vojenského filmu." *Národní listy,* October 27, 1923.

Kopaněvová, Galina. "Kontexty nového československého filmu." *Film a doba,* no. 8 (August 1967): 396–397.

Kopaněvová, Galina, Antonín Novák, and Jan Svoboda. "Hovoříme v přítomném čase o československém armádním filmu." *Film a doba,* no. 8 (August 1966): 434–437.

kt. "Vojenské kino ve VVT." *Obrana lidu,* August 9, 1949.

Kuba, Oldřich. "Propaganda jako zbraň." *Branná politika* 1, no. 1 (May 28, 1938): 23–24.

Kučera, Jan. "Advertising and Cinematic Art." In Anděl and Szczepanik, *Cinema All the Time,* 181–182.

Lehovec, Jiří. "Dokumentaristé sněmovali (Původní zpráva z Bruselu)." *Filmové noviny,* no. 25 (June 2, 1947): 1.

"Lidová armáda pochoduje: Film o přehlídce Čs. armády, Sboru národní bezpečnosti a Lidových milic v Praze, dne 6. května 1951." *Kino,* no. 14 (1951): 328.

Liehm, Antonín. "Argument." *Literární noviny,* no. 17 (April 25, 1964): 3.

———. "Author's Foreword: On Culture, Politics, Recent History, the Generations—and also on Conversations." In *The Politics of Culture,* edited by Antonín Liehm, 41–92. New York: Grove Press, 1968.

———. "Nad Tankovou brigádou." *Literární noviny,* no. 42 (October 15, 1955): 5.

Linhart, Lubomír. "The Proletarian Film Struggle in Czechoslovakia." In Anděl and Szczepanik, *Cinema All the Time*, 187–188.

Mňačko, Ladislav. *Kde končia prašné cesty.* Bratislava: Vydavateľstvo osveta, 1963.

"Naše filmy do New Yorku." *Filmový kurýr*, no. 6 (February 10, 1939): 2.

Navrátil, Antonín. "Dny krátkého filmu: Renesance dokumentárního filmu?" *Rudé právo*, March 27, 1964.

———. "Je dokumentarismus mrtev?," *Film a doba*, no. 8 (August 1968): 396–398.

———. *Jiří Lehovec.* Prague: Československý filmový ústav, 1984.

———. "Jiří Lehovec: Portrét dokumentaristy—kus historie a dneška." *Film a doba*, no. 6 (1959): 381–389.

———. "Krátkařské aktuality." *Film a doba*, no. 3 (March 1964): 154.

———. "Krátkařské aktuality." *Film a doba*, no. 4 (April 1964): 205.

———. "Na závěr dnů krátkého filmu: Dobrý rok dokumentaristů." *Rudé právo*, April 3, 1966.

———. "Prokleté měsíce." *Film a doba*, no. 3 (March 1965): 162–163.

Nezval, Vítězslav. "*Photogénie.*" In Anděl and Szczepanik, *Cinema All the Time*, 165–169.

"Obrana lidu volá Čs. armádní film. Odpovídá vedoucí dramaturg ČAF Roman Hlaváč." *Obrana lidu*, August 22, 1961.

O. K. "Současnost a budoucnost krátkého filmu v ČSR." *Filmová práce*, no. 21 (October 12, 1945): 4.

"O publicistice a dogmatismu: Hovoříme s Ladislavem Mňačkem." *Kulturní život*, January 1, 1964, 7.

"Pojízdné kino u vojáků." *Obrana lidu*, July 15, 1949.

Purš, Jiří. *Obrysy vývoje československé znárodněné kinematografie (1945–1980).* Prague: Československý filmový ústav, 1985.

Rubáš, Fr. "O nové organisaci v laboratořích na Barrandově." *Záběr*, no. 6 (1956): 5–6.

Šajmovič, Juraj. *Duch času: Mezi fotografií a filmem.* Prague: Národní filmový archiv, 2003.

Sequens, Jiří. "O poslání a odpovědnosti evropského filmového realismu." *Kino*, no. 17 (1948): 324–325.

Sís, Vladimír, and Josef Vaniš. "Natáčeli jsme v Tibetu." *Obrana lidu*, March 30, 1955.

Soeldner, Ivan. "K současnému stavu krátkého filmu: Třetí Dny krátkého filmu v Karlových Varech (20.–27. ledna 1962)." *Film a doba*, no. 3 (March 1962): 113–114.

———. "Mělo by se něco stát." *Kino*, no. 23 (1961): 354.

———. "Vojáci se tuží." *Kulturní tvorba*, November 26, 1964, 12.

Stašek, Bohumil. "Stát a kinematografie." *Filmový kurýr*, no. 25 (June 18, 1937): 5.

Štoll, Ladislav. *30 let bojů za československou socialistickou poesii.* Prague: Orbis, 1950.

Struska, Jiří. "Československý krátký film." *Film a doba*, no. 4 (April 1960): 230–233.

———. "Hledání těžiště." *Divadelní noviny*, no. 20 (April 22, 1964): 6.

Strusková, Eva. "*Svědectví.*" *Kino*, no. 21 (1961): 327.

"Studio ČAF—tendence a tvůrci." *Zprávy Svazu československých filmových a televizních umělců*, no. 12 (December 7, 1967): 1–2.

"Světová unie filmových dokumentaristů." *Rudé právo*, July 24, 1948, 3.

Tallents, Stephen G. *The Projection of England.* London: Olen Press for Film Centre Ltd, 1955.

Teige, Karel. "Photo Cinema Film." In Anděl and Szczepanik, *Cinema All the Time*, 123–144.

ts. "V nový život." *Filmový kurýr*, no. 51 (December 23, 1938): 4.

Tunys, Ladislav. "Kdyby těch schodů nebylo." *Československý voják*, no. 3 (1965): 30–31.

————. "S Romanem Hlaváčem o celovečerním dokumentu, který vzniká v ČAF." *Film a doba*, no. 11 (1968): 597–599.

Tvrzník, Jiří. "Hledají a nalézají." *Film a doba*, no. 11 (November 1965): 613.

Vančura, Vladislav. *Marketa Lazarová*. Rev. ed. 1961; reprint, Prague: Dauphin, 1997.

"Vítězná posádka." *Kino*, no. 17 (1953): 262–263.

Voskovec, Jiří. "*Photogenie* and Suprareality." In Anděl and Szczepanik, *Cinema All the Time*, 161–164.

Weiss, Jiří. "Film se rodí." *Kulturní politika*, October 12, 1945.

————. "Krátký film—Umění nebo propaganda?," *Kulturní politika*, October 19, 1945.

Werich, Jan. *Italské prázdniny*. Prague: Československý spisovatel, 1960.

Žalman, Jan. "Venkove, dočkal ses!" *Kino*, no. 5 (1955): 71.

Zhdanov, Andrei. "Speech to the Congress of Soviet Writers." In *Art in Theory 1900–2000: An Anthology of Changing Ideas*, edited by Charles Harrison and Paul Wood, 426–429. Malden, MA: Blackwell, 2003.

Zvoníček, Petr. "Dokumenty jako řemen." *Lidové noviny*, August 7, 1990.

Zvoníček, Stanislav. "O filmu 'Tanková brigáda.'" *Film a doba*, nos. 11–12 (1955): 522–526.

Secondary Sources

Abel, Richard, ed. *French Film Theory and Criticism: A History/Anthology, 1907–1939*. Vol. 2: *1929–1939*. Princeton, NJ: Princeton University Press, 1988.

Abrams, Bradley F. *The Struggle for the Soul of the Nation: Czech Culture and the Rise of Communism*. Lanham, MD: Rowman & Littlefield, 2004.

Acland, Charles R. "Celluloid Classrooms and Everyday Projectionists: Post–World War II Consolidation of Community Film Activism." In Orgeron, Orgeron, and Streible, *Learning with the Lights Off*, 377–396.

————. "Curtains, Carts, and the Mobile Screen." *Screen* 50, no. 1 (Spring 2009): 148–166.

Acland, Charles R., and Haidee Wasson, eds. *Useful Cinema*. Durham, NC: Duke University Press, 2011.

————. "Introduction: Utility and Cinema." In Acland and Wasson, *Useful Cinema*, 1–14.

Anděl, Jaroslav, and Petr Szczepanik, eds. *Cinema All the Time: An Anthology of Czech Film Theory and Criticism, 1908–1939*. Translated by Kevin B. Johnson. Prague: Národní filmový archiv, 2008.

————. "Czech Film Thought—An Introduction." In Anděl and Szczepanik, *Cinema All the Time*, 18–62.

Anderson, Benedict. *Imagined Communities*. New York: Verso, 1991.

Applebaum, Anne. *Iron Curtain: The Crushing of Eastern Europe, 1944–1956*. New York: Doubleday, 2012.

Bajkay, Éva. "Dessau." In Benson, *Central European Avant-Gardes*, 217–225.

Balázs, Béla. *Béla Balázs: Early Film Theory*. Edited by Erica Carter. Translated by Rodney Livingstone. New York: Berghahn, 2011.

————. "Three Addresses by Way of a Preface." In *Béla Balázs*, 3–8.

Barnouw, Eric. *Documentary: A History of the Non-fiction Film*. 2nd rev. ed. New York: Oxford University Press, 1993.

Batistová, Anna. "Cesta k soběstačnosti. Vývoj technického zázemí domácí sítě kin po roce 1945." In Skopal, *Naplánovaná kinematografie*, 427–467.

Bauer, Šimon. "Televize jako prostředek subvencování kinematografie: Vývoj smluvního rámce Československé televize a československého státního filmu z hlediska distribučních vztahů v letech 1953 až 1960." In Skopal, *Naplánovaná kinematografie*, 468–527.

Benjamin, Walter. "The Author as Producer." In *Understanding Brecht*, translated by Anna Bostock, introduction
by Stanley Mitchell, 85–104. New York:
Verso, 1998.

Benson, Timothy O., ed. *Central European
Avant-Gardes: Exchange and Transforma-
tion, 1910–1930*. Cambridge, MA: MIT
Press, 2002.

Biller, Maxim. *Bernsteintage: Sechs neue Ge-
schichten*. Munich: Deutscher Taschen-
buch Verlag, 2006.

Bláhová, Jindřiška. "Národní, mezinárodní,
globální. Proměny rolí filmového festivalu v Mariánských Lázních/Karlových
Varech, 1946 až 1959." In Skopal, *Naplánovaná kinematografie*, 255–311.

Blaive, Muriel. "L'ouverture des archives
d'une police politique communiste:
Le cas tchèque, de Zdena Salivarová à
Milan Kundera." In *Archives et histoire
dans les sociétés postcommunistes*, edited
by Sonia Combe, with Paul Gradvohl,
Charles Kecskeméti, Antoine Marès, and
Jean-Charles Szurek, 203–225. Paris: La
Découverte/BDIC, 2009.

————. *Une déstalinisation manquée: Tché-
coslovaquie, 1956*. Paris: Editions com-
plexe, 2005.

Bloom, Peter J. *French Colonial Documen-
tary: Mythologies of Humanitarianism*.
Minneapolis: University of Minnesota
Press, 2008.

Bottomore, Stephen, ed. "War and Militarism." Special issue, *Film History* 14, nos.
3–4 (2002).

Boym, Svetlana. *The Future of Nostalgia*.
New York: Basic Books, 2001.

Bren, Paulina. *The Greengrocer and His TV:
The Culture of Communism after the 1968
Prague Spring*. Ithaca, NY: Cornell Uni-
versity Press, 2010.

Bryant, Chad. "Either German or Czech:
Fixing Nationality in Bohemia and
Moravia, 1939–1946." *Slavic Review* 61,
no. 4 (Winter 2002): 683–706.

————. *Prague in Black: Nazi Rule and
Czech Nationalism*. Cambridge, MA:
Harvard University Press, 2007.

Čarnický, Michal. "'Zítra se bude
promítat všude'. Dějiny putovních kin v
československé zestátněné distribučních
síti." In Skopal, *Naplánovaná kinematografie*, 359–390.

Carter, Erica. Introduction to Balázs, *Béla
Balázs: Early Film Theory*, xv–xlvi.

Česálková, Lucie. *Film před tabulí:
Idea školního filmu v prvorepub-
likovém Československu. Studie
Národohospodářského ústavu Josefa
Hlávky no. 4*, 2010.

————. "Film v místech 'nevyužitého
času.'" *Iluminace* 23, no. 1 (2011): 111–117.

————. "Nedostižné tempo růstu a
zbrzděná avantgarda. Kompatibilita
krátkometrážní filmové produkce s
plánovaným hospodářstvím ČSR (1945
až 1960)." In Skopal, *Naplánovaná kinematografie*, 192–231.

————. "Noví noví lidé. Budovatelská
tematika v produkci Krátkého filmu v
letech 1945 až 1954." In *Film a dějiny 3:
Politická kamera—Film a stalinismus*, edited by Kristian Feigelson and Petr Kopal, 449–460. Prague: Casablanca, 2012.

————. "Oběť ve státním zájmu: Kulturně-
propagační dodatek a filmová politika
30. let." *Iluminace* 21, no. 2 (2009):
135–155.

————. "Žánrové varianty českého
předválečného nonfikčního filmu." *Iluminace* 21, no. 2 (2009): 184–203.

Clark, Katerina. "Socialist Realism *with*
Shores: The Conventions for the Positive
Hero." In Lahusen and Dobrenko, *Social-
ist Realism without Shores*, 27–50.

————. *The Soviet Novel: History as Ritual*.
3rd ed. Bloomington: Indiana University
Press, 2000.

Clybor, Shawn. "Laughter and Hatred Are
Neighbors: Adolf Hoffmeister and E. F.
Burian in Stalinist Czechoslovakia,

1948–1956." *East European Politics and Societies* 26, no. 3 (2012): 589–615.

Coates, Paul. *The Red and the White: The Cinema of People's Poland*. New York: Wallflower, 2005.

Conley, Tom. *Cartographic Cinema*. Minneapolis: University of Minnesota Press, 2007.

Connelly, John. *Captive University: The Sovietization of East German, Czech, and Polish Higher Education, 1945–1956*. Chapel Hill: University of North Carolina Press, 2000.

Cunningham, John. *Hungarian Cinema: From Coffee House to Multiplex*. New York: Wallflower, 2004.

De Grazia, Victoria. "Mass Culture and Sovereignty: The American Challenge to European Cinemas, 1920–1960." *Journal of Modern History* 61, no. 1 (March 1989): 53–87.

Demetz, Peter. *Prague in Black and Gold: Scenes in the Life of a European City*. New York: Hill & Wang, 1997.

———. *Prague in Danger: The Years of German Occupation, 1939–45: Memories and History, Terror and Resistance, Theater and Jazz, Film and Poetry, Politics and War*. New York: Farrar, Straus, & Giroux, 2008.

Dobrenko, Evgeny. *Political Economy of Socialist Realism*. Translated by Jesse M. Savage. New Haven, CT: Yale University Press, 2007.

Dobrenko, Evgeny, and Eric Naiman, eds. *The Landscape of Stalinism*. Seattle: University of Washington Press, 2003.

Druick, Zoë. *Projecting Canada*. Montreal: McGill-Queen's University Press, 2007.

———. "'Reaching the Multimillions': Liberal Internationalism and the Establishment of Documentary Film." In Grieveson and Wasson, *Inventing Film Studies*, 66–92.

Dufek, Antonín. "Fotografie, 1939–1948." In *Dějiny českého výtvarného umění V. 1939–1958*, edited by Rostislav Švácha

and Marie Platovská, 409–433. Prague: Academia, 2005.

Elsaesser, Thomas. "Archives and Archaeologies: The Place of Non-fiction Film in Contemporary Media." In Hediger and Vonderau, *Films That Work*, 19–34.

Fehrenbach, Heide. *Cinema in Democratizing Germany: Reconstructing National Identity after Hitler*. Chapel Hill: University of North Carolina Press, 1995.

Ferro, Marc. "Y a-t-il 'trop de démocratie' en URSS?" *Annales ESC* 40, no. 4 (July–August 1985): 811–827.

Fiedler, Jiří, and Václav Sluka. "Vojenský technický a letecký ústav." In *Encyklopedie branné moci Republiky československé 1920–1938*, edited by Jiří Fiedler and Václav Sluka, 703. Prague: Nakladatelství Libri, 2006.

Fitzpatrick, Sheila. "Revisionism in Retrospect: A Personal View." *Slavic Review* 67, no. 3 (Fall 2008): 682–704.

Frey, Mattias. "Cultural Problems of Classical Film Theory: Béla Balázs, 'Universal Language' and the Birth of National Cinema." *Screen* 51, no. 4 (Winter 2010): 324–340.

Frick, Caroline. *Saving Cinema: The Politics of Preservation*. New York: Oxford University Press, 2011.

Frommer, Benjamin. *National Cleansing: Retribution against Nazi Collaborators in Postwar Czechoslovakia*. New York: Cambridge University Press, 2005.

Garton Ash, Timothy. *The File: A Personal History*. New York: Random House, 1997.

Geyer, Michael, and Sheila Fitzpatrick. *Beyond Totalitarianism: Stalinism and Nazism Compared*. New York: Cambridge University Press, 2009.

Giustino, Cathleen M. "Industrial Design and the Czechoslovak Pavilion at EXPO '58: Artistic Autonomy, Party Control and Cold War Common Ground." *Journal of Contemporary History* 47, no. 1 (2012): 185–212.

Gladstone, Kay. "The APFU: The Origins of British Army Combat Filming during the Second World War." In Bottomore, "War and Militarism," 316–331.

Glassheim, Eagle. "Ethnic Cleansing, Communism, and Environmental Devastation in Czechoslovakia's Borderlands, 1945–1989." *Journal of Modern History* 78, no. 1 (March 2006): 65–92.

———. *Noble Nationalists: The Transformation of the Bohemian Aristocracy.* Cambridge, MA: Harvard University Press, 2005.

Grieveson, Lee. "The Cinema and the (Common) Wealth of Nations." In *Empire and Film,* edited by Lee Grieveson and Colin MacCabe, 73–113. London: BFI, 2011.

———. *Policing Cinema: Movies and Censorship in Early-Twentieth-Century America.* Berkeley: University of California Press, 2004.

Grieveson, Lee, and Colin MacCabe, eds. *Film and the End of Empire.* London: BFI, 2011.

Grieveson, Lee, and Haidee Wasson, eds. *Inventing Film Studies.* Durham, NC: Duke University Press, 2008.

Griffiths, Alison. *Wondrous Difference: Cinema, Anthropology, and Turn-of-the-Century Visual Culture.* New York: Columbia University Press, 2002.

Groening, Stephen. "'We Can See Ourselves as Others See Us': Women Workers and Western Union's Training Films in the 1920s." In Acland and Wasson, *Useful Cinema,* 34–58.

Groys, Boris. "The Art of Totality." In Dobrenko and Naiman, *The Landscape of Stalinism,* 96–122.

Gunning, Tom. "Before Documentary: Early Nonfiction Films and the 'View' Aesthetic." In *Uncharted Territory: Essays on Early Nonfiction Film,* edited by Daan Hartogs and Nico De Klerk, 9–24. Amsterdam: Stichting Nederlands Filmmuseum, 1997.

———. *D. W. Griffith and the Origins of American Narrative Film.* Urbana: University of Illinois Press, 1993.

Gupta, Akhil. *Red Tape: Bureaucracy, Structural Violence, and Poverty in India.* Durham, NC: Duke University Press, 2012.

Hagener, Malte. *Moving Forward, Looking Back: The European Avant-Garde and the Invention of Film Culture, 1919–1939.* Amsterdam: Amsterdam University Press, 2007.

Hames, Peter, ed. *The Cinema of Central Europe.* New York: Wallflower, 2004.

———. *The Czechoslovak New Wave.* 2nd ed. New York: Wallflower, 2005.

Hanuš, Milan. *Podoby Františka Vláčila.* Prague: Československý filmový ústav, 1984.

"Hauptpreise in Leipzig, 1955–1996." In Leipziger DOK Filmwochen GmbH, *Weiße Taube auf dunklem Grund,* 216–227.

Havel, Ludvík. "'O nového člověka, o dokonalejší lidstvo, o nový festival.' Filmový festival pracujících, 1948 až 1959." In Skopal, *Naplánovaná kinematografie,* 312–358.

Havelka, Jiří. *Čs. filmové hospodářství, 1945–1950.* Prague: Československý filmový ústav, 1970.

———. *Čs. filmové hospodářství, 1951–1955.* Prague: Československý filmový ústav, 1972.

———. *Čs. filmové hospodářství, 1956–1960.* Prague: Československý filmový ústav, 1973.

———. *Čs. filmové hospodářství, 1961–1965.* Prague: Československý filmový ústav, 1975.

———. *Čs. filmové hospodářství, 1966–1970.* Prague: Československý filmový ústav, 1975.

———. *Čs. krátké filmy, 1945–1970.* Prague: Československý filmový ústav, 1977.

———. *Československý krátký film v letech 1922–45.* Unpublished manuscript. Print, National Film Archive, Prague.

———. *Kdo byl kdo v československém filmu před r. 1945.* Prague: Československý filmový ústav, 1979.

———. *Kronika našeho filmu, 1898–1965.* Prague: Filmový ústav, 1967.

Hediger, Vinzenz, and Patrick Vonderau, eds. *Films That Work: Industrial Film and the Productivity of Media.* Amsterdam: Amsterdam University Press, 2009.

———. "Record, Rhetoric, Rationalization: Industrial Organization and Film." In Hediger and Vonderau, *Films That Work,* 35–49.

Hejzlar, Zdeněk, and Vladimír Kusin. *Czechoslovakia, 1968–1969: Chronology, Bibliography, Annotation.* New York: Garland, 1975.

Heller, Leonid. "A World of Prettiness: Socialist Realism and its Aesthetic Categories." In Lahusen and Dobrenko, *Socialist Realism without Shores,* 51–75.

Higson, Andrew, and Richard Maltby, eds. *"Film Europe" and "Film America": Cinema, Commerce and Cultural Exchange, 1920–1939.* Exeter: University of Exeter Press, 1999.

Holt, Jennifer, and Alisa Perren. "Introduction: Does the World Really Need One More Field of Study?" In *Media Industries: History, Theory, and Method,* edited by Jennifer Holt and Alisa Perren, 1–16. Malden, MA: Wiley-Blackwell, 2009.

Horak, Jan-Christopher, ed. *Lovers of Cinema: The First American Avant-Garde, 1919–1945.* Madison: University of Wisconsin Press, 1985.

———. "A Neglected Genre: James Sibley Watson's Avant-Garde Industrial Films." In "Experiment in Film before World War II," ed. John Fullerton. Special issue, *Film History* 20, no. 1 (2008): 35–48.

Horne, Jennifer. "Experiments in Propaganda: Reintroducing James Blue's Colombia Trilogy." *The Moving Image* 9, no. 1 (Spring 2009): 183–200.

Horníček, Jiří. "The Institutionalization of Classroom Films in Czechoslovakia between the Wars." In "Nontheatrical Film," ed. Dan Streible, Martina Roepke, and Anke Mebold. Special issue, *Film History* 19, no. 4 (2007): 384–391.

Hull, Matthew S. "Documents and Bureaucracy." *Annual Review of Anthropology* 41 (2012): 251–267.

———. *Government of Paper: The Materiality of Bureaucracy in Urban Pakistan.* Berkeley: University of California Press, 2012.

Imre, Anikó, ed. *A Companion to Eastern European Cinemas.* Malden, MA: Wiley-Blackwell, 2012.

———, ed. *East European Cinemas.* New York: Routledge, 2005.

———. "Introduction: Eastern European Cinema from *No End* to the End (As We Know It)." In Imre, *A Companion to Eastern European Cinemas,* 1–22.

Imre, Anikó, Timothy Havens, and Kati Lustyik, eds. *Popular Television in Eastern Europe during and since Socialism.* New York: Routledge, 2013.

Iordanova, Dina. "Showdown of the Festivals: Clashing Entrepreneurships and Post-Communist Management of Culture." *Film International* 4, no. 23 (2006): 25–37.

Janoušek, Pavel, ed. *Dějiny české literatury, 1945–1989. Vol. 2: 1948–1958.* Prague: Academia, 2007.

———. *Dějiny české literatury, 1945–1989. Vol. 3: 1958–1969.* Prague: Academia, 2009.

Jiras, Pavel, and Zdeněk Mareš, eds. *František Vláčil: Zápasy.* Prague: Správa Pražského hradu and Barrandov Studio, 2008.

Judt, Tony. *Postwar: A History of Europe since 1945.* New York: Penguin, 2005.

Kafka, Ben. *The Demon of Writing: Powers and Failures of Paperwork.* New York: Zone Books, 2012.

———. "Paperwork: The State of the Discipline." *Book History* 12 (2009): 340–353.

Kahana, Jonathan. *Intelligence Work: The Politics of American Documentary*. New York: Columbia University Press, 2008.

Kalinová, Lenka. *Společenské proměny v čase socialistického experimentu: K sociálním dějinám v letech 1945–1960*. Prague: Academia 2007.

Kaplan, Karel. *Kronika komunistického Československa: Doba tání, 1953–1956*. Brno: Barrister & Principal, 2005.

———. *Sovětští poradci v Československu, 1949–1956*. Prague: Ústav pro soudobé dějiny AV ČR, 1993.

Kenez, Peter. *Cinema and Soviet Society from the Revolution to the Death of Stalin*. New York: I. B. Tauris, 2001.

King, Jeremy. *Budweisers into Czechs and Germans: A Local History of Bohemian Politics, 1848–1948*. Princeton, NJ: Princeton University Press, 2002.

Kittler, Friedrich A. *Gramophone, Film, Typewriter*. Translated by Geoffrey Winthrop-Young and Michael Wutz. Stanford, CA: Stanford University Press, 1999.

Klimeš, Ivan. "Edice a materiály: Komunistická moc v Československu: Vzrušený rok 1959," *Iluminace* 16, no. 4 (2004): 129–138.

———. "K povaze historismu v hraném filmu poúnorového období." In *Filmový sborník historický 2: 90 let vývoje čs. kinematografie—příspěvky z konference*, 81–86. Prague: Československý filmový ústav, 1991.

———. "Stát a filmová kultura." *Iluminace* 11, no. 2 (1999): 125–136.

Knapík, Jiří. *Únor a kultura: Sovětizace české kultury, 1948–1950*. Prague: Nakladatelství Libri, 2004.

———. *V zajetí moci. Kulturní politika, její systém a aktéři 1948–1956*. Prague: Nakladatelství Libri, 2006.

Koszarski, Richard. "Subway Commandos: Hollywood Filmmakers at the Signal Corps Photographic Center." In Bottomore, "War and Militarism," 296–315.

Kouba, Karel. "Průvodce po krajinách sorely—Vše, co jste chtěli vědět o budovatelském románu." *A2*, no. 22 (2007).

Kovács, András Bálint. *Screening Modernism: European Art Cinema, 1950–1980*. Chicago: University of Chicago Press, 2007.

Kovaly, Heda Margolius. *Under a Cruel Star: A Life in Prague, 1941–1968*. Cambridge, MA: Plunkett Lake Press, 1986.

Kusák, Alexej. *Kultura a politika v Československu, 1945–1956*. Prague: Torst, 1998.

Kusin, Vladimir V. *The Intellectual Origins of the Prague Spring: The Development of Reformist Ideas in Czechoslovakia*. New York: Cambridge University Press, 1971.

Květová, Hana. "Filmové jaro na vesnici 1951 až 1956. Historie kulturně-osvětové akce na českém venkově v 50. letech dvacátého století." In Skopal, *Naplánovaná kinematografie*, 391–426.

Kýn, Oldřich. "Market and Price Mechanism in Socialist Countries: The Rise and Fall of Economic Reform in Czechoslovakia." In "Papers and Proceedings of the Eighty-second Annual Meeting of the American Economic Association." Special issue, *American Economic Review* 60, no. 2 (May 1970): 300–306.

Lahusen, Thomas, and Evgeny Dobrenko, eds. *Socialist Realism without Shores*. Durham, NC: Duke University Press, 1997.

Langerová, Marie, Josef Vojvodík, Anja Tippnerová, and Josef Hrdlička, eds. *Symboly obludností: Mýty, jazyk a tabu české postavantgardy 40.–60. let*. Prague: Malvern, 2009.

Larkin, Brian. *Signal and Noise: Media, Infrastructure, and Urban Culture in Nigeria*. Durham, NC: Duke University Press, 2008.

Lebow, Katherine. "Kontra Kultura: Leisure and Youthful Rebellion in Stalinist Poland." In *Pleasures in Socialism: Leisure and Luxury in the Eastern Bloc*, edited by

David Crowley and Susan E. Reid, 71–92. Evanston, IL: Northwestern University Press, 2010.

Leff, Carol Skalnik. *The Czech and Slovak Republics: Nation versus State.* Boulder, CO: Westview Press, 1997.

Leipziger DOK Filmwochen GmbH. *Weiße Taube auf dunklem Grund: 40 Jahre Internationales Leipziger Festival für Dokumentar- und Animationsfilm.* Berlin: Henschel, 1997.

Lenin, Vladimir I. *What Is to Be Done?* In *Collected Works*, vol. 5, 349–529. London: Lawrence & Wishart, 1961.

Levi, Pavle. *Disintegration in Frames: Aesthetics and Ideology in the Yugoslav and Post-Yugoslav Cinema.* Stanford, CA: Stanford University Press, 2007.

Leyda, Jay. *Films Beget Films.* New York: Hill & Wang, 1964.

Liehm, Antonín. *Closely Watched Films: The Czechoslovak Experience.* White Plains, NY: International Arts and Sciences Press, 1974.

Liehm, Antonín, and Mira Liehm. *The Most Important Art: East European Film after 1945.* Berkeley: University of California Press, 1977.

Littell, Robert, ed. *The Czech Black Book.* Prepared by the Institute of History of the Czechoslovak Academy of Sciences. New York: Praeger, 1969.

Lovejoy, Alice. "From Ripples to Waves: Bazin in Eastern Europe." In *Opening Bazin: Postwar Film Theory and its Afterlife*, edited by Dudley Andrew with Hervé Joubert-Laurencin, 302–307. New York: Oxford University Press, 2011.

Malitsky, Joshua. "Esfir Shub and the Film Factory-Archive: Soviet Documentary from 1925–1928." *Screening the Past* 17 (2004).

———. *Post-revolution Nonfiction Film: Building the Soviet and Cuban Nations.* Bloomington: Indiana University Press, 2013.

Mansbach, S. A. "Methodology and Meaning in the Modern Art of Eastern Europe." In Benson, *Central European Avant-Gardes*, 288–306.

Margry, Karel. "Newsreels in Nazi-Occupied Czechoslovakia: Karel Peceny and His Newsreel Company *Aktualita*." *Historical Journal of Film, Radio and Television* 24, no. 1 (2004): 69–117.

McCarthy, Anna. "Screen Culture and Group Discussion in Postwar Race Relations." In Orgeron, Orgeron, and Streible, *Learning with the Lights Off*, 397–423.

McDermott, Kevin. "A 'Polyphony of Voices'? Czech Popular Opinion and the Slánský Affair." *Slavic Review* 67, no. 4 (Winter 2008): 840–865.

Mückenberger, Christiane. "Zur Geschichte des Leipziger Festivals." In Leipziger DOK Filmwochen GmbH, *Weiße Taube auf dunklem Grund*, 9–24.

Musil, Jiří. "Poznámky o české sociologii za komunistického režimu." *Sociologický časopis* 40, no. 5 (2004): 573–595.

Musser, Charles, in collaboration with Carol Nelson. *High-Class Moving Pictures: Lyman Howe and the Forgotten Era of Traveling Exhibition, 1880–1920.* Princeton, NJ: Princeton University Press, 1991.

Navrátil, Antonín. *Cesty k pravdě či lži: 70 let československého dokumentárního filmu.* Prague: AMU, 2002.

Nichols, Bill. "Documentary Film and the Modernist Avant-Garde." *Critical Inquiry* 27, no. 4 (Summer 2001): 580–610.

Obraz vojenského prostředí v kinematografii mezivalečného Československa. Prague: Historický ústav Československé armády and Český filmový ústav, 1992.

Orgeron, Devin, Marsha Orgeron, and Dan Streible, eds. *Learning with the Lights Off: Educational Film in the United States.* New York: Oxford University Press, 2012.

Orzoff, Andrea. *Battle for the Castle: The Myth of Czechoslovakia in Europe,*

1914–1948. New York: Oxford University Press, 2009.

Ostrowska, Dorota. "An Alternative Model of Film Production: Film Units in Poland after World War II." In Imre, *A Companion to Eastern European Cinemas*, 453–465.

Owen, Jonathan L. *Avant-Garde to New Wave: Czechoslovak Cinema, Surrealism, and the Sixties*. New York: Berghahn, 2011.

Paštéková, Jelena. "Reportáž ako pokus o zmenu paradigmy fikcie. Prvá a druhá generácia ľudovodemokratickej literatúry." In *Literatura socialistického realismu: Východiska, struktury a kontexty totalitního umění*, edited by Petr Šámal, 149–158. Prague: ÚČL AV ČR, 2009.

Pernes, Jiří, Jaroslav Pospíšil, and Antonín Lukáš. *Alexej Čepička: Šedá eminence rudého režimu*. Prague: Nakladatelství Brána, 2008.

Petišková, Tereza. *Československý socialistický realismus, 1948–1958*. Prague: Gallery Rudolfinum, 2002.

Pittaway, Mark. *Brief Histories: Eastern Europe, 1939–2000*. London: Hodder Arnold, 2004.

Pozner, Valérie. "Le 'réalisme socialiste' et ses usages pour l'histoire du cinéma soviétique." In *Caméra politique: Cinéma et stalinisme*, edited by Kristian Feigelson, 11–17. Paris: Presses Sorbonne nouvelle, 2005.

Pudovkin, Vsevolod. "The *Naturschchik* instead of the Actor." In *Vsevolod Pudovkin: Selected Essays*, edited by Richard Taylor, translated by Richard Taylor and Evgeni Filippov, 158–162. New York: Seagull Books, 2006.

Pullmann, Michal. *Konec experimentu: Přestavba a pád komunismu v Československu*. Prague: Scriptorium, 2011.

Rak, Jiří. *Bývalí Čechové*. Prague: H & H, 1994.

———. "Úvodem k synopsi legionářského filmu." *Iluminace* 5, no. 1 (1993): 115–122.

Reid, Susan E. "The Soviet Art World in the Early Thaw." *Third Text* 20, no. 2 (2006): 161–175.

Reid, Susan E., and David Crowley, eds. *Style and Socialism: Modernity and Material Culture in Post-war Eastern Europe*. New York: Berg, 2000.

Rentschler, Eric. "Appendix A: Films and Events, 1933–1945." In *The Ministry of Illusion: Nazi Cinema and Its Afterlife*. 3rd printing, Cambridge, MA: Harvard University Press, 2002. Originally published 1996.

Rice, Condoleezza. "The Problem of Military Elite Cohesion in Eastern Europe." *Air University Review*. January–February 1982. www.airpower.maxwell.af.mil /airchronicles/aureview_toc/AUReview 1982/AUReview1982Jan-Feb.htm (accessed January 30, 2014).

———. *The Soviet Union and the Czechoslovak Army, 1948–1983: Uncertain Allegiance*. Princeton, NJ: Princeton University Press, 1984.

Rosen, Philip. "Border Times and Geopolitical Frames." *Canadian Journal of Film Studies* 15, no. 2 (Fall 2006): 2–19.

Rothschild, Joseph. *East Central Europe between the Two World Wars*. Seattle: University of Washington Press, 1974.

Rothschild, Joseph, and Nancy M. Wingfield. *Return to Diversity: A Political History of East Central Europe since World War II*. 3rd ed. New York: Oxford University Press, 2000.

Ryklin, Mikhail. "'The Best in the World': The Discourse of the Moscow Metro in the 1930s." In Dobrenko and Naiman, *The Landscape of Stalinism*, 261–276.

Sabrow, Martin. "Time and Legitimacy: Comparative Reflections on the Sense of Time in the Two German Dictatorships." *Totalitarian Movements and Political Religions* 6, no. 3 (2005): 351–369.

Sarkisova, Oksana. "Building the Past: Archival Footage in Documentary and Fictional Film." *Trans* 17 (March 2010). www.inst.at/trans/17Nr/7-11/7-11

_sarkisova17.htm (accessed January 30, 2014).

Sayer, Derek. *The Coasts of Bohemia: A Czech History.* Princeton, NJ: Princeton University Press, 1998.

Sharma, Aradhana, and Akhil Gupta. "Introduction: Rethinking Theories of the State in an Age of Globalization." In *The Anthropology of the State: A Reader,* edited by Aradhana Sharma and Akhil Gupta, 1–42. Oxford: Wiley-Blackwell, 2006.

Shell, Hanna Rose. *Hide and Seek: Camouflage, Photography, and the Media of Reconnaissance.* New York: Zone Books, 2012.

Shore, Marci. "Engineering in the Age of Innocence: A Genealogy of Discourse within the Czechoslovak Writers' Union, 1949–1967." *East European Politics and Societies* 12, no. 3 (1998): 397–441.

———. *The Taste of Ashes: The Afterlife of Totalitarianism in Eastern Europe.* New York: Crown, 2013.

Siefert, Marsha. "East European Cold War Culture(s)? Alterities, Commonalities, and Film Industries." In *Cold War Cultures: Perspectives on Eastern and Western European Societies,* edited by Annette Vowinckel, Marcus M. Payk, and Thomas Lindenberger, 23–54. New York: Berghahn, 2012.

Sís, Peter. "The Story behind the Book: A Very Short Version in the Author's Own Words." *Tibet through the Red Box.* www.petersistibet.com/tibetstory.htm.

Skilling, H. Gordon. *Czechoslovakia's Interrupted Revolution.* Princeton, NJ: Princeton University Press, 1976.

Skoller, Jeffrey. *Shadows, Specters, Shards: Making History in Avant-Garde Film.* Minneapolis: University of Minnesota Press, 2005.

Skopal, Pavel. "Filmy z nouze. Způsoby rámcování filmových projekcí a divácké zkušenosti v období stalinismu." *Iluminace* 21, no. 3 (2009): 70–91.

———, ed. *Naplánovaná kinematografie: Český filmový průmysl, kulturní politika a státní plánování, 1945–1960.* Prague: Academia, 2012.

Škvorecký, Josef. *All the Bright Young Men and Women: A Personal History of the Czech Cinema.* Translated by Michael Schonberg. Toronto: Peter Martin Associates, 1971.

Šmidrkal, Václav. *Armáda a stříbrné plátno: Československý armádní film, 1951–1999.* Prague: Naše vojsko, 2009.

Štabla, Zdeněk. *Data a fakta z dějin čs. kinematografie, 1896–1945.* Vol. 2. Prague: Československý filmový ústav, 1989.

Štingl, Pavel. "Lidstvo se nikdy nepoučí z vlastní historie . . . : Manipulace v dokumentárním filmu." In *Film a dějiny,* edited by Petr Kopal, 331–342. Prague: Nakladatelství Lidové noviny, 2004.

Streible, Dan, Martina Roepke, and Anke Mebold. "Introduction: Nontheatrical Film." In "Nontheatrical Film," ed. Dan Streible, Martina Roepke, and Anke Mebold. Special issue, *Film History* 19, no. 4 (2007): 340–341.

Švoma, Martin. *Karel Vachek, etc.* Prague: AMU, 2008.

Szczepanik, Petr. *Konzervy se slovy: Počátky zvukového filmu a česká mediální kultura 30. let.* Brno: Host, 2009.

———. "'Machři' a 'diletanti'. Základní jednotky filmové praxe v době reorganizací a politických zvratů 1945 až 1962." In Skopal, *Naplánovaná kinematografie,* 27–101.

———. "Modernism, Industry, Film: A Network of Media in the Baťa Corporation and the Town of Zlín in the 1930s." In Hediger and Vonderau, *Films That Work,* 349–376.

Taborsky, Edward. *Communism in Czechoslovakia, 1948–1960.* Princeton, NJ: Princeton University Press, 1961.

Trumpener, Katie. "*La guerre est finie:* New Waves, Historical Contingency, and the GDR 'Rabbit Films'." In *The Power of Intellectuals in Contemporary Germany,* edited by Michael Geyer, 113–137. Chicago: University of Chicago Press, 2001.

———. *The Divided Screen: German Cinema, 1930–*. Princeton, NJ: Princeton University Press, forthcoming.

Urbanová, Eva, et al. *Český hraný film I. 1898–1930*. Prague: Národní filmový archiv, 1995.

———. *Český hraný film III. 1945–1960*. Prague: Národní filmový archiv, 2001.

Uricchio, William. "The *Kulturfilm*: A Brief History of an Early Discursive Practice." In *Before Caligari: German Cinema, 1895–1920*, edited by Paolo Cherchi Usai and Lorenzo Codelli, 356–379. Pordenone: Edizioni Biblioteca dell'Immagine, 1990.

Vatulescu, Cristina. *Police Aesthetics: Literature, Film, and the Secret Police in Soviet Times*. Stanford, CA: Stanford University Press, 2010.

Verdery, Katherine. *What Was Socialism, and What Comes Next?* Princeton, NJ: Princeton University Press, 1996.

Vinogradova, Maria. "Between the State and the Kino: Amateur Film Workshops in the Soviet Union." *Studies in European Cinema* 8, no. 3 (2012): 211–225.

Virilio, Paul. *War and Cinema*. New York: Verso, 1989.

Vojtech, Miloslav. "Ladislav Mňačko." In *Portréty slovenských spisovateľov 3*, edited by Ján Zambor, 40–50. Bratislava: Univerzita Komenského, 2003.

Waller, Gregory A. "Cornering *The Wheat Farmer* (1938)." In Orgeron, Orgeron, and Streible, *Learning with the Lights Off*, 249–270.

———. "Projecting the Promise of 16mm, 1935–45." In Acland and Wasson, *Useful Cinema*, 125–148.

Wasson, Haidee. *Museum Movies: The Museum of Modern Art and the Birth of Art Cinema*. Berkeley: University of California Press, 2005.

———. "The Other Small Screen: Moving Images at New York's World's Fair, 1939."

Canadian Journal of Film Studies 22, no. 1 (2012): 81–103.

———. "Protocols of Portability." *Film History* 25, nos. 1–2 (2013): 236–247.

Waters, Leslie. "National Displacement, Political Revolution, and Social Consequences: The Hungarian–Slovak Population Exchange." Paper presented at "Postwar as Revolution? Rethinking Power in Eastern Europe after World War II," University of California, Berkeley, April 3–5, 2014.

Waugh, Thomas. "Beyond Verité: Emile de Antonio and the New Documentary of the 70s." *Jump Cut*, nos. 10–11 (1976): 33–39.

Wees, William C. "From Compilation to Collage: The Found-Footage Films of Arthur Lipsett: The Martin Walsh Memorial Lecture 2007." *Canadian Journal of Film Studies* 16, no. 2 (2007): 2–22.

Widdis, Emma. *Visions of a New Land: Soviet Film from the Revolution to the Second World War*. New Haven, CT: Yale University Press, 2003.

Williams, Kieran. *The Prague Spring and Its Aftermath: Czechoslovak Politics, 1968–1970*. New York: Cambridge University Press, 1997.

Wingfield, Nancy M. *Flag Wars and Stone Saints: How the Bohemian Lands Became Czech*. Cambridge, MA: Harvard University Press, 2007.

———. "The Politics of Memory: Constructing National Identity in the Czech Lands, 1945–1948." *East European Politics and Societies* 14, no. 2 (2000): 246–267.

Winston, Brian. *Claiming the Real: The Griersonian Documentary and Its Legitimations*. London: British Film Institute, 1995.

Witkovsky, Matthew S. *Foto: Modernity in Central Europe, 1918–1945*. Washington, D.C.: National Gallery of Art, 2007.

Woll, Josephine. *Real Images: Soviet Cinema and the Thaw*. New York: I.B. Tauris, 2000.

Zabloudilová, Jitka. "Film a fotografie v čs. vojsku v Rusku, 1914–1920," *Iluminace* 7, no. 2 (1995): 111–128.

Zahra, Tara. *Kidnapped Souls: National Indifference and the Battle for Children in the Bohemian Lands, 1900–1948.* Ithaca, NY: Cornell University Press, 2008.

Zarecor, Kimberly Elman. *Manufacturing a Socialist Modernity: Housing in Czechoslovakia, 1945–1960.* Pittsburgh: University of Pittsburgh Press, 2011.

Zeman, Pavel. "Stát a filmová propaganda ve třicátých letech," *Iluminace* 11, no. 1 (1999): 85–88.

Zimmermann, Yvonne. "What Hollywood Is to America, the Corporate Film Is to Switzerland: Remarks on Industrial Film as Utility Film." In Hediger and Vonderau, *Films That Work*, 101–117.

Zryd, Michael. "The Academy and the Avant-Garde: A Relationship of Dependence and Resistance." *Cinema Journal* 45, no. 2 (Winter 2006): 17–42.

———. "Experimental Film and the Development of Film Study in America." In Grieveson and Wasson, *Inventing Film Studies*, 182–216.

Zusi, Peter. "Tendentious Modernism: Karel Teige's Path to Functionalism."

Slavic Review 67, no. 4 (Winter 2008): 821–839.

DIGITAL SOURCES

"Národní divadlo, 'Prodaná nevěsta (Opera).'" Soupis repertoáru od roku 1883, http://archiv.narodni-divadlo.cz/default.aspx?jz=cs&dk=Inscenace.aspx&ic=3548&pn=256affcc-f102-1000-85ff-c11223344aaa (accessed April 23, 2012).

"'Since then I have believed in fate . . .': Transports of Protectorate Jews to the Baltic States, 1942." www.jewish museum.cz/en/abelivein.htm (accessed June 18, 2014).

"Tomáš Škrdlant—Filmografie." *Stránky Tomáše Škrdlanta.* www.tomasskrdlant .info/Stranky_Tomase_Skrdlanta/ Filmografie.html (accessed January 30, 2014).

UNPUBLISHED MATERIALS

Jansen, Huub. "Inventory of the W.U.D.-A.I.D. Collection." European Foundation Joris Ivens/Municipal Archives Nijmegen, 2004.

FILMOGRAPHY

Introduction

This filmography both provides details on the films discussed in this book and offers an overview of the thematic and generic range of Czechoslovak military nonfiction, newsreel, and instructional film production between 1919 and 1969. It does not include the Czechoslovak Ministry of Defense's secret or top-secret productions, full records of which I have been unable to locate, nor does it include films produced by other studios and dubbed by Army Film or its precursors into Czech or Slovak.

Although the full extent of the Czechoslovak Ministry of Defense's film production during these fifty years is unknown, in *The Army and the Silver Screen*, Václav Šmidrkal offers a rough overview of the scale of production in selected postwar years. In 1954, the studio's productions totaled approximately 18,500 meters (calculated in terms of 35mm films; of which circa 35 percent were fiction and nonfiction films produced for the Main Political Administration [HPS], 20 percent periodical productions—including newsreels—for the HPS, and 65 percent instructional films for the Combat Training Directorate [SBP]).

In 1959, the studio produced approximately 28,000 meters of film (30 percent for the HPS, 35 percent periodicals for the HPS, and 55 percent for the SBP); in 1963, approximately 30,000 meters (20 percent for the HPS, 35 percent periodicals for the HPS, 40 percent for the SBP, and 5 percent commissions for other organizations); and in 1968, approximately 49,000 meters (23 percent for the HPS; 17 percent periodicals for the HPS, 50 percent for the SBP, and 10 percent commissions). The number of films produced in the interwar period was considerably smaller. Not all films are extant; existing films are held by the Army Film Archive (a division of the Military History Institute in Prague) and the Czech National Film Archive.

The filmography is organized chronologically and alphabetically. Each entry contains the following details (where known): the film's genre; color (black and white or color); length (in meters—35mm, unless otherwise indicated—or minutes); details on coproductions or commissions; director; screenwriter or author of the original text; cinematographer; sound recordist; editor; and composer. Information is often incomplete and is in most cases reproduced as given in published sources (Havelka, *Čs. krátké filmy, 1945–1970*, and *Československý krátký film v letech 1922–45*; Šmidrkal, *Armáda a stříbrné plátno*) or archival documents. The orthography of Chinese names is reproduced from Havelka, *Čs. krátké filmy, 1945–1970*.

Films Produced by the Czechoslovak Ministry of Defense

1920

U slovenské vlády v Žilině (At the Slovak Government in Žilina)
Actuality, B&W

1921

Pohřeb čtyřiceti dvou popravených italských legionářů v Praze (The Funeral of Forty-Two Executed Italian Legionnaires in Prague)
Topical, B&W, 896 m.
Screenplay: Rudolf Medek

1922

Postavení pontonového mostu přes Dunaj (Constructing a Pontoon Bridge over the Danube)
B&W

1923

Škodovy závody průmyslové (The Škoda Industrial Works)
B&W, 225 m.

Zpomalený snímek dělostřeleckého cvičení (Slowed-Down Recording of Artillery Training)
B&W

1924

Mezinárodní armádní a lyžařské závody čs. branné moci (International Military and Skiing Championships of the Czechoslovak Armed Forces)
B&W, 532 m.

Přehlídka baterie proti letadlům presidentem republiky (Review of the Anti-Aircraft Battery by the President of the Republic)
B&W, 304 m.
Director: Lt. Brázda; Cinematography: Vojtěch Vyšín

Traktory a jejich použití (Tractors and Their Use)
Educational, B&W, 160 m.

1925

Československá armáda (The Czechoslovak Army)
Compilation, B&W, 2480 m.
Director: Vojtěch Vyšín; Cinematography: Vladimír Studecký

Letecký den v Praze (Aviation Day in Prague)
Topical, B&W, 240 m.

Slavnostní otevření domova čs. legionářů invalidů na Jenerálce (Ceremonial Opening of the Czechoslovak Legionnaire House at Jenerálka)
Topical, B&W, 230 m.

1926

Ukázka polního tělocviku (Example of Field Training)
Reportage, B&W, 150 m.

1927

Obrázky z bratrského království Srbů, Chorvatů a Slovinců (Images from the Brotherly Kingdom of Serbs, Croats, and Slovenes)
B&W, 250 m.

Slavia L-Brox (Románek letcův) (Slavia L-Brox [A Pilot's Romance])
Fiction feature, B&W, 2104 m.
Director and Screenplay: Vladimír Studecký; Cinematography: Vojtěch Vyšín

1928

Aeroplán (Aeroplane)
Technical, B&W, 230 m.

Tatry v zimě (The Tatras in Winter)
Promotional, B&W, 370 m.

Vítězné lety české aeronautiky (Champion Flights of Czech Aeronautics)
Topical, B&W, 450 m.

Vysoké Tatry (The High Tatras)
Nature film, B&W, 975 m.

Za československý stát (For the Czechoslovak State)
Fiction feature, B&W, 2004 m.
Director: Vladimír Studecký; Screenplay: Rudolf Medek, Vladimír Studecký; Cinematography: Vojtěch Vyšín

1929

Horské volání S.O.S. (Mountain Cry S.O.S.)
Fiction feature, B&W, 2523 m. Coproduction with Elektajournal.
Director: Leo Marten, Vladimír Studecký; Screenplay: František Horký, Vojtěch Vyšín, Vladimír Studecký; Cinematography: Karel Kopřiva, Vladimír Studecký, Jan Stallich

Technika vojenského lyžařství (Military Skiing Techniques)
Educational, B&W, 975 m.
Director: Miloš Frgal; Cinematography: Vladimír Studecký

1930

Dvanáct let presidentem ČSR (Twelve Years as President of the Czechoslovak Republic)
Documentary, B&W, 590 m.

Násilím či rozumem (Jak zacházeti se zlými, vzdorovitými koňmi) (By Force or by Reason [How to Handle Unruly, Cantankerous Horses])
Educational, B&W, 2560 m.

Výcvik vojenských psů (Training Military Dogs)
Educational, B&W, 1045 m.
Director: František Kunce

1931

Závěrečná cvičení jezdectva (Final Cavalry Exercises)
Topical, B&W, 800 m.

1932

Účast vojska o IX. sletě všesokolském v Praze 1932 (Soldiers' Participation in the Twelfth Sokol Slet in Prague, 1932)
Topical, B&W, 140 m.

1933

S řidičem na vojně (Jeho výcvik a školení) (With Drivers in the Military [Their Training and Education])
Educational, B&W, 2795 m.

Vítězný den našeho armádního letectva (Triumphant Day for our Military Aviation)
Topical, B&W, 335 m.

Vojenské oslavy 15. výročí republiky (Military Celebrations for the Fifteenth Anniversary of the Republic)
Topical, B&W, 395 m.

1934

Ráno v kasárnách (Morning in the Barracks)
Reportage, B&W, 1095 m.
Director: Jiří Jeníček

1935

Naši vojáci (Our Soldiers)
Propaganda, B&W, 1680 m.
Director: Jiří Jeníček; Cinematography: Alois Čuřík, Zdeněk Hofbauer

1936

Péče o koně (The Care of Horses)

Instructional, B&W, 270 m. Coproduction with Lloydfilm and AB.
Director and Screenplay: Jiří Jeníček; Cinematography: Zdeněk Hofbauer and Jiří Jeníček; Sound: František Šindelář

Praktické příklady ze strážní služby (Practical Examples of Guard Duty)

Instructional, B&W
Director: Jiří Jeníček

1937

Armádní letecký den 1936 (Military Aviation Day 1936)

Topical, B&W, 320 m.

Naše armáda (Our Army)

Documentary, B&W, 265 m.
Director and Screenplay: Jiří Jeníček; Cinematography: Zdeněk Hofbauer, Jiří Lehovec, Vladimír Novotný; Sound: František Šindelář, Josef Zora; Editor: Vladimír Novotný; Music: E. F. Burian

1938

Ukázky z cizích armád (Examples from Foreign Armies)

Compilation, B&W, 3430 m.
Director: Miloš Staněk

Válka ve Španělsku (The War in Spain)

Topical, B&W, 670 m.
Director: Miloš Staněk

V nový život (In a New Life)

Documentary, B&W, 285 m. Produced in collaboration with AB.
Director, Screenplay, and Cinematography: Jiří Jeníček; Text: Josef Knap; Sound: Vilém Taraba; Editor: Vladimír Novotný; Music: Jiří Srnka

Vojáci v horách (Soldiers in the Mountains)

Educational, B&W, 360 m.

Director and Screenplay: Jiří Jeníček; Cinematography: Jiří Lehovec, Vladimír Novotný; Sound: Vilém Taraba; Editor: Vladimír Novotný; Music: Jiří Srnka

1945

Cesta domů (The Journey Home)

Reportage, B&W, 1065 m.
Director and Screenplay: Miroslav Tiller; Cinematography: Miroslav Tiller, Miloš Novák, Václav Kepák, Kurt Goldberger; Sound: Ken Cameron; Editor: Josef Dobřichovský; Music: Jiří Šust

Pod praporem svobody (Under Freedom's Flag)

Promotional, B&W, 453 m.
Director and Screenplay: František Rejlek; Cinematography: Jan Tuček, Míla Vích; Editor: František Rejlek, Jan Tuček

1946

Střežíme hranice (We Are Defending the Border)

Reportage, B&W, 1065 m.
Director and Screenplay: Jaroslav Váchal; Cinematography: Emil Háša, Jiří Sekera; Editor: Eduard Kadeřábek; Music: Jiří Šust

1948

Armádní den (Army Day)

Reportage, B&W, 515 m.
Director: Jaroslav Váchal; Cinematography: Emil Háša, Josef Pešek, Josef Vágner, J. Adam, František Jindra, M. Holík; Music: Jan Seechák

Mladá křídla nastupují (Young Wings Alight)

Promotional, B&W, 579 m.
Director: Jaroslav Váchal; Screenplay: Rudolf Holeček, Jaroslav Váchal; Cinematography: Emil Háša, Jiří Sekera, Eduard Kadeřábek; Sound: Jiří Židlický; Music: Jiří Srnka

1949

*Škola důstojnického dorostu
(Young Officers' School)*

Reportage, B&W, 380 m.
Director and Editor: Jaroslav Váchal;
Screenplay: Lubomír Možný; Cinema-
tography: Josef Pešek, Jiří Tarantík;
Sound: Jan Lerch

1950

*Budujeme, jdeme vpřed (We Shall
Build, We Shall Advance)*

Reportage, B&W, 353 m.
Director: Jaroslav Váchal; Cinematography: Jiří Tarantík

Vítězná cesta (Victorious Journey)

Documentary (compilation), B&W, 282 m.
Director and Editor: Ivo Toman; Narra-
tion: Miloš Nesvadba; Sound: Miloslav
Hůrka

Výsadkáři (Paratroopers)

Promotional, B&W, 490 m.
Director: Jaroslav Váchal; Screenplay: Jiří
Brenner; Cinematography: Jiří Tarantík,
Rudolf Stahl, Jaroslav Trojan; Sound:
Miloslav Hůrka; Music: Otakar Maršík

1951

*Alexandrovci u nás (The Alexandrov
Ensemble in Czechoslovakia)*

Reportage, B&W, 1387 m.
Director and Cinematography: Ivan
Frič; Screenplay: Ivan Frič and Roman
Hlaváč; Sound: Karel Cajthaml and Jo-
sef Zavadil; Editor: Josef Dobřichovský;
Music: Jiří Šust

*Armádní sportovní hry (Army
Sports Matches)*

Documentary (sports), B&W, 320 m.
Director and Screenplay: Karel Baroch;
Cinematography: Jan Čuřík

Ocel písní kalená (Song-Hardened Steel)

Reportage, B&W, 435 m.
Director and Screenplay: Karel Baroch;
Cinematography: Jan Čuřík; Sound:
Karel Cajthaml; Editor: Dana Němcová;
Music: Miloš Smatek

Přehlídka 1951 (Military Parade 1951)

Reportage (military parade), B&W, 1695 m.
Director: Ivo Toman; Screenplay: Ivo To-
man, Ivan V. Frič; Cinematography:
Ivan V. Frič, Jan Čuřík, Václav Hanuš,
Václav Huňka, Jan Jiráček, Svatopluk
Malý, Jan Novák, Vladimír Novotný,
Josef Pešek, Přemysl Prokop, Rudolf
Stahl, Jiří Tarantík, Josef Vaniš; Sound:
František Černý, Josef Zavadil; Editor:
Josef Dobřichovský; Music: Jiří Šust,
AUS Orchestra

Šetřte potravinami (Conserve Provisions)

Agitka, B&W, 122 m.
Director: Zbyněk Brynych

*Slyší tě nepřítel (The Enemy
Is Listening to You)*

Agitka, B&W, 380 m.
Director: Zbyněk Brynych; Screenplay: Jiří
Beneš, Vratislav Blažek; Cinematogra-
phy: Jan Čuřík; Music: Jiří Šust

1952

*Armádní filmový festival (The
Army Film Festival)*

Reportage, B&W, 242 m.
Director: Karel Baroch

Křídla vlasti (Wings of the Homeland)

Reportage (aviation), B&W, 259 m.
Director: Stanislav Brožík; Cinematogra-
phy: Jan Jaroš, Miroslav Fojtík; Editor:
Jiří Sobotka

*Letní armádní spartakiáda (The
Army's Summer Spartakiada)*

Reportage (sports), B&W, 340 m.
Director: Miroslav Dufek, Lubomír Marek

Neprojdou (They Shall Not Pass)
Documentary, Color, 398 m.
Director: Zbyněk Brynych, Roman Hlaváč;
  Screenplay: Roman Hlaváč, Zbyněk
  Brynych; Cinematography: Jan Čuřík;
  Sound: Karel Cajthaml; Editor: Miloslav
  Hájek; Music: Jiří Šust

*Neprojdou (Korea) (They
Shall Not Pass [Korea])*
Compilation, B&W, 430 m.
Director: Václav Hapl

*Olympijský vítěz Jánko Zachara
(Jánko Zachara's Olympic Victory)*
Documentary (sports), B&W, 216 m.
Director: Ľubomír Marek; Cinematogra-
  phy: Jan Jiráček

*Věda jde s lidem (Science
Goes with the People)*
Reportage, B&W, 621 m.
Director and Screenplay: Pavel Háša;
  Cinematography: Vojtěch Jasný, Karel
  Kachyňa, Miloslav Fojtík, Jan Jaroš,
  Alois Jiráček; Sound: Karel Cajthaml;
  Editor: Dana Lukešová; Music: Jiří
  Pauer

Vítězný pochod (Triumphant March)
Documentary (military parade), Color,
  1929 m.
Director and Screenplay: Ivan V. Frič; Cin-
  ematography: Ivan V. Frič et al.; Sound:
  Karel Cajthaml; Editor: Jan Chaloupek;
  Music: Jiří Šust

*Zimní armádní spartakiáda (The
Army's Winter Spartakiada)*
Reportage (sports), B&W, 332 m.
Director: Karel Baroch

1953

*Armádní umělecké divadlo (The
Army Artistic Theater)*
Documentary, B&W, 781 m.

Director and Screenplay: Pavel Háša; Cin-
  ematography: Jaroslav Kučera; Sound:
  Karel and Stanislav Cajthaml; Editor:
  Dana Lukešová; Music: Jiří Pauer

*Divadlo čs. armády (The
Czechoslovak Army Theater)*
Documentary, B&W, 559 m.
Director and Screenplay: Ján Lacko; Cin-
  ematography: Josef Illík; Sound: Karel
  Cajthaml; Editor: Dana Lukešová; Mu-
  sic: Václav Dobiáš

Jsme připraveni (We Are Prepared)
Reportage, Color, 735 m.
Director: Ján Lacko; Cinematography: Jo-
  sef Illík; Sound: Karel Cajthaml; Editor:
  Jiří Sobotka; Music: Jiří Šust

JVS (Josef Vissarionovich Stalin)
B&W, 565 m.

*Létání bez vidu podle systému OSP
(Flying Blind Using System OSP)*
Instructional, Color, 1395 m.
Director and Screenplay: František Vláčil;
  Cinematography: Josef Illík; Sound:
  Karel Cajthaml; Editor: Vlasta Plotěná;
  Animation: Josef Bůžek, Vladimír
  Dvořák

Lidé jednoho srdce (People of One Heart)
Documentary, Color, 2694 m.
Director and Screenplay: Vojtěch Jasný and
  Karel Kachyňa, Čchu Paj-in, Tüng Siao-
  wu; Cinematography: Vojtěch Jasný,
  Karel Kachyňa, Čchao Tin-jün, Tchien
  Li; Sound: Svatopluk Havelka, Miloš
  Vacek; Editor: Jan Chaloupek

Modrý den (Blue Day)
Reportage, Color, 706 m.
Director: Vladimír Sís; Screenplay:
  František Vláčil, Vladimír Sís; Cinema-
  tography: Jan Čuřík; Music: Rudolf
  Kubín; Editor: Miroslav Hájek

Na stráži (On Guard)

Instructional, B&W, 411 m.

Director and Cinematography: Vojtěch Jasný and Karel Kachyňa; Screenplay: Karel Krejčí; Editor: Jiří Sobotka

Naše vojsko (Our Army)

Documentary, B&W, 275 m.

Director: Ivan V. Frič; Screenplay: Karel Krejčí; Cinematography: Miroslav Fojtík

Pevný břeh (Ironclad Border)

Documentary, Color, 337 m.

Director: Vladimír Sís; Cinematography: Jan Čuřík; Sound: Karel Cajthaml; Editor: Dana Lukešová; Music: Jiří Šust

Rektifikace (Rectification)

Instructional, B&W

Director: Jaroslav Váchal

Rozloučení s Klementem Gottwaldem (Farewell to Klement Gottwald)

Documentary, Color, 1507 m.

Director: Ivo Toman; Text: Pavel Kohout; Cinematography: Army Film and State Film cameramen; Editor: Jaromír Janáček

Sportovní odpoledne na Strahově (Athletic Afternoon at Strahov)

Reportage (sports), B&W, 318 m.

Director: Stanislav Barabáš

Stará čínská opera (Old Chinese Opera)

Documentary, Color, 326 m.

Director and Screenplay: Vojtěch Jasný, Karel Kachyňa, Čchao Tin-jün, Tchien Li; Music: Miloš Vacek; Sound: Josef Zavadil; Editor: Jan Chaloupek

1954

Armádní divadlo Martin (The Army Theater in Martin)

Documentary, B&W, 425 m.

Director and Screenplay: Oldřich Holíček; Cinematography: Josef Illík; Sound:

Stanislav Cajthaml; Editor: Dana Lukešová; Music: Dezider Kardoš

Ať žije Mao Ce-tung (Long Live Mao Zedong)

Documentary, B&W, 195 m.

Director: Ján Lacko; Cinematography: Josef Illík

Budující Korea (Building Korea)

Documentary (compilation), B&W, 365 m.

Director: Karel Krejčí

Cesta vede do Tibetu (The Road Leads to Tibet)

Reportage, Color, 1664 m. Coproduction with, and commissioned by, the Chinese People's Army film studio.

Director: Vladimír Sís, Chu Čchi, Li Ťün, Wang Ping; Cinematography: Josef Vaniš, Feng Ťin, Ťiang Š, Wu-Ti, Čchen Č-Čhiang, Čang Jün; Sound: Karel Cajthaml; Editor: Vlasta Plotěná; Music: Miloš Vacek

Čs. nemocnice v Koreji (The Czechoslovak Hospital in Korea)

Reportage, B&W, 370 m.

Director: Jiří Ployhar; Text: Roman Hlaváč; Cinematography: Ivan Frič, Jiří Ployhar; Sound: Karel Cajthaml; Editor: Jiří Sobotka; Music: Jiří Šust

Dnes večer všechno skončí (Everything Ends Tonight)

Fiction feature, Color, 2202 m.

Director: Vojtěch Jasný, Karel Kachyňa; Screenplay: Lubomír Možný; Cinematography: Jaroslav Kučera; Sound: František Fabián; Editor: Jan Chaloupek; Music: Svatopluk Havelka

Odminování průchodu III (Demining a Passage III)

Instructional, B&W, 864 m.[?]

Director: Václav Hapl

*Opičí císař dostává zbraň v paláci Dračího
císaře (The Monkey Emperor Receives a
Weapon at the Palace of the Dragon Emperor)*
Documentary, Color, 319 m.
Director: Ján Lacko, Dzei Čo; Cinematog-
raphy: Josef Illík, Milan Nejedlý; Sound:
Stanislav Cajthaml; Editor: Dana
Lukešová

Vojenská přehlídka (Military Parade)
Reportage (military parade), Color, 481 m.
Director: Pavel Háša; Cinematography: Jo-
sef Illík et al.; Editor: Miroslav Hájek

Vzpomínka (Memory)
Documentary, Color, 541 m.
Director and Screenplay: František Vláčil;
Cinematography: Jan Čuřík; Sound:
Karel Cajthaml; Editor: Dana Lukešová;
Music: Jiří Šust

Za lidovou armádu (For the People's Army)
Compilation, B&W, 420 m.
Director and Screenplay: Ivan V. Frič

*Z čínského zápisníku (From
a Chinese Notebook)*
Reportage, Color, 353 m.
Director: Vojtěch Jasný, Karel Kachyňa,
Čchu Paj-im; Cinematography: Vojtěch
Jasný, Karel Kachyňa, Tchien Li, Čchao
Tin-Jü; Editor: Jan Chaloupek; Music:
Svatopluk Havelka

1955

*IV. armádní spartakiáda (Lyžařské
přebory) (IV. Army Spartakiada
[Skiing Championships])*
Reportage (sports), B&W, 386 m.
Director and Text: Vladimír Horák; Cin-
ematography: Karel Hollegcha, Miroslav
Fojtík, Jan Jaroš, Jaroslav Kadlec, Ivan
Koudelka; Editor: Vlasta Plotená; Mu-
sic: Jiří Šust

10 let (10 Years)
Documentary (compilation), B&W, 480 m.

Director and Screenplay: Karel A. Krejčí

Bez obav (Fearless)
Documentary (military parade), Color,
669 m.
Director and Screenplay: Vojtěch Jasný;
Cinematography: Jiří Ployhar; Sound:
Karel Cajthaml; Editor: Jiří Sobotka;
Music: Svatopluk Havelka

*Choreografické prvky pro nácvik
I. celostátní spartakiády (Choreographic
Elements for Training for the First
All-Country Spartakiada)*
Instructional, Color, 475 m.
Director: Jaroslav Váchal

Hygiena tábora (Camp Hygiene)
Instructional, Color, 320 m.
Director and Screenplay: Václav Hapl

Letecký den 1955 (Aviation Day 1955)
Reportage (aviation), Color, 369 m.
Director and Screenplay: Karel Krejčí; Cin-
ematography: Ivan V. Frič, Karel Hol-
legcha, Josef Illík, Jaroslav Kadlec, Ivan
Koudelka, Josef Vaniš; Sound: Karel
Cajthaml; Editor: Dana Lukešová; Mu-
sic: Jiří Šust

*Lidově demokratický stát—stát dělníků
a rolníků (The People's Democratic
State—A State of Workers and Farmers)*
Compilation, B&W, 490 m.
Director and Screenplay: Oldřich Holíček

Mistr Jan Hus (Master Jan Hus)
Documentary, Color, 673 m.
Director: Pavel Háša; Screenplay: Pavel
Háša, Josef Illík; Cinematography: Josef
Illík, Josef Josefík; Music: Jiří Pauer

*Mne sa to nemôže stat' (It
Can't Happen to Me)*
Agitka, B&W, 340 m.
Director and Screenplay: Ján Lacko; Cin-
ematography: Karel Hollegcha; Editor:
Dana Lukešová

*Odběr infekčního materiálu I
(Epidemiologie I) (Collecting Infectious
Material I [Epidemiology I])*

Instructional, Color, 270 m.
Director and Screenplay: Jaromír
Dvořáček; Cinematography: Miroslav
Fojtík

*Pozdrav veliké země (Greetings
to a Great Land)*

Documentary, Color, 2366 m.
Director: Ján Lacko, Čaj Čchao; Text:
Vojtěch Jasný; Cinematography: Josef Il-
lík, Yang Čchaj; Sound: Karel Cajthaml
and Stanislav Cajthaml, Sue Čhen-Sün;
Editor: Dana Lukešová; Music: Jiří Šust,
Chuang Šchin

Rozdělená země (Divided Land)

Documentary, Color, 681 m.
Director: Ivan Frič; Cinematography:
Ivan Frič, Jiří Ployhar; Sound: Karel
Cajthaml; Editor: Jiří Sobotka; Music:
Jiří Šust

Ztracená stopa (The Lost Track)

Fiction feature, B&W, 2232 m.
Director: Karel Kachyňa; Screenplay:
Jiří Beneš; Cinematography: Jaroslav
Kučera; Editor: Dana Lukešová, Jiří
Sobotka; Sound: Karel Cajthaml; Music:
Miloš Vacek

1956

Anestesie v poli (Field Anesthesia)

Instructional, Color, 300 m.
Director and Screenplay: Vlastimil Fiala

*Atomy a jejich složení II, III (Atoms
and Their Constitution II, III)*

Educational, B&W, 400 m. / 450 m.
Director and Screenplay: Vlastimil Fiala;
Cinematography: Jan Jiráček

Berlín 1956

Reportage, Color, 351 m. Coproduction
with DEFA.

Director: Stanislav Brožík; Cinematography: Karel Hollegcha, Ivan Koudelka;
Sound: Karel Cajthaml; Editor: Jiří Sobotka; Music: Jiří Šust

Brodění tanků (Wading Tanks)

Instructional, B&W, 359 m.
Director: Jaroslav Trojan

Daleko od Prahy (Far from Prague)

Documentary, B&W, 319 m.
Director, Screenplay, Cinematography:
Ivan V. Frič; Text: Jiří Ployhar; Nar-
ration: Jiří Šrámek; Sound: Karel
Cajthaml; Editor: Jiří Sobotka; Music:
Archival (arr. Jiří Šust)

Devět za devět (Nine by Nine)

Agitka, B&W, 280 m.
Director: Stanislav Brožík; Cinematography: Jaroslav Kadlec

Dopis z fronty (Letter from the Front)

Reportage, B&W, 380 m.
Director: František Vláčil; Cinematog-
raphy: Jan Čuřík; Editor: Jiří Sobotka;
Music: Vladimír Sommer

Gymnastika žen (Women's Gymnastics)

Educational, 300 m.
Director: Jaroslav Trojan, Jaroslav Váchal

Křivé zrcadlo (Crooked Mirror)

Agitka, Color, 490 m.
Director and Screenplay: Karel Kachyňa;
Cinematography: Josef Vaniš; Editor:
Vlasta Plotěná

*Měření výškového větru (Measuring
Altitudinal Wind)*

Instructional, B&W, 200 m.
Director and Screenplay: Jaromír Dvořáček

*Naši sportovní střelci v Číně (Czechoslovak
Sport Shooters in China)*

Reportage, Color, 220 m.
Director: František Vláčil; Cinematography: Josef Illík

Ochranný léčebný režim na ošetřovně (Prophylactic Therapeutic Regime in the Infirmary)

Instructional, Color, 330 m.
Director and Screenplay: Jaroslav Váchal

Operace mozkového aneurysmatu (Operating on Brain Aneurysms)

Instructional (medical), Color, 1491 m.
Director and Screenplay: Jaromír Dvořáček; Cinematography: Miroslav Fojtík; Editor: Vlasta Plotěná; Music: Archival (arr. Jiří Šust)

Palba na vzdušné cíle z ručních zbraní (Shooting at Air Targets from Hand Weapons)

Instructional, B&W, 300 m.
Director and Screenplay: Miroslav Fojtík

Posádka na štítě (The Crew on the Peak)

Educational, Color, 328 m.
Director and Screenplay: František Vláčil; Cinematography: Jan Čuřík; Sound: Karel Cajthaml; Editor: Vlasta Plotěná; Music: Vladimír Sommer

První závod vítězství (First Competition for Victory)

Reportage, Color, 292 m.
Director and Screenplay: Stanislav Brožík; Cinematography: Karel Hollegcha, Jan Čuřík, Miroslav Fojtík, Josef Vaniš; Sound: Karel Cajthaml; Editor: Jiří Sobotka; Music: Jiří Šust

Příležitost (Opportunity)

Agitka, B&W, 400 m.
Director and Screenplay: Vojtěch Jasný; Cinematography: Josef Illík; Sound: Karel Cajthaml; Editor: Dana Lukešová; Music: Svatopluk Havelka

Puška—tvůj kamarád (The Rifle—Your Friend)

Agitka, B&W, 320 m.
Director and Screenplay: Ivo Toman; Cinematography: Jan Čuřík

Služební pes (Service Dog)

Instructional, Color, 300 m.
Director and Screenplay: Jaroslav Váchal

Sportovci ÚDA v Berlíně (The Athletes of ÚDA in Berlin)

Reportage (sports), Color, 380 m.
Director: Stanislav Brožík; Cinematography: Ivan Koudelka, Karel Hollegcha

Stalo se jedné noci (It Happened One Night)

Agitka, B&W, 519 m.
Director: Pavel Háša; Screenplay: Pavel Háša, Josef Illík; Cinematography: Josef Illík; Sound: Karel Cajthaml; Editor: Vlasta Plotěná; Music: Jiří Šust

Střelecké závody v Pekinu (Shooting Competitions in Peking)

Reportage, Color, 531 m.
Director and Screenplay: František Vláčil, Chao Kuan, Josef Illík, Sue Paj-Ching; Sound: Karel Cajthaml; Editor: Vlasta Plotěná; Music: Jiří Šust

Stroje pro zemní práce (Machines for Earthwork)

Instructional, B&W, 300 m.
Director and Screenplay: Miroslav Dufek

Svazarm v Číně (Svazarm in China)

Documentary, B&W, 280 m.
Director: František Vláčil; Cinematography: Josef Illík

Tanková brigáda (The Tank Brigade)

Fiction feature, Color, 2602 m.
Director: Ivo Toman; Screenplay: Jaroslav Klíma; Cinematography: Jan Čuřík; Sound: Karel Cajthaml; Editor: Jiřina Lukešová

Technika skladování automobilního a traktorového materiálu (Techniques for Storing Automobile and Tractor Material)

Instructional, B&W, 359 m.
Director and Screenplay: Jaroslav Váchal

Umělé srdce (Artificial Heart)

Educational (medical), Color, 240 m.
Director and Screenplay: Vlastimil Fiala;
Cinematography: Jaroslav Kadlec

Úvod do světa atomů (Introduction to the World of Atoms)

Educational (popular-scientific), 590 m.
Director and Text: Václav Hapl; Screenplay: Ivan Sedláček, Václav Hapl; Cinematography: Alois Jiráček; Editor: Vlasta Plotěná

Velká zkouška (The Great Trial)

Reportage, Color, 486 m.
Director, Screenplay, Cinematography: Jiří Ployhar; Sound: Karel Cajthaml; Editor: Vlasta Plotěná; Music: Svatopluk Havelka

Vývoj polních zbraní (The Development of Field Weapons)

Documentary, B&W, 330 m.
Director: Vladimír Sís; Cinematography: Josef Vaniš

Zabraňte úrazům (Prevent Injuries)

Agitka, B&W, 160 m.
Director and Screenplay: Ivo Toman; Cinematography: Jan Čuřík

Zbraň, kterou ztratíš (The Weapon You Lose)

Agitka, B&W, 290 m.
Director and Screenplay: Ivo Toman; Cinematography: Jan Čuřík

Zimní spartakiáda (Lyžování) (Winter Spartakiada [Skiing])

Reportage (sports), B&W, 320 m.
Director and Screenplay: Vladimír Horák

1957

Částečná anestesie (Local Anesthesia)

Instructional, Color, 360 m.
Director and Screenplay: Vlastimil Fiala

Celková anestesie (General Anesthesia)

Instructional, Color, 300 m.

Director and Screenplay: Vlastimil Fiala

Charakteristiky turbokompresorového motoru (Characteristics of the Turbocompressor Motor)

Instructional, B&W, 430 m.
Director: Karel Baroch, Josef Hančar

Co nevíte o sportovní střelbě (All You Need to Know about Sport Shooting)

Instructional, B&W, 350 m.
Director and Screenplay: Ivo Toman

Exploatace buldozeru (The Use of Bulldozers)

Instructional, B&W, 300 m.
Director and Screenplay: Miroslav Dufek

Hygiena nohou (Foot Hygiene)

Instructional, B&W, 290 m.
Director and Screenplay: Oldřich Holíček

Hygienické zásady zásobování vojsk pitnou vodou (Hygienic Fundaments of Providing Troops with Potable Water)

Instructional, Color, 330 m.
Director and Screenplay: Oldřich Holíček

Lovci perel (Pearl Hunters)

Agitka, B&W, 394 m.
Director and Screenplay: Oldřich Holíček; Cinematography: Karel Hollegcha; Sound: Karel Cajthaml; Editor: Dana Lukešová; Music: Jiří Šust

Minuty v Paříži (Minutes in Paris)

Documentary, Color, 455 m.
Director and Screenplay: Vladimír Sís; Cinematography: Josef Vaniš; Editor: Jiří Sobotka; Music: Miloš Vacek

Modrá a zlatá (Blue and Gold)

Agitka, B&W, 315 m.
Director: Pavel Háša; Screenplay: Pavel Háša, Roman Hlaváč; Cinematography: Josef Illík; Editor: Jiří Sobotka; Music: Jiří Šust

Nebezpečné paprsky (Dangerous Rays)
Popular-scientific, B&W, 300 m.
Director and Screenplay: Vladimír Horák;
   Cinematography: Jiří Ployhar

*Palivová instalace turbokompresorového
motoru (Fuel Installation of the
Turbocompressor Motor)*
Instructional, B&W, 400 m.
Director: Karel Baroch, Josef Hančar

*Plachtařská mistrovství světa
(Yachting World Championships)*
Reportage (sports), B&W, 547 m.
Director: Milan Čumpelík, Petr Gryner;
   Cinematography: Jan Eisner, Miroslav
   Pflug, Ivan Wurm; Music: Archival (arr.
   František Belfín)

*Poranění krční páteře a nový způsob fixace
hlavy (Injury to the Cervical Spine and
New Means of Immobilizing the Head)*
Educational (medical), Color, 370 m.
Director and Screenplay: Jaromír Váchal;
   Cinematography: Jaroslav Kadlec

*Princip a popis staničního tlakoměru
(Principles and Description of
the Station Barometer)*
Instructional, B&W, 300 m.
Director and Screenplay: Jaromír Dvořáček

*Rozdělené město (Berlín 1957)
(Divided City [Berlin 1957])*
Documentary, Color, 452 m.
Director, Screenplay, Text: Ivo Toman;
   Cinematography: Jan Jaroš, Jan Čuřík;
   Narration: Jiří Šrámek; Editor: Dana
   Lukešová; Music: Jiří Šust

Sen (Dream)
Agitka, B&W, 300 m.
Director and Screenplay: Karel Kachyňa;
   Cinematography: Miroslav Fojtík; Edi-
   tor: Vlasta Plotěná; Music: Miloš Vacek

Skleněná oblaka (Glass Skies)
Documentary, Color, 400 m.

Director and Screenplay: František Vláčil;
   Cinematography: Josef Vaniš; Editor:
   Jiří Sobotka; Music: Miloš Vacek

*Startování vozidel za nízkých teplot
(Starting Vehicles in Low Temperatures)*
Instructional, B&W, 300 m.
Director and Screenplay: Vlastimil Fiala

Strahov, 9. května 1957 (Strahov, May 9, 1957)
Reportage (military parade), B&W, 265 m.
Director: Vladimír Sís; Cinematography:
   Josef Vaniš; Editor: Jiří Sobotka; Music:
   Archival (arr. Jiří Šust)

Střelba z vozidel (Shooting from Vehicles)
Instructional, B&W, 410 m.
Director: Vladimír Horák

*Tajemství gyroskopu (The
Mystery of the Gyroscope)*
Instructional, B&W, 280 m.
Director and Screenplay: František
   Karásek; Cinematography: Miroslav
   Fojtík; Editor: Vlasta Plotěná

*Technické ošetřování automobilů:
Vstřikovací zařízení, I–IV (Technical Care
of Automobiles: Injector Equipment, I–IV)*
Popular-scientific, Color (I) and B&W, 808
   m./469 m./489 m./508 m.
Director and Screenplay: Karel Baroch

*Technika jízdy automobilem
(Techniques for Driving a Car)*
Instructional, B&W, 430 m.
Director and Screenplay: Karel Baroch

Útěk (Escape)
Documentary, B&W, 380 m.
Director and Screenplay: Václav Hapl; Cin-
   ematography: Josef Vaniš; Editor: Vlasta
   Plotěná; Music: Svatopluk Havelka

*Vojenská požární ochrana
(Military Fire Prevention)*
Instructional, B&W, 380 m.
Director and Screenplay: Miroslav Dufek

Vojenský pozdrav (The Military Salute)
Instructional, B&W, 240 m.
Director and Screenplay: Vlastimil Fiala

Vývoj a činnost turbokompresorového motoru (The Development and Function of the Turbocompressor Motor)
Instructional, B&W, 430 m.
Director: Karel Baroch, Josef Hančar

Zápisník z NDR (Notebook from West Germany)
Documentary, Color, 440 m.
Director and Screenplay: Ivo Toman; Cinematography: Jan Čuřík, Jan Jaroš

Zápisník z Tibetu (Notebook from Tibet)
Documentary, Color, 400 m.
Director, Screenplay, Cinematography: Jiří Ployhar; Editor: Vlasta Plotěná; Music: Svatopluk Havelka

Zbraň ve strážní službě (The Gun in Guard Duty)
Instructional, B&W, 350 m.
Director and Screenplay: Karel Baroch

1958

Aerodynamika I: Základní zákony aerodynamiky (Aerodynamics I: Fundamental Laws of Aerodynamics); II: Křídla letounu (II: Airplane Wings), III. Mechanisace křídla letounu (III: The Mechanization of Airplane Wings)
Popular-scientific, B&W, 643 m./1029 m./670 m.
Director and Screenplay: Karel Baroch; Cinematography: Jan Jaroš; Sound: Karel Cajthaml; Editor: Vlasta Plotěná; Music: Archival (arr. Miloš Smatek)

Co dokáže tarasnice (What a Bazooka Can Do)
Instructional (popular-scientific), B&W, 415 m.
Director and Screenplay: Vladimír Horák; Cinematography: Jan Jiráček; Sound: Karel Cajthaml; Editor: Jiří Sobotka; Music: Archival (arr. Jiří Šust)

Čtyřikrát o Bulharsku (Four Times about Bulgaria)
Nature film, Color, 246 m.
Director and Screenplay: Karel Kachyňa; Cinematography: Jan Jaroš; Sound: Karel Cajthaml; Editor: Jiří Sobotka; Music: Archival (arr. Miloš Vacek)

Lyžařský výcvik (Ski Training)
Instructional (sports), B&W, 544 m.
Director and Screenplay: Stanislav Brožík; Cinematography: Ivan Koudelka; Sound: Karel Cajthaml; Editor: Jiří Sobotka; Music: Archival (arr. Jiří Šust)

Miluj svou zbraň (Love Your Weapon)
Instructional, B&W, 1929 m.
Director: Ivan V. Frič

Návštěva korejské vojenské delegace v Československu (The Korean Military Delegation's Visit to Czechoslovakia)
Reportage, B&W, 234 m.
Director and Screenplay: Jiří Ployhar; Cinematography: Jiří Ployhar, Miroslav Fojtík; Sound: Karel Cajthaml; Editor: Jiří Sobotka; Music: Archival (arr. Jiří Šust)

Nekrvavá bitva (Bloodless Battle)
Documentary, Color, 374 m.
Director and Screenplay: Jiří Ployhar; Cinematography: Jiří Ployhar, Miroslav Fojtík; Sound: Karel Cajthaml; Editor: Jiří Sobotka; Music: Archival (arr. Jiří Šust)

Organofosfáty (Organophosphates)
Popular-scientific, Color, 584 m.
Director: Václav Hapl; Screenplay: Jiří Tulach, Miroslav Sajda, František Karásek; Cinematography: Miroslav Fojtík; Sound: Karel Cajthaml; Editor: Vlasta Plotěná; Music: Archival (arr. Jiří Šust)

Péče o zraněné s míšním poškozením (Caring for Casualties with Spinal Injuries)

Instructional (exemplary), B&W, 492 m.

Director: Vlastimil Fiala; Screenplay: Vladimír Beneš, Vlastimil Fiala; Cinematography: Jaroslav Kadlec; Sound: Karel Cajthaml; Editor: Vlasta Ploténá; Music: Archival (arr. Jiří Šust)

Přetlakové dýchání (Pressurized Breathing)

Educational, Color, 308 m.

Director: Jaromír Dvořáček; Screenplay: Dr. Otakar Černoch, Jaromír Dvořáček; Cinematography: Josef Vaniš; Music: Archival (arr. Miloš Vacek)

Sebeobrana (Self-Defense)

Instructional, B&W, 300 m.

Director: František Vláčil; Screenplay: Vladimír Sís; Cinematography: Josef Vaniš; Sound: Karel Cajthaml; Editor: Jiří Sobotka; Music: Archival (arr. Miloš Vacek)

Spolehlivá zbraň (A Reliable Weapon)

Educational, B&W, 437 m.

Director and Screenplay: Vladimír Horák; Cinematography: Jiří Ployhar; Sound: Karel Cajthaml; Editor: Jiří Sobotka; Music: Archival (arr. Jiří Šust)

Technika jízdy automobilem za zhoršených podmínek (Techniques for Driving a Car in Poor Conditions)

Instructional (exemplary), B&W, 1040 m.

Director and Screenplay: Karel Baroch; Cinematography: Jan Jaroš; Sound: Karel Cajthaml; Editor: Vlasta Ploténá; Music: Archival (arr. Miloš Smatek)

Vnější balistika (Exterior Ballistics)

Popular-scientific, B&W, 633 m.

Director: Miroslav Burger; Cinematography: Miroslav Fojtík, Jaroslav Kadlec; Narration: Jiří Šrámek; Sound: Karel Cajthaml; Editor: Vlasta Ploténá; Music: Archival (arr. Jiří Šust)

Ze soboty na neděli (From Saturday to Sunday)

Agitka, B&W, 354 m.

Director and Screenplay: Vladimír Sís; Cinematography: Josef Vaniš; Sound: Karel Cajthaml; Editor: Jiří Sobotka; Music: Miloš Vacek

1959

650 milionů (650 Million)

Reportage, B&W, 410 m.

Director and Screenplay: Ivo Toman; Cinematography: Jaroslav Kadlec, Miroslav Fojtík; Sound: Karel Cajthaml; Editor: Jiří Sobotka; Music: Archival (arr. Jiří Šust)

Antény I (Teoretická část) (Antennas I [Theoretical Section])

Educational, Color, 601 m.

Director: František Karásek; Screenplay: František Karásek, Jaroslav Tichý; Cinematography: Jaroslav Šmajsl; Sound: Karel Cajthaml; Editor: Vlasta Ploténá; Music: Archival (arr. Jiří Šust)

Černé světlo (Black Light)

Popular-scientific, B&W, 348 m.

Director and Screenplay: Vladimír Horák; Cinematography: Jiří Ployhar; Sound: Karel Cajthaml; Editor: Vlasta Ploténá; Music: Archival (arr. Jiří Šust)

Dva muži a balon (Two Men and a Balloon)

Agitka, B&W, 802 m.

Director: Pavel Háša; Screenplay: Roman Hlaváč, Pavel Háša; Cinematography: Jaroslav Kadlec; Sound: Karel Cajthaml; Editor: Jiří Sobotka; Music: Jiří Šust

Jak bojovat v noci (How to Fight at Night)

Instructional, B&W, 440 m.

Director and Screenplay: Vladimír Horák; Cinematography: Jaroslav Šmajsl; Sound: Karel Cajthaml; Editor: Jiří Sobotka; Music: Archival (arr. Jiří Šust)

Kyjevská vzpomínka (Kiev Memory)

Documentary, Color and B&W, 286 m.

Director, Screenplay, Cinematography: Jiří Ployhar, Pavel Háša, Roman Hlaváč; Sound: Karel Cajthaml; Editor: Jiří Sobotka; Music: Archival (arr. Jiří Šust)

Metodika a technika sebeobrany (Methods and Techniques of Self-Defense)

Instructional, B&W, 789 m.

Director and Screenplay: Jaromír Dvořáček; Cinematography: Jaroslav Kadlec; Sound: Karel Cajthaml; Editor: Jiří Sobotka; Music: Archival (arr. Jiří Šust)

Mise dobré vůle (The Goodwill Mission)

Reportage, B&W, 1304 m.

Director and Screenplay: Ivo Toman; Cinematography: Jaroslav Kadlec, Miroslav Fojtík; Sound: Karel Cajthaml; Editor: Jiří Sobotka; Music: Archival (arr. Jiří Šust)

Naše setkání (Our Meeting)

Documentary, B&W, 258 m.

Director and Screenplay: Pavel Háša; Cinematography: Archival footage and Jaroslav Šmajsl; Sound: Karel Cajthaml; Editor: Jiří Sobotka; Music: Archival (arr. Jiří Šust)

Rakety (Rockets)

Popular-scientific, B&W, 454 m.

Director and Screenplay: Vladimír Horák; Cinematography: Jiří Ployhar; Narration: Jiří Šrámek; Sound: Karel Cajthaml; Editor: Vlasta Plotěná; Music: Archival (arr. Jiří Šust)

Sokolovo (Sokolovo)

Documentary, B&W, 399 m.

Director, Screenplay, Cinematography: Jiří Ployhar; Sound: Karel Cajthaml; Editor: Jiří Sobotka; Music: Archival (arr. Jiří Šust)

Vždy připraveni (Always Prepared)

Reportage, B&W, 311 m.

Director and Screenplay: Karel Baroch; Cinematography: Jan Jaroš; Sound: Karel Cajthaml; Editor: Vlasta Plotěná; Music: Archival (arr. Miloš Smatek)

Zbraně v našich rukách (Weapons in Our Hands)

Compilation, B&W, 352 m.

Director, Screenplay, Editor: Jiří Sobotka; Music: Archival (arr. Jiří Šust)

Život Maďarské lidové armády (Life of the Hungarian People's Army)

Compilation, B&W, 430 m.

Director: Václav Hapl; Sound: Karel Cajthaml; Editor: Vlasta Plotěná; Music: Archival (arr. Václav Lídl)

1960

9. květen 1960 (May 9, 1960)

Reportage (military parade), Color, 385 m.

Director and Screenplay: Ivo Toman; Cinematography: Jiří Ployhar; Narration: Jiří Šrámek; Sound: Karel Cajthaml; Editor: Jiří Sobotka; Music: Archival (arr. Jiří Šust)

Agent K vypovídá (Agent K Speaks)

Documentary, B&W, 775 m. Coproduction with DEFA.

Director and Cinematography: Jiří Ployhar; Screenplay: Roman Hlaváč; Sound: Karel Cajthaml; Editor: Jiří Sobotka; Music: Archival (arr. Jiří Šust)

Branné cvičení na školách 2. cyklu I, II (Defense Education in Secondary Schools I, II)

Instructional, B&W, 600 m. / 728 m.

Director and Screenplay: Karel Baroch; Cinematography: Jan Jaroš; Sound: Karel Cajthaml; Editor: Věra Kutilová; Music: Archival (arr. Miloš Smatek)

Den tělovýchovy a sportu (Day of Physical Education and Sport)

Documentary (compilation), B&W, 328 m.
Director and Screenplay: Karel Baroch; Sound: Karel Cajthaml; Editor: Věra Kutilová; Music: Archival (arr. Miloš Smatek)

Dopravní nehody (Transportation Accidents)

Educational, B&W, 375 m.
Director and Screenplay: Stanislav Brožík; Cinematography: Ivan Koudelka; Sound: Karel Cajthaml; Editor: Věra Kutilová; Music: Archival (arr. Jiří Šust)

Festival souboru Maďarské lidové armády (The Hungarian People's Army Choral Festival)

Reportage (compilation), B&W, 425 m.
Director: Vladimír Horák; Sound: Karel Cajthaml; Editor: Jiří Sobotka; Music: Archival (arr. Jiří Šust)

Hydraulická instalace (Hydraulic Installation)

Instructional (methodological), Color, 911 m.
Director and Screenplay: Karel Baroch; Cinematography: Jan Jaroš; Sound: Karel Cajthaml; Editor: Věra Kutilová; Music: Archival (arr. Miloš Smatek)

Jižní pevnost (Southern Fortress)

Documentary (tourist), Color, 444 m.
Director and Cinematography: Jiří Ployhar; Text: Roman Hlaváč, Jiří Ployhar; Sound: Karel Cajthaml; Editor: Jiří Sobotka; Music: Archival (arr. Jiří Šust)

Křižáci XX. století (Battleships of the Twentieth Century)

Documentary (compilation), B&W, 1019 m.
Director and Screenplay: Vladimír Horák; Sound: Karel Cajthaml; Editor: Vlasta Ploténá; Music: Archival (arr. Jiří Šust)

Letecký den 1960 (Aviation Day 1960)

Reportage (aviation), Color, 413 m.

Director: Zbyněk Brynych; Cinematography: Jiří Ployhar; Sound: Karel Cajthaml; Editor: Jiří Sobotka; Music: Archival (arr. Jiří Šust)

Návštěva čs. vojenské delegace v Maďarsku (The Czechoslovak Military Delegation's Visit to Hungary)

Documentary (compilation), B&W, 300 m.
Director and Screenplay: Pavel Háša; Sound: Karel Cajthaml; Editor: Jiří Sobotka; Music: Archival (arr. Jiří Šust)

Opravy hydraulické instalace letounu MIG-15 bis I, II (Repairing the Hydraulic Fittings on a MIG-15 bis, I, II)

Instructional, B&W, 996 m. / 887 m.
Director and Screenplay: Karel Baroch; Cinematography: Jan Jaroš; Narration: Jiří Šrámek; Sound: Karel Cajthaml; Editor: Věra Kutilová; Music: Archival (arr. Miloš Smatek)

Příběh o mé cestě (Horníci) (The Tale of My Journey [Miners])

Agitka, B&W, 415 m.
Director and Screenplay: Milan Růžička; Cinematography: Jaroslav Kadlec; Sound: Karel Cajthaml; Editor: Věra Kutilová; Music: Archival (arr. Jiří Šust)

Rehabilitace ruky po úrazech (Rehabilitating Hands after an Injury)

Educational, B&W, 552 m.
Director and Screenplay: Vlastimil Fiala; Cinematography: Jaroslav Kadlec; Narration: Jiří Šrámek; Sound: Karel Cajthaml; Editor: Vlasta Ploténá; Music: Archival (arr. Miloš Smatek)

Tajná zbraň—bakterie (Secret Weapon—Bacteria)

Popular-scientific, B&W, 434 m.
Director and Screenplay: Vladimír Horák; Cinematography: Jaroslav Šmajsl; Sound: Karel Cajthaml; Editor: Jiří Sobotka; Music: Archival (arr. Jiří Šust)

1961

Iluze za letu (Illusion of Flight)
Instructional (methodological), Color,
555 m.
Director and Screenplay: František
Karásek; Cinematography: Jaroslav
Kadlec; Sound: Karel Cajthaml; Editor:
Vlasta Plotěná; Music: Archival (arr.
Miloš Vacek)

*Pohádka o zámečku, dětech a
spravedlnosti (A Fairy Tale about a
Castle, Children, and Justice)*
Documentary (compilation), B&W, 297 m.
Director and Screenplay: Rudolf Krejčík;
Cinematography: Zbyněk Olmer; Edi-
tor: Jiří Sobotka; Music: Aleš Jermář

*První zimní spartakiáda spřátelených
armád (The First Winter Spartakiada
of the Brotherly Armies)*
Reportage, B&W, 559 m. Coproduction
with Czołówka.
Director and Screenplay: Sergius Sprudin;
Cinematography: Adolf Forbert; Sound:
Karel Cajthaml; Editor: Jiří Sobotka

*Svědectví I, II: Zrada, Vítězství
(Witness I, II: Betrayal, Victory)*
Compilation (documentary), B&W, 2521 m.
/ 2225 m.
Director: Pavel Háša, Ivo Toman; Screen-
play: Pavel Háša, Roman Hlaváč, Ivo To-
man; Sound: Karel Cajthaml; Editor: Jiří
Sobotka; Music: Jiří Šust

Umělé dýchání (Artificial Respiration)
Popular-scientific, B&W, 506 m.
Director and Screenplay: Vlastimil Fiala;
Cinematography: Jaroslav Kadlec;
Sound: Karel Cajthaml; Editor: Věra
Kutilová; Music: Archival (arr. Miloš
Vacek)

Včera neděle byla (Yesterday Was Sunday)
Agitka, B&W, 271 m.

Director and Screenplay: Jozef Sedláček;
Cinematography: Jiří Ployhar; Sound:
Karel Cajthaml; Editor: Jiří Sobotka;
Music: Archival (arr. Jiří Šust)

1962

*Bundeswehr pochoduje
(Budeswehr on the March)*
Documentary (compilation), B&W, 468 m.
Director and Screenplay: Vladimír Horák;
Cinematography: Zbyněk Olmer;
Sound: Karel Cajthaml; Editor: Jiří So-
botka; Music: Archival (arr. Jiří Šust)

Generálův meč (The General's Sword)
Compilation, B&W, 722 m.
Director: Ivan Balaďa; Screenplay: Jiří
Gold, Ivan Balaďa; Cinematography:
Archival footage and Zbyněk Olmer;
Sound: Karel Cajthaml; Editor: Jiří So-
botka; Music: Archival (arr. Jiří Šust)

Havana-Praha (Havana-Prague)
Reportage, B&W, 183 m.
Director and Screenplay: Milan Růžička;
Cinematography: Jan Jiráček; Sound:
Karel Cajthaml; Editor: Jiří Sobotka;
Music: Archival (arr. Jiří Šust)

Hovoří Varšava (Warsaw Speaking)
Documentary (compilation), B&W, 1251 m.
Director and Editor: Jiří Sobotka; Screen-
play: Roman Hlaváč; Sound: Karel
Cajthaml

*O vteřinu a přátelství (On a
Moment and Friendship)*
Reportage (sports), Color, 523 m.
Director and Screenplay: Pavel Háša;
Cinematography: Jaroslav Kadlec et al.;
Sound: Karel Cajthaml; Editor: Jiří So-
botka; Music: Archival (arr. Jiří Šust)

Pátá kolona (The Fifth Column)
Documentary, B&W, 1084 m.
Director and Screenplay: Rudolf Krejčík;
Cinematography: Zbyněk Olmer;
Sound: Karel Cajthaml; Editor: Jiří So-
botka; Music: Jiří Šust

Přehlídka (Military Parade)
Reportage (military parade), B&W, 250 m.
Director and Screenplay: Milan Růžička;
Cinematography: Jan Jiráček; Sound:
Karel Cajthaml; Editor: Dagmar Strán-
ská; Music: Archival (arr. Jiří Šust)

Tatíci (Old Codgers)
Reportage, B&W, 400 m.
Director and Screenplay: Milan Růžička;
Cinematography: Ivan Koudelka;
Sound: Karel Cajthaml; Editor: Antonín
Zelenka; Music: Jiří Šust

Varšavský koncert (Warsaw Concert)
Reportage (compilation), B&W, 581 m.
Director, Screenplay, Editor: Jiří Sobotka;
Sound: Karel Cajthaml; Music: Archival
(arr. Jiří Šust)

1963

*Cintorín bez mena: Requiem Aeternam
(Unnamed Cemetery: Requiem Aeternam)*
Documentary, B&W, 521 m.
Director: Ivan Balaďa; Screenplay: Ivan
Balaďa, Jiří Gold; Cinematography:
Juraj Šajmovič; Sound: Karel Cajthaml;
Editor: Vlasta Plotěná; Music: Jiří Šust,
Tomáš Gálik

*Hrdinové, na které nezbyl čas (Heroes
for Whom No Time Remained)*
Documentary, B&W, 710 m.
Director and Screenplay: Ivo Toman; Cin-
ematography: Jiří Ployhar; Sound: Karel
Cajthaml; Editor: Jiří Sobotka; Music:
Jiří Šust

Legenda (Legend)
Documentary, B&W, 281 m.

Director and Screenplay: Jozef Sedláček,
Bruno Šefranka; Cinematography: Ivan
Koudelka; Sound: Karel Cajthaml; Edi-
tor: Jiří Sobotka; Music: Wiliam Bukový

Náboj (The Cartridge)
Fiction, B&W, 502 m.
Director: Ivo Toman; Screenplay: Vladimír
Kalina; Cinematography: Jiří Ployhar;
Sound: Karel Cajthaml; Editor: Jiří So-
botka; Music: Jiří Šust

Pamět' našeho dne (Memory of Our Day)
Documentary, B&W, 275 m.
Director and Screenplay: Jan Němec; Cinematography: Archival footage and Jaroslav Šofr; Sound: Karel Cajthaml; Editor: Zdeněk Stehlík; Music: Jan Klusák

Reportér (Reporter)
Documentary, B&W, 669 m.
Director and Screenplay: Pavel Háša; Cin-
ematography: Jaroslav Kadlec; Sound:
Karel Cajthaml; Editor: Jiří Sobotka;
Music: Jiří Šust

1964

Člověk vo velkej hale (Man in a Great Hall)
Documentary, B&W, 521 m.
Director: Ivan Balaďa; Screenplay: Ivan
Balaďa, Jiří Gold; Cinematography:
Juraj Šajmovič; Sound: Karel Cajthaml;
Editor: Vlasta Plotěná; Music: Archival,
with compositions by J. S. Bach

*Dobrá rada je nad zlato (Good Advice
Is Worth Its Weight in Gold)*
Fiction, B&W, 395 m.
Director and Screenplay: Milan Růžička;
Cinematography: Ivan Koudelka;
Sound: Karel Cajthaml; Editor: Vlasta
Plotěná; Music: Jiří Šust

Elektrografie (Electrography)
Educational, B&W, 429 m.
Director and Screenplay: Stanislav Brožík;
Cinematography: Jaroslav Kadlec;

Sound: Karel Cajthaml; Editor: Vlasta Plotěná; Music: Jiří Šust

"Letci" ("Flyers")

Documentary, B&W, 446 m.

Director and Screenplay: František Karásek; Cinematography: Juraj Šajmovič, Jiří Lebeda; Sound: Karel Cajthaml; Editor: Vlasta Plotěná; Music: Jiří Šust

Nejhezčí řeka (The Loveliest River)

Promotional (tourist), Color, 417 m.

Director and Screenplay: Václav Hapl; Cinematography: Zbyněk Olmer; Sound: Karel Cajthaml; Editor: Vlasta Plotěná; Music: Archival (arr. Jiří Šust)

Pohár z New Yorku (The New York Cup)

Documentary, Color, 794 m.

Director and Screenplay: Jiří Sobotka, Ivan Koudelka; Cinematography: Ivan Koudelka; Sound: Karel Cajthaml; Editor: Jiří Sobotka; Music: Wiliam Bukový

Protitankové řízené střely (Anti-Tank Missiles)

Popular-scientific, B&W, 319 m.

Director and Screenplay: Vladimír Horák; Cinematography: Zbyněk Olmer; Sound: Karel Cajthaml; Editor: Vlasta Kutilová

Přeprava vysouvacího zařízení I-P nosníků (The Preparation of Extension Apparatus I-P Carriers)

Instructional, B&W, 420 m.

Director and Screenplay: Karel Baroch; Cinematography: Ivan Koudelka; Sound: Karel Cajthaml; Editor: Vlasta Plotěná; Music: Archival (arr. Miloš Smatek)

Příčiny sportovních úrazů (The Reasons for Sports Injuries)

Educational (exemplary), B&W, 348 m.

Director and Screenplay: Jozef Sedláček; Cinematography: Jan Jiráček; Sound:

Karel Cajthaml; Editor: Vlasta Plotěná; Music: Jiří Šust

Případ Daniela (The Daniela Case)

Fiction, B&W, 1526 m.

Director: Pavel Háša; Screenplay: Roman Hlaváč, Pavel Háša; Cinematography: Jaroslav Kadlec; Sound: Karel Cajthaml; Editor: Zdeněk Stehlík; Music: Jiří Šust

Sedmnáct hodin (Tankisté) (Seventeen Hours [Tankists])

Documentary, B&W, 495 m.

Director and Screenplay: Milan Růžička; Cinematography: Jaromír Šofr; Sound: Karel Cajthaml; Editor: Jiří Sobotka; Music: Archival (arr. Jiří Šust)

1965

Ať žije republika (Já, Julina a konec velké války) (Long Live the Republic [Me and Julina and the End of the Great War])

Fiction, B&W, 3754 m. Coproduction with Film Studio Barrandov.

Director: Karel Kachyňa; Screenplay: Jan Procházka, Karel Kachyňa; Cinematography: Jaromír Šofr; Sound: Jiří Lenoch; Editor: Miroslav Hájek; Music: Jan Novák

Geneze strachu (The Genesis of Fear)

Educational, B&W, 550 m.

Director and Screenplay: František Karásek; Cinematography: Jiří Lebeda; Sound: Karel Cajthaml; Editor: Alois Fišárek; Music: Miloš Vacek

Katetrizační angiografie (Catheterizing Angiography)

Instructional (exemplary), B&W, 443 m.

Director: Vlastimil Fiala; Screenplay: Vlastimil Fiala, Josef Roschl; Cinematography: Jaroslav Kadlec; Sound: Karel Cajthaml; Editor: Vlasta Kutilová

Lidice (Lidice)

Documentary (compilation), B&W, 1054 m.
Director and Screenplay: Pavel Háša;
  Cinematography: Archival footage and
  Jaroslav Kadlec; Sound: Karel Cajthaml;
  Editor: Zdeněk Stehlík; Music: Jiří Šust

*Malý raketový přírodopis (A Short
Natural History of Rockets)*

Educational, B&W, 446 m.
Director and Screenplay: Vladimír Horák;
  Cinematography: Jiří Ployhar; Sound:
  Karel Cajthaml; Editor: Zdeněk Stehlík;
  Music: Archival (arr. Jiří Šust)

*Obrněný transportér 64 (OT-64)
(Armored Transporter 64)*

Instructional, B&W, 578 m.
Director and Screenplay: Vlastimil
  Fiala; Cinematography: Zbyněk Olmer;
  Sound: Karel Cajthaml; Editor: Marie
  Vosová; Music: Jiří Šust

*Od Azovského mora pod Tatry (From
the Azov Sea under the Tatras)*

Documentary (compilation), B&W, 760 m.
Director and Screenplay: Jozef Sedláček;
  Cinematography: Archival footage and
  Jaroslav Kadlec; Sound: Karel Cajthaml;
  Editor: Jiřina Skalská; Music: Jiří Šust

Před očima všech (Before the Eyes of All)

Documentary (sports), B&W, 1017 m.
Director and Screenplay: Václav Hapl;
  Cinematography: Zbyněk Olmer et al.;
  Sound: Karel Cajthaml; Editor: Zdeněk
  Stehlík; Music: Jiří Šust

Přehlídka (Military Parade)

Reportage (military parade), B&W, 300 m.
Director and Screenplay: Miroslav Burger;
  Cinematography: Jaroslav Kadlec et al.;
  Sound: Karel Cajthaml; Editor: Jan Cha-
  loupek; Music: Jiří Šust

Stoletá voda (Hundred-Year Flood)

Documentary, B&W, 830 m.
Director: Karel Vachek, Ivan Koudelka;
  Screenplay: Karel Vachek; Cinematog-

raphy: Ivan Koudelka; Sound: Karel
  Cajthaml; Editor: Jiřina Skalská; Music:
  Jiří Šust

Život po 90 minutách (Life after 90 Minutes)

Documentary (sports), B&W, 806 m.
Director and Screenplay: Jan Schmidt;
  Cinematography: Jiří Lebeda, Zbyněk
  Olmer; Sound: Karel Cajthaml; Editor:
  Jiřina Skalská; Music: Archival (arr. Jiří
  Šust)

1966

15 let Studia ČAF (15 Years of Studio ČAF)

Reportage (compilation), B&W, 313 m.
Director and Screenplay: Pavel Háša;
  Cinematography: Karel Hložek; Sound:
  Karel Cajthaml; Editor: Jiřina Skalská

Čas křídel (The Time of Wings)

Documentary (aviation), B&W, 1591 m.
Director and Screenplay: Pavel Mertl;
  Cinematography: Jiří Macák, Jaroslav
  Kadlec; Sound: Karel Cajthaml; Editor:
  Josef Dobřichovský; Music: Archival
  (arr. Jiří Šust)

Čas náš vezdejší (Our Daily Time)

Documentary, B&W, 572 m.
Director: Milan Růžička; Screenplay: Milan Růžička and Karel Rychtařík; Cinematography: Ivan Koudelka; Sound:
  Karel Cajthaml; Editor: Alois Fišárek

*Čekání na vlak, který přijede podle
jízdního řádu (Waiting for a Train
That Comes according to Schedule)*

Documentary, B&W, 448 m.
Director and Screenplay: Ivan Balaďa; Cin-
  ematography: Juraj Šajmovič; Sound:
  Karel Cajthaml; Editor: Jiřina Skalská;
  Music: Archival (arr. Jiří Šust)

*Československo, země neznámá
(Czechoslovakia, an Unknown Land)*

Promotional, Color, 858 m. Produced for
  Government Tourist Board.
Director and Cinematography: Jiří Ploy-
  har; Screenplay: Jiří Ployhar, Alois Svo-

boda; Sound: Karel Cajthaml; Editor: Jiřina Lukešová; Music: Jiří Šust

Frontový kameraman (Front Cameraman)

Documentary (compilation), B&W, 454 m.

Director and Screenplay: Milan Růžička; Cinematography: Ivan Koudelka; Sound: Karel Cajthaml; Editor: Alois Fišárek; Music: Miloš Vacek

Hra pro chlapy (A Game for Guys)

Documentary, B&W, 643 m.

Director and Screenplay: Jan Schmidt; Cinematography: Jiří Macháně; Sound: Karel Cajthaml; Editor: Zdeněk Stehlík; Music: Jiří Šust

Konec srpna v hotelu Ozon (The End of August at the Hotel Ozone)

Fiction, B&W, 2218 m.

Director: Jan Schmidt; Screenplay: Pavel Juráček, Jan Schmidt; Cinematography: Jiří Macák; Sound: František Fabián, Bohumír Brunclík (sound effects); Editor: Miroslav Hájek; Music: Jan Klusák

Na vlně ČAF (On the Wave of ČAF)

Documentary (compilation), B&W, 1795 m.

Director and Screenplay: Ivo Toman; Cinematography: Jaroslav Kadlec; Sound: Karel Cajthaml; Editor: Jiřina Skalská

Otázky (o armádě) (Questions [about the Army])

Documentary, B&W, 460 m.

Director and Screenplay: Miroslav Burger; Cinematography: Ivan Koudelka; Sound: Karel Cajthaml; Editor: Alois Fišárek

Pohlednice od Baltu (Postcard from the Baltic)

Reportage, B&W, 301 m.

Director and Screenplay: Karel Forst; Cinematography: Zbyněk Olmer; Sound: Karel Cajthaml; Editor: Vlasta Kutilová; Music: Archival (arr. Jiří Šust)

Přebor čs. armády v lyžování (The Czechoslovak Army Championship in Skiing)

Reportage (sports), B&W, 303 m.

Director and Screenplay: Rudolf Adler; Cinematography: Jan Jiráček; Sound: Karel Cajthaml; Editor: Alois Fišárek, Jiřina Skalská

Pro blaho země (Afghánistán) (For the Sake of the Earth [Afghanistan])

Documentary, B&W, 850 m. Produced for the Afghan government.

Director and Screenplay: Jiří Ployhar, Antonín Hajdušek; Sound: Karel Cajthaml; Editor: Alois Fišárek; Music: Jiří Šust

Speciální tělesná příprava letců (The Special Physical Preparation of Pilots)

Educational, B&W, 363 m.

Director: František Karásek; Screenplay: Jiří Žára, František Karásek; Cinematography: Jiří Macák; Sound: Karel Cajthaml; Editor: Jiřina Skalská; Music: Archival (arr. Miloš Vacek)

Vítězství nad korozí (Victory over Rust)

Instructional (exemplary), Color, 445 m.

Director and Screenplay: František Karásek; Cinematography: Jan Jiráček; Sound: Karel Cajthaml; Editor: Vlasta Kutilová

V pátek se stěhujeme (We Move on Friday)

Documentary, B&W, 371 m.

Director and Screenplay: Ivan Balaďa; Cinematography: Juraj Šajmovič; Sound: Karel Cajthaml; Editor: Alois Fišárek; Music: Archival (arr. Jiří Šust)

Výchova mladého psa (The Training of a Young Dog)

Instructional, B&W, 240 m.

Director and Screenplay: Karel Forst; Cinematography: Jan Jiráček; Sound: Karel Cajthaml; Editor: Zdeněk Stehlík; Music: Archival (arr. Jiří Šust)

1967

Anestézie při hromadném výskytu raněných (Anesthesia for Mass Injuries)

Instructional (exemplary), Color, 1042 m.
Director and Screenplay: Vlastimil Fiala; Cinematography: Zbyněk Olmer; Sound: Karel Cajthaml; Editor: Vlasta Plotěná; Music: Archival (arr. Jiří Šust)

Cecoslovacco buono (The Good Czechoslovak)

Documentary, B&W, 470 m.
Director and Screenplay: Milan Růžička; Cinematography: Ivan Koudelka; Sound: Karel Cajthaml; Editor: Alois Fišárek; Music: Jiří Šust

Činnost vestibulárního systému (The Function of the Vestibular System)

Instructional (exemplary), Color, 518 m.
Director and Screenplay: Václav Hapl; Cinematography: Zbyněk Olmer; Sound: Karel Cajthaml; Editor: Vlasta Plotěná; Music: Archival (arr. Jiří Šust)

Den armády (Army Day)

Reportage (compilation), B&W, 283 m.
Director and Screenplay: Stanislav Brožík; Sound: Karel Cajthaml; Editor: Vlasta Plotěná

Devět kapitol ze starého dějepisu (Nine Chapters from Ancient History)

Documentary (compilation), B&W, 2763 m.
Director: Pavel Háša; Screenplay: Roman Hlaváč, Pavel Háša; Cinematography: Jaroslav Kadlec; Sound: Karel Cajthaml; Editor: Alois Fišárek; Music: Jiří Šust

Docela jiná noc (A Rather Different Night)

Documentary (tourist), Color, 455 m. Produced for Czechoslovak Television.
Director: Milan Růžička; Narration: Vlastimil Brodský

Hudba v srdci Evropy (Music in the Heart of Europe)

Promotional, Color, 582 m. Produced for Government Tourist Board.
Director, Screenplay, Cinematography: Jiří Ployhar; Sound: Karel Cajthaml; Editor: Jiřina Lukešová

*Infračervené záření (Infrared Light):
I. Fyzikální principy (I. Physical Principles),
II. Technické využití (II. Technical Use)*

Instructional (methodological), Color, 656 m. / 485 m. / 485 m.
Director and Screenplay: Karel Baroch; Cinematography: Juraj Šajmovič; Sound: Karel Cajthaml; Editor: Alois Fišárek; Music: Archival (arr. Jiří Šust)

Jak se stát neviditelným (How to Become Invisible)

Educational, Color, 425 m.
Director and Screenplay: Vladimír Horák; Cinematography: Andrej Barla; Sound: Karel Cajthaml; Editor: Vlasta Plotěná; Music: Jiří Šust

Krumlovské proměny (Krumlov Transformations)

Promotional, Color, 290 m. Produced for Government Tourist Board.
Director, Screenplay, Cinematography: Jiří Ployhar; Sound: Karel Cajthaml; Editor: Jiřina Lukešová; Music: Jiří Šust

Linková technika I–III (The Technology of Communication Lines I–II)

Educational, 700 m. / 665 m. / 581 m.
Director and Screenplay: Miroslav Burger; Cinematography: Jan Jiráček; Sound: Karel Cajthaml; Editor: Jiřina Skalská; Music: Archival (arr. Jiří Šust)

Na hranici skutečnosti (On the Edge of Reality)

Educational, B&W, 457 m.
Director and Screenplay: Stanislav Brožík; Cinematography: Juraj Šajmovič; Sound:

Karel Cajthaml; Editor: Vlasta Ploténá; Music: Archival (arr. Jiří Šust)

Ničení selhané a nevybuchlé munice (The Demolition of Failed and Unexploded Munitions)

Instructional, B&W, 819 m.

Director and Screenplay: Václav Hapl; Cinematography: Petr Polák; Sound: Karel Cajthaml; Editor: Vlasta Ploténá

Od startu do přistání (From Start to Takeoff)

Reportage (aviation), B&W, 260 m.

Director and Screenplay: Karel Baroch; Cinematography: Karel Hložek, Petr Polák; Sound: Karel Cajthaml; Editor: Jiřina Skalská; Music: Archival (arr. Jiří Šust)

Odvaha (Courage)

Documentary, B&W, 452 m.

Director and Screenplay: Jan Schmidt; Cinematography: Zbyněk Olmer; Sound: Karel Cajthaml; Editor: Jiřina Skalská; Music: Archival (arr. Jiří Šust)

Orlík

Promotional, Color, 144 m. Produced for Government Tourist Board.

Director, Screenplay, Cinematography: Jiří Ployhar; Sound: Karel Cajthaml; Editor: Jiřina Lukešová; Music: Archival (arr. Jiří Šust)

Schůzky s Dianou (Dates with Diana)

Promotional, Color, 279 m. Produced for Government Tourist Board.

Director, Screenplay, Cinematography: Jiří Ployhar; Sound: Karel Cajthaml; Editor: Jiřina Lukešová; Music: Jiří Šust

To je bundeswehr (That Is the Bundeswehr)

Documentary (compilation), B&W, 480 m. (revision of 1962 film *Bundeswehr on the March*)

Veliká pout' (Great Pilgrimage)

Documentary, B&W, 581 m.

Director and Screenplay: Pavel Háša; Cinematography: Jaroslav Kadlec; Sound: Karel Cajthaml; Editor: Zdeněk Stehlík; Music: Archival (arr. Jiří Šust)

Vltava 1966

Reportage, B&W, 513 m.

Director and Screenplay: Stanislav Brožík; Cinematography: Zbyněk Olmer; Narration: Richard Honzovič; Sound: Karel Cajthaml; Editor: Vlasta Ploténá; Music: Archival (arr. Jiří Šust)

Vyprávění o Kalevi Liiva (The Story of Kalevi Liiva)

Documentary, B&W, 630 m.

Director and Screenplay: Ivan Balaďa; Cinematography: Juraj Šajmovič; Sound: Karel Cajthaml; Editor: Alois Fišárek; Music: Archival (arr. Jiří Šust)

Vzpomínka na tři rána v českém lese (Setkání) (Memory of Three Mornings in a Czech Meadow [Meeting])

Documentary, Color, 496 m.

Director and Screenplay: Ivan Balaďa; Cinematography: Juraj Šajmovič; Sound: Karel Cajthaml; Editor: Alois Fišárek; Music: Jiří Šust

Zdravotní ochrana proti BBP (biologickým bojovým prostředkům) (Protecting against Biological Weapons)

Educational, Color, 583 m.

Director and Screenplay: Karel Baroch; Cinematography: Jaroslav Kadlec; Sound: Karel Cajthaml; Editor: Vlasta Ploténá

Země pod křídly racků (jižní Čechy) (Land under the Wings of Gulls [Southern Bohemia])

Promotional, Color, 520 m. Produced for Government Tourist Board.

Director and Cinematography: Jiří Ployhar; Screenplay: Jiří Ployhar, Milan Pavlík; Sound: Karel Cajthaml; Editor: Jiřina Lukešová; Music: Archival (arr. Jiří Šust)

Znojemské historické vinobraní
(Historical Vendange in Znojmo)

Promotional, Color, 490 m. Produced for Czechoslovak Television.

Director and Screenplay: Petr Ruttner, Andrej Barla; Cinematography: Andrej Barla; Sound: Karel Cajthaml; Editor: Ludvík Pavlíček; Music: Josef Ceremuga

1968

Dedovia, otcovia, synovia (Historie armády) (Grandfathers, Fathers, Sons [A History of the Army])

Documentary (compilation), B&W, 846 m.

Director and Screenplay: Jozef Sedláček; Sound: Karel Cajthaml; Editor: Ludvík Pavlíček; Music: Archival (arr. Jiří Šust)

Hanácké Athény (Hanák Athens)

Documentary, Color, 266 m. Produced for Government Tourist Board.

Director and Cinematography: Jiří Ployhar; Sound: Karel Cajthaml; Editor: Eva Kloboukowá, Jiří Ployhar; Music: Archival (arr. Jiří Šust)

Krajem stříbrných vod (Through the Land of Silver Waters)

Promotional, Color, 320 m. Produced for Government Tourist Board.

Director, Screenplay, Cinematography: Jiří Ployhar; Sound: Karel Cajthaml; Editor: Jiřina Lukešová; Music: Archival (arr. Jiří Šust)

Lekce (Lesson)

Documentary, B&W, 417 m.

Director and Screenplay: Vladimír Drha; Cinematography: Karel Hložek; Sound: Karel Cajthaml; Editor: Daniela Zachariášová; Music: Archival (arr. Jiří Šust)

Metrum (Panychida 36)

Documentary, B&W, 280 m.

Director and Screenplay: Ivan Balaďa; Cinematography: Juraj Šajmovič; Sound:

Karel Cajthaml; Editor: Alois Fišárek; Music: Archival (arr. Jiří Šust)

Na tý louce zelený (On That Green Meadow)

Documentary, B&W, 260 m.

Director: Milan Růžička, Jan Jiráček; Screenplay: Milan Růžička; Cinematography: Jan Jiráček; Sound: Karel Cajthaml; Editor: Jan Chaloupek; Music: Archival (arr. Jiří Šust)

Pout' k bohyním a drakům (Pilgrimage to Goddesses and Dragons)

Documentary, Color, 215 m. Produced for Government Tourist Board.

Director, Screenplay, Cinematography: Jiří Ployhar; Sound: Karel Cajthaml; Editor: Jiřina Lukešová; Music: Archival (arr. Jiří Šust)

Pražský dekameron (Prague Decameron)

Promotional, Color, 545 m. Produced for Government Tourist Board.

Director, Screenplay, Cinematography: Jiří Ployhar; Sound: Karel Cajthaml; Editor: Jiřina Lukešová; Music: Archival (arr. Jiří Šust)

Rána pod pás (A Blow below the Belt)

Fiction, B&W, 324 m.

Director and Screenplay: Ivo Toman; Cinematography: Jan Jiráček; Sound: Karel Cajthaml; Editor: Alois Fišárek; Music: Archival (arr. Jiří Šust)

Rozkaz (Order)

Documentary, B&W, 300 m.

Director and Screenplay: Miroslav Burger; Cinematography: Ivan Koudelka; Sound: Karel Cajthaml; Editor: Ludvík Pavlíček; Music: Archival (arr. Jiří Šust)

Stopy vedou k petrochemii (Plastické hmoty) (The Tracks Lead to Petrochemicals [Plastic Materials])

Educational, B&W, 530 m.

Director and Screenplay: Stanislav Brožík; Cinematography: Jaroslav Kadlec;

Sound: Karel Cajthaml; Editor: Vlasta Ploténá; Music: Archival (arr. Jiří Šust)

V hodině strachu (In the Hour of Fear)

Fiction, B&W, 1487 m. Produced for Czechoslovak Television.

Director and Screenplay: Milan Růžička; Cinematography: Juraj Šajmovič; Sound: Pavol Sásik; Editor: Alois Fišárek; Music: Zdeněk Liška

Vyšetřování činnosti vestibulárního ústrojí (Examination of the Functions of the Vestibular Mechanism)

Popular-scientific, Color, 649 m.

Director and Screenplay: Václav Hapl; Cinematography: Zbyněk Olmer; Sound: Karel Cajthaml; Editor: Vlasta Ploténá

Za vojačka mňa vzali (They Took Me for a Soldier)

Documentary, B&W, 470 m.

Director and Screenplay: Rudolf Adler; Cinematography: Ivan Koudelka; Sound: Karel Cajthaml; Editor: Alois Fišárek; Music: Archival (arr. Jiří Šust)

1969

Člověk je tvor elektrický (Elektroanestézie) (Man Is an Electric Being [Electroanesthesia])

Educational, B&W, 401 m.

Director and Editor: Stanislav Brožík; Cinematography: Jaroslav Kadlec; Sound: Karel Cajthaml; Editor: Vlasta Ploténá; Music: Archival (arr. Jiří Šust)

Čtyři bílé stěny (Four White Walls)

Educational, Color, 491 m.

Director and Screenplay: Miroslav Burger; Cinematography: Karel Hložek; Sound: Karel Cajthaml; Editor: Alois Fišárek

Drapte, drapte, drapulenky (Tear, Tear Away, Little Featherbed Makers)

Educational, B&W, 444 m.

Director and Screenplay: Rudolf Adler; Cinematography: Ivan Koudelka;

Sound: Karel Cajthaml; Editor: Alois Fišárek

Farbotlač/Barvotisk (Color Wheel)

Documentary, Color, 373 m.

Director and Screenplay: Vladimír Drha; Cinematography: Karel Hložek; Sound: Karel Cajthaml; Editor: Dana Zachariášová; Music: Josef Ceremuga

Korunovační klenoty Království českého (The Crown Jewels of the Czech Kingdom)

Documentary, Color, 338 m. Produced for Government Tourist Board.

Director and Cinematography: Jiří Ployhar; Screenplay: Alois Svoboda, Jiří Ployhar; Editor: Josef Valušiak; Music: Archival (arr. Jiří Šust)

Les (Forest)

Documentary, B&W, 412 m.

Director and Screenplay: Ivan Balaďa; Cinematography: Juraj Šajmovič, Ivan Koudelka, Karel Hložek, Ivan Vojnar; Sound: Karel Cajthaml; Editor: Alois Fišárek; Music: Štěpán Koníček, Kühnův dětský sbor

Návštěva (Helsinki) (Visit [Helsinki])

Documentary, B&W, 220 m. Coproduction with Yleisradio (Finland).

Director and Screenplay: Kaisa Karikoski, Rudolf Adler, Bohuslav Blažek; Cinematography: Ivan Koudelka; Sound: Karel Cajthaml, Lasse Litovaara; Editor: Jiřina Skalská; Music: Finnish music and Jiří Šust

Patenty přírody (Nature's Patents)

Educational, B&W, 426 m.

Director and Screenplay: Vladimír Horák; Cinematography: Zbyněk Olmer; Narration: Vladimír Fišer; Sound: Karel Cajthaml; Editor: Jiřina Skalská; Music: Archival (arr. Jiří Šust)

Pes u boudy (Kenneled Dog)

Documentary, B&W, 527 m.
Director and Screenplay: Karel Forst; Cinematography: Jan Jiráček; Sound: Karel Cajthaml; Editor: Vlasta Plotěná; Music: Archival (arr. Jiří Šust)

Potomci (The Descendants)

Documentary, B&W, 386 m. Coproduction with Czechoslovak Television.
Director and Screenplay: Angelika Hannauerová, Tomáš Škrdlant; Cinematography: Ivan Vojnár; Sound: Karel Cajthaml; Editor: Alois Fišárek

Pozůstalost 38 (The Legacy of 38)

Documentary, B&W, 565 m.
Director and Screenplay: Tomáš Škrdlant; Cinematography: Ivan Vojnár; Sound: Karel Cajthaml; Editor: Alois Fišárek; Music: Archival (arr. Jiří Šust)

Setkání s vrchním velitelem (Meeting with the Commander-in-Chief)

Documentary, B&W, 340 m.
Director and Screenplay: Karel Forst; Cinematography: Karel Hložek; Sound: Karel Cajthaml; Editor: Jiřina Skalská; Music: Archival (arr. Jiří Šust)

Snové scény (Dream Scenes)

Documentary, B&W, 673 m.
Director and Screenplay: Vladimír Drha; Cinematography: Karel Hložek; Sound: Zbyněk Mader, Karel Cajthaml; Editor: Jaromír Janáček; Music: Josef Ceremuga

Tandemová pec (Tandem Furnace)

Educational, Color, 358 m.
Director and Screenplay: Stanislav Brožík; Cinematography: Jaroslav Kadlec; Sound: Karel Cajthaml; Editor: Vlasta Plotěná; Music: Archival (arr. Jiří Šust)

Třicet čtyři ženy (Thirty-Four Women)

Documentary, B&W, 330 m.
Director and Screenplay: Vladimír Drha; Cinematography: Karel Hložek; Sound: Karel Cajthaml; Editor: Dana Zachariášová

U komory stál (15 let ČAF) (He Stood by the Pantry [15 Years of ČAF])

Documentary, B&W, 312 m.
Director and Screenplay: Milan Růžička; Cinematography: Ivan Koudelka; Sound: Karel Cajthaml; Editor: Jiřina Skalská; Music: Archival (arr. Jiří Šust)

Ves (Village)

Documentary, B&W, 304 m.
Director and Screenplay: Vladimír Drha; Cinematography: Karel Hložek; Sound: Karel Cajthaml; Editor: Dana Zachariášová; Music: Archival (arr. Josef Ceremuga)

Voda stoupá (Jeden den a každý druhý) (The Water Is Rising [Today and Every Other Day])

Documentary, B&W, 311 m.
Director and Screenplay: Petr Ruttner; Cinematography: František Vlček; Sound: Karel Cajthaml; Editor: Milada Sádková; Music: Josef Ceremuga

Vyučovací stroje (Teaching Machines)

Educational, Color, 416 m.
Director and Screenplay: František Karásek; Cinematography: Ivan Koudelka; Sound: Karel Cajthaml; Editor: Jiřina Skalská; Music: Archival (arr. Václav Lídl)

Zamyšlení nad aerosalónem (Musings on an Aerosalon)

Reportage (aviation), B&W, 460 m.
Director and Screenplay: Vladimír Novák; Cinematography: Zbyněk Olmer; Sound: Karel Cajthaml; Editor: Vlasta Plotěná; Music: Jiří Šust

Ztišení (Jurmo) (Quieting [Jurmo])

Documentary, B&W, 316 m. Coproduction with Yleisradio (Finland).
Director and Screenplay: Bohuslav Blažek, Rudolf Adler, Pentii Riuttu; Cinematography: Ivan Koudelka; Sound: Karel Cajthaml; Editor: Jiřina Skalská

1970

Člověk neumírá žízní (Halucinogeny) (Man Will Not Die of Thirst [Hallucinogens])
Popular-scientific, Color, 616 m.
Director and Screenplay: Václav Hapl;
Cinematography: Jiří Šimůnek; Sound:
Karel Cajthaml; Editor: Václav Hapl,
Vlasta Plotěná; Music: Archival (arr. Jiří
Šust)

Czechoslovak Military Newsreels

Only newsreels produced during the period this book examines are listed below.

Vojenský zpravodaj (Military Bulletin)
1–4 issues per year, 1930–1937

Armádní zpravodaj (Army Bulletin)
Monthly and biweekly, 1946[?]–1965

Naše vojsko (Our Army)
Monthly, 1951–1953

Bojová technika kapitalistických armád (Battle Technology of the Capitalist Armies)
Yearly, 1957–1990

Armádní filmový měsíčník (Army Newsreel)
Monthly, 1962–1965

Armádní technický magazín (Army Technical Newsreel)
1–4 issues per year, 1965–1969

Magazín ČAF (ČAF Magazine)
Monthly, 1966–1972

Films Produced outside the Czechoslovak Ministry of Defense

1930

Das Deutsche Land an der Saar (The German Land on the Saar)
Kulturfilm, B&W, 2035 m. Produced by
Bundesfilm AG (Germany).

1933

Windmill in Barbados
Documentary, B&W, 9 min. Produced
by Empire Marketing Board Film Unit
(United Kingdom).
Director, Cinematography, and Editor: Basil Wright; Sound: E.A. Pawley, Alberto
Cavalcanti

Zem spieva (The Earth Sings)
Ethnographic, B&W, 66 min. Produced by
Ladislav Kolda and Matice slovenská
(Czechoslovakia).
Director: Karol Plicka; Cinematography:
Karol Plicka; Editor: Alexander Hackenschmied; Music: František Škvor

1934

Chapayev
Fiction feature, B&W, 95 min. Produced by
Lenfilm (Soviet Union).
Director: Georgi Vasilyev, Sergei Vasilyev;
Screenplay: Anna Furmanov, Dmitri
Furmanov (original novel), Georgi Vasilyev, Sergei Vasilyev; Cinematography:
Aleksandr Ksenofontov, Aleksandr
Sigaev; Sound: Aleksandr Bekker; Music: Gavriil Popov

Pett and Pott
Promotional, B&W, 29 min. Produced by
General Post Office Film Unit (United
Kingdom).
Director: Alberto Cavalcanti; Screenplay:
Alberto Cavalcanti, Stuart Legg; Cinematography: John Taylor; Sound: John
Cox; Editor: Alberto Cavalcanti; Music:
Walter Leigh

Weather Forecast
Documentary, B&W, 18 min. Produced by
General Post Office Film Unit (United
Kingdom).
Director: Evelyn Spice; Cinematography:
George Noble

1936

Dejte nám křídla (Give Us Wings)

Documentary, B&W, 340 m. Produced by AB (Czechoslovakia).

Director and Screenplay: Jiří Weiss; Camera: Václav Hanuš; Music: Jiří Srnka

1937

Filosofská historie (A Philosophical History)

Fiction feature, B&W, 2523 m. Produced by Moldavia (Czechoslovakia).

Director and Screenplay: Otakar Vávra; Cinematography: Otto Heller, Ferdinand Pečenka; Sound: Vilém Taraba; Editor: Jan Kohout; Music: Jan Branberger

Píseň o smutné zemi (Song of a Sad Land)

Nature film, B&W, 295 m. Produced by AB (Czechoslovakia).

Director, Screenplay, Editor: Jiří Weiss; Text: K. M. Walló; Cinematography: Václav Hanuš; Music: Jiří Srnka

Přístav vzdušného moře (Harbor in a Sea of Air)

Documentary, B&W, 280 m. Produced by AB (Czechoslovakia).

Director, Screenplay, Editor: Jiří Weiss; Camera: Václav Hanuš; Sound: František Šindelář; Music: Jiří Srnka

Svět patří nám (The World Belongs to Us)

Fiction feature, B&W, 2625 m. Produced by AB (Czechoslovakia).

Director: Martin Frič; Cinematography: Otto Heller; Sound; František Šindelář; Editor: Jan Kohout; Music: Jaroslav Ježek

1943

Listen to Britain

Documentary, B&W, 19 min. Produced by Crown Film Unit (United Kingdom).

Director and Editor: Humphrey Jennings, Stewart McAllister; Cinematography: H. E. Fowle; Sound: Ken Cameron

1949

Pierwse lata (The First Years)

Documentary, B&W, 99 min. Produced by Československý státní film (Czechoslovakia), Wytwórnia filmów dokumentalnych (Poland), Bulgarfilm (Bulgaria).

Director: Joris Ivens; Screenplay: Marion Michelle; Cinematography: Ivan V. Frič, Zachari Shandov, Wladislaw Forbert et. al.; Editor: Joris Ivens, Karel Höschl; Music: Jan Kapr

1951

Kierunek—Nowa Huta! (Destination—Nowa Huta!)

Documentary, B&W, 13 min. Produced by Wytwórnia filmów dokumentalnych (Poland).

Director: Andrzej Munk; Screenplay: Artur Międzyrzecki; Cinematography: Jerzy Chluski, Romuald Kropat; Editor: L. Protasiewicz; Music: Tadeusz Baird

1954

Johnny Guitar

Fiction feature, Color, 110 min. Produced by Republic Pictures (United States).

Director: Nicholas Ray; Screenplay: Philip Yordan; Cinematography: Harry Stradling, Sr.; Sound: T. A. Carman, Howard Wilson; Editor: Richard L. Van Enger; Music: Victor Young, Peggy Lee

Vánoce hokejistů (The Hockey Players' Christmas)

Documentary, B&W, 487 m. Produced by Krátký Film—Documentary Film (Czechoslovakia).

Director and Screenplay: Jindřich Ferenc; Cinematography: Alois Jiráček, Josef Pešek; Sound: Josef Šlingr; Editor: Jaromír Janáček

1956

Du und mancher Kamerad (You and Many a Comrade)

Compilation, B&W, 98 min. Produced by DEFA (German Democratic Republic).

Director: Andrew and Annelie Thorndike; Commentary: Günther Rücker, Andrew and Annelie Thorndike, Karl-Eduard von Schnitzler; Cinematography: Ernst and Vera Kunstmann; Sound: Georg Gutschmidt et al.; Editor: Ella Ulrich; Music: Paul Dessau

Zářijové noci (September Nights)

Fiction feature, B&W, 2388 m. Produced by Film Studio Barrandov (Czechoslovakia).

Director: Vojtěch Jasný; Screenplay: Pavel Kohout, František Daniel, Vojtěch Jasný; Cinematography: Jaroslav Kučera; Sound: Milan Novotný; Editor: Jan Chaloupek; Music: Svatopluk Havelka

1957

Smultronstället (Wild Strawberries)

Fiction feature, B&W, 91 min. Produced by Svensk Filmindustri (Sweden).

Director and Screenplay: Ingmar Bergman; Cinematography: Gunnar Fischer; Sound: Aaby Wedin; Editor: Oscar Rosander; Music: Erik Nordgren

1958

Hvězda jede na jih (A Star Goes South)

Fiction feature, Color, 2718 m. Produced by Film Studio Barrandov (Czechoslovakia).

Director: Oldřich Lipský; Screenplay: Oldřich Lipský, Jiří Síla, Vladimír Škutina; Cinematography: Ferdinand Pečenka; Sound: Josef Vlček; Editor: Miloslav Hájek; Music: Jiří Bauer, Miloslav Ducháč, Vlastimil Hála, Evžen Klen

Malá neznámá země (A Small, Unknown Land)

Compilation, B&W, 1087 m. Produced by Krátký Film—Documentary Film (Czechoslovakia).

Director and Screenplay: Emanuel Kaněra, Jiří Mrázek; Sound: Josef Franěk; Editor: Josef Pejsar; Music: Archival

Tři přání (Three Wishes)

Fiction feature, B&W, 2877 m. Produced by Film Studio Barrandov (Czechoslovakia).

Director: Ján Kadár, Elmar Klos; Screenplay: Vratislav Blažek, Ján Kadár, Elmar Klos; Cinematography: Rudolf Stahl; Sound: František Černý; Editor: Josef Dobřichovský; Music: Jiří Sternwald

Zde jsou lvi (Hic Sunt Leones)

Fiction feature, B&W, 2529 m. Produced by Film Studio Barrandov (Czechoslovakia).

Director: Václav Krška; Screenplay: Oldřich Daněk; Cinematography: Jaroslav Tuzar; Sound: Adolf Böhm; Editor: Jan Kohout; Music: Jan F. Fischer

1959

Hiroshima mon amour

Fiction feature, B&W, 90 min. Produced by Argos Films, Como Films, Daiei Studios, Pathé Entertainment (France, Italy, Japan).

Director: Alain Resnais; Screenplay: Marguerite Duras; Cinematography: Michio Takahashi, Sacha Vierny; Editor: Jasmine Chasney, Henri Colpi, Anne Sarraute; Music: Georges Delerue, Giovanni Fusco

1960

Holubice (The White Dove)

Fiction feature, B&W, 2080 m. Produced by Film Studio Barrandov (Czechoslovakia).
Director and Screenplay: František Vláčil; Cinematography: Jan Čuřík; Sound: František Fabián; Editor: Miloslav Hájek; Music: Zdeněk Liška

Primary

Documentary, B&W, 60 min. Produced by Drew Associates, Time (United States).
Director: Robert Drew; Cinematography: Richard Leacock, Albert Maysles; Sound: Robert Drew, D. A. Pennebaker; Editor: Robert Drew et al.

1961

Ďáblova past (The Devil's Trap)

Fiction feature, B&W, 2438 m. Produced by Film Studio Barrandov (Czechoslovakia).
Director: František Vláčil; Screenplay: F. A. Dvořák and M. V. Kratochvíl; Cinematography: Rudolf Milič; Sound: František Fabián; Editor: Miroslav Hájek; Music: Zdeněk Liška

La notte

Fiction feature, B&W, 115 min. Produced by Nepi Film, Silver Films, Sofitedip (Italy).
Director: Michelangelo Antonioni; Screenplay: Michelangelo Antonioni, Ennio Flaiano, Tonino Guerra; Cinematography: Gianni Di Venanzo; Sound: Claudio Maielli; Editor: Eraldo Da Roma; Music: Giorgio Gaslini

Ochránci (Guardians)

Compilation, B&W, 447 m. Produced by Krátký Film—Documentary Film (Czechoslovakia).
Director and Screenplay: Josef Kořán; Cinematography: Josef Čepelák; Sound: Miroslav Letenský; Editor: Josef Pejsar; Music: Archival

1962

Schaut auf diese Stadt (Look at this City)

Documentary, B&W, 85 min. Produced by DEFA Studio for Documentary Films (German Democratic Republic).
Director and Screenplay: Karl Gass; Cinematography: Hans Dumke, Hans E. Leupold; Editor: Christel Hemmerling; Music: Jean-Kurt Forest

Slnko v sieti (The Sun in a Net)

Fiction feature, B&W, 2577 m. Produced by Štúdio hraných filmov, Bratislava-Koliba (Czechoslovakia).
Director: Štefan Uher; Screenplay: Alfonz Bednár; Cinematography: Stanislav Szomolányi; Sound: Rudolf Pavlíček; Editor: Bedřich Voděrka; Music: Ilja Zeljenka

1963

Až přijde kocour (Cassandra Cat)

Fiction feature, Color, 2823 m. Produced by Film Studio Barrandov (Czechoslovakia).
Director: Vojtěch Jasný; Screenplay: Jiří Brdečka, Vojtěch Jasný; Cinematography: Jaroslav Kučera; Sound: Dobroslav Šrámek et al.; Editor: Jan Chaloupek; Music: Svatopluk Havelka

Konkurs (Competition)

Fiction feature, B&W, 1310 m. Produced by Film Studio Barrandov (Czechoslovakia).
Director: Miloš Forman; Screenplay: Miloš Forman, Ivan Passer; Cinematography: Miroslav Ondříček; Sound: Adolf Böhm, Josef Vlček; Editor: Miroslav Hájek; Music: Jiří Suchý, Jiří Šlitr

O něčem jiném (Another Way of Life)

Fiction feature, B&W, 2284 m. Produced by Film Studio Barrandov (Czechoslovakia).
Director and Screenplay: Věra Chytilová; Cinematography: Jan Čuřík; Sound:

Miloslav Hůrka; Editor: Miroslav Hájek; Music: Jiří Šlitr

Smrt si říká Engelchen (Death Is Called Engelchen)

Fiction feature, B&W, 3681 m. Produced by Film Studio Barrandov (Czechoslovakia).
Director and Screenplay: Ján Kadár, Elmar Klos; Cinematography: Rudolf Milič; Sound: František Černý, Bohumír Brunclík (sound effects); Editor: Jaromír Janáček; Music: Zdeněk Liška

Všední dny velké říše (Every Day in the Great Reich)

Compilation, B&W, 1250 m. Produced by Krátký Film—Popular-Scientific Film (Czechoslovakia).
Director and Screenplay: Rudolf Krejčík; Sound: Jan Kindermann, Benjamin Astrug; Editor: Milada Sádková; Music: Jiří Šust

1964

Démanty noci (Diamonds of the Night)

Fiction feature, B&W, 1814 m. Produced by Film Studio Barrandov (Czechoslovakia).
Director: Jan Němec; Screenplay: Arnošt Lustig, Jan Němec; Cinematography: Jaroslav Kučera; Sound: František Černý, Bohumír Brunclík (sound effects); Editor: Miroslav Hájek; Music: Ladislav Janský et al.

1965

Každý mladý muž (Every Young Man)

Fiction feature, B&W, 2328 m. Produced by Film Studio Barrandov (Czechoslovakia).
Director and Screenplay: Pavel Juráček; Cinematography: Ivan Šlapeta; Sound: Jiří Pavlík; Editor: Josef Dobřichovský; Music: Karel Svoboda, Jaromír Vomáčka

Lásky jedné plavovlásky (Loves of a Blonde)

Fiction feature, B&W, 2195 m. Produced by Film Studio Barrandov (Czechoslovakia).
Director: Miloš Forman; Screenplay: Jaroslav Papoušek, Miloš Forman, Ivan Passer; Cinematography: Miroslav Ondříček; Sound: Adolf Böhm; Editor: Miroslav Hájek; Music: Evžen Illín

Obyknovennyy fashizm (Ordinary Fascism)

Documentary (compilation), B&W, 138 min. Produced by Mosfilm (Soviet Union).
Director: Mikhail Romm; Screenplay: Yuri Khanyutin, Mikhail Romm, Maya Turovskaya; Cinematography: German Lavrov; Editor: Valentina Kulagina, Mikhail Romm; Sound: Sergei Minervin, Boris Vengerovsky; Music: Alemdar Karamanov

Perličky na dně (Pearls of the Deep)

Fiction feature (omnibus), B&W/Color, 2905 m. Produced by Film Studio Barrandov (Czechoslovakia).
Director: Věra Chytilová, Jaromil Jireš, Jiří Menzel, Jan Němec, Evald Schorm; Screenplay: Bohumil Hrabal and directors; Cinematography: Jaroslav Kučera; Sound: Bernard Blažej; Editor: Miroslav Hájek, Jiřina Lukešová; Music: Jan Klusák, Jiří Šust

1966

Ostře sledované vlaky (Closely Watched Trains)

Fiction feature, B&W, 2535 m. Produced by Film Studio Barrandov (Czechoslovakia).
Director: Jiří Menzel; Screenplay: Bohumil Hrabal, Jiří Menzel; Cinematography: Jaromír Šofr; Sound: Jiří Pavlík; Editor: Jiřina Lukešová; Music: Jiří Šust

Sedmikrásky (Daisies)

Fiction feature, B&W/Color, 2069 m. Produced by Film Studio Barrandov (Czechoslovakia).

Director: Věra Chytilová; Screenplay: Ester Krumbachová, Věra Chytilová; Cinematography: Jaroslav Kučera; Sound: Ladislav Hausdorf; Editor: Miroslav Hájek; Music: Jiří Šust, Jiří Šlitr

1967

Marketa Lazarová

Fiction feature, B&W, 4522 m. Produced by Film Studio Barrandov (Czechoslovakia).

Director: František Vláčil; Screenplay: František Vláčil and František Pavlíček; Cinematography: Bedřich Baťka; Sound: František Fabián; Editor: Miroslav Hájek; Music: Zdeněk Liška

Rozmarné léto (Capricious Summer)

Fiction feature, Color, 2058 m. Produced by Film Studio Barrandov (Czechoslovakia).

Director: Jiří Menzel; Screenplay: Václav Nývlt, Jiří Menzel; Cinematography: Jaromír Šofr; Sound: Jiří Pavlík; Editor: Jiřina Lukešová; Music: Jiří Šust

Údolí včel (Valley of the Bees)

Fiction feature, B&W, 2738 m. Produced by Film Studio Barrandov (Czechoslovakia).

Director: František Vláčil; Screenplay: Vladimír Körner, František Vláčil; Cinematography: František Uldrich; Sound: František Fabián; Editor: Miroslav Hájek; Music: Zdeněk Liška

1968

Farářův konec (The End of a Priest)

Fiction feature, B&W, 2717 m. Produced by Film Studio Barrandov (Czechoslovakia).

Director: Evald Schorm; Screenplay: Josef Škvorecký, Evald Schorm; Cinematography: Jaromír Šofr; Sound: František Fabián; Editor: Jiřina Lukešová; Music: Vlastimil Brodský

Spalovač mrtvol (The Cremator)

Fiction feature, B&W, 2724 m. Produced by Film Studio Barrandov (Czechoslovakia).

Director: Juraj Herz; Screenplay: Ladislav Fuks, Juraj Herz; Cinematography: Stanislav Milota; Sound: František Černý; Editor: Jaromír Janáček; Music: Zdeněk Liška

Spříznění volbou (Elective Affinities)

Documentary, B&W, 2390 m. Produced by Krátký Film—Popular-Scientific Film (Czechoslovakia).

Director: Karel Vachek; Cinematography: Jozef Ort-Šnep; Sound: Zbyněk Mader; Editor: Jiřina Skalská

Všichni dobří rodáci (All My Good Countrymen)

Fiction feature, Color, 3271 m. Produced by Film Studio Barrandov (Czechoslovakia).

Director and Screenplay: Vojtěch Jasný; Cinematography: Jaroslav Kučera; Sound: Dobroslav Šrámek; Editor: Miroslav Hájek, Jan Kučera; Music: Svatopluk Havelka

Žert (The Joke)

Fiction feature, B&W, 2199 m. Produced by Film Studio Barrandov (Czechoslovakia).

Director: Jaromil Jireš; Screenplay: Milan Kundera, Jaromil Jireš; Cinematography: Jan Čuřík; Sound: Adam Kajzar; Editor: Josef Valušiak; Music: Zdeněk Pololáník

2011

Zlatá šedesátá: Ivan Balaďa (The Golden Sixties: Ivan Balaďa)

Documentary, Color, 57 min. Coproduction of První veřejnoprávní (Čestmír Kopecký), Czech Television, and the Slovak Film Institute (Czech Republic, Slovakia).

Director: Martin Šulík, Cinematography: Martin Štrba

COMPANION DVD CONTENTS

1. V nový život (In a New Life)

Czechoslovakia / 1938 / B&W / 10 min.
Director, Screenplay, and Cinematography:
Jiří Jeníček
35mm transfer courtesy National Film Ar-
chive, Prague
Reproduced with kind permission of Olga
Krejčová and Pavel Najman

2. Neprojdou (They Shall Not Pass)

Czechoslovakia / 1952 / Color / 13 min.
Director and Screenplay: Zbyněk Brynych,
Roman Hlaváč / Cinematography: Jan
Čuřík
Digital transfer courtesy Military History
Institute, Prague
Reproduced with kind permission of JUDr.
Olga Kalivodová, Anna
Votavová, and Romana
Konrádová-Hlaváčová

3. Příležitost (Opportunity)

Czechoslovakia / 1956 / B&W / 15 min.
Director and Screenplay: Vojtěch Jasný /
Cinematography: Josef Illík
Digital transfer courtesy Military History
Institute, Prague
Reproduced with kind permission of Prof.
Vojtěch Jasný and Jarmila Illíková

4. Křivé zrcadlo (Crooked Mirror)

Czechoslovakia / 1956 / Color / 14 min.
Director and Screenplay: Karel Kachyňa /
Cinematography: Josef Vaniš
35mm transfer courtesy National Film Ar-
chive, Prague
Reproduced with kind permission of Karolína
Kachyňová, Mgr. Alena Mihulová, and
Eliška Nová

5. Útěk (Escape)

Czechoslovakia / 1957 / B&W / 15 min.
Director and Screenplay: Václav Hapl /
Cinematography: Josef Vaniš
Digital transfer courtesy Military History
Institute, Prague
Reproduced with kind permission of Jan Vaniš
and Pavel Vaniš

6. Člověk vo veľkej hale
(Man in a Great Hall)

Czechoslovakia / 1964 / B&W / 10 min.
Director: Ivan Balaďa / Screenplay: Ivan
Balaďa, Jiří Gold / Cinematography:
Juraj Šajmovič
35mm transfer courtesy of National Film Ar-
chive, Prague
Reproduced with kind permission of Ivan
Balaďa and Juraj Šajmovič

7. Armádní filmový měsíčník 3/1965 (Army Newsreel 3/1965)

Czechoslovakia / 1965 / B&W / 14 min.
Director: Karel Vachek
Digital transfer courtesy Military History Institute, Prague
Reproduced with kind permission of Prof. Karel Vachek

8. Metrum

Czechoslovakia / 1968 / B&W / 10 min.
Director and Screenplay: Ivan Baláda /
  Cinematography: Juraj Šajmovič
35mm transfer courtesy of National Film Archive, Prague
Reproduced with kind permission of Ivan Baláda and Juraj Šajmovič

9. Lekce (Lesson)

Czechoslovakia / 1968 / B&W / 15 min.
Director and Screenplay: Vladimír Drha /
  Cinematography: Karel Hložek
35mm transfer courtesy National Film Archive, Prague
Reproduced with kind permission of Vladimír Drha and Mgr. Karel Hložek

10. Les (Forest)

Czechoslovakia / 1969 / B&W / 12 min.
Director and Screenplay: Ivan Baláda /
  Cinematography: Juraj Šajmovič, Ivan
Koudelka, Karel Hložek, Ivan Vojnar
35mm transfer courtesy of National Film Archive, Prague
Reproduced with kind permission of Ivan Baláda and Juraj Šajmovič

11. 34 ženy (34 Women)

Czechoslovakia / 1969 / B&W / 11 min.
Director and Screenplay: Vladimír Drha /
  Cinematography: Karel Hložek
35mm transfer courtesy National Film Archive, Prague
Reproduced with kind permission of Vladimír Drha and Mgr. Karel Hložek

12. Farbotlač (Color Wheel)

Czechoslovakia / 1969 / Color / 11 min.
Director and Screenplay: Vladimír Drha /
  Cinematography: Karel Hložek
35mm transfer courtesy National Film Archive, Prague
Reproduced with kind permission of Vladimír Drha and Mgr. Karel Hložek

13. Ves (Village)

Czechoslovakia / 1969 / B&W / 11 min.
Director and Screenplay: Vladimír Drha /
  Cinematography: Karel Hložek
Digital transfer courtesy Military History Institute, Prague
Reproduced with kind permission of Vladimír Drha and Mgr. Karel Hložek

For full credits to each film, please see this book's filmography.

Permissions

All films on this DVD, including their soundtracks, are reproduced with kind permission of the Military History Institute (Vojenský historický ústav), National Film Archive (Národní filmový archiv), OSA (Ochranný svaz autorský pro práva k dílům hudebním, z.s.), Prague, and the authors and their heirs. All reasonable efforts have been made to identify and contact copyright holders for the films on this DVD.

The copyright holders have licensed the films on this DVD (including their soundtracks) for home use only. All other rights are reserved. Any unauthorized use or distribution of this DVD or any part thereof is strictly prohibited.

Credits

DVD produced by Alice Lovejoy
Authoring and encoding by Cine-O-Matic
  Subtitles for *Army Newsreel 3/1965* and *Crooked Mirror* by Nataša Ďurovičová. Subtitles for all other films by Alice Lovejoy.

Acknowledgements

The author gratefully acknowledges the enthusiasm and generous help of all those who contributed to this DVD. Special thanks to the filmmakers and their heirs; David Černý, Milan Hrubý, and Aleš Knížek (Military History Institute); Michal Bregant, Iwona Łyko, and Eva Pavlíková (National Film Archive); Jiří Srstka and Jitka Tomešová (DILIA, divdelní, literární, audiovizuální agentura, o.s.); Martina Hollá (LITA, autorská spoločnosť); Karel Fořt and Marie Zelbová (OSA); Jakub Forst (Copyright Partners); and Nataša Ďurovičová.

Funding for this DVD was generously provided by the University of Minnesota's Center for Austrian Studies, Imagine Fund, and Grant-in-Aid program.

INDEX

ALICE LOVEJOY

is McKnight Land-Grant Assistant Professor in the Department of Cultural Studies and Comparative Literature and the Moving Image Studies program at the University of Minnesota. Her work has appeared in, among others, *Screen, The Moving Image, East European Politics and Societies and Cultures,* and *Film Comment,* where she has also worked as an editor. The dissertation on which this book is based was awarded honorable mention in the 2011 Society for Cinema and Media Studies dissertation awards.